Women's Writing and Historiography in the GDR

HELEN BRIDGE

CLARENDON PRESS · OXFORD

OXFORD
UNIVERSITY PRESS

Great Clarendon Street, Oxford, OX2 6DP

Oxford University Press is a department of the University of Oxford.
It furthers the University's objective of excellence in research, scholarship,
and education by publishing worldwide in

Oxford New York

Auckland Bangkok Buenos Aires Cape Town Chennai
Dar es Salaam Delhi Hong Kong Istanbul Karachi Kolkata
Kuala Lumpur Madrid Melbourne Mexico City Mumbai Nairobi
São Paulo Shanghai Taipei Tokyo Toronto

Oxford is a registered trade mark of Oxford University Press
in the UK and certain other countries

Published in the United States
by Oxford University Press Inc., New York

British Library Cataloguing in Publication Data

Data available

Library of Congress Cataloging in Publication Data

Data available

ISBN 0-19-925592-X

1 3 5 7 9 10 8 6 4 2

Typeset in Baskerville
by Regent Typesetting, London
Printed in Great Britain
on acid-free paper by
Biddles Ltd, Guildford and King's Lynn

ACKNOWLEDGEMENTS

I would like to thank all those who have given me help and encouragement during my work on this book, which is a revised version of a doc-
toral thesis submitted to the University of Oxford in 1999. I am particularly indebted to my supervisor Karen Leeder, for providing invalu-
able feedback, inspiration, and support over four years. Thanks are
also due to colleagues and friends who took an interest in my work and
offered advice and encouragement: Ray Ockenden, Elizabeth Boa,
Katrin Kohl, Tom Kuhn, Helen Watanabe-O'Kelly, Peter Grieder,
and Simon Ward. For financial support while writing the thesis I am
grateful to Wolfson College, Oxford; grants from the Gerrans Fund
and the Arts and Humanities Research Board of the British Academy
enabled me to make several visits to the Deutsches Literaturarchiv in
Marbach and the Staatsbibliothek in Berlin. Over the past two years
my colleagues at Exeter have been very supportive; I am especially
grateful to Chloe Paver and Dave Horrocks, who read drafts of my
work and provided very helpful constructive criticism.

An earlier version of my analysis of Irmtraud Morgner's *Amanda* in
Chapter 3 appeared as an article in *German Life and Letters* in 1998. I
am grateful to Blackwell Publishers for permission to reproduce this
material.

CONTENTS

LIST OF ABBREVIATIONS

The following abbreviations are used in references throughout the book:

ABNG	Amsterdamer Beiträge zur neueren Germanistik
CG	*Colloquia Germanica*
DD	*Diskussion Deutsch*
DS	*Deutsche Studien*
FMLS	*Forum for Modern Language Studies*
GLL	*German Life and Letters*
GM	German Monitor
GSR	*German Studies Review*
GR	*Germanic Review*
LGS	*London German Studies*
MDU	*Monatshefte für den deutschen Unterricht*
NDH	*Neue deutsche Hefte*
NDL	*Neue deutsche Literatur*
SF	*Sinn und Form*
WB	*Weimarer Beiträge*
WIGY	*Women in German Yearbook*
ZG	*Zeitschrift für Germanistik*

INTRODUCTION

WRITING THE LITERARY HISTORY OF THE GDR AFTER 1989

The collapse of the GDR has given rise to extensive reflection, amongst literary scholars as well as historians and journalists, on the question of how now to approach the history of the GDR and its literature. Three areas of the discussion are of particular relevance for the present study. Firstly, attention has been focused on the questions of what constitutes 'GDR literature', whether the term corresponds to a definable literary entity, and what value such a category might have for literary historiography. Whereas terms like 'English literature' or 'German literature' might be defined (although not unproblematically) either according to the use of a common language or in relation to an idea of nation based on cultural, if not always political, identity, 'GDR literature' is a category defined by a political entity with clear historical and geographical boundaries. These state boundaries had a special relevance for literature because of the unusual ideological constraints which governed cultural production, circulation, and reception within them. However, they proved permeable to literature in a number of ways, raising questions about how to delimit 'GDR literature'.[1] Should the category include a text like Anna Seghers's *Das siebte Kreuz*, which played a prominent and influential role in the literary life of the early GDR, yet was first published seven years before its foundation? Are texts of the 1990s which deal with the experience of life in the GDR and are read primarily by citizens of the new *Bundesländer* still in some sense 'GDR literature'? Did the many writers who left the GDR in the late 1970s and 1980s continue to produce 'GDR literature' although they lived and wrote in the West? Debates about the various possible meanings of the term are nothing new, but in recent years critical reflection on its validity has been prompted by a widespread recognition of the primarily political motivations which determined its usages in East and West respectively up to 1989. Critics including Ursula

[1] See Wolfgang Emmerich, *Kleine Literaturgeschichte der DDR*, rev. edn. (Leipzig: Kiepenheuer, 1996), 21–2; Marc Silberman, 'Whose Story Is This? Rewriting the Literary History of the GDR', in *Contentious Memories: Looking Back at the GDR*, ed. Jost Hermand and Marc Silberman (New York: Lang, 1998), 25–57 (32).

Heukenkamp and Rainer Rosenberg have argued that it is futile to continue to work with a category which was created to fulfil a political function in each of the post-war German states:

Zwanzig Jahre lang hat das Paradigma von der Existenz der zwei deutschen Literaturen in den beiden deutschen Staaten gegolten. Nun hat es ausgedient. Unter den Bedingungen der Zweistaatlichkeit erwies es sich als nützlich, ermöglichte es doch übersichtliche Einteilungen und war zudem auf je wechselnde Art auch politisch vernünftig.[2]

Jede geschichtliche Gestalt erscheint, wenn sie vergangen ist, in einem anderen Licht. So wird auch aus dem Untergang der DDR eine neue Sicht auf die DDR-Literatur gewonnen werden. Als eine eigenständige deutschsprachige Literatur neben der westdeutschen oder österreichischen wird man das, was in den Grenzen dieses Staates geschrieben wurde, in Zukunft wohl kaum noch verhandeln.[3]

While in future it will undeniably be necessary to rethink the relationship between literature written in the GDR and that of other German-speaking states, a thorough understanding of the position, functions, and achievements of literature within its immediate social and political context is necessary before any meaningful comparisons can be drawn between literatures written under markedly different conditions. It is my aim to enhance such an understanding; I therefore retain a belief in the validity and value of the term 'GDR literature'. Because my focus is on the functions literature can take on in a totalitarian state as one in a nexus of strictly controlled discourses, I shall work with a narrow definition of 'GDR literature', focusing primarily on texts which were both written and published under the constraints of the GDR system.

A second area of discussion since 1989 has centred on the relationship between politics and aesthetics, and the need for a critical reassessment of the way GDR literature related to the political and cultural political history of the state. The criticisms which Bernhard Greiner made in 1983 of western GDR literary studies in general have found widespread acceptance amongst scholars since the fall of the Berlin Wall.[4] Greiner attacked the excessive politicization of GDR literature and the adoption of an unnecessarily narrow range of approaches.

---

[2] Ursula Heukenkamp, '*Eine* Geschichte oder *viele* Geschichten der deutschen Literatur seit 1945? Gründe und Gegengründe', *ZG*, NS 5 (1995), 1, 22–37 (22).

[3] Rainer Rosenberg, 'Was war DDR-Literatur? Die Diskussion um den Gegenstand in der Literaturwissenschaft der Bundesrepublik Deutschland', *ZG*, NS 5 (1995), 1, 9–21 (19).

[4] Bernhard Greiner, 'DDR-Literatur als Problem der Literaturwissenschaft', *Jahrbuch zur Literatur in der DDR*, 3 (1983), 233–54.

Extending Greiner's critique in the 1996 edition of his *Kleine Literatur-geschichte der DDR*, Wolfgang Emmerich, the principal authority on GDR literary history, argues that:

Interesse an der DDR-Literatur war häufig weit *mehr aus dem Interesse am Experiment Sozialismus als an der Literatur* an sich geboren. Natürlich war dieses Interesse allemal legitim und bleibt es auch. Folgenschwer war die *Verwechslung* der beiden Interessen, oder doch zumindest ihre permanente *Vermischung*. Literarische Texte wurden so nur selten als *Texte* untersucht und weit häufiger als Widerspiegelung gesellschaftlich-politischer Verhältnisse—oder umgekehrt (was methodologisch wenig ändert): als Protest gegen sie.[5]

New simplifications of the relationship between aesthetics and ideology have gained currency since 1989. As Thomas C. Fox has pointed out, the new paradigm proposed by Ulrich Greiner and other participants in the 'Literaturstreit' is as inadequate for understanding the relationship between GDR authors and the state as the paradigm it was supposed to replace. A one-sided view of the author as a heroic voice of opposition has been countered with an equally one-sided condemnation of GDR literature as 'Gesinnungsästhetik' subordinat-ing aesthetic values to social, political, and moral concerns, and as the product of a co-dependency between author and state.[6]

While studies prior to 1989 all too often read GDR literature as a direct consequence of cultural policy and so neglected the aesthetic qualities of literary texts, the complex relationship between literature and its GDR context remains an important subject for analysis. Questions of aesthetics are, in the GDR as in other societies and historical periods, inextricably bound up with ideological positions. Recognizing that literary texts use aesthetic means to construct imaginative worlds and versions of reality, rather than fulfilling a straightforward documentary function, does not mean that the politi-cal implications of different aesthetic choices have to be neglected. In the case of the GDR, where cultural policy overtly politicized aesthetics, any account of literature based solely on aesthetic criteria would be, in Emmerich's words, 'historisch verfehlt'.[7] Examining how particular aesthetic qualities of literature enabled it to articulate new ideological positions, the present study aims to shed light on the

---

[5] Emmerich, *Kleine Literaturgeschichte*, 17–18.

[6] Thomas C. Fox, 'Germanistik and GDR Studies: (Re)Reading a Censored Literature', *MDU* 85 (1993), 3, 284–94 (284). See also Ulrich Greiner, 'Die deutsche Gesinnungsästhetik: Noch einmal: Christa Wolf und der deutsche Literaturstreit. Ein Zwischenbilanz', in *'Es geht nicht um Christa Wolf': Der Literaturstreit im vereinigten Deutschland*, ed. Thomas Anz, rev. edn. (Frankfurt am Main: Fischer, 1995), 208–16.   [7] Emmerich, *Kleine Literaturgeschichte*, 19.

complex relationships between literature and other discourses in the GDR, including official cultural policy, while avoiding overly simple models which seek causes in the history of policy and effects in literary texts.

The third subject of debate in GDR studies since 1989, of particular interest here, is one which is symptomatic of recent western thinking about history more broadly, and concerns the validity of historical narratives. At the centre of the debate is a tension between the value, even necessity, of narrative as a means of structuring historical accounts and offering explanations for historical events, and an awareness of the untenability of the 'grand narratives' which characterized traditional historiography.[8] This tension is manifest in Emmerich's *Kleine Literaturgeschichte der DDR*, as well as in many recent contributions to debates about the future of GDR studies.

Emmerich criticizes the use of teleological models to describe literary historical developments, particularly amongst GDR scholars, in their use of metaphors such as 'Abschied', 'Ankunft', and 'Anwesendsein'. He expresses his intention, 'der Vielheit und Uneindeutigkeit der (literar-)historischen Prozesse Rechnung zu tragen', and draws on the model of literary history established by Uwe Japp, in order to emphasize the inconsistencies and ruptures which characterize literary developments.[9] These ideas, already evident in Emmerich's work prior to the GDR's demise, are outlined more fully in an essay of 1988:

> Literatur entfaltet sich weder linear noch stetig, noch auf irgendein Telos hin. Es gibt nicht *eine* literarische Entwicklung, sondern ein System widerspruchsvoller, interferierender Bewegungen. Verschiedene ästhetische Strategien und Praxen existieren nebeneinander, konkurrieren miteinander.[10]

While thus recognizing the inadequacy of a single historical narrative to do justice to the complexities of literary history, Emmerich insists that in order to write meaningful literary histories it is necessary to relate developments to an overarching macrothesis:

> Nun ist es beim Geschäft einer ja auch erzählenden Literaturgeschichtsschreibung beinahe unmöglich, ganz ohne einen roten Faden oder doch wenigstens eine überschaubare, stets reduktive Zahl von wenigen kräftigeren

---

[8] Cf. Georg G. Iggers, *Historiography in the Twentieth Century: From Scientific Objectivity to the Postmodern Challenge* (Hanover, NH, and London: Wesleyan University Press, 1997), 6–16.

[9] Emmerich, *Kleine Literaturgeschichte*, 20–4.

[10] Wolfgang Emmerich, 'Gleichzeitigkeit: Vormoderne, Moderne und Postmoderne in der Literatur der DDR', in *Die andere deutsche Literatur: Aufsätze zur Literatur aus der DDR* (Opladen: Westdeutscher Verlag, 1994), 129–50 (130).

Leit-Fäden auszukommen. Keine Literaturgeschichte läßt sich ohne eine, 'wie auch immer implizit bleibende, Makrothese über den Verlauf literarhistorischer Prozesse' (J. Fohrmann), ohne eine 'idealtypische Konstruktion' (S. Scherer) schreiben.[11]

The macrothesis of the *Kleine Literaturgeschichte* is, 'daß ein erheblicher Teil der Literatur aus der DDR im Lauf von vier Jahrzehnten eine Emanzipationsbewegung vollzieht'. Emmerich defines this process primarily in aesthetic terms, as a shift from didacticism towards 'Haltungen des erkennenden Experimentierens, zum ästhetischen Text als Differenz zur Wirklichkeit, nicht als deren planes Abbild', but his choice of metaphor ('Emanzipation') reveals the inseparability of aesthetics and politics. While the central hypothesis of his work is essentially unchanged from the 1988 edition, the new edition aims at 'eine differenzierte und insgesamt skeptischere Darstellung gerade des Unstimmigen an diesem Prozeß'.[12]

Discussions about the project of writing GDR literary history and suggestions of new contexts in which to understand GDR literature have been particularly prominent in US Germanists' responses to the events of 1989. There, what Patricia Herminghouse has called a 'healthy skepticism about all attempts to produce literary history' has resulted, for many, in a broad shift of agenda.[13] Like Emmerich, many US scholars have questioned the approaches to GDR literature which dominated studies produced in the West before 1989. There has been a widespread call for self-reflection on the part of (American) critics, and for a critical re-examination of the ways GDR literature has been appropriated by US German Studies. Herminghouse describes the task facing those who work on the GDR as,

more than a mere remapping of the parameters which had contained the study of GDR literature within the American academic landscape: confronting the need to reexamine the political and professional interests circumscribing its domain also entails acknowledging factors which shaped our own engagement with this particular strain of writing in the German language.[14]

Such methodological meta-reflection is unquestionably necessary, but at times it threatens to eclipse literature as the object of study, and

---

[11] Emmerich, *Kleine Literaturgeschichte*, 21.
[12] Ibid.
[13] Patricia Herminghouse, 'New Contexts for GDR Literature: An American Perspective', in *Cultural Transformations in the New Germany: American and German Perspectives*, ed. Friederike Eigler and Peter C. Pfeiffer (Columbia, SC: Camden House, 1993), 93–101 (98).
[14] Ibid. 93.

to function as a pretext for not formulating any new hypotheses about the GDR. While some US critics, such as Thomas Fox, insist that 'as we historicize GDR literature, it will be essential to continue reconstructing the horizon of former readers',[15] others have proposed new starting-points for approaching GDR literature which often neglect the historical context of the GDR, in order to relate literary texts to contexts regarded as more relevant to American readers. Marc Silberman's article 'Whose Story is This? Rewriting the Literary History of the GDR' exemplifies this trend in US criticism. Treating GDR literature as 'an especially salient object for illustrating how we construct tradition and how we endorse values that define continuity', Silberman does not offer his own 'grand narrative of GDR literature'—though he does suggest starting-points for one—but examines instead 'the obstacles, typologies, and strategies pertinent to such an undertaking'.[16] This involves a theoretical discussion which shares the tension central to Emmerich's introduction. Silberman, too, questions the 'linear construction' of literary history and criticizes the 'rigidly teleological organizing schemes' which have, in his view, tended to characterize GDR literary history. On the other hand, like Emmerich, he accepts the necessity of 'abstract, retrospective concepts' as a means of ordering and analysing material:

Needless to say, the problematization of literary history does not obviate the need to pursue synthesizing retrospectives. Without the selectivity of a literary canon the evaluation of genres, authors, and individual works can not proceed, and without historicizing periods and phases comparisons become all but impossible. The point is to define our expectations and limitations when contemplating the past [. . .][17]

This sounds remarkably close to Emmerich's position, as outlined in his introduction, yet Silberman's discussion of the 1996 *Kleine Literaturgeschichte* is a polemical attempt to discredit it by revealing inconsistencies in Emmerich's methodology. He accuses him, for example, of basing his work on 'the same teleology of increasing autonomy and subjectivity that characterized his previous work':

From this perspective the forty-year history of GDR literature traces a progressive evolution from a pre-modern, closed society under the extra-literary control of dogmatic censorship that produced works of socialist realism to modern forms of resistance and systemic critique that culminated in experimental and avantgarde aesthetics.[18]

---

[15] Fox, 286.   [16] Silberman, 28.   [17] Ibid. 30–2.   [18] Ibid. 46.

It is true that Emmerich's preference for avantgarde experimentalism determines his construction of GDR literary history. However, the 'new cultural paradigm' which Silberman proposes as an alternative framework within which to read post-1945 German literature, namely the 'global economy of advanced capitalism', in which 'autonomous history disappears, traditional regimes of political power no longer function, and national boundaries become superfluous', could arguably be seen as equally teleological:

The similarities between modern forms of culture and organization—capitalism, socialism, fascism—emerge now in high relief. [. . .] There were fundamental differences in how these socio-political systems squandered human and natural resources or in how they controlled access to power, but they also constitute the shared past out of which the new globalization of art and culture has been emerging.[19]

A new grand narrative which flattens out the differences between capitalism, socialism, and fascism, and claims the meaninglessness of history, political power, and national boundaries, can scarcely hope to do justice to GDR literature as a historically specific phenomenon, constrained by very real boundaries, both geographical and political.

A central premiss of my analysis is that Emmerich's macrothesis that GDR literature gradually emancipated itself from the ideological constraints imposed on it remains a valid and helpful framework which does justice to the special features of this literature within its historical context. While accepting this broad historical narrative, however, I shall draw out the complexities and inconsistencies which Emmerich highlights in his introduction, but tends to suppress in his later discussion of literary texts. The present study focuses on one strand of the literary history of the last two decades of the GDR's existence, that is, the development of critical approaches to history in narrative fiction by women. While women were not the only authors to expand the boundaries of historical debate in the GDR, this study will show how the increasing centrality of gender to their critiques means that they made a special and significant contribution to GDR public discourses. When texts by a variety of authors are juxtaposed, the idea that a single chronological narrative is adequate for describing developments in literature appears problematic. The authors to be discussed were born between the late 1920s and the mid-1940s, a time-span within which even generations born only ten or fifteen years apart could be separ-

---

[19] Ibid. 47–8.

ated by considerably different experiences of the GDR. As soon as any literary history takes account of the careers of more than one author, a plurality of developments is inevitable. This plurality took a special form in the GDR, where the privileges granted to prominent and internationally successful authors—permission to travel to the West and consequently access to western discourses, for example—were withheld from less established writers. Furthermore, as David Bathrick has argued, an élite group of well-known authors occupied a position of political power as institutions within the GDR public sphere:

Dabei erwies sich, daß eben diese zentrale Position des Kultursektors erfolgreichen und etablierten Autoren nicht nur eine gewisse Macht, sondern auch eine politische Autonomie verlieh, die in den anderen gesellschaftlichen Bereichen dieser Öffentlichkeit ohne Beispiel ist. Das gilt besonders für Autoren von Weltrang wie etwa Bertolt Brecht, Heiner Müller, Christa Wolf, Stefan Heym, Stephan Hermlin und Volker Braun. Sie alle wurden auf diese Weise gewissermaßen zu Institutionen, die direkt oder indirekt für die Artikulation von gesellschaftlichen Interessen, aber auch für Formen der Dissidenz oder Opposition sorgten.[20]

As Julia Hell has pointed out, Emmerich's model of GDR literary history is implicitly centred on the career of Christa Wolf.[21] He does not problematize the relationship between the texts of those authors who might be regarded as social institutions in Bathrick's analysis, and those by writers who did not have this status. Instead, he attempts to fit the latter into a pattern established by more prominent writers. There are good reasons why accounts of GDR literature have tended to focus on Wolf. Besides the quality of her writing (an argument which could be made for other writers who never gained a status comparable with hers), her works participate in a number of discourses which were of political and intellectual interest to many in East and West especially from the late 1960s onwards: utopian socialism, feminism, environmentalism, and the peace movement. Wolf belonged to a group of writers who produced what many, in East and West, saw as the most interesting and 'representative' GDR texts of the 1970s and 1980s. Neither dogmatically affirmative of the SED state nor radically dis-

[20] David Bathrick, 'Kultur und Öffentlichkeit in der DDR', in *Literatur der DDR in den siebziger Jahren*, ed. P. U. Hohendahl and P. Herminghouse (Frankfurt am Main: Suhrkamp, 1983), 53–81 (64).
[21] Julia Hell, 'Critical Orthodoxies, Old and New, or The Fantasy of a Pure Voice: Christa Wolf', in *Contentious Memories: Looking Back at the GDR*, ed. Hermand and Silberman, 65–101 (66).

sident, Wolf, Braun, Müller, and others shared the ideals of socialism and advocated reforms of the state system from within. The fact that Wolf has been made more central to GDR literary histories than any other author in this category has two probable reasons. Firstly, her texts were frequently the earliest prominent and highly successful attempts in GDR prose literature to explore new topics and literary techniques which subsequently became popular with other authors, although in drama Müller played a similar role. Secondly, her career spans the last three decades of the GDR, and manifests an unusually clear progression in ideas and literary technique. Her shift from historical optimism and socialist realist dogmatism to positions of increasing subjectivity, feminism, pessimism, and criticism of the course history has taken, lends itself as a narrative framework for understanding broader developments in GDR literature.

Since 1989 there have been calls for greater attention to be paid to GDR women writers who have hitherto been excluded from a canon centring on Wolf and Irmtraud Morgner.[22] Recent research projects have focused on women of a younger generation who never identified with the socialist state and who, often unable to publish their works in the GDR, did not participate in public discourse in the way that the older women did.[23] Because the present study is concerned with the ways in which literature can reconfigure the boundaries imposed on public discourses in a totalitarian state, it will deal primarily with that strand of GDR literature which aimed at reforming socialism from within. It aims to strike a balance between acknowledging the importance of the literary career of Wolf, as one of the most prominent and influential writers of the GDR, and suggesting that the literary history of the GDR is not a single story determined by the work of one author. Whereas Wolf and Morgner have often been grouped together as canonical authors of the same generation with broadly similar concerns, this study will draw out differences between their aesthetics and ideas, as well as showing how their works relate to those of less established writers.

---

[22] See, for example, Karen Jankowsky, 'Canons Crumble Just Like Walls: Discovering the Works of GDR Women Writers', in *Cultural Transformations in the New Germany*, ed. Eigler and Pfeiffer, 102–16.

[23] For example, Birgit Dahlke, *Papierboot: Autorinnen aus der DDR—inoffiziell publiziert* (Würzburg: Königshausen and Neumann, 1997). A canonical writer is compared with a marginalized one in Beth V. Linklater, *'Und immer zügelloser wird die Lust': Constructions of Sexuality in East German Literatures. With Special Reference to Irmtraud Morgner and Gabriele Stötzer-Kachold* (Berne: Lang, 1998).

LITERATURE AND HISTORIOGRAPHY IN THE GDR: THE
DIVERGENCE OF THEORY AND PRACTICE

In his *Kleine Literaturgeschichte*, Emmerich uses the term 'geschichts-
philosophischer Paradigmenwechsel' to describe a set of fundamental
shifts which transformed GDR literature during the 1970s and 1980s:
'Das vom Marxismus in seiner orthodoxen Version vermittelte Fort-
schrittsdenken wird von den kritischen Künstlern verworfen, der
Glaube an ein gesetzmäßig gesichertes Ankommen im Sozialismus
und endlich Kommunismus geht verloren.'[24] A prominent and substantial sector of GDR literature moved beyond its officially prescribed
role as a voice for the state ideology, to become instead a forum for
the articulation of plural, critical, and subversive viewpoints. The relationship between literature and history was, as Emmerich's formulation suggests, central to this shift. The SED understood literature as a
means of influencing the course of history: by reflecting the progress of
socialist society in accordance with Marx's model of history, literary
works were to instil a socialist historical consciousness in readers and so
inspire them to work actively towards bringing about communism.
However, as many GDR writers began to reject this optimistic understanding of history as progress towards a teleological goal, their works
increasingly transformed the way history was understood and written
about in the GDR, as well as calling for transformations of historical
reality in ways quite different from those envisaged by the SED.
Literature assumed a special and important role as a medium in which
more critical approaches to history, taboo in other kinds of GDR
public discourse, could be explored.

The cultural and political developments of the 1970s resulted in a
paradoxical situation for literature. Although Honecker seemed to
promise greater ideological and aesthetic freedom for writers in 1971,
the limitations of this liberalization quickly became apparent, as critical works by writers including Braun, Heym, and Müller continued
to be suppressed. After Wolf Biermann's expatriation in 1976, state
control of literature intensified, with the consequence that writers'
power to voice criticisms in the public sphere was diminished, yet their
attitude to the state was more critical than ever before. For a subsector
of society, literature continued to offer a space in which increasingly
critical positions were articulated. This study takes as its starting-point
the increasing tendency, from the 1970s onwards, for literature by

[24] Emmerich, *Kleine Literaturgeschichte*, 273.

many of the major writers in the GDR to challenge the official Party line and broaden the parameters of historical debate. By analysing the shifts in literature alongside developments in academic work on history and in literary criticism, it asks why literature in particular has the potential to subvert the requirements imposed on it in a totalitarian state where all public discourses are subject to strict ideological regulation and censorship. It begins by outlining a model of the relationships between GDR literature, academic discourses on history and on literature, and a prescriptive official discourse which outlined roles for each of these.

The SED authorized a model of history based on Marx's writings. However, as is generally the case when considering official GDR policy, it is essential to recognize the discrepancy between the Party's claims concerning the theory on which the regime was ostensibly based, and the actual appropriation of this theory in practice. The empirical quality of Marx's ideas about history and his emphasis on the progression towards a communist future, to be achieved by political activity, were played down. Instead, the SED instrumentalized and dogmatized this model of history as an understanding of the past with the primary aim of legitimizing the GDR and discrediting the capitalist West. In order to achieve this, the dialectical concept of progress central to Marx's thought was reduced to a polarized view of the past in terms of progressive and reactionary elements, introduced by the SED as the official interpretation of the past in 1951.[25] By positioning its own regime at a stage in Marx's model of society's development after the proletarian revolution, the SED changed the emphasis of this model from a progression towards a future goal, to the justification and preservation of present conditions. This represents a significant divergence from the ideas of Marx and Engels, for in 'Die deutsche Ideologie' they assert that communism is to be understood not as a static ideal condition to be attained, but as a dynamic process of continuing progress: 'Der Kommunismus ist für uns nicht ein *Zustand*, der hergestellt werden soll, ein *Ideal*, wonach die Wirklichkeit sich zu richten haben [wird]. Wir nennen Kommunismus die *wirkliche* Bewegung, welche den jetzigen Zustand aufhebt.'[26] The West German historian

---

[25] Alexander Fischer and Günther Heydemann, 'Weg und Wandel der Geschichtswissenschaft und des Geschichtsverständnisses in der SBZ/DDR seit 1945', in *Geschichtswissenschaft in der DDR*, 2 vols., ed. Fischer and Heydemann (Berlin (FRG): Duncker and Humblot, 1988), i. *Historische Entwicklung, Theoriediskussion und Geschichtsdidaktik*, 3–30 (9).

[26] Karl Marx and Friedrich Engels, 'Die deutsche Ideologie', in *Ausgewählte Werke*, 6 vols. (Berlin: Dietz, 1970–2), i (1970), 201–77 (226).

Hermann Weber has shown how the SED instrumentalized Marx's
model of history in order to legitimize its own policies. GDR historians,
he asserts, were obliged—in practice, if not in the official rhetoric—to
treat history as 'rückprojizierte Gegenwart', that is, 'die aktuelle Politik
in die Vergangenheit zu transformieren'.[27] Certain elements in Marx's
writings made his theory of history particularly susceptible to this kind
of appropriation. In particular, his claim to a scientifically objective
theory of history, his emphasis on the need to make the study of history
politically productive for the present, and his understanding of history
as a course of progress determined by laws, were adopted in a dogmatically binding form in the GDR and used as a basis for an approach to
history which served primarily to legitimize the regime and its policies
in the present.

   The official functions of both professional history and literature in
the GDR were determined by this understanding of history. Although
the precise nature of the limitations and prescriptions imposed on
the activities of historians and writers varied during the course of
the GDR's development, the ultimate functions attributed to them
remained constant.[28] Historians had the task of illustrating and re-
inforcing the theoretical, ostensibly Marxist model of history proposed
by the SED, by demonstrating how individual periods, figures, and
events fitted into it. Literature, meanwhile, was given an overtly
historical and didactic role as a tool of socialist enlightenment.
Fictional works were to influence the course of history by enabling
readers to recognize and fulfil their roles in history. Literature was
assigned a function comparable to that of history, in interpreting
historical events according to a schema regarded as the only objective
and true way of understanding the course of history. While professional
history was to lend academic authority to this official model of history,
literature was to make it comprehensible to the public, particularly in
its implications for the present.[29]

---

[27] Hermann Weber, '"Weiße Flecken" und die DDR-Geschichtswissenschaft', in
Zwischen Parteilichkeit und Professionalität: Bilanz der Geschichtswissenschaft der DDR, ed. Konrad H.
Jarausch (Berlin: Akademie Verlag, 1991), 139–53 (140).

[28] Fischer and Heydemann, 'Weg und Wandel', 6–7. See also Peter Lübbe, 'Zur Funktion
der Geschichtswissenschaft im staatlich etablierten Sozialismus', *DS* 25 (1987), 292–300 (292,
297).

[29] Walter Schmidt, 'Geschichtsbewußtsein und sozialistische Persönlichkeit bei der
Gestaltung der entwickelten sozialistischen Gesellschaft', in *Geschichtsbewußtsein und sozialistische Gesellschaft: Beiträge zur Rolle der Geschichtswissenschaft, des Geschichtsunterrichts und der
Geschichtspropaganda bei der Entwicklung des sozialistischen Geschichtsbewußtseins*, ed. Helmut Meier
and Walter Schmidt (Berlin: Dietz, 1970), 8–41 (9).

In the earliest years of the GDR, literature was regarded as an essential medium for antifascist re-education. It was given a central role in state planning, as an effective means of achieving and cementing social change. Walter Ulbricht announced in 1951, 'Die Kunst hat im Fünfjahrplan eine hohe Aufgabe. Sie kann Großes leisten, um die Menschen zu echtem Patriotismus, zum Geiste des Friedens, der Demokratie und des Fortschritts zu erziehen.'[30] In an attempt to attain socialism without the class struggles and socio-economic revolutions from below which were central to Marx's model of history, the SED placed enormous faith in the humanist literary heritage as a substitute means of achieving historical progress quickly.[31] Cultural policy aimed to introduce the masses to German Classical art and literature, while writers were to help create a 'sozialistische Nationalkultur' based on the development of 'alles Große, Humanistische, Fortschrittliche, das die Kultur unseres Volkes in der Vergangenheit hervorgebracht hat', as well as 'den kulturellen Traditionen des mehr als hundert-jährigen revolutionären Kampfes der deutschen Arbeiterklasse'.[32] As Emmerich has commented, such policies were founded on naïve assumptions about how a historical 'Erbe' could be made productive for the present: 'Geistig-literarische Produktionen der Vergangenheit wurden als "Güter" oder "Schätze" wahrgenommen, die man sich "aneignen", von denen man "Besitz ergreifen" müsse.'[33]

During the later decades of the GDR's history, both historiography and literature were able to negotiate a broadening of the boundaries within which they worked, loosening the restrictions imposed on them and effecting reformulations of the official state discourse which they were obliged to support. Significant changes in historiography were initiated by a reconsideration of the relationship between the SED and historians in the late 1960s. Party control of the activities of historians had been particularly strict during the politically tense 1950s: at the fortieth anniversary of the 1918 revolution, academics were reprimanded for their 'wrong' interpretations of this event.[34] By the late 1960s, nearly all professional historians were members of the Party, so

---

[30] 'Aufgaben der Kunst', in *Dokumente zur Kunst-, Literatur- und Kulturpolitik der SED*, ed. Elimar Schubbe (Stuttgart: Seewald, 1972), 213–15 (213).

[31] Wolfram Schlenker, *Das 'Kulturelle Erbe' in der DDR: Gesellschaftliche Entwicklung und Kulturpolitik 1945–1965* (Stuttgart: Metzler, 1977), 67.

[32] 'Die sozialistische Nationalkultur als die Erfüllung der humanistischen Kultur des deutschen Volkes', in *Dokumente zur Kunst-, Literatur- und Kulturpolitik der SED*, ed. Schubbe, 781–2 (781).

[33] Emmerich, *Kleine Literaturgeschichte*, 84.

[34] Fischer and Heydemann, 'Weg und Wandel', 10.

this degree of policing was no longer felt to be necessary, although research remained subject to five-year planning.[35] At the Seventh Party Congress of the SED in 1967, greater significance was accorded to academic disciplines. Consequently, historical studies were able to develop away from their former purely ideological function, towards a greater emphasis on academic research. With the foundation of the Rat für Geschichtswissenschaften in 1968, a new, dialogic form of communication between the Party and historians was introduced. This was accompanied by demands for a broader theory and method-ology of history.[36]

These changed conditions of historical research, together with the abandonment of hope for a reunification of Germany into a single, socialist state, led to changes in the official interpretation of the past in the 1970s. The emphasis shifted from Germany's national past to parallels in the historical development of the GDR and other socialist states, while the differences between the Federal Republic and the GDR were now highlighted to a greater degree. Proletarian inter-nationalism and socialist patriotism were now regarded as comple-mentary and wholly compatible, so the focus on the GDR's place in a world revolutionary process was accompanied by the new view that the GDR was heir to the entire German past. A new, more integral approach to German history began, in the late 1970s, to replace the previous highly selective treatment. Ingrid Mittenzwei's essay of 1978, 'Die zwei Gesichter Preußens' is representative of, and played an important part in, this change. Mittenzwei challenges the simplistic polarity between progressive and reactionary elements in history which had previously dominated the official approach to the past, arguing instead for a more differentiated assessment of key historical episodes. She criticizes the tendency to focus on certain aspects of history and ignore others, and asserts that the whole of history must be addressed, including elements which are problematic for the GDR, such as Prussia's authoritarian past: 'Preußen ist Teil unserer Geschichte, nicht nur Weimar. Ein Volk kann sich seine Traditionen nicht aussuchen; es muß sich ihnen stellen, und es sollte dies auf unter-schiedliche Weise tun.'[37]

The ideas raised by Mittenzwei's essay formed the basis of a discus-

[35] Mary Fulbrook, *German National Identity after the Holocaust* (London: Polity, 1999), 131.

[36] Fischer and Heydemann, 'Weg und Wandel', 15–18.

[37] Ingrid Mittenzwei, 'Die zwei Gesichter Preußens', *Forum*, 32 (1978), 19, 8–9; repr. in *Erbe und Tradition: Die Diskussion der Historiker*, ed. Helmut Meier and Walter Schmidt (Cologne: Pahl-Rugenstein, 1989), 72–8 (72).

sion of heritage and tradition amongst GDR historians, beginning in the late 1970s. The term 'Erbe' was broadened to refer to the entire legacy of history in its complexity and its contradictions, while 'Tradition' was used to denote those elements of the 'Erbe' which could be evaluated positively from the perspective of the GDR and were therefore considered to have a function in solving historical problems faced in the present.[38] The schematic division of the German national past into 'progressive' elements which could serve as a foundation for the GDR, and 'reactionary' elements allegedly leading to the Federal Republic, was thus replaced by a more differentiated examination of the GDR's relation to the whole of German history. Although this new approach meant that a broader range of historical episodes and figures were considered worthy of academic attention, a fundamental continuity in the role and the methodology of GDR historical studies is apparent. Helmut Meier and Walter Schmidt outline the new tasks facing historians:

Unser Traditionsverständnis hebt daher stets zwei Aspekte des Verhältnisses der sozialistischen DDR zur deutschen Geschichte in ihrer Gesamtheit hervor: *erstens* die *Fortsetzung* und Vollendung der progressiven, humanistischen und revolutionären Traditionen des Volkes und *zweitens* den entschiedenen, endgültigen *Bruch* mit der deutschen Reaktion.[39]

A polarized conception of a positive and a negative line of historical development is maintained here, although both of these are now related solely to the GDR, rather than to the opposition between East and West Germany. Similarly, the function of historiography in legitimizing the GDR as the lawful end-product of a positive tradition of revolutionary progress remained essentially unchallenged. Any significant dissent from this official model could, even in the 1980s, only be voiced privately, and did not find expression in published academic work.[40]

As in all academic disciplines in the GDR, there were niches where individual scholars could pursue research in a relatively undogmatic way. Academics employed by the Akademie der Wissenschaften had

---

[38] Ulrich Neuhäußer-Wespy, 'Erbe und Tradition in der DDR: Zum gewandelten Geschichtsbild der SED', in *Geschichtswissenschaft in der DDR*, ed. Fischer and Heydemann, i. 129–53.

[39] Helmut Meier and Walter Schmidt, 'Zum marxistisch-leninistischen Traditionsverständnis in der DDR', in *Erbe und Tradition: Die Diskussion der Historiker*, ed. Meier and Schmidt, 27–57 (31).

[40] *Marxist Historiography in Transformation: East German Social History in the 1980s*, ed. Georg G. Iggers, trans. Bruce Little (New York and Oxford: Berg, 1991), 8.

greater freedom than those working at universities, because they were not required to teach. In the words of Rainer Eckert, who worked at the Institut für deutsche Geschichte at the Akademie, 'es ging [. . .] nicht um den Nachwuchs, der einseitig ideologisch geprägt werden sollte'.[41] Since these historians were required to produce research which would gain the GDR international prestige, they also had access to western publications, and were able to meet western academics at international conferences.[42] However, most historians at the Akademie were members of the SED and so were subject to Party disciplinary measures if their work did not support the accepted interpretation of history sufficiently. These ranged from a reprimand to a ban on publications, removal from an academic position, or even a prison sentence. Studies of ancient and medieval history were freer from ideological control than those of more modern (and politically relevant) periods. At the Zentralinstitut für Alte Geschichte und Archäologie of the Akademie, for example, only 10 per cent of the employees belonged to the SED.[43]

As Mary Fulbrook has suggested, in the later years of the GDR many historians moved away from committed dogmatic positions: 'Many East German historians adopted the "sandwich principle": a rich and nutritious empirical filling could be safely topped and tailed by a little dry bread of Marxist-Leninist theory in the introductory and concluding sections.'[44] By the late 1980s, GDR historians such as Jürgen Kuczynski, Hartmut Zwahr, Jan Peters, and Sigrid Jacobeit had also produced some varied and undogmatic work on topics in social history and *Alltagsgeschichte*.[45] However, such work was regarded as a serious threat to mainstream political history, and gained what freedom it had from its marginalization. As Harald Dehne has com-

---

[41] 'Ohne Vergangenheitsbewältigung gibt es keinen demokratischen Neubeginn: Gespräch mit Dr Rainer Eckert, Historiker, 1972 von der Humboldt-Universität relegiert wegen Teilnahme an einer staatsfeindlichen Gruppierung', in *Hure oder Muse? Klio in der DDR: Dokumente und Materialien des Unabhängigen Historiker-Verbandes*, ed. Rainer Eckert, Ilko-Sascha Kowalczuk, and Isolde Stark (Berlin: Gesellschaft für sozialwissenschaftliche Forschung und Publizistik, 1994), 115–19 (119).

[42] Ibid. See also Therese Hörnigk, 'Contours of a New Academic Landscape: Research Institutes and the University System in the New German States', in *Cultural Transformations in the New Germany*, ed. Eigler and Pfeiffer, 172–9 (176).

[43] Isolde Stark, 'Warum ein Unabhängiger Historiker-Verband?', in *Hure oder Muse?*, ed. Eckert, Kowalczuk, and Stark, 11–20 (12).

[44] Fulbrook, *German National Identity*, 132.

[45] A seminal work was Jürgen Kuczynski, *Geschichte des Alltags des deutschen Volkes*, 5 vols. (Berlin: Akademie Verlag, 1980–2). Other examples of such work are collected in *Marxist Historiography in Transformation*, ed. Iggers.

mented in an illuminating 1992 postscript to an essay written for publication in the West in 1989, 'as long as everyday-historical questions remained shunted off onto the sidetrack of marginal disciplines, they continued to be tolerated as an object of interest pursued by what were deemed to be harmless "exotics".'[46] Nevertheless, as Dehne makes clear in his comments on his own essay, work on these topics was sometimes severely compromised by political expediency.

It was only in the final years of the GDR that any significant cracks began to show in the seemingly monolithic block of historical studies.[47] When, in 1988, Gorbachev extended *glasnost* to include the 'blank spots of history' and the October issue of the Soviet journal *Sputnik*, devoted to the taboo-breaking topic 'Stalin and the War', was banned in the GDR, some young historians protested, and were consequently disciplined.[48] This diversity of opinion, however, only entered the historical profession when the GDR was on the point of collapse, and even then remained a marginal phenomenon. On the whole, GDR historians continued to produce work which served to legitimize the state until the very end of the state's existence.

While historians reformulated their task in order to broaden the areas of study considered legitimate, but did not challenge the fundamental role and structure of their discipline as established in the early decades of the GDR, literature transformed historical debate in more radical ways from the late 1960s onwards. Until this time most literature, like historiography, had fulfilled the function assigned to it by the SED. Conforming to the socialist realist doctrine, GDR literature of the 1950s and early 1960s generally reflected the official conception of history and encouraged readers to play their part in helping to establish the socialist state. During the 1960s, however, a fundamental shift occurred in the world view of some of the most prominent writers in the GDR. From the mid-1960s onwards literary texts began to appear which questioned the prescribed aesthetic models which had hitherto been willingly adopted, and instead expressed growing scepticism

[46] Harald Dehne, 'Have We Come Any Closer to *Alltag*? Everyday Reality and Workers' Lives as an Object of Historical Research in the German Democratic Republic', in *The History of Everyday Life: Reconstructing Historical Experiences and Ways of Life*, ed. Alf Lüdtke, trans. William Templer (Princeton: Princeton University Press, 1995), 116–48 (141).

[47] Rainer Eckert, 'Zwischen den Scherben einer zerbrochenen Welt: Hoffnung auf einen Neubeginn. Die Probleme der Historiker in den Neuen Bundesländern', in *Hure oder Muse?*, ed. Eckert, Kowalczuk, and Stark, 133–8 (135).

[48] Patricia Herminghouse, 'Confronting the "Blank Spots of History": GDR Culture and the Legacy of "Stalinism"', *GSR* 14 (1991), 2, 345–65 (347); *Marxist Historiography in Transformation*, ed. Iggers, 5.

concerning the inflexible *Weltanschauung* of the SED. In texts such as Christa Wolf's 'Juninachmittag' (1965) and *Nachdenken über Christa T.* (1968) and Fritz Rudolf Fries's *Der Weg nach Oobliadooh* (published in the Federal Republic, 1966) the schematic and closed narrative forms of socialist realism are rejected in favour of modernist modes of narration which give voice to a loss of faith in the possibility of comprehending reality as a totality and reflecting this totality objectively in literature.[49] This direction became more marked and more widespread after the Eighth Party Congress of the SED in 1971. Honecker's announcement that there were no taboos for art providing it proceeded from socialist principles created an atmosphere—albeit shortlived—of new hopes for a liberalization of cultural policy. Texts written in the 1960s but at that time regarded as too subversive for publication were now able to appear.

The first two chapters of this book analyse this divergence in the respective developments of literature and historiography from the 1970s onwards. The first chapter discusses the treatment of the National Socialist past, showing how literature was able to challenge the foundation narrative of antifascism by introducing new perspectives based on specifically female experiences of fascism. The second chapter shows how feminist approaches to women's place in history were explored by GDR literary writers, but remained taboo for historians. In each case, I ask what it was that enabled literature to broaden the boundaries of historical debate, and whether developments in the literary sphere had any impact on academic discourses dealing with the same topics. The third chapter examines a group of texts which adopt a rather different approach to history, employing fantasy and myth.

The relationship between the three chapters is not always one of chronological continuity, although a variety of literary developments over the course of the 1970s and 1980s will emerge. Rather, each chapter is concerned with history on a different level. In the first, authors reclaim a personal and collective past which represented an enormous psychological and moral burden, and which had been denied by the SED. The second chapter is also concerned with the recovery of histories excluded from the official state notion of its heritage, but in this case the focus is on women's experience as a reservoir of ideals which should be made productive for the present.

---

[49] Wolfgang Emmerich, 'Der verlorene Faden: Probleme des Erzählens in den siebziger Jahren', in *Die andere deutsche Literatur*, 46–78 (50–60).

This project is continued by some of the texts in Chapter 3, but here several new elements are introduced. Writers explore new ways of making history productive by incorporating fantasy into their works, while explorations of women's experience excluded from conventional notions of 'history' are complemented by panoramic reinterpretations of the whole of western history.

THEORETICAL APPROACHES TO THE RELATIONSHIP BETWEEN LITERARY AND HISTORICAL DISCOURSES

Two broad problems—or groups of problems—must be addressed in the attempt to create a model of the way literature and historiography functioned in the GDR. Firstly, a theory of GDR culture must be able to account for the ways in which political developments, official state discourse, literature, and academic writing interacted to produce changes in the cultural and intellectual spheres over the course of GDR history. Secondly, the differing developments of literary and historical discourses in the GDR raise important questions more generally about the relationship between literature and historiography. How was literature able to voice fundamental critiques of the orthodox discourse, while historiography achieved only more limited reformulations of the officially sanctioned approach to history? An obvious factor is the different extents to which literature and historiography were institutionalized in the GDR. Whereas historians had to work within an institution, whether the Akademie der Wissenschaften, a university, or another institute of higher education, writers did not necessarily need to belong to the Schriftstellerverband in order to produce literature. However, most mainstream writers did belong to the Schriftstellerverband and were bound by its statute to a role of subordination to state cultural policy. Furthermore, all published literature was subject to institutional control in so far as it was dependent on the Hauptverwaltung Verlage und Buchhandel, which functioned as a censoring body with the power to decide whether or not a book could be submitted for publication. In view of these means of institutional control and the harsh disciplinary measures to which writers could be subjected for any action perceived as against the interests of the state, the different institutional positions of historians and writers cannot fully account for the differing developments of the two discourses.[50]

[50] Cf. David Bathrick, 'The End of the Wall Before the End of the Wall', *GSR* 14 (1991), 2, 297–311 (304).

This section will consider a variety of western theoretical discussions of literature and history which are fruitful for understanding how GDR discourses in particular functioned.

The history of GDR literature has been understood—by Emmerich, among others—in terms of a progression away from the officially sanctioned master discourse in order to become an effective critical counter-discourse.[51] It might seem tempting to contrast literature, as a counter-discourse, with historiography, which remained within the boundaries of the master discourse, but—as David Bathrick has shown in his discussion of GDR literature—there are problems with a binary model such as this:

The facile juxtaposition of master discourse (*Leitdiskurs*, monosemia, or encrastic language) to counterdiscourse (countertext, polysemia, etc.) suggests a discreteness of separation that denies the truly contextual and historical nature of the problem we are addressing. The struggle to rewrite and reinscribe the master plot is precisely a process by which one as writer is textually engaged in stretching or realigning cultural political mappings. For example, Christa Wolf continually invokes and at the same time violates a set of formal and ideological codes and in so doing renders those very boundaries historically transfigured. Is she inside or out? On one side or the other?[52]

Similar problems arise when this binary opposition is applied to GDR historiography. Although historians did not publicly subvert or challenge the official discourse on history to the same extent as writers of literature, a similar process of broadening the debate and redefining its terms from within the confines imposed on it transformed academic work on history during the 1970s. Taking Bathrick's comments as a starting-point, this study will work with a model which sees the various kinds of GDR public discourse (literature, historiography, literary criticism, etc.) as a series of interrelated spaces, each centred on official state policy and operating within boundaries imposed by this official discourse. However, both literature and academic writings were able to reconfigure these discursive spaces and to rewrite the master plot—to use Bathrick's terminology—which formed their centre. By examining specific examples of this process, I aim to establish why literature was able to accomplish more momentous transformations of discursive space than academic work, and how far the reconfiguration of one discourse could trigger changes in others.

[51] Emmerich, 'Status melancholicus: Zur Transformation der Utopie in vier Jahrzehnten', in *Die andere deutsche Literatur*, 175–89 (180).

[52] David Bathrick, *The Powers of Speech: The Politics of Culture in the GDR* (Lincoln, Neb., and London: University of Nebraska Press, 1995), 19.

Pierre Bourdieu's theory of cultural production—although written primarily with France in mind and so in its detail often not appropriate for describing GDR practice—provides some broad notions which are helpful for conceptualizing the GDR cultural and intellectual spheres. His concept of the cultural field with its own specific economy based on a particular set of beliefs concerning what constitutes a cultural work and its aesthetic or social value offers a valuable way of approaching GDR culture.[53] The fields of literature and literary criticism are, according to Bourdieu, sites where the authority to determine the legitimate definition of the literary work is at stake. In order to understand the significance of a particular literary work, it must be analysed in relation to the structure of the field at the time when it was produced. These ideas seem particularly appropriate with reference to GDR literature, where the official regulation of culture meant that contests over the definition and role of literature were able to shape the field of cultural production in unusually overt ways. Dissent from the accepted value system could, for example, result in censorship and even imprisonment for the artist. An understanding of the rules of this particular field is unquestionably necessary for recognizing the significance of individual works produced within it.

Bourdieu's model of how the structure of a field changes over time is also particularly apt for the GDR. A field's structure is determined by the relational system of positions occupied by agents within the field. This system is dynamic: whenever a new position asserts itself, for example as a result of political change, this 'determines a displacement of the whole structure and leads to changes in the position-takings of the occupants of other positions'.[54] This model is very fruitful for understanding how the interrelated fields of literature, literary criticism, and historiography developed over time in the GDR, despite the attempt to regulate their roles from above. The first chapter of this study, for example, shows how the publication of Christa Wolf's *Kindheitsmuster*, by creating a new position within the field, altered the structure of the field as a whole and made it possible for other authors and literary critics to take up new positions. As Randal Johnson comments, for Bourdieu the central dialectic of change in the cultural field is a 'broad conflict between orthodoxy and heresy'.[55] If 'orthodoxy' is understood as adherence to the official state discourse and 'heresy'

---

[53] Pierre Bourdieu, *The Field of Cultural Production: Essays on Art and Literature*, ed. and trans. Randal Johnson (Cambridge and Oxford: Polity, 1993), 9.

[54] Ibid. 58.

[55] Ibid. 17.

as dissidence, then this struggle is clearly central to the broadening of discursive boundaries in the GDR.

Bourdieu's model of the cultural field offers a productive way of approaching the dynamics of change in GDR literature and historiography. However, the central question of why these two discourses diverged so significantly in their developments remains unanswered. The project of comparing historiography and prose fiction presupposes a certain degree of common ground between the two. In recent decades, critical theory has highlighted the permeable nature of the boundary between written history and prose fiction. Each uses language, and in most instances narrative, to create a discourse which combines a referential relationship to reality with elements of fictionality. The textual nature of historiography has been emphasized. Keith Jenkins, for example, argues that a fundamental disjunction must be acknowledged between the past as a reality, which is inaccessible, and the discursive traces of this reality which provide the only criterion for assessing the truth of any particular historical discourse.[56] Hayden White has suggested that historiography employs literary rhetoric and plot structures to give meaning to the events of the past, which 'do not offer themselves as stories':[57]

Insofar as historical stories can be completed, can be given narrative closure, can be shown to have had a plot all along, they give to reality the odor of the ideal. [. . .] The demand for closure in the historical story is a demand, I suggest, for moral meaning, a demand that sequences of real events be assessed as to their significance as elements of a moral drama.[58]

While a total erasure of the boundary between literature and historiography—of which White has frequently been accused[59]—is clearly absurd, acknowledging the fictional elements in historical narratives is particularly helpful for approaching GDR historiography. White's analysis, based on nineteenth-century political historiography, does not do justice to many developments in twentieth-century approaches to history, but is extremely apt in the case of an ideologically controlled historical profession where historians' work was required to conform to a prescribed master narrative of history. White argues that histori-

---

[56] Keith Jenkins, *On 'What is History?': From Carr and Elton to Rorty and White* (London and New York: Routledge, 1995), 18.
[57] Hayden White, *The Content of the Form: Narrative Discourse and Historical Representation* (Baltimore and London: Johns Hopkins University Press, 1987; repr. 1990), 4.
[58] Ibid. 21.
[59] See, for example, Paul Michael Lützeler, *Klio oder Kalliope? Literatur und Geschichte: Sondierung, Analyse, Interpretation* (Berlin: Schmidt, 1997), 12–13.

ans have failed to acknowledge the constructed nature of historical stories, presenting them instead as empirically found. He distinguishes between 'a historical discourse that narrates and a discourse that narrativizes': while the former 'openly adopts a perspective that looks out on the world and reports it', the latter 'feigns to make the world speak itself and speak itself as a story', thus concealing the act of construction involved in the presentation of the past.[60] With its claims to scientific objectivity and empirical verifiability, GDR historiography is a prime example of the latter.

While the mixture of fact and fiction—or real events and imaginary contexts[61]—contained in both literature and historiography provides a basis for a comparison, a number of important differences between the two discourses might help to account for their differing developments in the GDR. White's reduction of historiography to an ultimately fictional discourse is a helpful way of approaching the process by which GDR historians accommodated historical figures and events within an authoritative grand narrative of history. However, this equation of historiography with fiction risks obscuring the fact that the two discourses are traditionally expected to fulfil very different functions with regard to notions of reality and truth. As Karin J. MacHardy concludes in a paper on 'The Boundaries of History and Literature', historiography is subject to criteria of verifiability which do not apply to literary writing:

The most important of these differences is that historians do not have the freedom to invent occurrences or persons of the past, nor can they narrate their inner dialogues. [. . .] Unlike fiction writers, historians have to verify their stories with evidence from other texts, such as archival sources and other historical studies. Nevertheless, this verification of consistency does not in itself objectify historians' work as it is thereby not contradicted by reality itself but by other texts. It must be stressed that fiction writing cannot be contradicted in this manner.[62]

If plot structures which are ultimately imaginary are employed by historians, then this occurs with the aim of finding as truthful a way as possible of making sense of real events in the past. Prose fiction can

---

[60] White, 2. This idea can be traced back to Barthes's work in the 1960s. See Roland Barthes, 'Historical Discourse', trans. Peter Wexler, in *Structuralism: A Reader*, ed. Michael Lane (London: Cape, 1966), 145–55 (153).

[61] See Jenkins, 19.

[62] Karin J. MacHardy, 'The Boundaries of History and Literature', in *Fact and Fiction: German History and Literature 1848–1924*, ed. Gisela Brude-Firnau and Karin J. MacHardy (Tübingen: Francke, 1990), 11–25 (25).

focus on imaginary events as well as real ones, and is free to combine
the two in ways historiography is not. Literature deals with possibilities, rather than the actual events of history. This difference has important consequences for any attempt to control the notions of 'truth'
embodied in literature and historiography respectively. Literature is
not subject to the requirement to depict a single, consistent world,
which R. G. Collingwood defines as a condition for history and Lionel
Gossman regards rather as a regulative constraint in the conventions
of historical discourse: 'that all history must be consistent with itself,
since there is only one historical world, whereas fictional universes,
being autonomous, need not agree, and cannot clash.'[63] Literature
thus allows a plurality of fictional worlds and narratives because it is
regarded as an ultimately imaginative discourse, while historiography,
understood as the representation of a reality conceived to be monolithic, is confined to a single world and, in a totalitarian state such as the
GDR, to a single overarching narrative.

Since literature is an imaginary narrativization of both real and
imaginary events, any relation it might bear to the past is not one of
straightforward correspondence. Both this more opaque relationship
to reality and the inevitable plurality of fictional worlds and plots from
one text to another make it more difficult to control literature's conformity to a single definitive narrative than is the case with history.
Literature also has a far greater potential for ambiguity and plurality
within an individual text than historiography. A literary text may present contradictory meanings or a subversive subtext far more easily
than a historical account, which is required to be internally consistent,
and where the convention of a more transparent identity of narrator
and author corresponds to a reading practice based on the straightforward equation of statements on the page with authorial opinion.
A polyphony of voices and the possibilities of irony are among the
features which make authorial views much harder to locate in a novel.

In attempting to impose similar constraints on literature and historiography, the SED also overlooked fundamental differences in their
traditions as institutions. Whereas history is generally practised within
state institutions and so has often had the task of writing the official
story of the past, from the perspective of a particular state, literature

---

[63] R. G. Collingwood, *The Idea of History* (Oxford: Clarendon, 1946), 246. Cited in Lionel
Gossman, 'History and Literature: Reproduction or Signification', in *The Writing of History:
Literary Form and Historical Understanding*, ed. Robert H. Canary and Henry Kozicki (Madison:
University of Wisconsin Press, 1978), 3–39 (30).

has a long tradition of commenting critically on society from an outside perspective. The subjective experience of the writer, conventionally suppressed in historical accounts, is traditionally the basis and subject of a large proportion of world literature. Bathrick has argued that in the GDR literature was more able than any other discourse, 'einen authentischen Kontakt zwischen der öffentlichen und der privaten Sphäre zu vermitteln'.[64] Elizabeth Mittman has described the consequences of the tension between a tradition of literary autonomy and the SED's attempts at institutionalizing and controlling literature in the following terms:

As a site for the production and communication of subjectivity, for the expression of the non-collective, in and through the voice of the writer, literature produced under the structural conditions of state socialism bears witness to a persistence of dissonances between two antagonistic discursive realms—the official discourse of the state and a plethora of other, 'private' voices that would, through their public articulation, contest the dominant discourse.[65]

Finally, the different developments of literature and historiography in the GDR may be related to a more widespread divergence of the two discourses from the late nineteenth century onwards, particularly with regard to the question of how language and narrative relate to reality. Dominick LaCapra sees the 'tremendous explosion of exploratory approaches to narrative' in the novel since Flaubert as a phenomenon from which modern historiography could fruitfully learn.[66] While literature began to question the transparency of language as a medium for reflecting reality and to challenge the closed narratives and omniscient narrators of realism, such reflective and self-critical impulses remained absent from mainstream western historiography:

Narrative in history tends, with some exceptions, to remain set in its nineteenth-century ways. [. . .] There is relatively little self-consciousness about the problem of voice or point of view; the narrator tends to be omniscient and to rely on the convention of unity not only of narrative voice but between narrative and authorial voice; and the story is typically organized in accordance with a chronologically arranged, beginning-middle-end structure.[67]

---

[64] Bathrick, 'Kultur und Öffentlichkeit', 65.
[65] Elizabeth Mittman, 'Locating a Public Sphere: Some Reflections on Writers and *Öffentlichkeit* in the GDR', in *WIGY 10*, ed. Jeanette Clausen and Sara Friedrichsmeyer (Lincoln, Neb., and London: University of Nebraska Press, 1995), 19–37 (23).
[66] Dominick LaCapra, *History and Criticism* (Ithaca, NY, and London: Cornell University Press, 1985; repr. 1996), 123.   [67] Ibid. 122.

Despite its attempt to impose on literature narrative conventions of this kind, in the form of socialist realism, the SED was not able in the long term to prevent writers from taking up modernist literary traditions which challenge monolithic and unified narratives, and undermine faith in the directly mimetic capacity of language. Most of the texts to be discussed in the present study incorporate a degree of narrative self-reflection, in order to highlight the limitations of language and literary form as means of representing a past reality. They thus implicitly, and at times explicitly, challenge the premises of the official version of history. Historiography, meanwhile, had no such tradition of self-reflection or scepticism about language and narrative. GDR historians' writing was generally characterized not only by the kind of language traditional in academic work; a language which, despite its rootedness in a particular time and place, is confident that it has access to an objective truth, and which denies its origin in a thinking and organizing subject, and values reason to the neglect of imagination. Historians also adopted the rigid terminology of official SED discourse, a language which made imaginative input and rigorous intellectual enquiry difficult by providing a fixed set of concepts embodying a preconceived truth which all work had to support. As Georg Iggers has argued, Marxist–Leninist ideology 'led to the ritualization of language in the form of a terminological code that prevented intellectually honest communication'.[68]

The SED's attempt to appropriate literature as a form of ideological support to disseminate the authorized version of history to the public undoubtedly helped to create a literature which was highly conscious of its role as a commentator on history. However, the various factors I have outlined—literature's opaque relationship to reality, its potential for plurality and ambiguity, its capacity for self-reflection, its tradition of critical commentary on society, and its roots in subjective, individual experience—help to explain why literature was able to develop away from supporting state-sponsored historiography, to become an alternative discourse on history.

FEMINISM IN THE GDR

Feminism represents one of the most significant and fundamental challenges to the orthodox model of history voiced by GDR literature

---

[68] *Marxist Historiography in Transformation*, ed. Iggers, 7.

of the 1970s and 1980s. It can be seen as an area of intersection between two different kinds of discourse which questioned this orthodox model: those created by political movements, such as environmentalism and the peace movement, and more theoretical bodies of thought, for example, the postmodern scepticism about history which has pervaded the work of many western intellectuals in recent decades. Not only is feminism both a political practice and a body of theories,[69] but, in a variety of forms, it also overlaps with, draws from, and feeds into all of these other discourses.

Gender relations in the GDR were characterized by the discrepancy between official proclamations and experienced reality which generally structured all areas of public and private life. The SED based its policies concerning women and gender equality on the writings of Marx, Engels, Bebel, and Zetkin, all of whom saw women's oppression under patriarchy as a problem subordinate to the oppression of the working classes under capitalism. Sonja Hilzinger identifies three fundamental ideas common to these socialist thinkers: 'daß sie im Privateigentum die Ursache der Versklavung der Arbeiter wie der Frauen sehen, daß sie die Frauen-Emanzipationsbewegung der Arbeiterbewegung unterordnen und daß sie in der Einführung sozialistischer Produktionsverhältnisse das Ende beider Ausbeutungsverhältnisse sehen.'[70]

The assumption that women's oppression was rooted in capitalism meant that the establishment of a socialist state was regarded as a foundation on which gender equality would automatically develop. Legislation, motivated at least in part by economic necessity in the post-war years, aimed at enabling women to combine motherhood with a career. Equality was defined in terms of women's participation in paid employment. Women were thus encouraged to play the same role as men in the public sphere, though in practice they generally occupied less prestigious and lower paid positions. Sociological research has shown that, in the private sphere, conventional gender roles continued to prevail, a finding which is frequently reflected in literature by women.[71]

One important consequence of the official claim to have achieved

[69] Cf. Chris Weedon, *Feminist Practice and Poststructuralist Theory* (Cambridge, Mass., and Oxford: Blackwell, 1987; repr. 1994), 1–6.

[70] Sonja Hilzinger, *'Als ganzer Mensch zu leben . . .': Emanzipatorische Tendenzen in der neueren Frauen-Literatur der DDR* (Frankfurt am Main: Lang, 1985), 10–11.

[71] See, for example, Morgner's *Trobadora Beatriz*. For more detailed accounts of the legal provisions for GDR women and sociological evidence, see Hilzinger, *'Als ganzer Mensch zu leben . . .'*, 10–28; Mechthild M. Matheja-Theaker, *Alternative Emanzipationsvorstellungen in der DDR-Frauenliteratur (1971–1989): Ein Diskussionsbeitrag zur Situation der Frau* (Stuttgart: Heinz, 1996), 15–19.

gender equality was the taboo status accorded to the notion of feminism. There could be no autonomous, public women's movement in the GDR, since this would have challenged the idea that gender inequality was a consequence of class inequality, and had therefore been eradicated under 'real existierender Sozialismus'. There was thus no public forum for the discussion of women's needs, problems, and continuing subordination to men, particularly in the private domain. Feminism was regarded as the product of western capitalist relations, and therefore dismissed as irrelevant to the GDR. A narrow understanding of feminism as an expression of women's antagonism towards men was widespread. Eva Kaufmann has shown how, 'in der DDR jede selbständige Regung und Bewegung von Frauen als "Emanzentum" verpönt und politisch denunziert wurde'.[72] Small academic discussion groups were formed during the 1980s to explore feminist approaches to research, for example by the Berlin cultural scientist Irene Dölling.[73] However, such groups were few in number and marginal, occupying a semi-official space within institutions. They were also perceived as a threat: in 1986, a research group on women's issues in German literature at the Akademie der Wissenschaften was dissolved, because its members were thought to have strayed too far from the Party line.[74] Even writers like Wolf and Morgner were eager to distance themselves from 'feminism' as it was widely understood. In an interview of 1976 with Ursula Krechel, Morgner persistently rejects the label 'DDR-Feministin', arguing that 'der Feminismus ist eine Reaktion auf eine frauenfeindliche Umgebung. Mein Staat ist frauenfreundlich', and defining herself as 'eine Kommunistin, die die speziellen Forderungen der Frauen außerordentlich bewegen'.[75] Similarly, in her essay 'Berührung', written as a preface for Maxie Wander's Guten Morgen, du Schöne, Wolf stresses the distinction between Wander's work and 'bestimmte Frauengruppen in kapitalistischen Ländern, denen man ihren oft fanatischen Männerhaß vorwirft'.[76] However, Wolf goes on to

[72] Eva Kaufmann, 'Irmtraud Morgner, Christa Wolf und andere: Feminismus in der DDR-Literatur', in Literatur in der DDR: Rückblicke, ed. Heinz Ludwig Arnold and Frauke Meyer-Gosau (Munich: text + kritik, 1991), 109–16 (113).
[73] Gabriele Jähnert, 'Das Zentrum für interdisziplinäre Frauenforschung (ZiF) an der Humboldt-Universität zu Berlin', ZG, NS 9 (1999), 1, 118–22 (118).
[74] Hörnigk, 'Contours of a New Academic Landscape', 176.
[75] 'Die täglichen Zerstückelungen: Gespräch mit Ursula Krechel', in Irmtraud Morgner: Texte, Daten, Bilder, ed. Marlis Gerhardt (Frankfurt am Main: Luchterhand, 1990), 24–33 (24–5).
[76] Christa Wolf, 'Berührung: Maxie Wander', in Die Dimension des Autors: Essays und Aufsätze, Reden und Gespräche 1959–1985, 2 vols. (Frankfurt am Main: Luchterhand, 1987; repr. 1990), i. 196–209 (205).

blame social conditions—the lack of a strong workers' movement—for this variety of feminism, and to conclude that GDR women might be able to learn something from the solidarity, initiative, imagination, and plurality which she perceives in western women's movements.

The reluctance of these writers publicly to identify themselves with feminism may have been partly motivated by pragmatic political considerations, and represented in any case a rejection of a popular and ideologically motivated image of *Feminismus* which corresponded only to a small strand in the heterogeneous and constantly developing body of ideas produced by feminists internationally since the early 1970s. While it is clearly not unproblematic to apply the term 'feminist' to works by writers who expressly distanced themselves from this label, I shall use the term in a broad sense, as a useful shorthand to describe positions which criticize gender relations under patriarchy.

Feminism, in all its manifestations, presented a number of challenges to official SED discourse. By highlighting women's continuing oppression in the present and calling for political action to overcome patriarchy, it questioned the legitimacy of the GDR as a state where gender equality had been realized. By encouraging critical reflection on the meanings of terms like 'gender equality' and 'women's needs', it questioned the goals the GDR had set itself, determined as they were by an assimilation of women to male norms, rather than a questioning of those norms. Feminist critiques of patriarchy and its manifestation in the traditional nuclear family revealed the inadequacy of the SED's policy of integrating women into existing patriarchal structures. Most generally, by promoting gender as an independent category of analysis, feminism challenged the strict subordination of gender to class in GDR discourse.

Because of the importance of feminism as a challenge to the Party line, examining the degree to which feminist ideas became absorbed into different kinds of discourse in the GDR is an effective way of assessing the different rules which governed literature and academic writing, and the varying extents to which each was able to subvert official ideology. The different feminist approaches adopted by the various texts discussed here may correspond to different stages and perspectives in the debates which have taken place in western feminism since the 1970s. However, it is not the aim of this study to establish a teleology based on the history of western feminist theory, nor to assess literary texts according to criteria provided by a particular set of feminist ideas. Instead, the emphasis is on the variety of ways in which women writers broadened the boundaries of GDR public discourse by focusing on gender.

APPROACHES TO NARRATIVE PROSE BY GDR WOMEN

The literary texts which form the focus of the chapters to follow have hitherto been examined in the contexts of three different kinds of critical study. Firstly, attention has been focused on women's writing in the GDR, sometimes within broader surveys of GDR literature. Secondly, in the case of the more prominent writers, that is, Wolf and to a lesser extent Morgner, a number of author-based studies have appeared. Thirdly, texts have been grouped by topic, often together with literature by men and/or literature from the other German-speaking states, and analysed accordingly. Studies have thus focused on literary representations of the National Socialist past, biographical fiction, or writers' employment of mythical themes and forms. This study is the first to combine the examination of these different topics, in order to show the variety and the developments in the ways GDR women's writing transformed approaches to history in the 1970s and 1980s.

Two critical approaches dominate this body of secondary literature. Firstly, literature by GDR women has repeatedly been read as a straightforward reflection of, or comment on, the social conditions governing women's lives under 'real existierender Sozialismus'. An insistence on the social basis and intent of this literature characterizes the work of critics within the GDR. In assessing how the terms 'Frauenliteratur' and 'weibliches Schreiben' might be helpful for approaching writing in the GDR, for example, Ilse Nagelschmidt defines them in exclusively sociological terms:

Im Prozeß der sozialistischen Revolution, in dessen Verlauf die noch bestehenden nichtantagonistischen sozialen Widersprüche zwischen den Klassen und Schichten abgebaut werden, verstehen wir die sozialistische Frauenliteratur als eine besondere Möglichkeit und Notwendigkeit der künst-lerischen Artikulation, auf bestehende Probleme aufmerksam zu machen, wirkliche Verhältnisse und Verfahrensweisen analytisch darzustellen, um so den differenzierten Annäherungsvorgang der Geschlechter zu forcieren.[77]

---

[77] Ilse Nagelschmidt, 'Sozialistische Frauenliteratur: Überlegungen zu einem Phänomen der DDR-Literatur in den siebziger und achtziger Jahren', *WB* 35 (1989), 3, 450–71 (459).

In the West, too, sociological approaches—albeit with a different accent—dominated criticism throughout the 1970s and 1980s. The sociological bias which Emmerich perceives in research on GDR literature in general was, and remains, particularly prominent in work on women's writing. Emmerich's own treatment of texts by women in the 1996 edition of the *Kleine Literaturgeschichte* persists in regarding the notion of 'women's writing' as a sociologically determined phenomenon concerned solely with analysing the society in which it was written. Although texts by women, especially Wolf and Morgner, are central to Emmerich's narrative of literary history at a number of points, only once in the section on the literature of the last two decades of the GDR does he focus specifically on 'Frauenliteratur' as a category worthy of special attention. He limits the category to those texts which present the everyday experiences of GDR women, and discusses 'Frauenliteratur' in the context of a series of topics dealt with under the heading 'Die neue Herrlichkeit: DDR-Alltag als Sujet'.[78] This categorization implies that female authorship is of consequence or particular interest only in so far as a literary text can be read as a comment on social conditions for women in the present. This sociologically oriented approach is also the most common one to be found in feminist work specifically on GDR women writers. Throughout the 1970s and 1980s studies of GDR women's writing were invariably framed with a discussion of the theory and reality of gender equality in the GDR, and literary texts were read largely as a commentary on social conditions.[79]

Despite the widespread criticism, since the demise of the GDR, of approaches to its literature which neglected the aesthetic and textual qualities of works in order to read them as social documents, sociological approaches to GDR women's writing have proliferated since 1989. Three recent full-length studies, by Mechthild M. Matheja-Theaker, Gabriele Müller-Rückert, and Kornelia Hauser, analyse texts by

---

[78] Emmerich, *Kleine Literaturgeschichte*, 298–301.

[79] Examples include Patricia Herminghouse, 'Wunschbild, Vorbild oder Porträt? Zur Darstellung der Frau im Roman der DDR', in *Literatur und Literaturtheorie in der DDR*, ed. Peter Uwe Hohendahl and Patricia Herminghouse (Frankfurt am Main: Suhrkamp, 1976), 281–334, '"Der Autor nämlich ist ein wichtiger Mensch": Zur Prosa', in *Frauen Literatur Geschichte: Schreibende Frauen vom Mittelalter bis zur Gegenwart*, ed. Hiltrud Gnüg and Renate Möhrmann (Stuttgart: Metzler, 1985; repr. Frankfurt am Main: Suhrkamp, 1989), 338–53; Sara Lennox, '"Nun ja! Das nächste Leben geht aber heute an": Prosa von Frauen und Frauenbefreiung in der DDR', in *Literatur der DDR in den siebziger Jahren*, ed. Hohendahl and Herminghouse, 224–58. Two longer studies relate developments in GDR women's writing to conditions for women in the GDR, but go beyond purely sociological readings in their literary analysis: Dorothee Schmitz-Köster, *Trobadora und Kassandra und . . . : Weibliches Schreiben in der DDR* (Cologne: Pahl-Rugenstein, 1989); Hilzinger, *'Als ganzer Mensch zu leben . . .'*.

women as sources of sociological evidence. Matheja-Theaker examines the relationship between literary texts, the findings of sociological research, and the official presentation of women in GDR discourses.[80] Müller-Rückert offers sociological analyses of the female protagonists of works by Ursula Hörig, Brigitte Martin, Erika Paschke, Gerti Tetzner, and Hedda Zinner.[81] Hauser reads texts by Wolf, Morgner, Brigitte Reimann, Gerti Tetzner, and Monika Maron as sources of information about gender relations in the GDR, in order then to draw out the utopian potential which she feels they still have to offer society, even after the dissolution of the context in which they were produced.[82]

The second critical approach which has been used to analyse the texts to be discussed here is common in topic-based studies and in some work on individual authors, and came to prominence in the late 1980s. Texts are read in relation to an 'international' (i.e. western) theoretical context, usually feminist, with at most a cursory reference to the specific political and cultural conditions of the GDR. An example of this approach is Stephanie Bird's *Recasting Historical Women: Female Identity in German Biographical Fiction* (1998).[83] Bird outlines social conditions for women and the development of women's writing in the GDR in a brief paragraph in her introductory chapter, then analyses texts by Wolf, Brigitte Struzyk, Sigrid Damm, and Volker Ebersbach alongside works by the West German writers Karin Reschke, Ria Endres, and Sibylle Knauss. In her literary analysis and qualitative judgements she employs categories from western feminist theory, and pays little attention to the significantly different historical contexts in which, and for which, the texts were written.

The present study is based on the conviction that, for all their particular merits, neither of these two dominant critical approaches does justice to the achievements of GDR women's literature in transforming the public discourse of the state by opening a space in which feminist ideas could modify and subvert official notions of society in the present and of history. It is undeniable that GDR women's texts provide a unique insight into, and analysis of, conditions of life for

[80] Matheja-Theaker, *Alternative Emanzipationsvorstellungen in der DDR-Frauenliteratur*.

[81] Gabriele Müller-Rückert, *Frauenleben und Geschlechterverhältnis in der ehemaligen DDR: Weibliche Lebenswelten im Spiegel literarischer 'Frauengeschichten' und sozialwissenschaftlicher Auswertung* (Bielefeld: Kleine, 1993).

[82] Kornelia Hauser, *Patriarchat als Sozialismus: Soziologische Studien zu Literatur aus der DDR* (Hamburg: Argument-Verlag, 1994).

[83] Stephanie Bird, *Recasting Historical Women: Female Identity in German Biographical Fiction* (Oxford and New York: Berg, 1998).

women under 'real existierender Sozialismus'. They also unquestionably have much to contribute to an international feminist discourse. However, approaches which focus exclusively on either of these aspects risk reducing literature to either its historical context or a set of theoretical ideas. Literary analysis tends towards sociology or philosophy respectively, and in either case the distinct qualities of texts as literature get lost. It is the aim of this study to show how literature negotiates between a historical context and the realm of ideas. Texts by GDR women respond to social and political reality not just by describing that reality, but also by reconfiguring the discourses—about history and gender, for example—which belonged to it. The alternatives which Ute Brandes observes in American work on GDR women writers are therefore a false dichotomy:

Die Texte von DDR-Schriftstellerinnen werden [. . .] zum einen analysiert als Dokumente politischer Haltungen, die in der Kultur des Herkunftlandes verankert sind und von denen sich eine Autorin jeweils abgrenzt oder nicht; zum anderen als grenzüberschreitender Ausdruck von weiblichen Lebenszusammenhängen und feministischen Befreiungsutopien.[84]

In an article of 1988, Genia Schulz proposes an approach which reads the various feminist aesthetics of GDR authors as a response to the dominant discourse of state socialism: 'beansprucht wird die künstlerische Lizenz, den Herrschaftsdiskurs zu durchbrechen, zu ironisieren oder ihn zu negieren. All dies sind Bewegungen, die die Mitarbeit an der gesellschaftlichen Sinnproduktion in Frage stellen.'[85] Responding to this stimulus, the present study will focus on the significance which feminism had in GDR literature, as an example of a counter-discourse capable of transforming the cultural and intellectual spheres under state socialism.

---

[84] Ute Brandes, 'Einleitung', in *Zwischen gestern und morgen: Schriftstellerinnen der DDR aus amerikanischer Sicht*, ed. Ute Brandes (Berlin: Lang, 1992), 7–16 (1).
[85] Genia Schulz, 'Kein Chorgesang: Neue Schreibweisen bei Autorinnen (aus) der DDR', in *Bestandsaufnahme Gegenwartsliteratur: Bundesrepublik Deutschland, Deutsche Demokratische Republik, Österreich, Schweiz*, ed. Heinz Ludwig Arnold (Munich: text + kritik, 1988), 212–25 (223).

'DAS VERGANGENE IST NICHT TOT': NEW APPROACHES TO NATIONAL SOCIALISM IN LITERATURE OF THE 1970S

HISTORICAL AND LITERARY TREATMENTS OF NATIONAL SOCIALISM PRIOR TO THE 1970S

National Socialism tested—and revealed—the limits of GDR historiography to a greater degree than almost any other topic. As in all areas of historical study, work on the Third Reich involved subordinating evidence to an unquestioned orthodox Marxist master narrative of history. This master narrative, based on an economic understanding of social developments, determined the aspects of Hitler's regime which were privileged in historians' accounts, and resulted in a highly selective approach to the era. Even in the later years of the GDR, when historians were generally questioning rigid orthodoxies, explanations of this period remained unconvincingly dogmatic and one-sided.

The unsatisfactory nature of GDR work on the fascist past is due ultimately to the way 'fascism' had to be understood in order to give it an unproblematic and fully explicable place in the officially prescribed Marxist model of history. Georgi Dimitroff's 1935 definition of 'Faschismus' as 'die offene, terroristische Diktatur der reaktionärsten, am meisten chauvinistischen, am meisten imperialistischen Elemente des Finanzkapitals' was adopted and remained officially valid until the GDR's demise.[1] Fascism was thus reduced to an extreme manifestation of capitalism, which can be fully explained in purely economic terms. The ideas of human agency and individual or mass responsibility were marginalized. The specific characteristics of German National Socialism were neglected, and instead fascism was studied as a universal manifestation of capitalism in its late stages, attempting to defend itself against the threat of a socialist revolution. By implication, it was assumed that the replacement of capitalist economic structures

---

[1] See Christel Berger, *Gewissensfrage Antifaschismus: Traditionen der DDR-Literatur. Analysen—Interpretationen—Interviews* (Berlin: Dietz, 1990), 20.

by socialist ones must necessarily destroy fascism.[2] However, fascism was perceived as an ongoing danger in the present for the capitalist world.

The officially binding model of German history as a 'progressive' tradition culminating in the GDR and a 'reactionary' course of development leading to the Federal Republic had the ideologically desirable effects of associating Hitler's regime with West Germany and denying any historical continuity between the Third Reich and the GDR. As a socialist state, the GDR could claim an alternative, positive tradition as its history; that of resistance to Hitler, particularly by communists. This identification with the heroic deeds of antifascists allowed the recent German past to be seen not as a burden needing to be 'bewältigt', but instead as something already triumphantly overcome. As Stephan Hermlin commented in 1979, the GDR's self-designation as 'Sieger der Geschichte' had the effect of absolving its citizens from guilt concerning their past.[3] 'Antifascism' became a foundation myth of the GDR, used to differentiate the new socialist state from both the National Socialist German nation and the newly founded Federal Republic.[4]

Although even in the 1950s literary authors and critics showed an awareness of both the need for an honest and thorough confrontation with the fascist past and the potential of literature to achieve this, such views did not properly find their way into GDR literary practice until the 1970s.[5] In 1953 Bertolt Brecht warned of the dangers of attempting to build a new society without first dealing with the problems of the past: 'Wir haben allzufrüh der unmittelbaren Vergangenheit den Rücken zugekehrt, begierig, uns der Zukunft zuzuwenden. Die Zukunft wird aber abhängen von der Erledigung der Vergangenheit.'[6]

---

[2] Berger still subscribes to this view in her work of 1990. Ibid. 19.

[3] Klaus Wagenbach, 'Wo sind wir zu hause? Gespräch mit Stephan Hermlin', *Freibeuter*, 1 (1979), 1, 47–55 (49–50).

[4] See Emmerich, *Kleine Literaturgeschichte*, 29; Bathrick, *The Powers of Speech*, 13, 17–18. More detailed accounts of antifascism are provided by Konrad H. Jarausch, 'The Failure of East German Antifascism: Some Ironies of History as Politics', *GSR* 14 (1991), 1, 85–102; Petra Boden, 'Ornamente und Tabus: Antifaschismus als Herrschaftsdiskurs', *WB* 41 (1995), 1, 104–19; Antonia Grunenberg, *Antifaschismus: Ein deutscher Mythos* (Reinbek: Rowohlt, 1993), 120–44.

[5] See Patricia Herminghouse, 'Vergangenheit als Problem der Gegenwart: Zur Darstellung des Faschismus in der neueren DDR-Literatur', in *Literatur der DDR in den siebziger Jahren*, ed. Hohendahl and Herminghouse, 259–94 (265–9).

[6] Bertolt Brecht, 'Kulturpolitik und Akademie der Künste', in *Werke* (Große kommentierte Berliner und Frankfurter Ausgabe), ed. Werner Hecht, Jan Knopf, *et al.*, 30 vols. (Berlin: Aufbau; Frankfurt am Main: Suhrkamp, 1988–2000), xxiii (1993). 256–60 (259).

This might seem an odd statement, considering that fascism and the Second World War were prominent themes in GDR literature from the very beginning. The work of returning exiled authors such as Anna Seghers, Johannes R. Becher, and Alexander Abusch, dealing primarily with experiences during the National Socialist era, was published in the Soviet Occupied Zone in the late 1940s.[7] The topic continued to be prominent in works produced by these and other authors throughout the 1950s and 1960s. However, like GDR historiography of Hitler's regime, this literature tended not to present the past as a problem needing to be confronted, but instead used a highly selective and mythologizing view of the past as a source of ideals and role models for the present.

Two literary models recur in the novels of this period which deal with the fascist past. Firstly, stories about the heroic deeds of (usually communist) members of the antifascist resistance are told. Anna Seghers's *Das siebte Kreuz* functioned as a model for this literature, which was produced primarily by authors who had been committed communists during the Third Reich, and who had experienced either exile or imprisonment in concentration camps. This category includes works by Bodo Uhse, Otto Gotsche, Stephan Hermlin, and Ludwig Renn. These texts helped to create the myth of a heroic tradition of humane behaviour in the name of socialism. They focus on exemplary cases and adopt an optimistic perspective, suggesting that the essential goodness of human nature continues to hold sway, even in circumstances of extreme brutality. As Patricia Herminghouse has pointed out, this model did not correspond to the experiences of the vast majority of GDR citizens, for whom 'nichts anderes übrig blieb, als ihre eigenen, andersartigen Erfahrungen und ihre Einsicht, wie sehr sie sich selbst in den Kriegsjahren kompromittiert hatten, zu verdrängen'.[8]

A second group of works, written by younger authors whose commitment to socialism had more recent roots, features protagonists, often soldiers, who are supporters of the fascist regime, but then gain an insight into its injustice and inhumanity, and quickly convert to socialism. Such *Wandlungsromane* were produced by Herbert Otto, Dieter Noll, Franz Fühmann, Max Walter Schulz, and Günter de Bruyn, among others.[9] This variant on the socialist realist *Bildungs-*

---

[7] See Emmerich, *Kleine Literaturgeschichte*, 81.

[8] Herminghouse, 'Vergangenheit als Problem der Gegenwart', 263.

[9] See Ingrid Dinter, *Unvollendete Trauerarbeit in der DDR-Literatur: Ein Studium der Vergangenheitsbewältigung* (New York: Lang, 1994), 59.

roman was discussed by Hermann Kant and Frank Wagner in their paper at a conference on the topic 'Widerspiegelung des zweiten Weltkriegs in der Literatur', held in October 1957, and by Christa Wolf in her subsequent report on the conference.[10] Kant and Wagner are highly critical of certain schematic approaches to fascism which they identify in the works of Egon Günther, Kurt David, Werner Steinberg, Klaus Herrmann, Martin Müller, and Herbert Otto. In particular, they criticize the use of protagonists who, even as fascist soldiers, possess the seeds of antifascist insight and socialist commitment:

all diese zweifelnden, ahnenden oder gar wissenden Soldaten sind eben nicht Abbilder jenes Soldaten der deutschen Wehrmacht, der sich so schmählich von den Faschisten mißbrauchen ließ. Damit aber begibt man sich der großen Chance, einen echten Konflikt zu gestalten; der wahrhaft erregende, aufwühlende und lehrreiche Prozeß der echten Wandlung wird eingetauscht gegen Schein- oder Halbkonflikte, gegen abenteuerliche und unglaubhafte Konstruktionen.[11]

Wolf is similarly critical of the schematism of existing works and of authors' reluctance, 'den tieferen Konflikt eines von der faschistischen Ideologie betörten jungen Menschen in den Mittelpunkt zu stellen'.[12]

Literary works depicting 'den Prozeß der Wandlung in seiner ganzen Schwere und Kompliziertheit', as demanded by Kant and Wagner, did not appear in the GDR until the 1970s. A curious discrepancy thus seems to have arisen, between theoretical calls for an honest and complex treatment of the past, and a literature reluctant to move beyond the schematic approaches of the immediate post-war years. Two factors help to explain this anomaly. Firstly, as Kant and Wagner acknowledge, writing truthfully about experiences during the war requires a certain openness to self-criticism.[13] Historical distance is likely to be necessary before honest self-scrutiny can be achieved.

Secondly, a closer examination of Kant and Wagner's paper reveals that the authors are still working within the kind of schematic approach which their rhetoric condemns. In calling for more complex presentations of change, they are not criticizing the model of character development underlying literary plots, nor the didactic function of the

[10] Hermann Kant and Frank Wagner, 'Die große Abrechnung: Probleme der Darstellung des Krieges in der deutschen Gegenwartsliteratur', *NDL* 5 (1957), 12, 124–39; Christa Wolf, 'Vom Standpunkt des Schriftstellers und von der Form der Kunst', *NDL* 5 (1957), 12, 119–24.
[11] Kant and Wagner, 128.
[12] Wolf, 'Vom Standpunkt des Schriftstellers', 121.
[13] Kant and Wagner, 127.

positive hero with whom the reader can identify. Instead, they are concerned primarily with the credibility of the presentation. For instance,
they criticize the popular use of the 'old Communist' figure as an 'ideologischer Lehrmeister', yet the 'realistic' presentation of socialist antifascist resistance fighters remains central to their demands.[14] Their call
for presentations of the kind of soldier, 'der sich so schmählich von den
Faschisten *mißbrauchen ließ*' (emphasis added), implicitly exonerates the
soldiers from guilt by removing their agency and responsibility. The
didactic and schematic model of the immediate post-war years is thus
being refined here, rather than overthrown. While calling for realistic,
believable, and complex presentations of change, Kant and Wagner
still require autobiographical experience to be moulded into the
orthodox patterns of historical understanding which had determined
literary works up to this point:

Wir drängen auf eine Überwindung der nur autobiographischen Methode in
Richtung auf eine umfassendere und tiefere Darstellung der Gesellschaft und
ihrer Prozesse. Notwendig ist eine vernichtende literarische Kritik der
imperialistischen Volksfeinde. Hinter dem Schrecken des Krieges möchten
wir die Schuldigen entdecken. [. . .] Das Schwerste ist die Darstellung des
Fortschritts in jenen finsteren Zeiten. Hier muß man mit der Isoliertheit der
kämpfenden Avantgarde des deutschen Antifaschismus vom deutschen Volk
rechnen. Dabei gilt es gerade, diese Vorkämpfer mit dem Leben, mit der
Geschichte der Massen, der Nation in Verbindung zu bringen.[15]

Such tightly prescriptive demands on literature encourage precisely
the kind of schematic plots and characters which Kant and Wagner
condemn. As long as authors were required to subordinate their own
experience of the past to such prescribed models of understanding, it is
not surprising that, as Herminghouse has commented, literature continued to propagate 'den Mythos einer prompten Desillusionierung
der jungen Faschisten und ihre bereitwillige Wandlung zu Arbeitern
am Sozialismus'.[16]

A striking, yet rarely mentioned characteristic of both these literary
models—the heroic antifascist resistance novel and the *Wandlungsroman*—is their gender specificity.[17] With the exception of Seghers, the

---

[14] Kant and Wagner, 132.   [15] Ibid. 138.
[16] Herminghouse, 'Vergangenheit als Problem der Gegenwart', 269.
[17] Julia Hell has, however, offered a compelling psychoanalytical analysis of novels by
Bredel, Seghers, and Gotsche as contributions to a GDR foundation narrative of antifascism
which centred on the figure of the communist father. See Julia Hell, *Post-Fascist Fantasies:
Psychoanalysis, History, and the Literature of East Germany* (Durham, NC, and London: Duke
University Press, 1997).

authors of these works are exclusively male. More importantly, their protagonists are male. In this respect Seghers is a very interesting case. *Das siebte Kreuz* not only has a male protagonist, but consistently presents men as actors and decision-makers. Female characters are intuitive and emotional rather than rational, and capable only of complying with decisions made by men, often without fully understanding the implications of their behaviour. The female characters in the novel are seen primarily in relation to men, as daughters, mothers, wives, and lovers.

Autobiographical experience is the basis for *Das siebte Kreuz* and the heroic communist resistance novels of the early GDR years which it inspired, as well as for the slightly later *Wandlungsromane*. The marginalization of female perspectives in these works can be seen as further evidence of the way personal experiences of the Nazi era and the war had to be moulded into certain acceptable narrative patterns. The ideologically determined prescriptions for writing about this era, as expressed in Kant's and Wagner's paper, pertain primarily to male experience. This is particularly apparent in the case of the *Wandlungsroman*, where the experience of being a soldier under Hitler generally causes ideological change. The domestic experience of National Socialism common to the majority of women who later became GDR citizens was not a fruitful basis for telling heroic tales of resistance activity or defections to communism. Even a woman whose experience deviated from this norm, such as Seghers, upheld conventional gender roles in her work and wrote about this experience from a male perspective. Seghers presumably hoped this would lend greater validity to her protagonists as role models and prevent her from being regarded as an author belonging to the marginalized and trivialized category of 'Frauenliteratur'.[18] This exclusive interest in generally male experience undoubtedly explains the scarcity of works by women dealing with National Socialism until the 1970s, when a number of political and literary shifts created a climate more favourable to the discussion of women's experience.

---

[18] Cf. Christiane Zehl Romero, '"Vertreibung aus dem Paradies?"': GDR Women's Writing Reconsidered', in *Retrospect and Review: Aspects of the Literature of the GDR 1976–1990*, ed. Robert Atkins and Martin Kane, GM 40 (Amsterdam and Atlanta: Rodopi, 1997), 108–25 (113).

SHIFTING PERSPECTIVES ON THE NATIONAL SOCIALIST PAST IN 1970S
LITERATURE AND HISTORIOGRAPHY

A renewed interest in the National Socialist past is one of the striking features of GDR literature of the 1970s.[19] The treatment of the topic underwent substantial qualitative changes around this time. The new wave of texts demonstrates the emancipation of literary writers from the schematic models of interpretation which had formed a consensual basis for earlier literature dealing with this subject. Women's perspectives, as both authors and protagonists, now become markedly more prominent. There are several reasons for these changes. One is that the National Socialist past was now written about for the first time by a younger generation of writers, who had experienced Hitler's regime from the perspective of childhood. The very different content of their biographies meant that new ways of writing about this era had to be found.

This fact alone does not account for the emergence of new literary narratives which are not merely adaptations or refinements of the earlier models, but represent rather a change of direction. The new approaches to the German past must be seen in the context of the broader literary and political shifts which significantly altered the role and functioning of literary discourse within GDR public life from the late 1960s onwards. The changed literary climate after the Eighth Party Congress of the SED had several important consequences in terms of the possibilities open to writers for exploring the National Socialist past. The increased acceptability of experimental and modernist literary forms had the effect of freeing writers from the schematic narrative models of earlier decades. The emphasis on subjective perspectives which had formerly been taboo, and the turn to personal experience as the guarantor of truth, meant that overtly autobiographical approaches to the past, frowned upon by Kant and Wagner in 1957, now became popular. The documentation of everyday experience became a central task of GDR literature. This meant that typically female experience was now, for the first time, considered worthy of attention.

As Heiner Müller commented in 1975, it was 'der gewöhnliche Faschismus' which was now of greatest interest to writers.[20] With the

[19] See Berger, *Gewissensfrage Antifaschismus*, 96.

[20] Heiner Müller, 'Brief an die Redaktion', *Theater der Zeit*, 30 (1975), 8, 58–9 (58). In West Germany, this perspective on National Socialism had been brought into literature in the late 1950s by writers like Günter Grass and Heinrich Böll. For a detailed account of the treatment

relaxation of Cold War tensions in the 1970s, the need for literary presentations of fascism to provide the GDR with legitimate roots and discredit western capitalism became less urgent. Within the GDR this was an era of reflection on the achievements and the failures of 'real existierender Sozialismus', resulting in a more sober recognition of the distance still remaining between GDR society and its communist goal. The GDR Germanist Christel Berger has persuasively shown how these new circumstances in the present changed the perception of history and created a 'Nachholbedarf' with regard to understanding the National Socialist past.

Die Erkenntnis von einem noch sehr langen Weg zum Kommunismus, den im Unterschied zu den Anfangsphasen allmähliche Veränderungen kennzeichnen, der Gewöhnung braucht und diese wiederum in Frage stellt [. . .] trug dazu bei, Geschichtsbewußtsein umfassender als Wissen um langwährende und -wirkende komplizierte Prozesse durchzusetzen. Das Gefühl, nun intensiver und für lange mit dem Gewohntsein und der Gewöhnung an den Alltag dieser Gesellschaft leben zu müssen, bewirkte ein gestiegenes Interesse am Alltäglichen, unter anderem auch an seiner Existenzform im Faschismus.[21]

Just as open literary forms replaced the earlier closed models, the National Socialist past was now increasingly seen not as a closed and finished period of history, but as 'unvollendete Geschichte' which had implications for, and continuities with, the present.

These tendencies are apparent in works by both male and female authors in the 1970s. However, it is my contention that the female authors to be discussed here—Helga Schütz and Christa Wolf—made a rather different contribution to the GDR discourse about the fascist past from that of male authors at the same time. Klaus Schlesinger's *Michael* of 1971, Franz Fühmann's *22 Tage oder Die Hälfte des Lebens* of 1973, and Hermann Kant's *Der Aufenthalt* of 1977 exemplify the major developments in male writers' treatment of this era during the 1970s.[22]

Schlesinger's text consists of the inner monologue of Michael Berger over the course of three hours, as he contemplates his relationship with his father. Michael had found a photograph of Polish hostages being executed in a book about war crimes, and had thought he recognized

of this era in West German public discourses, see Fulbrook, *German National Identity*, 75–7, 113–29, 170.

[21] Berger, *Gewissensfrage Antifaschismus*, 135–6.

[22] Klaus Schlesinger, *Michael* (Rostock: Hinstorff, 1971), Franz Fühmann, *22 Tage oder Die Hälfte des Lebens* (Rostock: Hinstorff, 1973; repr. Frankfurt am Main: Suhrkamp, 1978) and Hermann Kant, *Der Aufenthalt: Roman* (Berlin: Rütten and Loening, 1977; repr. Aufbau, 1994).

his father in one of the soldiers present. However, immediately prior to the opening of his narrative, he has received a letter from Poland stating that the man in the photo was not his father. These experiences lead Michael to reflect on his father's past—an average life marked by successive conformity to two opposing ideological systems, rather than any fundamental ideological change—and on his relationship with his father.[23]

Fühmann's *22 Tage* is a travel diary which records the authorial narrator's experiences and thoughts during a stay in Budapest in an open essay form. His past as a member of the SA and the process of change initiated by antifascist re-education in the Soviet Union quickly emerge as central themes of the work. Fühmann rejects the notion of swift and simple ideological conversion which was central to his earlier works on the subject, and attempts instead to confront his past more thoroughly and honestly in order to do justice to his experience of change as a complex and difficult process.[24]

Kant's *Der Aufenthalt*, like both Fühmann's and Schlesinger's works, explores the issue of change, and asserts a new model of gradual and complex re-education in the place of the earlier simplifications of the 1950s and 1960s *Wandlungsromane*. Kant's protagonist Mark Niebuhr narrates his own learning process, initiated by the experience of imprisonment in Poland under suspicion of being involved in war crimes. The accusation is false, and Mark—unlike Fühmann's narrator—was never an enthusiastic fascist, yet the experience triggers a gradual acknowledgement of German guilt and his own personal responsibility.[25]

In these three works, the processes of change and of reflection on the past are associated with extreme forms of experience and direct personal involvement in momentous historical events. It is the idea that his father has murdered Poles which triggers Michael Berger's reassessment of the past. Fühmann's narrator reflects on the idea that it was pure coincidence which prevented him from joining the SS and being sent to Auschwitz, as his friend W. was (*22 Tage*, 206). Kant's Mark

[23] For more detailed discussions of *Michael* see Berger, *Gewissensfrage Antifaschismus*, 123–6; J. H. Reid, *Writing Without Taboos: The New East German Literature* (New York: Berg, 1990), 132–5.

[24] For more detailed discussions of *22 Tage* see Berger, *Gewissensfrage Antifaschismus*, 100–5; Dinter, 77–92; Uwe Wittstock, *Über die Fähigkeit zu trauern: Das Bild der Wandlung im Prosawerk von Christa Wolf und Franz Fühmann* (Frankfurt am Main: Athenäum, 1987).

[25] For more detailed discussions of *Der Aufenthalt* see Berger, *Gewissensfrage Antifaschismus*, 105–17; Reid, *Writing Without Taboos*, 140–4.

Niebuhr is prompted by the extreme experiences of false accusation and imprisonment to reflect on German atrocities and his own part in them.

Obviously, no absolute distinction can be drawn between everyday life under Nazism and personal involvement in the more significant events which have entered history books about the period. Everyday experience of fascism plays a far greater role in Schlesinger's, Fühmann's, and Kant's works than in earlier GDR novels, while characters' involvement in National Socialist crimes against humanity and in the war features at the margins of Schütz's and Wolf's works. However, both women writers primarily explore the experience of female children whose involvement in fascism—while passionate in the case of Wolf's protagonist, Nelly Jordan—was restricted to the sphere of everyday domestic and local life. Fascism and war had a profound and lasting psychological impact not only on those actively involved as soldiers or directly affected as victims, but also on the millions of (mainly) women and children who experienced the course of history very differently and for the most part from a greater distance. In focusing on these people's experience, Schütz and Wolf explore forms of guilt which are rather less tangible than the guilt associated with murdering Poles or realizing that chance alone saved one from involvement in Auschwitz atrocities. Ideological change, too, occurs in different ways when typically male experiences such as imprisonment or Soviet re-education play no role in the process.

Since the 1970s, numerous surveys of GDR writers' presentation of the National Socialist past have been produced, in both East and West. Besides full-length studies of the topic by Christel Berger and Ingrid Dinter, shorter contributions have been made by Karl-Heinz Hartmann, Therese Hörnigk, Hans Jürgen Geerdts, Wolfgang Emmerich, Alexander Stephan, Nancy A. Lauckner, Patricia Herminghouse, and Dennis Tate, among others.[26] This secondary literature has repeatedly

---

[26] Dinter, *Unvollendete Trauerarbeit in der DDR-Literatur*; Karl-Heinz Hartmann, 'Das Dritte Reich in der DDR-Literatur: Stationen erzählter Vergangenheit', in *Gegenwartsliteratur und Drittes Reich: Deutsche Autoren in der Auseinandersetzung mit der Vergangenheit*, ed. Hans Wagener (Stuttgart: Reclam, 1977), 307–28; Therese Hörnigk, 'Das Thema Krieg und Faschismus in der Geschichte der DDR-Literatur', *WB* 24 (1978), 5, 73–105; Hans Jürgen Geerdts, 'Zur Thematik des Antifaschismus in der Geschichte der DDR-Prosa', *ZG* 1 (1980), 71–81; Wolfgang Emmerich, 'Der ganz gewöhnliche Faschismus: Die Auseinandersetzung mit der nationalsozialistischen Vergangenheit', in *Die andere deutsche Literatur*, 38–45; Alexander Stephan, 'Von Aufenthalten, Hosenknöpfen und Kindheitsmustern: Das Dritte Reich in der jüngsten Prosa der DDR', in *Studies in GDR Culture and Society 6*, ed. Margy Gerber (Washington: University Press of America, 1981), 127–39; Nancy A. Lauckner, 'The

identified those features which resulted in a new variety of literary *Vergangenheitsbewältigung* in the GDR in the 1970s. Therese Hörnigk perceives 'eine deutliche Akzentverschiebung' in the early 1970s, which she defines in terms of a new focus on the relationship between the past and the present: 'Die Vergangenheit wird direkter in die Gegenwart geholt und ist ein immanenter Teil von ihr.'[27] Hans Jürgen Geerdts discusses authors' new acknowledgement of the complex nature of ideological change.[28] Berger devotes a chapter to this aspect of 1970s literature, followed by one dealing with writers' new-found interest in everyday experiences of fascism.[29]

Although Wolf's *Kindheitsmuster* and, to a lesser extent, Helga Schütz's texts are prominent in these studies, little attention has hitherto been paid to the relationship between gender and the way the fascist past is represented. Most of the secondary literature regards Wolf's and Schütz's works as typical of broader trends in literary presentations of the past in 1970s GDR literature, but considers neither the gender specificity of the orthodox narratives about fascism, nor the distinctly new female perspective on the topic which these writers introduced. Exceptions are Marie-Luise Gättens's *Women Writers and Fascism: Reconstructing History* and Julia Hell's *Post-Fascist Fantasies: Psychoanalysis, History, and the Literature of East Germany*.[30] Hell combines a critical reading of texts' explicit political discourse with a psychoanalytical approach, thus regarding literary texts as part of GDR culture's production of unconscious fantasies. She shows how family sagas in early GDR literature functioned as foundation narratives of antifascism, and how identification with the communist father's body in these works resulted in the fantasy of the post-fascist body. She then argues that Wolf's works continued to write the central story of socialist realism, connecting the fantasy of a 'pure' post-fascist body to a fantasy of the 'pure' post-fascist voice. Hell's work is innovative in its

Treatment of Holocaust Themes in GDR Fiction from the Late 1960s to the Mid-1970s: A Survey', in *Studies in GDR Culture and Society 6*, 141–54; Herminghouse, 'Vergangenheit als Problem der Gegenwart'; Dennis Tate, 'Writing in the Shadow of Auschwitz: Literary Perspectives on the GDR's Failure to Overcome its Past', in *Reconstructing the Past: Representations of the Fascist Era in Post-War European Culture*, ed. Graham Bartram, Maurice Slawinski, and David Steel (Keele: Keele University Press, 1996), 118–34.

[27] Hörnigk, 'Das Thema Krieg und Faschismus', 100. See also Herminghouse, 'Vergangenheit als Problem der Gegenwart', 288–9.

[28] Geerdts, 79.

[29] Berger, *Gewissensfrage Antifaschismus*, 96–163.

[30] Marie-Luise Gättens, *Women Writers and Fascism: Reconstructing History* (Gainesville, Fla.: University Press of Florida, 1995); Hell, *Post-Fascist Fantasies*.

NEW APPROACHES TO NATIONAL SOCIALISM

approach, and provides a valuable complement to the present study. Whereas Hell traces continuities in narratives of legitimation present in literature as unconscious fantasies, I am concerned with the diversification of stories told by GDR literature in the last two decades.

Gättens's study places texts by GDR women—Wolf's *Kindheitsmuster*, Helga Schubert's *Judasfrauen*, and Monika Maron's *Stille Zeile Sechs*—in a broader context, by examining not only a West German work—Ruth Rehmann's *Der Mann auf der Kanzel*—but also Virginia Woolf's 1930s analysis of the relationship between gender and fascism, in *Three Guineas*. Gättens examines how the four post-1945 texts present 'the historical experiences of a specific group of women, primarily middle-class "German" women whose position within National Socialism is characterized simultaneously by exclusion and inclusion'.[31] She discusses the female narrators' reconstruction of the past, showing how their activity as female historians serves as a critique of dominant practices of historiography in their (masculine) gender specificity. She offers close textual analyses which focus on how the various writers present the relationship between fascism and patriarchy, as well as on how they address the complex intersection of resistance and complicity which characterized women's relation to the National Socialist state. Gättens reads the texts by Wolf, Schubert, and Maron as responses to the official GDR discourse of history, showing the varying degrees to which they challenge and criticize the latter. However, she treats each text as a relatively autonomous response to its context, and her project is not concerned with the effects which literary presentations of the past had on GDR historical debate, nor with the changing limits to the discourse on fascism over the course of GDR history. The aim of this chapter is to show not just how individual literary texts responded to the official GDR interpretation of the National Socialist past, but how literature interacted with its context in such a way as to reconfigure it.

'DER GEWÖHNLICHE FASCHISMUS': HELGA SCHÜTZ'S JETTE/JULIA NOVELS

Helga Schütz was one of the first authors to introduce new perspectives on the National Socialist past into GDR literature in the early 1970s. Born in 1937, she is typical of a new generation of writers who

---

[31] Gättens, 4.

experienced fascism only as children, and who began around this time to incorporate this very different perspective on the era into their work. Schütz's début of 1970, *Vorgeschichten oder Schöne Gegend Probstein*, set in the final months of the Second World War, was followed by a series of texts developing the characters established here in the settings of both post-war German states: *Das Erdbeben bei Sangerhausen* (1972), *Festbeleuchtung* (1974), *Jette in Dresden* (1977), and *Julia oder Erziehung zum Chorgesang* (1980).[32] In an interview with Leonore Krenzlin in 1976, Schütz attributes the renewed interest in the period around 1945 shown in contemporary writing to the experiences of her generation, now beginning to write, and to a universal concern with childhood:

Ich finde, zu allen Zeiten haben Schriftsteller ihre Stoffe aus der eigenen Kindheit bezogen, jüngere und ältere. Daß es jetzt augenfällig geworden ist, mag an dem gewaltigen Entwicklungssprung liegen, den viele Deutsche nach 45 gemacht haben, und daran, daß eben jetzt die Generation zu schreiben beginnt, die diesen Sprung als letzte, und zwar als Kind, miterlebt und erfahren hat. Die Erfahrung soll schnell festgehalten werden, und zwar im heutigen Lichte, da eventuell gerade die eigenen Kinder heranwachsen. Andere Gründe sehe ich nicht.[33]

While political expediency may be playing a role here—the last sentence quoted seems uncharacteristically adamant—the idea that personal experience should be the basis for writing about the fascist past recurs throughout the interviews Schütz gives, and is central to her literary work. She does not set out primarily to revise interpretations of the past—although her works achieve this—but instead to arrive at an understanding of her own childhood. She stresses the very personal motivations for her writing, and—in an interview with Joachim Walther—defines the task as 'dieses Sich-selber-ergründen-Wollen'.[34] The phrase echoes the quotation from Johannes R. Becher which Christa Wolf used as a motto for *Nachdenken über Christa T.*—'dieses Zu-sich-selber-Kommen des Menschen'—and connotes a similar emphasis on the individual subject. However, the temporal perspective is

---

[32] Helga Schütz, *Vorgeschichten oder Schöne Gegend Probstein* (Berlin and Weimar: Aufbau, 1970; repr. 1987), *Das Erdbeben bei Sangerhausen und andere Geschichten* (Berlin and Weimar: Aufbau, 1972), *Festbeleuchtung: Erzählung* (Berlin and Weimar: Aufbau, 1973; repr. Darmstadt: Luchterhand, 1982), *Jette in Dresden* (Berlin and Weimar: Aufbau, 1977; repr. Berlin: Aufbau, 1994), *Julia oder Erziehung zum Chorgesang* (Berlin and Weimar: Aufbau, 1980; repr. Darmstadt: Luchterhand, 1988).

[33] Leonore Krenzlin, 'Interview mit Helga Schütz', *WB* 22 (1976), 2, 77–89 (79).

[34] Joachim Walther, *Meinetwegen Schmetterlinge: Gespräche mit Schriftstellern* (Berlin: Verlag Der Morgen, 1973), 112.

different: while Becher's phrase signals a process leading to a future goal, Schütz's emphasis is on understanding the present self through an exploration of its past. This archaeological approach to the subject anticipates Wolf's later work about childhood under National Socialism, *Kindheitsmuster*.

In the same interview with Walther, Schütz describes how it was only through the process of writing about her memories of childhood that she realized that the underlying theme of this experience was 'der gewöhnliche Faschismus'. In a necessarily vague reference to 'Theorie', she hints at the gulf between official GDR understandings of this era and her own personal experience of it: 'Zudem spielte sich meine Kindheit zu einer Zeit ab, die mir bis heute, trotz aller Theorie, unbegreiflich ist.'[35] By starting from the perspective of the individual, whose experience becomes indicative of broader social developments, Schütz is able to challenge such 'Theorie' and present new, very different narratives of the fascist past.

Vorgeschichten oder Schöne Gegend Probstein, the only complete text actually set in National Socialist times, relates individual lives to the great events of history in a way which, in 1970, was new for GDR literature, particularly with regard to this era. Earlier works dealing with the Third Reich and the Second World War invariably focus on characters whose actions, whether as resistance fighters or as Nazi soldiers, contribute directly to events which have entered the history books. These characters are, or at least become, fully aware of the historical significance of their behaviour, and their decisions and dilemmas have direct consequences for the course of history. Schütz's text focuses on the everyday lives and concerns of very ordinary people living in the rural village of Probstein in Silesia.[36] The momentous political events of the time are presented in terms of their consequences, of varying severity, for these characters. For the seven-year-old Jette, the war means being sent to Probstein to live with her grandparents so that, with a household of three people, they are allowed to keep all the meat from their pig, instead of having to give half of it to the state (*Vorgeschichten*, 7–10). The child's perspective, prominent in the text, helps to create a naïve world view in which the political is seen merely as an infringement on the personal. When Jette's older friends, Christoph and Gabriel, are called up to fight, Jette cries because they

[35] Ibid. 105

[36] A corruption of 'Probsthain', the name 'Probstein' emphasizes the representative quality of the village. Like a touchstone, or *Probierstein*, the community serves as a means of measuring more general truths and values.

will no longer be able to meet secretly in their dugout to eat cinnamon cake and tell adventure stories (*Vorgeschichten*, 97). Such political naïvety is, however, shared by most of the adults in the text. Just as Jette finds herself presented with developments whose causes she does not understand, and which she cannot change, the adults regard the war as a circumstance brought about by fate, which they cannot influence, but which requires them to adapt in their needs and expectations:

Die Umstände sind: In Deutschland dieser Krieg, den, wie man sagt, die Vorsehung vorgesehen hat und gegen den mithin nichts zu machen ist, und dieser Haushalt von zwei Personen, zuwenig für eine Sau im großen und ganzen. (*Vorgeschichten*, 7)

The juxtaposition of the historical and the domestic here is characteristic of the text as a whole.

Most of the Probsteiner have a pragmatic approach to politics typical of the *Mitläufer* masses who enabled Hitler's state to function. Only a minority of Schütz's characters are convinced National Socialists who actively and deliberately support the regime. Even these tend to be motivated by a desire for power or status, rather than by ideological principles. Brinkfriede Hahn has an air of importance because of her proven Aryan blood: as Jette's grandmother, Berta Mann, puts it, 'Die Hahn ist eine besondere Nummer. Die hat einen Stammbaum' (*Vorgeschichten*, 22). She keeps 'einen belgischen Feind', the prisoner of war Leopold, to whom she is domineering and cruel. Leopold is an attractive character for Jette, Christoph, and Gabriel because of his generosity with chewing-gum. When Brinkfriede angrily separates Jette and Leopold, but Jette still manages to get a piece of chewing-gum because Christoph and Gabriel have already visited Leopold, the narrator comments, 'Was weiß denn Brinkfriede, welche unterirdischen Kanäle in Probstein bestehn' (*Vorgeschichten*, 25). The ironic use of a phrase which might be expected to refer to an organized underground resistance movement highlights the absence of any such movement in Probstein. Adult opposition to characters like Brinkfriede or to the regime itself tends to be no more ideologically grounded than the young people's efforts to obtain chewing-gum. When the Gestapo officer Tiefenbach questions Kutz, the miller, about his neighbour, Petzold— one of the few characters to express a principled opposition to National Socialism—Kutz's main concern is self-preservation. With the thought, 'Soll ich die Hand, die mich schlägt, beißen, damit sie mich erdrosselt? Ich wäre schön dämlich', he acts pragmatically. Rather than refusing to answer the questions of the Gestapo, he lies to protect Petzold and bribes Tiefenbach with a bag of flour (*Vorgeschichten*, 162–3). For Kutz, self-preservation is thus not a matter of autonomy, but one of accommodation with power. Towards the end of the novel Heinrich Mann, Jette's grandfather, stumbles across a secret nocturnal meeting of men from Probstein and neighbouring villages who are not supporters of the Nazi regime. Again, though, no heroic acts of resistance are being planned. Instead the talk is of news heard on foreign radio implying that Probstein is about to be evacuated (*Vorgeschichten*, 179–87).

In Schütz's text, opposition to fascism is motivated purely by the desire to save one's own skin. Heinrich Mann is presented as a typical citizen whose moral and political principles prevent him from actively supporting the regime, but are not strong enough to preclude his participation in a system he knows to be unjust, when it is able to meet his needs. When he has a heavy crop of apples needing to be picked quickly, he takes on a Polish boy, Adam, as a source of free labour. When Petzold looks disapprovingly at him, Heinrich attempts to justify his action and ease his conscience:

Na, was denn, denkt Heinrich, was denn, was denn. Ob der nun bei mir arbeitet, oder er schuftet im Gut. Das bleibt sich doch ein und dasselbe. Da möcht ich ja sagen, da is der bei mir besser dran als bei denen. Viel besser. (*Vorgeschichten*, 103)

Here the central principle underlying the behaviour of most of Schütz's characters is clear: the Probsteiner refuse to look beyond the small world of their own needs to perceive the broader meanings of their actions. This principle is reflected formally: the work consists of sixty relatively independent sections of text, most of which relate everyday incidents. These small-scale stories are not subordinated to any unifying and overarching plot which might serve as a broader picture to give meaning to individual details. As a village, Probstein represents this limited perspective on the world. Most of the characters find it difficult to imagine a world outside Probstein. When Heinrich Mann points out a red kite to Jette and says that the bird is 'vorzeitig zurück nach Europa', the narrator ironically comments, 'Denn: Probstein ist Europa' (*Vorgeschichten*, 165). When civilians are told to leave the area, Heinrich resists for as long as possible, unable to acknowledge a necessity greater than the concerns of his everyday existence: 'Ich will nischt verteidigen und nischt verteidigt ham, verstehn Se, hat Heinrich gesagt' (*Vorgeschichten*, 195).

A further way of understanding this equation of Probstein with Europe, or the world, is suggested at the end of the work. The penultimate section of text consists of five letters which, because of the postmaster's flight from Probstein, are never delivered. One is from Gabriel Tischer to Jette. He writes of a reunion with their favourite fantasy figure, Captain Bräccer:

> Wir gehen oft gemeinsam spazieren und unterhalten uns über Probstein und die Welt, das heißt, er macht gar keinen Unterschied. Er sagt: Probstein ist die Welt. Aber das wissen wir, Du und ich, besser: Probstein ist nicht die Welt, bei uns gibt es zum Beispiel keine Palmen und keine Oliven. (*Vorgeschichten*, 206–7)

As the letter continues, Marxist views are attributed to Bräccer, and Gabriel contrasts this philosophy favourably with the Christianity of his upbringing:

> Er gehöre zu denen, die da sagen: Gewürgte Lämmer aller Länder vereinigt euch! Ich sagte, Du und ich, wir Probsteiner, kennen den Satz vom Zorn des Lammes von meinem Vater, dem Kantor selig. Aber der war kein Prophet und keiner von den Inspirierten. Die besseren Wisser sind in den großen Städten. (*Vorgeschichten*, 207)

In the light of this, Bräccer's supposed comment that Probstein is the world can be understood to mean that Probstein is a microcosm of the world, which functions according to the same principles as society at large. This echoes Schütz's comments in interviews, where she describes how the personal functions as an example for more broadly manifest phenomena.[37] Gabriel's suggestion that 'die besseren Wisser' are to be found in the cities points to the urban nature of the new philosophy. As Bräccer's substitution of 'Lämmer' for 'Proletarier' comically suggests, Marxism has to be translated into rural language if agricultural workers are to be persuaded by it. Gabriel, a highly positive character who is imaginative and writes poetry, has clearly undergone a political learning process very similar to that which was central to the earlier GDR *Wandlungsroman*. However, his story is marginal to the text. Its outcome is conveyed only in a letter which, within the fiction, never finds a reader.

Krenzlin has compared Schütz's works with those of Seghers, showing how both are concerned with 'die Nahtstellen zwischen Alltag und Geschichte', but treat this boundary in very different ways:

> Anna Seghers verwendet alle Sorgfalt darauf, jene Momente herauszuarbeiten, in denen das Handeln ihrer Figuren im Alltag geschichtliche

---

[37] See Krenzlin, 'Interview', 79.

NEW APPROACHES TO NATIONAL SOCIALISM   51

Relevanz erreicht. [. . .] Helga Schütz verfährt anders, sie schildert Menschen, die im platten Alltag befangen bleiben und ihr Erleben zumeist falsch, kurzschlüssig verallgemeinern.[38]

Krenzlin does not mention the very striking contrast in gender perspectives between Seghers and Schütz. The world of the wives and daughters which is marginal in *Das siebte Kreuz* becomes the primary focus in Schütz's works. Fascism and the Second World War are presented here from the perspective of women, children, and elderly men who are unable to fight. Schütz is not interested in heroic action and dramatic political developments, but in forms of suffering and loss which were a predominantly female experience. The experiences of the young men of Probstein as soldiers are not presented in any detail. Instead, their mothers' perspective on events is shown. When Christoph Klose is called up, his mother spends the day cleaning the house for his departure: 'Martha Klose hat sich den Kummer vertreiben wollen. Hat das Unglück günstiger gestalten wollen. Aber das geht nicht. So sagt sich Martha, wenn er fort muß, dann geht er aus einem sauberen Haushalt' (*Vorgeschichten*, 95). When news of his death arrives, the women of Probstein offer each other support. Martha goes straight to Berta Mann, who comforts her, then they go together to see Selma, who joins them in their mourning. The men, meanwhile, try to persuade themselves that there is still hope: since Christoph never returned from no man's land, maybe he is imprisoned, or has defected (*Vorgeschichten*, 119). There is no consciously feminist attempt to challenge this somewhat stereotypical construction of women as emotional and men as rational. However, Jette's behaviour in this scene points up the degree of socialization behind both the men's and the women's behaviour. Only the child is able to pronounce the words, 'Christoph ist tot'. This breaking of a taboo provokes a shocked reaction from Selma, whose response to the news conforms to social expectations: 'Mädel, was sagst du denn! Selma fällt in den Jammer. Der ist groß und vergeht nicht' (*Vorgeschichten*, 119).

Schütz's privileging of a female perspective on the events of the Second World War is particularly apparent in the way she presents the story of the twins, Rudolph and Richard Reichhardt. A relatively long section of text gives a detailed account of their mother Antonie's experience of their births, narrated in her voice (*Vorgeschichten*, 61–4). This very personal and specifically female story is followed by two

---

[38] Leonore Krenzlin, 'Helga Schütz' Erzählweise', *WB* 22 (1976), 2, 90–8 (93).

brief sections of text describing the deaths of Rudolph and Richard in objective and emotionally uninvolved language (*Vorgeschichten*, 65–6). The deaths are set in a context of the mass destruction involved in well-known historical events:

> 1940 hat die deutsche Luftwaffe über England siebenunddreißigtausend Tonnen Bomben abgeworfen. Bordschütze in einer He III war Richard Reichhardt. Sein Bomber wurde auf dem Rückflug von Coventry von einem Spitfire-Jäger getroffen. Die Besatzung kam ums Leben. (*Vorgeschichten*, 66)

This meeting point of history and individual fate derives its meaning in the text from its place in Antonie's life, not from its place in history. No further details about the bombing of Coventry are given, and the twins' own perspectives are absent from the text. Instead, the reader has just been presented with Antonie's own story, and so empathizes with her.

The time of Schütz's birth is undoubtedly an important factor in allowing her to introduce this new, female perspective into GDR literature about National Socialism. Living through the war as a child meant witnessing the experiences of women and not those of the majority of men. Schütz's generation's memories of the time before 1945 thus share a perspective closer to that of women. This, together with a new interest in the private sphere and everyday life, may explain why Schütz was able to focus on areas of experience under Nazism which had not until then been regarded as worthy of attention.

In the interview with Walther, Schütz insists that her texts deal not only with historical material, but simultaneously with the present: 'ich beschreibe Gegenwärtiges vom ersten bis zum letzten Satz. Das Geschriebene ist sowohl der Versuch, eine bestimmte historische Situation lebendig zu machen als auch eine Beschreibung meines Zustandes während des Schreibens'.[39] In Schütz's works prior to *Julia oder Erziehung zum Chorgesang*, however, no overt present perspective on past events is presented. Unlike Schlesinger's *Michael* or Wolf's *Kindheitsmuster*, these texts do not use memory and narrative reflection to create a relationship between the past and the present. Instead, it is above all the relations between Schütz's texts which open out the past experiences presented and suggest their relevance for the present. The title, '*Vorgeschichten* oder Schöne Gegend Probstein' [emphasis added] indicates the status of the stories told in this work: they are not self-contained and complete, but are to be read as the seeds of later stories.

---

[39] Walther, III.

Such stories are developed in Schütz's subsequent works and, in *Julia oder Erziehung zum Chorgesang*, are shown to lead to a present in the 1970s.

By presenting the stories of the Probstein characters in a series of short pieces of prose, Schütz creates a pluralized and open-ended notion of history. Her texts tend to consist of short and detailed descriptions of individual episodes which, because of the absence of an overarching plot structure, make no claim to wholeness. At the end, questions are left open, which will only be answered by a later text. Even *Festbeleuchtung* (1973), the text which comes closest to a plot-driven structure, creates open spaces where a character's story is hinted at, but not told. Jette, for example, is marginal to this text, which concerns the wedding of Rosemarie Blümel and Gustav Gottschling, both former Probsteiner now living in Spitzbergen in the Harz. It is not until *Jette in Dresden* (1977) that Schütz fills in the details of Jette's experiences in the immediate post-war years. Schütz uses a narrative voice which explicitly stresses the multiple possibilities of perspective and emphasis, and the selections which narration involves. At the beginning of *Festbeleuchtung*, for example, a series of conditional statements is used to highlight the idea that this story actually consists of many stories and could be told in many different ways:

Wir könnten jetzt lang und breit die etwas reife, aber jung gebliebene Braut bewundern, und über den Bräutigam könnten wir ein paar anerkennende oder vielmehr tadelnde Sätze machen.
Wir könnten den Gasthof Zander beschreiben.
Oder wir könnten uns fragend an x-beliebige Gäste wenden, wir könnten um Auskunft bitten über Befinden und Herkunft. (*Festbeleuchtung*, 5)

Each of Schütz's works throughout the 1970s makes these selections in a different way, so that the history of a group of characters is presented as a series of stories which never close. In response to a question from Krenzlin about her use of short prose forms rather than the novel, Schütz highlights this effect of her aesthetic: 'Es ist so, daß ich das Gefühl habe, es ist eine Geschichte, aber es schließt sich auch nicht derartig ab, daß ich nicht das Gefühl hätte, ich dürfte den Figuren ruhig noch etwas andichten.'[40]

The relation of the National Socialist past to present concerns, implicit in Schütz's earlier works, becomes clear in *Julia oder Erziehung zum Chorgesang*. In this work Jette, now known as Julia, is around forty. Her husband Ulrich's adultery has led her to leave him and move to

[40] Krenzlin, 'Interview', 81.

Berlin, and has triggered a more general crisis in her understanding of herself and her role in society. In a rather disorienting manner, the novel juxtaposes scenes in the present with Julia's memories of earlier experiences. Ricarda Schmidt has shown how Schütz omits 'the logical pointers of conventional story-telling' and instead imitates 'the metonymic structures of thinking, feeling and of language itself'.[41] Other critics have responded less positively to the narrative technique, arguing that the complexity of the novel is its weakness. Dorothee Schmitz-Köster complains, not without justification, 'häufig wirken Übergänge unmotiviert, Rückgriffe funktionslos, der Wechsel der Erzählperspektive unverständlich'.[42] Julia thinks back over her life in order to trace the origins of her crisis in the present. The main focus of her reflections is her time as a student at the Arbeiter-und-Bauern-Fakultät in the 1950s. It is during this period, on meeting Ulrich, that the behavioural patterns of conformity to the norm and subordination to the collective, represented by singing in the choir, become firmly established in Julia (Julia, 239). In making a fresh start in the present, it is these ways of behaving which she seeks to overcome.

Although Julia oder Erziehung zum Chorgesang deals primarily with an individual's experience of the GDR, earlier memories from Julia's childhood in Probstein are also included. A continuity is thus suggested between experiences under National Socialism and later ones in the GDR: both have played a part in forming Julia's personality and deter-mining her behaviour in the present. Although Julia was too young to understand the political environment of pre-1945 Germany—her understanding of the statement 'Wir sind in Polen einmarschiert!' as a reference to a nearby hill is characteristic (Julia, 21–2)—the episodes which she remembers demonstrate a socialization which clearly created a basis for her later behaviour in the GDR. While she may have escaped indoctrination with National Socialist ideology, she did learn feminine modes of behaviour which prepared her for her later role as self-sacrificing wife and mother. The gender roles prevailing in the society of Julia's childhood are highlighted in the opening chapter, in the first of the remembered episodes from this time. While playing with her cousin, Gabriel Hielscher, Julia cuts off her pigtails and

[41] Ricarda Schmidt, 'Im Schatten der Titanin: Minor GDR Women Writers—Justly Neglected, Unrecognised or Repressed?', in Geist und Macht: Writers and the State in the GDR, ed. Axel Goodbody and Dennis Tate, GM 29 (Amsterdam and Atlanta: Rodopi, 1992), 151–62 (155).
[42] Schmitz-Köster, 45. See also Brigitte Weyhmann, 'Helga Schütz: Erziehung zum Chorgesang', NDH 28 (1981), 2, 365–8.

demands that they exchange clothes. Their natural physical resemblance enables them thus to swap roles. For the young Julia, this usurpation of male identity means acquiring the power to exert her will through language:

In seinen Federn habe ich das Wort wieder. Ich habe endgültig das Wort: Ich heiße Gabriel, und du bist Julietta. (*Julia*, 13)

Although she is the instigator of this prank and Gabriel remains passively compliant throughout, the adults are unable to imagine that a girl could be responsible and so take Gabriel to be the guilty party, chastising him in particular for his 'shameful' adoption of a feminine role:

Er allein bekommt die Unart angemessen. Es war zum Schämen, auf welche Gedanken so ein Lümmel kommen konnte und wozu er mich, Julietta, verleitet hatte. In falschen Kleidern gehn, man findet keine Worte, sich zum Mädchen machen, so eine Schande. Betrug. Heuchelei. Falsch Zeugnis. Sünde irgendwie. (*Julia*, 14)

In later episodes remembered from her childhood, Julia shows an increasing internalization of the notions of femininity with which she is brought up. In an attempt to impress Gabriel and demonstrate her superiority over him, she pretends to have learnt to knit. When her grandmother calls for help in feeding the rabbits, she parades her obedience and helpfulness as similarly impressive abilities: 'Dies kommt nun noch zu meinen Fähigkeiten: mein flinker Gehorsam. Alles gehört zu meiner Kunst und Überlegenheit: wie ich eilfertig vom Wagen herunterspringe, wie ich über die Wiese renne' (*Julia*, 81). Along with this desire to obey the will of others, Julia learns a specifically feminine form of guilt from her grandmother, her closest female role model. Berta Mann blames herself for everything that goes wrong in the household, even when it is actually Julia's fault or a natural misfortune (*Julia*, 98–100). These are qualities which are particularly conducive to the self-denial underlying Julia's later conformity to conditions and expectations in the GDR.

Schütz's works show how the National Socialist era continued to act as a burden for GDR citizens in the present, and therefore must be seen in continuity with the early socialist years. Even for her generation, too young to be politically involved in Hitler's regime, the society of their childhood had lasting effects in determining potentially life-long patterns of behaviour. Schütz presents National Socialism primarily in terms of its everyday impressions on a very young child. However, towards the end of *Julia oder Erziehung zum Chorgesang*, there is a passage which hints at Julia's increasing concern with the political implications of childhood experiences which she was unable to understand fully at the time. She remembers a Jewish woman called Sarah who used to come to her grandparents' house after dark for food and clothes (*Julia*, 232–7). As a young child she was receptive to the sense of secrecy and taboo surrounding these nocturnal visits, but was unable to make sense of them. She writes to Gabriel Tischer and her mother to ask what they know about Sarah, and is disappointed by her mother's insistence that nobody could have done anything to save Sarah when she was among the last Jews to be sent to a concentration camp (*Julia*, 237–8). Julia's assessment of her past in order to overcome her present crisis evidently encompasses the need to investigate the political circumstances of her childhood. Schütz's works, however, do not address this issue in any depth. Her achievement lies in her examination of the effects of everyday fascism on a developing child, a subject new to GDR literature when *Vorgeschichten oder Schöne Gegend Probstein* appeared.

Schütz was awarded the Heinrich-Mann-Preis by the Akademie der Künste in 1973, in a somewhat delayed recognition of *Vorgeschichten*. Despite this apparent success, very little attention seems to have been paid to her works. She received regular, but generally brief reviews in *Neue deutsche Literatur*, but throughout the first half of the 1970s, with the exception of Walther's interview, no more serious criticism was devoted to her.[43] In 1976, however, *Weimarer Beiträge* published an interview alongside an article by Leonore Krenzlin on Schütz's narrative perspective.[44] This sudden display of interest came two years after the publication of Schütz's most recent work, *Festbeleuchtung*. A possible explanation for this is that the publication of a far more prominent text, Christa Wolf's *Kindheitsmuster*, gave the theme of Schütz's early work, that is, the fascist past, new topicality and so triggered a retrospective interest in these texts.

---

[43] Gerhard Rothbauer, 'Vorgeschichten, Nachgeschichten oder einfach Geschichten', *NDL* 20 (1972), 1, 163–6, 'Wir könnten so tun, als wäre alles beim alten', *NDL* 23 (1975), 3, 151–4; Joachim Hannemann, 'Ein Stück von der Wahrheit', *NDL* 26 (1978), 11, 150–2; Dorothea Böck, 'Ein janusköpfiger Epilog', *NDL* 30 (1982), 3, 146–52.

[44] Krenzlin, 'Interview', 'Helga Schütz' Erzählweise'.

'WIE SIND WIR SO GEWORDEN, WIE WIR HEUTE SIND?': CHRISTA
WOLF'S *KINDHEITSMUSTER* AND ITS RECEPTION IN THE GDR

In certain central respects, Wolf's approach to the National Socialist
past in *Kindheitsmuster* resembles Schütz's in *Vorgeschichten oder Schöne
Gegend Probstein* and *Julia oder Erziehung zum Chorgesang*.[45] Both authors
use personal memories of a childhood under Hitler as a basis for
exploring everyday fascism as a past which is still relevant to a GDR
present. Just as Schütz regards her writing as a means of gaining a
better understanding of her childhood experiences, Wolf's notion of
'subjektive Authentizität', developed during her work on *Kindheitsmuster*, centres on the author's subjectivity and defines prose fiction as
an active process of exploring 'Erfahrung, die zu bewältigen ist'.[46] Wolf
is eight years older than Schütz and was consequently emotionally
involved in the National Socialist regime to a far greater degree at the
time of its collapse. This fact, as well as differences in Wolf's self-
perception and aims as a writer, result in a text which is politically
weightier, more ambitious, and much longer than Schütz's works.
As well as presenting everyday experience under fascism as Schütz
does, Wolf thematizes issues of memory, guilt, responsibility, and the
psychological consequences of fascism, which remain for the most part
beyond the scope of Schütz's texts. Much critical attention has been
paid to *Kindheitsmuster*, both within the GDR and internationally.[47] I
shall limit myself here to an outline of the innovative features of Wolf's
approach to the fascist past, before addressing an issue which has

---

[45] Christa Wolf, *Kindheitsmuster: Roman* (Berlin and Weimar: Aufbau, 1976; repr. Frankfurt
am Main: Luchterhand, 1988).

[46] Christa Wolf, 'Subjektive Authentizität: Gespräch mit Hans Kaufmann', in *Die Dimension des Autors*, ii. 773–805 (774).

[47] For a variety of recent contributions see, for example, Barbara Kosta, *Recasting Auto-
biography: Women's Counterfictions in Contemporary German Literature and Film* (Ithaca, NY, and
London: Cornell University Press, 1994); Joyce Crick, 'Dichtung und Wahrheit: Aspects of
Christa Wolf's *Kindheitsmuster*', *LGS* 2 (1983), 168–83; Sandra Frieden, '"Falls es strafbar ist,
die Grenzen zu verwischen": Autobiographie, Biographie und Christa Wolf', in *Christa Wolf:
Ein Arbeitsbuch. Studien, Dokumente, Bibliographie*, ed. Angela Drescher (Berlin and Weimar:
Aufbau, 1989; repr. Frankfurt am Main: Luchterhand, 1990), 121–39; and Catherine Viollet,
'Nachdenken über Pronomina: Zur Entstehung von Christa Wolfs *Kindheitsmuster*', in *Christa
Wolf: Ein Arbeitsbuch*, 101–13; Sabine Wilke, '"Worüber man nicht sprechen kann, darüber
muß man allmählich zu schweigen aufhören": Vergangenheitsbeziehungen in Christa Wolfs
Kindheitsmuster', *GR* 66 (1991), 4, 169–76; Jörn Rietsch, 'Versuch über einen Versuch:
Gedanken über den Blick auf Geschichte in Christa Wolfs Roman *Kindheitsmuster*', *WB* 38
(1992), 1, 68–84; Lothar Baier, 'Wo habt ihr bloß alle gelebt: Christa Wolfs "Kindheitsmuster", 1994 wiedergelesen', in *Christa Wolf*, ed. Heinz Ludwig Arnold, Text + Kritik, 46,
4th rev. edn. (Munich: text + kritik, 1994), 59–67.

not been adequately analysed by the secondary literature, that is, the impact the work had on other discourses in the GDR public sphere which were concerned with this aspect of German history.

As in Schütz's works, the narrative perspective in *Kindheitsmuster* is female. Wolf presents everyday domestic life under National Socialism through the eyes of the child Nelly. This naïve perspective is relativized not only by irony, as in Schütz's texts, but by explicit comment and analysis by the adult narrator figure. This juxtaposition of perspectives allows Wolf to explore and reflect on the interplay and overlaps between individual experience and history as a narrative of world events. Hearing news of the mobilization of troops in Israel and Egypt in October 1973, the narrator contrasts her present perspective with her experience of her father's conscription in 1939. This thought highlights the idea that any historical event is experienced and construed from multiple perspectives, some intimately involved and others distanced and analytical (*Kindheitsmuster*, 229–30). Wolf's narrator is aware that her presentation of historical events adopts a new, female perspective which has not featured in earlier accounts in the GDR. Both within the novel and in the discussion following readings from the unfinished work at the Akademie der Künste in 1975, Wolf dwells on the fact that the flight westwards in 1945 has scarcely been written about. She speculates that a chief reason for this is that it was predominantly a female experience, while those who later wrote about their experiences were generally men (*Kindheitsmuster*, 431).[48] There are obviously other, political reasons why the East Germans' flight from the Red Army had not been prominent in GDR accounts of the end of the war. Wolf's comment highlights the taboo-breaking potential of female experience as a subject for literature.

In comparison with Schütz's works, *Kindheitsmuster* offers a much more thorough exploration of the ways in which the private life of a professedly 'non-political' family was inextricably connected with more overtly political manifestations of fascism in the public sphere. The prosperity of the Jordans' petit-bourgeois existence, for example, is directly dependent on Hitler's military policy: their shop thrives because of its 'geschäftsgünstige Lage', close to the barracks (*Kindheitsmuster*, 155). Wolf focuses in particular on the role which language played in enabling fascist ideology to pervade the private sphere.[49] As

[48] Christa Wolf, 'Erfahrungsmuster: Diskussion zu *Kindheitsmuster*', in *Die Dimension des Autors*, ii. 806–43 (813).

[49] While this is one of the first literary treatments of the subtle ideological effects of language under National Socialism, two of the earliest philological investigations of the topic

a child, Nelly is aware of a series of terms which structure her parents' thinking, but which are surrounded by a sense of taboo which prevents her from asking about their meanings. These 'Glitzerworte'— 'unnormal', 'triebhaft', 'Schwindsucht', 'verdorben', 'artfremd', and 'unfruchtbar', among others—convey a bourgeois morality in the service of the National Socialist world view. Ideological language of this kind permeates Nelly's early life both at home and at school and, in its intertwining of 'Schuld und Verschweigen', provides her with a set of unquestionable precepts (*Kindheitsmuster*, 83). As Gättens has argued, *Kindheitsmuster* 'dismantles the myth that the private life of ordinary middle-class German people could be lived innocently and untouched by the racial policies of the regime'.[50] This had particularly important implications in the GDR context, since the subtle ideological effects of fascism on the German population at large had been notably lacking from discussions of National Socialism prior to the publication of *Kindheitsmuster*.

As a consciously gendered exploration of the National Socialist past, *Kindheitsmuster* goes beyond depicting historical events which were experienced primarily by women. In its presentation of Nelly's development throughout childhood and adolescence, the work is a study in female socialization under Nazism. Like other GDR writers of the 1970s, Wolf focuses on the psychological effects of living in Hitler's Germany, which were neglected by earlier works about the era.[51] Many of the tendencies which Wolf perceives in Germans of her generation and which she attributes to the ideological context of their childhood—excessive dependency on authority, a lack of trust, fear, the repression of past experience, conformity to social norms—transcend gender divisions.[52] However, her work is the first to deal also with the differences in the ways Nazi ideology affected men and women—a result of the very marked gender roles of the Third Reich— and to explore the particular consequences for female subjects.

By juxtaposing events in Nelly's personal development with incidents reflecting the ideology of the time, Wolf shows how the two are

had been published in the GDR much earlier: Victor Klemperer, *LTI: Notizbuch eines Philologen* (Berlin: Aufbau, 1949); Eugen Seidel and Ingeborg Seidel-Slotty, *Sprachwandel im Dritten Reich* (Halle: Sprache und Literatur, 1961).

[50] Gättens, 101.

[51] Cf. for example Schlesinger, *Michael*, Fühmann, *22 Tage oder Die Hälfte des Lebens*, and Kant, *Der Aufenthalt*.

[52] Cf. Christa Wolf, 'Unerledigte Widersprüche: Gespräch mit Therese Hörnigk', in *Im Dialog: Aktuelle Texte* (Frankfurt am Main: Luchterhand, 1990), 24–68 (26).

interwoven in Nelly's experience. The early stages of Nelly's adolescence, marked by the onset of menstruation and her parents' decision that she can no longer share a bedroom with her brother, are presented amidst reflection on the female role models and constructs of femininity which Nelly encountered at that age (*Kindheitsmuster*, 288). The tragic story of Tante Trudchen, although not told to Nelly until several years later, is placed by the narrator just before the chapter dealing with Nelly's adolescent development. Here, it serves to highlight the expectations of women prevalent in the world of her earliest adulthood. After a secret backstreet abortion, undergone to protect the respectability of her family, Trudchen is unable to bear children. When her husband wants to divorce her in order to live with his lover, the law is on his side and regards women's function and value solely in terms of their reproductive capacities: 'Ein deutscher Mann, hat der Scheidungsrichter gesagt, soll mit der Frau zusammen leben, die ihm Kinder gebären kann' (*Kindheitsmuster*, 283).

The most influential role model for Nelly during her adolescence is her teacher, Julia Strauch. Constantly proclaiming Nazi ideology and yet herself dark-haired with Slavic features, unmarried, childless, and intellectual, Julia embodies the contradiction between the ideals professed by the National Socialists and the reality of their society (*Kindheitsmuster*, 298). Margarete Mitscherlich-Nielsen has shown that such a discrepancy characterizes the presentation of gender relations throughout the novel.[53] While Nazi ideology glorified the strong and dominant man and consigned women to a subservient role as wives and mothers, the actual men in the novel—Nelly's father, for instance—are presented as weak and often slightly ridiculous. It is the women—Nelly's mother and grandmothers—who have power and control within the family. It is also women—her mother, followed by Julia Strauch—who play the most important roles in Nelly's development.

Believing in an ideology whose ideals they cannot translate into reality is shown to have extremely destructive psychological effects on individual women. Julia Strauch responds to a female ideal consisting in 'Hingabe' and a purely domestic lifestyle she cannot aspire to, with misogynist self-hatred (*Kindheitsmuster*, 302). For Nelly, Julia represents the only female lifestyle she can imagine for herself, yet she finds it difficult to identify fully with her self-denying ideals. This results in feel-

[53] See Margarete Mitscherlich-Nielsen, 'Gratwanderung zwischen Anspruch und Verstrickung', in *Christa Wolf: Ein Arbeitsbuch*, ed. Drescher, 114–20 (117–18).

ings of her own inadequacy and a guilty conscience (*Kindheitsmuster*, 299–302). Like Christa T. in the early years of the GDR, Nelly responds to conflicts between her feelings and her society's demands of her by doubting herself rather than questioning the world around her.[54] Ultimately, this lack of self-love manifests itself in a pathologically disturbed relation to her physical self. Her movements are clumsy, betraying a lack of harmony with her body; she attempts to discipline herself by controlling her eating, but resorts to binges followed by physical punishment: 'Sie kann es körperlich spüren, wie ihre Achtung vor sich selbst weiter schwindet' (*Kindheitsmuster*, 339).

Several aspects of Wolf's treatment of gender in *Kindheitsmuster* prefigure her development of a more self-consciously feminist approach to history in *Kein Ort. Nirgends*, *Kassandra*, and *Medea*. In all four works, the relationship between different historical eras is explored through relationships between women of the past and the present. In *Kindheitsmuster* a female genealogy serves as an index of the mixture of continuity and change which characterizes the relationship between the 1970s present and the National Socialist past. In each of the later texts a female narrator's identification with historical, and then mythical, female figures enables her to relate more distant eras from the past to the present in a productive way. Mother–daughter relationships are central to *Kindheitsmuster*. The narrator focuses on her relationships with her mother Charlotte and her daughter Lenka, and repeatedly compares Lenka's behaviour with her own as a teenager. Cultural lines of continuity emerge, for example in details of children's games, demonstrating the degree of everyday 'normality' in a childhood even in the Third Reich (e.g. *Kindheitsmuster*, 166). However, Lenka has a capacity for independent, critical thinking and a sense of ethical responsibility which Nelly lacked at her age. Unlike Nelly, she openly protests about things in the world which are generally accepted as 'normal', but which she finds wrong, such as the working conditions for East German factory workers and the media's eagerness to photograph and report atrocities, without doing anything to help (*Kindheitsmuster*, 367, 215). The differences between Nelly and Lenka would seem to suggest a clear line of historical progress. However, Lenka's attitudes are not presented as typical of her generation. Indeed, it is her capacity to criticize her society and her contemporaries when they fall short of her (socialist) ideals—for example, when she hears young GDR tourists singing

---

[54] Cf. Christa Wolf, *Nachdenken über Christa T.* (Halle: Mitteldeutscher Verlag, 1968; repr. Frankfurt am Main: Luchterhand, 1991), 75.

racist songs in Czechoslovakia—which finds her mother's approval and admiration (*Kindheitsmuster*, 385). As Gättens has commented, 'it is in the figure of Lenka, who has grown up under socialism, that Wolf's ambivalent, critical, and yet loyal attitude toward the GDR of the 1970s shows itself most clearly'.[55]

The relationship between the narrator and Lenka also serves to highlight the difficulties for the narrator in communicating about her childhood, and the self-censorship mechanisms within her. The narrator frequently inserts 'Lenka', as addressee, into her accounts of the past (e.g. *Kindheitsmuster*, 204). This implies that she is reporting conversations which took place during the 1971 trip to Poland, but also creates the impression that the narrative as a whole is directed towards Lenka, as a representative of the younger generation. By reflecting on the problems she has in communicating the past to Lenka, as the first recipient of her story, the narrator is able to address issues raised by her project more broadly in its GDR context. In particular, she highlights the filtering mechanisms of self-censorship which limit her communication with Lenka, and presents her attempts to justify these: 'Alles kann und soll nicht gesagt werden, darüber muß Klarheit herrschen' (*Kindheitsmuster*, 170). Although she includes in the text details which she keeps from Lenka, such reflections can be read as an indirect admission that the work as a whole is also subject to these mechanisms, an idea which is made explicit at other points in the text (*Kindheitsmuster*, 312, 332).

The characterization in *Kindheitsmuster* suggests that men and women have different relationships to the dominant trends in history, an idea which is developed and reflected upon in Wolf's later texts. The men in the text tend to conform comparatively unquestioningly to the requirements of their society, while the women have a greater capacity for resistance and criticism, even if this is not translated into subversive action. Bruno Jordan easily suppresses his conscience in his desire to conform: when his rowing club becomes affiliated to the NSDAP he is relieved to be 'dabei' without having to make a personal decision (*Kindheitsmuster*, 64). Charlotte's conformist behaviour involves a far greater suppression of doubt and disagreement. Her more critical attitude emerges on occasions as sarcasm, for example when she hears about Nelly's religious education: 'Jesus Christus, sagt Herr Warsinski, wäre heute ein Gefolgsmann des Führers und würde die Juden hassen. —Hassen? sagte Charlotte Jordan. War wohl nicht gerade seine

Stärke' (*Kindheitsmuster*, 176). She is likened to Kassandra, revealing Wolf's interest, even at this stage, in female figures who, because they are not entirely integrated into the social order, have an especially clear-sighted insight into the course which events are likely to take (*Kindheitsmuster*, 223).

A similar gender contrast exists in the present between the narrator's brother Lutz, and Lenka and the narrator. Whereas Lenka and the narrator both have a critical perspective on a society which refuses to confront its past, and where 'progress' has resulted in large sections of the population's having to perform monotonous and repetitive tasks in inhuman conditions, Lutz shares this society's blind spots. His view of history is mechanistic, and allows no space for human agency or moral considerations. He argues against resistance of any kind, claiming that 'das Bestehende beweise einfach durch seine Existenz sein Recht auf Bestand' (*Kindheitsmuster*, 314). His arguments that human beings are merely products of their environment, and that 'es habe keinen Sinn, die Weltgeschichte allzu stark auf sich zu beziehen', serve to deny individual responsibility any role in history (*Kindheitsmuster*, 285, 251). As Gättens has shown, Lutz's view of history is strikingly different from the orthodox Marxist one in its mechanistic notion of mass behaviour and its neglect of the working class as the revolutionary subject of history, yet it has a similar function in providing explanations for National Socialism which allow an evasion of questions of personal involvement, guilt, and responsibility.[56] Lutz is one of the earliest of Wolf's male characters to embody a set of values—instrumental reason and faith in the progress enabled by technological advances— which Wolf regards as central to the dominant mode of thought in modern, industrial societies, and which in her later texts becomes increasingly associated with masculinity as it is constructed under patriarchy. In her Büchner Prize Speech of 1980, for example, she speaks of,

den vergegenständlichten Träumen jenes instrumentalen Denkens, das sich immer noch Vernunft nennt, aber dem aufklärerischen Ansatz auf Emanzipation, auf Mündigkeit hin, längst entglitt und als blanker Nützlichkeitswahn in das Industriezeitalter eingetreten ist.[57]

Like Schütz, Wolf uses a literary form which opens up the past and

---

[56] Ibid. 107–15.
[57] Christa Wolf, 'Von Büchner sprechen: Darmstädter Rede', in *Die Dimension des Autors*, ii. 611–25 (612).

makes it continuous with the present and still subject to new interpretations. While Schütz uses short prose forms to show that a completed and closed presentation of the past can never be reached, Wolf's explicit narratorial reflection serves to show how the past lives on in the present. The narrator's present perspective is overtly privileged, so that memory is presented not as a passive retrieval of fixed images belonging solely to the past, but instead as an active process of reconstruction in the present, which has to fight against the falsifying 'Medaillons' of the mind.[58] The narrator writes in the conviction that a dynamic dialogue between the past and present is an essential condition for a positive future:

Im Zeitalter universalen Erinnerungsverlustes (ein Satz, der vorgestern mit der Post kam) haben wir zu realisieren, daß volle Geistesgegenwart nur auf dem Boden einer lebendigen Vergangenheit möglich ist. Je tiefer unsere Erinnerung geht, um so freier wird der Raum für das, dem all unsere Hoffnung gilt: der Zukunft. (*Kindheitsmuster*, 209)

The past is therefore not of interest for its own sake, but as the prehistory which has formed the present, an idea encapsulated by the question 'Wie sind wir so geworden, wie wir heute sind?' (*Kindheitsmuster*, 284). Sabine Wilke has convincingly related Wolf's approach to history and memory in *Kindheitsmuster* to Walter Benjamin's ideas in his 'Thesen über den Begriff der Geschichte' and the fragment 'Ausgraben und Erinnern'.[59] For Wolf, as for Benjamin, history is 'Gegenstand einer Konstruktion, deren Ort nicht die homogene und leere Zeit sondern die von Jetztzeit erfüllte bildet'. Wolf's narrator's reflection on the process of writing makes this status of history as a construction very clear. Far from claiming to present the past directly, she shows the various levels of mediation which inevitably intervene between experience and the written account. Not only are memories often unreliable, but narrative form and even language itself require the organization and filtering of experience (*Kindheitsmuster*, 312, 366). The narrator is aware that her ideal of 'phantastische Genauigkeit',

<hr>

[58] Wolf uses this metaphor to refer to the way experience is transformed by memory into unchanging images. See Christa Wolf, 'Lesen und Schreiben', in *Die Dimension des Autors*, ii. 463–503 (478–81).

[59] Sabine Wilke, *Ausgraben und Erinnern: Zur Funktion von Geschichte, Subjekt und geschlechtlicher Identität in den Texten Christa Wolfs* (Würzburg: Königshausen and Neumann, 1993), 46–8; Walter Benjamin, 'Über den Begriff der Geschichte', in *Gesammelte Schriften*, ed. Rolf Tiedemann and Hermann Schweppenhäuser, 6 vols. (Frankfurt am Main: Suhrkamp, 1972–85), i (2). 691–704 (I refer here in particular to 696–7, 701), 'Ausgraben und Erinnern', in ibid. iv (1), 400–1.

whereby 'die Strukturen des Erlebens sich mit den Strukturen des Erzählens decken', is unattainable (*Kindheitsmuster*, 365).

In its understanding of history, *Kindheitsmuster* represents a challenge to the orthodox GDR discourse in several ways. Wolf's perspective on the Third Reich is not that of the triumphant 'Sieger der Geschichte' whose proud history is one of socialist resistance, but instead the guilt-laden position of a *Mitläufer* participant in Hitler's regime. In the ideological context of the GDR this is an instance of what Benjamin terms, 'die Geschichte gegen den Strich [. . .] bürsten'. He advocates a method of historiography which does not adopt the perspective of the victors of history, that is, 'die jeweils Herrschenden', but instead rewrites history from the viewpoint of the downtrodden victims of history. Instead of merely reproducing the social status quo, such a historiography fulfils a moral function by subverting a particular society's view of its history and by providing a critical perspective on that society in the present. In this way *Kindheitsmuster* challenges the self-understanding of the self-appointed 'Sieger der Geschichte' and offers instead a perspective which had previously been suppressed in GDR discourses. While Wolf never undermines the idea that the triumph of socialism in 1945 resulted in a state founded on antifascist ideals, she counters the plot structures of earlier GDR writings about this era with her own subjective experience, which had a very different shape:

Ein wenig stört mich, daß viele unserer Bücher über diese Zeit enden mit Helden, die sich schnell wandeln, mit Helden, die eigentlich schon während des Faschismus zu ziemlich bedeutenden und richtigen Einsichten kommen, politisch, menschlich. Ich will keinem Autor sein Erlebnis bestreiten. Aber mein Erlebnis war anders. Ich habe erlebt, daß es sehr lange gedauert hat, bis winzige Einsichten zuerst, später tiefergehende Veränderungen möglich wurden.[60]

Wolf's novel emphasizes the continuities between the Third Reich and the GDR which were denied by the SED. The orthodox notion of an easy and quick transition from Nazism to socialism is shown to have had disastrous effects in forcing a repression of the past and so masking underlying continuities within the subject, while imposing an artificial sense of psychological discontinuity. The narrator's inability to identify with her childhood self and tell her story in the first person is an indictment of the GDR for the way it has dealt with the national past. Continuities between Hitler's Germany and the GDR are not

---

[60] Wolf, 'Erfahrungsmuster', in *Die Dimension des Autors*, ii. 807.

confined to the level of the individual subject in Wolf's work. Several passages hint at political continuities between National Socialism and the Stalinism of the 1950s. The narrator describes her reluctance to mention a newspaper report about Stalin's show trials in 1937, aware that the taboos surrounding this aspect of the past are even greater than those associated with the Nazi era. The GDR of the 1950s, the narrator implies, is a further topic which, alongside Soviet Stalinism and German fascism, requires a more honest confrontation:

Was heißt das: sich verändern? Ohne Wahn auskommen lernen. Den Blicken der Kinder nicht ausweichen müssen, die unsere Generation treffen, wenn— selten genug—von 'früher' die Rede ist: Früher, in den dreißiger, früher, in den fünfziger Jahren. (*Kindheitsmuster*, 202)

In contrast with Schütz, Wolf does not leave her criticisms of orthodox GDR discourses about the past, whether literary or academic, implicit. In both *Kindheitsmuster* and the Akademie der Künste discussion, she describes the shortcomings of GDR school history books' presentation of the National Socialist era. In the non-fictional account in 'Erfahrungsmuster' she is careful to stress that these textbooks are factually correct: 'Es steht dort, wie es war.'[61] However, she is disturbed by the failure of these books and history teachers to arouse in young people any kind of emotional response to this topic in history. It is this impression which dominates in the fictional presentation in *Kindheitsmuster*. The narrator is shocked by her daughter's ability to regard a map of Germany depicting the locations of concentration camps with emotional detachment:

Soviel sie wisse, sagt Lenka, hatten die allermeisten aus ihrer Klasse—letzten Endes auch sie selbst—diese Karte nicht allzu gründlich, jedenfalls ohne tiefe Anteilnahme betrachtet. Es sei, sagt sie, nicht das Gefühl in ihnen aufgekommen (oder erweckt worden, denkst du), diese Karte ginge sie mehr an als andere Dokumente in diesem Buch. (*Kindheitsmuster*, 318–19)

In 'Erfahrungsmuster' Wolf defines a function for literature which is complementary to that of more factual discourses. Her work is attempting to create the kind of emotional and subjective relationship to the past which Lenka's textbook fails to inspire. She suggests that this individual reckoning with one's own past is an essential corrective to academic analyses in broad categories which enable the individual to evade an honest confrontation with his/her own experience:

---

[61] Wolf, 'Erfahrungsmuster', in *Die Dimension des Autors*, ii. 817.

Ich spreche jetzt von einer anderen Art der Bewältigung: die Auseinandersetzung des einzelnen mit seiner ganz persönlichen Vergangenheit, [...] Hier
versagt die Soziologie, die Statistik. Hier geht es um persönliche und
gesellschaftliche Moral und die Bedingungen, die beide außer Kraft setzen.
In diesem Sinne ist es nicht bewältigt. Das sehe ich an den Fragen junger
Leute, und das sehe ich an dem Schweigen meiner Altersgenossen und der
Älteren. Und sich dieser Fragen, dieses Schweigens anzunehmen—das kann
nur Literatur. Das ist kein Vorwurf gegen andere Medien, gegen Berichte und
Chroniken etwa, die das nicht tun, denn das ist nicht ihre Aufgabe. Aber es ist,
glaube ich, wirklich Aufgabe von Literatur, etwas Bewegung hineinzubringen
in die inneren Schichten, mit deren Unbeweglichkeit man sich gern beruhigt
[...].[62]

Although Wolf is careful here to avoid explicit criticism of the GDR's
writing of its prehistory, there are hints in the novel that she is aiming
not merely to complement, but to oppose certain tendencies in official
versions of the past. The narrator describes how she and a Moscow history professor discussed 'die verfluchte Verfälschung von Geschichte
zum Traktat' (*Kindheitsmuster*, 483), a phrase which reflects the tendency
of orthodox GDR historiography, as well as echoing the terms in
which Wolf rejected her own earlier work, *Moskauer Novelle*, in 1973.[63]
At another point in the work she hints at persisting taboos in the way
the Second World War has been treated:

Wir sind übereingekommen, über ein gewisses Bild des Krieges, in einem
gewissen Stil vom Kriege zu schreiben oder ihn zu verdammen, doch fühlt
man darin irgendein Verschweigen, ein Vermeiden jener Dinge, die immer
wieder eine seelische Erschütterung verursachen. (*Kindheitsmuster*, 232)

I would suggest that there are two main reasons why *Kindheitsmuster*
provoked more controversy and debate than any other literary work
about the fascist past throughout the history of the GDR. Firstly, Wolf
explicitly takes issue with the way the past had previously been presented in GDR discourses, and defines a role for literature which is not
merely supportive and illustrative of historiographical writing, but
serves as its corrective. The Polish critic Wlodzimierz Bialik has appro-
priately designated the novel an 'Abrechnung mit der Abrechnung'.[64]
    Secondly, the novel is pervaded by a sense that Wolf is speaking here

---

[62] Ibid. 811.
[63] See Christa Wolf, 'Über Sinn und Unsinn von Naivität', in *Die Dimension des Autors*, i.
42–53 (47).
[64] Wlodzimierz Bialik, 'Christa Wolfs Abrechnung mit der Abrechnung', in *Christa Wolf:
Ein Arbeitsbuch*, ed. Drescher, 78–90 (83).

not only about her own experience, but on behalf of her generation. Whereas Schütz's works seem modestly understated in their detailed focus on the everyday lives of typical Germans, Wolf's novel, while offering a convincing portrayal of an individual set of circumstances, loudly proclaims both the exemplary status of its narrator's experience and its political aims. The 'Muster' of the title and the narrator's address of herself in the second person are calculated to encourage readers to re-enact her process of remembering for themselves. The narrator, although unable to use the first person singular, frequently generalizes her own experience by using the first person plural: 'es wurde dir klar, daß gewisse Pflichten keinen Aufschub mehr dulden, unter ihnen die Pflicht, anzudeuten, was mit uns geschehen ist' (*Kindheitsmuster*, 200). The narrator's quest in writing is not only a personal, psychological one, but also quite overtly social and political. The novel is conceived as a contribution to *Vergangenheitsbewältigung* on a broad social level, a goal which Wolf hopes to achieve by offering a model of a subjective act of memory on an individual level.

The publication of *Kindheitsmuster* coincided with the aftermath of the Biermann affair, in which Wolf was prominently involved.[65] Although appearing with the publication date of 1976, the novel was not widely available in the GDR until 1977.[66] The reception of the work illustrates not only the nature of relations between literature and other, academic discourses in the GDR, but also the way current political events coloured the interpretation and appraisal of literary works.

During the course of 1977 individual reviews by Heinz Plavius, Sigrid Bock, Günther Cwojdrak, and Hermann Kant appeared in *Neue deutsche Literatur*, *Weimarer Beiträge*, *Die Weltbühne*, and *Sonntag* respectively.[67] The most heated debate surrounding the novel, however, took place on the pages of *Sinn und Form*. Here, reviews by Hans Richter and Monika Helmecke were followed up in the next issue by a lengthy attack on the work by Annemarie Auer. This provoked a number of letters from readers, some of which were subsequently printed.[68]

[65] See Emmerich, *Kleine Literaturgeschichte*, 252–63 for a detailed account of this episode.

[66] Berger, *Gewissensfrage Antifaschismus*, 153.

[67] Heinz Plavius, 'Gewissensforschung', *NDL* 25 (1977), 1, 139–51; Sigrid Bock, 'Christa Wolf: Kindheitsmuster', *WB* 23 (1977), 9, 102–30; Günther Cwojdrak, 'Kindheitsmuster— Ein Probestück', *Die Weltbühne*, 32 (1977), 18, 550–2; repr. in *Kritik 77: Rezensionen zur DDR-Literatur*, ed. Eberhard Günther, Werner Liersch, and Klaus Walther (Halle and Leipzig: Mitteldeutscher Verlag, 1978), 170–3; Hermann Kant, 'Kindheitsmuster', *Sonntag*, 31 (1977), 7, 5–6; repr. in *Kritik 77*, 174–82.

[68] Hans Richter, 'Moralität als poetische Energie', *SF* 29 (1977), 3, 667–78; Monika Helmecke, 'Kindheitsmuster', *SF* 29 (1977), 3, 678–81; Annemarie Auer, 'Gegenerinnerung',

Several surveys of the work's reception, in both the GDR and the Federal Republic, exist, but these serve primarily to summarize, rather than to analyse, the debate.[69]

Collectively, these assessments of the novel demonstrate the options open to GDR literary critics when dealing with a work of literature which presented a challenge to orthodox understandings of history and literature. *Kindheitsmuster* did not fit easily within the boundaries of what had hitherto been considered acceptable socialist literature, either in its literary form or in its construction of the relationship between the present and Germany's past. Critics could therefore either use it to broaden these boundaries, or reaffirm them by imposing the orthodox criteria on the novel.

Plavius, Richter, and Bock offer broadly positive assessments of the work which attempt to judge it by its own criteria and then use these criteria to reformulate expectations and demands concerning socialist literature. Plavius reads *Kindheitsmuster* as a class specific study of the petit-bourgeoisie, and shows how the novel answers the question, 'Ist das "Phänomen" Faschismus eine Sache der toten Vergangenheit?' in the negative, with reference to examples from the capitalist world. However, he then allows the work to broaden this orthodox understanding of fascism, by posing the same question in relation to GDR citizens:

Das Buch fragt selbstredend nicht nach der Zerschlagung und Überwindung des Systems Faschismus, es fragt nach den Wirkungen dieses Systems auf das Ich, auf den einzelnen, es sucht zu erforschen, was an Kindheitsmustern sich eingeprägt, möglicherweise festgesetzt hat und uns mit seinen Spätfolgen belastet.[70]

Richter argues that the narrative form of *Kindheitsmuster* is determined by, and appropriate to, Wolf's aims and the nature of the past she is exploring. His criticisms concern the work's presentation of the GDR recent past and present, which he finds 'schemenhaft, zufällig, willkürlich gesehen', and the narrator's tendency towards question-

SF 29 (1977), 4, 847–78; 'Briefe an Annemarie Auer', ed. Wilhelm Girnus, *SF* 29 (1977), 6, 1311–22; Bernd Schick, 'Brief eines Nachgeborenen: Zu Christa Wolf und Annemarie Auer', *SF* 30 (1978), 2, 422–6.

[69] See Norbert Schachtsiek-Freitag, 'Vom Versagen der Kritik: Die Aufnahme von "Kindheitsmuster" in beiden deutschen Staaten', in *Christa Wolf Materialienbuch*, ed. Klaus Sauer (Darmstadt and Neuwied: Luchterhand, 1979), 117–30; Gerd Krieger, 'Ein Buch im Streit der Meinungen: Untersuchungen literaturkritischer Reaktionen zu Christa Wolfs "Kindheitsmuster"', *WB* 31 (1985), 1, 56–75.

[70] Plavius, 147.

able generalizations, criticisms which are not without justification. He integrates the novel into a 'reiche Tradition antifaschistischer deutscher Literatur' and reads it as an expansion of the GDR's *Vergangenheitsbewältigung* hitherto:

Auf der dafür unentbehrlichen Grundlage dessen, was in der Deutschen Demokratischen Republik an radikaler Bewältigung der Vergangenheit geleistet worden ist, konnte sie [Wolf] an die Erledigung dieser Aufgabe auch mit der nötigen Aussicht auf Erfolg gehen.[71]

Richter's article was printed together with a brief response to the novel from Monika Helmecke. She does not share Richter's doubts about Wolf's generalizations, instead seeing the work's 'hohen Allgemeinheitsgrad und -anspruch' as its strength. Of all the critics who reviewed the book, she goes furthest in highlighting the critique of the GDR implicit in it. She is unusual in emphasizing not the class specificity of Wolf's account, but its generally representative status:

Nelly Jordan, ihre Eltern, Tanten und Onkel, das waren die deutschen Durchschnittsbürger, sie sind es. Es sind unsere Eltern, Tanten und Onkel, es sind die Älteren, die in der Kaufhalle neben uns stehen, die hinter uns die Treppe wischen, unsere Chefs, Wohnungs- und Gartennachbarn.[72]

Far from fearing western interpretations which could reflect unfavourably on the GDR, Helmecke herself boldly reads the text as an urgent warning against repetitions of the past in her own society. She relates a recent encounter with a fifteen year old whose curiosity about politics had been trained out of her in order to prevent difficulties at school, as an example of how the structures of thinking which enabled fascism to develop have continued into the GDR. This concern is undoubtedly a response to Biermann's expatriation and the draconian measures which the state adopted against those writers who voiced their protests. She concludes with praise for *Kindheitsmuster* as a vital corrective to orthodox GDR texts about the past: '*Kindheitsmuster* schließt bei weitem nicht die Lücke, die durch Einseitigkeit auf unserem Büchermarkt entstanden ist, aber es verringert sie.'[73] Rather than expanding the boundaries of what is acceptable in a socialist state in order to integrate Wolf's work into a tradition, Helmecke invokes a narrow orthodox notion of previously acceptable GDR literature, in order to position *Kindheitsmuster* favourably as a corrective to this tradition.

[71] Richter, 674–6.   [72] Helmecke, 679.   [73] Ibid. 681.

Bock is generally positive about the novel, though far more concerned to assess it according to orthodox socialist criteria than Helmecke. Indeed, Bock explicitly disagrees with Helmecke about the degree to which Wolf's characters can be regarded as socially representative. She reasserts their class specificity and criticizes the work for presenting their ways of behaviour as if they were universal responses to fascism. She dwells at some length on Wolf's own sense that she is offering a corrective to a prevalent one-sided view of history, but is careful to distance herself from these ideas:

Die Zuwendung zum Vergangenheitsstoff [. . .] richtet sich gegen eine, wie Christa Wolf meint, in unserem Leben vorherrschende 'einseitige Geschichtsbetrachtung', die den Faschismus als 'erledigt' behandele und sich fast ausschließlich auf die Tradition der Antifaschisten und Widerstandskämpfer berufe. [. . .] Abgesehen davon, daß die Autorin durch das Überspringen der objektiven Bedingungen des von ihr kritisierten Geschichtsdenkens der Gefahr nicht entgeht, in rigoroser Vereinfachung ein einseitiges Geschichtsbild aufzubauen, gilt es doch festzuhalten, daß sie sich mit dem Streben danach, im Bewußtsein eines Volkes keinerlei Lücken zu dulden, durchaus in der Tradition sozialistischer Schriftsteller befindet.[74]

Citing Anna Seghers, Bock proceeds to demonstrate continuities between Wolf's work and a socialist tradition of literature dealing with the fascist past. She claims that, despite Wolf's polemical rejection of the *Wandlungsroman* model, her work is a new development within the same tradition: 'Mit ihrer Arbeit steht sie auf den Schultern derjenigen, die mit einem Wandlungsroman ihrer Zeit Ausdruck gaben und geben, wird sie getragen von der Veränderung der gesellschaftlichen Verhältnisse.'[75]

If Bock responds to Helmecke's review by attempting to reintegrate *Kindheitsmuster* within the boundaries of a socialist tradition, Auer employs the opposite strategy. She assesses the work according to narrowly orthodox criteria, in order to suggest that it is lacking in every respect. The tone of her article is sarcastic and accusatory, and she wilfully misreads the text in order to voice personal criticisms of Wolf. Reaffirming the orthodox view of fascism as 'weiter nichts als die letzte Konsequenz jeglicher Klassenherrschaft', Auer ignores the historical specificity of the experience Wolf is presenting, and reduces the problems addressed by the novel to a matter of moving from one class to another. She responds to Wolf's criticism of the earlier *Wandlungsroman* by reasserting the model of a quick and simple shift from fascism to

[74] S. Bock, 'Kindheitsmuster', 109.   [75] Ibid. 113.

socialism and suggesting that there is something wrong with Wolf herself if she was unable to achieve such a smooth transition. She ridicules Wolf's focus on the individual and opposes it to historical and social categories, accusing Wolf of 'eine Art sittlicher Genugtuung an solchem In-sich-Hineinstarren' and an insufficiently worked out political standpoint. Repeating the very pronouncements which had hitherto determined literary presentations of fascism in the GDR, she stresses the importance of continuity for the cultural consciousness and so calls for accounts by antifascists:

Es fragt sich, ob unsere kulturelle Tradition nebst den Tugenden der wenigen, der Helden des aktiven Widerstands, ausschließlich auf die Charakterprägungen jener erbötigen, verblendeten Massen angewiesen ist, die Hitler erlagen. Ist wirklich die Wandelgeneration die exemplarische, die das Entscheidende über unser Volk und seine 'Lebensmuster' auszusagen hat?

Wenn das aber nicht, wo wären die Zeugnisse jener, die alltäglich unterm Faschismus zu leben hatten, ohne doch zu Faschisten zu werden. Was hielt sie? Welche Eigenschaften besaßen sie? Gab es sie überhaupt? Es gab sie. Aber ihre Bekundungen fehlen.[76]

Developing the idea of generational differences, Auer proceeds to accuse Wolf and her entire generation of 'literarische Geschichtsklitterung' because they were too young to know anything 'authentic' about National Socialism. Furthermore, their material comfort in the GDR gives them no right to the 'Klageton' which Auer perceives in Wolf's works. A reliable account of the fascist era, she claims, can only be given by her own generation. (Auer was born in 1913.) To fill in this alleged gap, she offers her own memories of the 'Befreiung' in 1945, in which Soviet soldiers feature as glowing heroes, 'unschuldig, prächtig und schön'. Auer underplays the fact that such experiences had been the basis of socialist literature about this period ever since—and even prior to—the foundation of the GDR. In response to Wolf's attempt to pluralize accounts of history, Auer's whole article aims at reducing history to a monolithic narrative once more. The complexities which Wolf brings into discussions about the past are reduced again to a simplistic black-and-white view: 'Um ein Nazi zu sein, mußte man entweder dumm sein oder schlecht.'[77]

As critics have pointed out, the tone and intensity of Auer's attack were undoubtedly due in large measure to the political circumstances at the time of the novel's publication. In her response to 'Gegenerinnerung', Leonore Krenzlin expresses gratitude to Auer for re-

[76] Auer, 'Gegenerinnerung', 856.   [77] Ibid. 873.

dressing a balance which she felt had been disturbed by political considerations in other reviews.[78] Dieter Schiller comments that Auer's review was 'vielleicht etwas ungerecht im einzelnen, aber tief notwendig im ganzen', for it was able to trigger a debate about the work.[79]

What is important about literary critics' response to *Kindheitsmuster* is the range of views articulated. Auer's strictly orthodox position was merely one end of a spectrum. While Wilhelm Girnus was able to read the work as a warning about the contemporary threat of fascism in capitalist countries,[80] other critics—notably Helmecke—used it to voice unmistakable criticisms of the GDR. By the mid-1970s, even directly after the Biermann affair, provocative works of literature were clearly able to facilitate a broadening of the boundaries within which literary critical discourse operated.[81] The reception of *Kindheitsmuster* illustrates the variety of roles played by GDR literary critics, as outlined by Therese Hörnigk in 1993. She argues that, while dominant voices were 'concerned with self-confirmation rather than critical analysis' and 'demanded arguments that supported predetermined conclusions', reviewers and scholars could also adopt more critical tactics:

On the other hand, literary studies in the GDR was an area of work that more than a few scholars used to circumvent the official discourse that dominated the academic world. [. . .] Supporting controversial books was a way to implicitly criticize aspects of society.[82]

A particularly interesting feature of the reception of *Kindheitsmuster* is the way critics defend the work by reformulating the relationship between literature and academic studies of history and sociology. By 1976 this relationship had in practice shifted away from the official model whereby literature served as a means of illustrating historians' findings with detailed individual examples. A recurring idea in the reviews of *Kindheitsmuster*—one which follows Wolf's own comments on the work—is the different, but complementary roles of literature and the social and historical sciences. Describing the work as 'eine Ergänzung zu wissenschaftlich-historischen Darstellungen dieser

---

[78] 'Briefe an Annemarie Auer', 1322. See also Berger, *Gewissensfrage Antifaschismus*, 153–5.

[79] 'Briefe an Annemarie Auer', 1321.

[80] Ibid. 1311–13.

[81] The debate surrounding *Kindheitsmuster* is only one example of this phenomenon. A notable earlier instance is the debate of 1972–3 following the publication of Ulrich Plenzdorf's *Die neuen Leiden des jungen W.*, SF 25 (1973), 1, 219–52; 25 (1973), 3, 672–6. See Emmerich, *Kleine Literaturgeschichte*, 249–51 for a summary of this debate.

[82] Hörnigk, 'Contours of a New Academic Landscape', 173.

Epoche und ihrer Voraussetzungen', Plavius argues that it 'will [. . .] nicht zulassen, daß die historische oder Klassenanalyse dieser Zeit als Schirm mißbraucht wird, hinter dem sich das Individuum auf bequeme Weise der Verantwortung entzieht'.[83] A space is thus opened for literature to do something which academic studies cannot do. The problems with the official GDR interpretation of the fascist past, in particular the use of abstract socio-economic categories as a means of denying individual responsibility, appear very clearly in Plavius's comments. However, no criticism of this kind of analysis is made. Instead, art is constructed as its necessary complement. Wolfgang Hegewald defends the work against Auer's criticisms by invoking important differences between literature and the social sciences, differences which he accuses Auer of not understanding:

Die Gesellschaftswissenschaft mag zu Recht 'Nelly und ihre Leute' 'Nutz-nießer des Regimes, wenn auch im Kleinstformat' [Auer] heißen, aber geht solche apodiktische Feststellung nicht am Kern der literarischen Erkundung vorbei? [. . .] Ein literarisches Buch leistet eben anderes auf andere Weise als eine historische Analyse. Der Autor wird sich allerdings den Ergebnissen der Sozialwissenschaften nicht verschließen; seine Aufgabe ist es jedoch nicht, diese zu wiederholen oder arabeskenhaft zu illustrieren.[84]

Here Hegewald distances himself quite explicitly from the earlier official model of literature's subordination to the Marxist social sciences.

The idea of a complementary relationship between literature and academic studies was a useful compromise for literary critics. It enabled them to broaden the role accorded to literature in order to do better justice to the works which more critical writers were now producing, and it allowed them to defend texts which did not adhere to the orthodox understanding of history. At the same time, it meant that due respect could be paid to the Marxist 'sciences', without the need to adopt their categories and criteria for analysing literature. Furthermore, directly oppositional challenges to the orthodox interpretation of the past could be conveniently veiled with the argument that literature had a special function of its own, and that this function was complementary to academic discourses. However, while broadening literary critical discourse and notions of acceptable socialist literature, this newly formulated complementary relationship may also have

---

[83] Plavius, 141. See also S. Bock, 'Christa Wolf: Kindheitsmuster', 111–12.
[84] 'Briefe an Annemarie Auer', 1316–17.

prevented the historical insights and critiques contained in literary texts from having any significant impact on the way historians approached the past. The acknowledgement of a new function for literature served, paradoxically, to preserve the orthodox role of the historical profession and to protect it from any criticisms which a work like *Kindheitsmuster* contained.

DEVELOPMENTS IN HISTORIANS' AND WRITERS' APPROACHES TO NATIONAL SOCIALISM AFTER *KINDHEITSMUSTER*

Although *Kindheitsmuster* expresses a clear critique of the way the fascist past had been treated by literary and historical discourses in the GDR, and breaks taboos which had previously acted as boundaries to discussions of the topic, there is little evidence of any significant change in historians' approach to the subject in the late 1970s and 1980s. While the late 1970s saw a general loosening of the schematic categories which had hitherto determined historians' work, most studies of National Socialism continued to be severely limited by a rigid methodology imposed from above, which distorted interpretations of empirical evidence. Acknowledging the psychological effects of fascism on the individual and the continuity of individuals' lives from Hitler's Germany to the GDR would have meant questioning fundamental ideological premises of the state.

Georg Iggers has claimed that, 'by 1989 GDR scholarship on Nazism and the Holocaust had reached the point where it could finally make its contribution to international scholarship'.[85] This statement needs qualifying. It is true that in the very last years of the GDR a small amount of socio-historical work on the era was produced which left the official dogma behind.[86] It is also true that some research in the later years of the GDR addressed new, formerly taboo topics and introduced new perspectives on the fascist past. The eminent professor at the Humboldt University in Berlin, Kurt Pätzold, was one of the first historians to address the issues of National Socialist racial policy and the Holocaust, generally played down by GDR historiography. His work from the mid-1970s onwards was acclaimed for challenging

---

[85] *Marxist Historiography in Transformation*, ed. Iggers, 16. See also Fulbrook, *German National Identity*, 133.

[86] See, for example, Sigrid Jacobeit, 'Clothing in Nazi Germany', in *Marxist Historiography in Transformation*, ed. Iggers, 227–45.

taboos and opening new fields of enquiry.[87] However, a close examination of his work reveals that racial policy and antisemitism remain firmly subordinated to the orthodox explanations of fascism based on the class struggle and monopoly capitalism. He insists, for example, that 'die Nazipartei war zuerst und vor allem imperialistischer Stoß-trupp gegen die Arbeiterklasse'.[88] According to this argument, Jews were persecuted because they were perceived as both the 'Erfinder der marxistischen Klassenkampflehre und -praxis' and the owners of growing capital. The racial ideology of Hitler's regime is granted no independent status. Instead, Pätzold argues that antisemitism was merely a tactic for diverting attention from the true struggle based on class:

Antisemitismus und Judenverfolgung waren in der Nazipartei seit ihrer Gründung ebenso billige wie wirkungsvolle Mittel, die eigenen meist aus dem Kleinbürgertum stammenden Anhänger von den sozialen Fragen abzulenken, sie an sozialen und politischen Scheinfronten zu gruppieren und dort 'kämpfen' zu lassen.

Joachim Petzold, working at the Akademie der Wissenschaften, offered a more challenging augmentation of the orthodox approach to fascism in his 1982 work, *Die Demagogie des Hitlerfaschismus: Die politische Funktion der Naziideologie auf dem Wege zur faschistischen Diktatur*. In a chapter entitled 'Die ideologischen und propagandistischen Methoden der Massenmobilisierung 1930–1932', he addresses the question, generally avoided by GDR historians, of why National Socialist ideology found the support of the masses, particularly in more rural areas. Antisemitism is granted a more central role than is usually the case in GDR accounts. Petzold devotes a large part of the chapter to an analysis of the pseudo-scientific racial theories propagated by the National Socialists. Admittedly, he adheres to the accepted view that antisemitism was merely a symptom of deeper, more 'real' class relations: 'Der objektive Antikapitalismus konnte gerade auf dem Lande in subjektiven Antisemitismus umgemünzt und abgewiegelt werden.'[89]

In 1989 a collection of essays about the years leading up to the Second World War appeared, edited by Dietrich Eichholtz and Kurt

[87] Fulbrook, *German National Identity*, 136.
[88] Kurt Pätzold, *Faschismus. Rassenwahn. Judenverfolgung: Eine Studie zur politischen Strategie und Taktik des faschistischen deutschen Imperialismus (1933–1935)* (Berlin: Deutscher Verlag der Wissenschaften, 1975), here in particular 14–17.
[89] Joachim Petzold, *Die Demagogie des Hitlerfaschismus: Die politische Funktion der Naziideologie auf dem Wege zur faschistischen Diktatur* (Berlin: Akademie Verlag, 1982), 288–328 (290).

Pätzold.[90] In their preface, the editors claim that the study fills a gap in GDR research by focusing attention on the immediate pre-war years of the Third Reich. The aim of the work, as outlined there, consists in an analysis 'der herrschenden imperialistischen Kreise in Deutschland', with a particular focus on 'führende Kreise des Finanzkapitals, der Wehrmacht und der faschistischen Partei'. The editors point out that further work is needed on areas including topics in social history and the history of everyday life, as are 'Untersuchungen des Inhalts und des Mechanismus der faschistischen Ideologisierung und Massenbeeinflussung'. Many of the contributions to the volume focus on economic and military history, and remain firmly within the confines of the orthodox approach to fascism. Racial policy and the Holocaust are barely mentioned, and where mass involvement in National Socialism is conceded, the notion of the innocent masses being manipulated by the 'aggressivsten und reaktionärsten imperialistischen und militaristischen Klassenkräfte' serves to exonerate the majority of Germans from responsibility.[91] Nevertheless, within this framework some interesting work is produced, particularly on aspects of social and ideological history. In an essay about the public celebrations for Hitler's fiftieth birthday, for example, Pätzold offers a wide-ranging and convincing analysis of 'die ausgefeilte Methodik [. . .], mit der in erster Linie Millionen Deutsche von der Macht des Faschismus, seiner Unüberwindbarkeit und Sieghaftigkeit überzeugt werden sollten'.[92]

Interestingly, two essays in the volume deal with the Hitler–Stalin Pact of August 1939, a taboo for GDR historians in earlier years.[93] However, both offer an interpretation of this event which confirms the notion of an absolute opposition between the progressive and peaceful Soviet Union, and the aggressive and imperialist Third Reich. Neither makes any mention of the secret protocols concerning the division of

---

[90] *Der Weg in den Krieg: Studien zur Geschichte der Vorkriegsjahre (1935/36 bis 1939)*, ed. Dietrich Eichholtz and Kurt Pätzold (Berlin: Akademie Verlag, 1989; repr. Cologne: Pahl-Rugenstein, 1989), here in particular pp. xi–xii.

[91] See, for example, Manfred Weißbecker and Gert Noack, ' "Die Partei als Rückgrat der inneren Front": Mobilmachungspläne der NSDAP für den Krieg (1937 bis 1939)', in *Der Weg in den Krieg*, ed. Eichholtz and Pätzold, 67–90 (72); Gerhart Hass, 'Krieg in Ost oder West? Zur Entscheidung über die Reihenfolge der faschistischen Aggressionen', in *Der Weg in den Krieg*, 151–81 (151–2).

[92] Kurt Pätzold, 'Hitlers fünfzigster Geburtstag am 20. April 1939', in *Der Weg in den Krieg*, ed. Eichholtz and Pätzold, 308–43 (308).

[93] Günter Rosenfeld, 'Die Sowjetunion und das faschistische Deutschland am Vorabend des zweiten Weltkrieges', in *Der Weg in den Krieg*, ed. Eichholtz and Pätzold, 345–80; Heinz Kühnreich, 'Der deutsch-sowjetische Nichtangriffsvertrag vom 23. August 1939 aus der zeitgenössischen Sicht der KPD', in *Der Weg in den Krieg*, 517–51.

eastern Europe.[94] Rosenfeld's explanation of Soviet policy as a clever tactic to protect socialist progress and prevent war is one which is supported by Kühnreich's analysis of contemporary KPD documents:

Daß es der Sowjetunion gelang, sich durch den Abschluß des Nichtangriffs-vertrages mit Hitlerdeutschland aus dem Krieg herauszuhalten und sich zunächst [. . .] vor dem früher oder später zu erwartenden Angriff Hitlerdeutschlands eine Atempause zu verschaffen, war für die Sicherung der Errungenschaften der Oktoberrevolution und des sozialistischen Aufbaus in dem ersten sozialistischen Lande der Welt von weitreichender Bedeutung und ein großer Erfolg der sowjetischen Diplomatie.[95]

A strikingly different perspective on this episode in history is offered by Wolf in a speech of 31 August 1989, illustrating the enormity of the gulf which had developed between writers and historians:

Erst von deutschen Kommunisten, zu der Zeit in Konzentrationslagern oder in der Emigration, erfuhr ich seit Ende der fünfziger Jahre von den qualvollen Konflikten, in die der Hitler-Stalin-Pakt sie stürzte, und es mag vor fünf-undzwanzig Jahren gewesen sein, daß mir ein litauischer Schriftsteller [. . .] von jenem heute nicht mehr bestrittenen Zusatzabkommen erzählte, das Polen und die baltischen Staaten zu Objekten zweier Großmächte machte [. . .][96]

In the case of work on National Socialism, Fulbrook's analysis of seemingly taboo-breaking ventures into new areas of historical research in the 1980s is apt:

It almost seems as if, in introducing previously taboo topics in order solely to reinsert them in older frameworks of interpretation, regime-sustaining histor-ians were practising something akin to historical innoculation: introducing a small dose of the heretical virus together with its ideologically sound antidote, such that the GDR citizen's theoretical defences would be ready if inadvert-ently exposed to similar themes in western publications.[97]

A small minority of GDR studies of fascism—Petzold's *Die Demagogie des Hitlerfaschismus*, for instance—might be said to operate the 'sand-wich principle', integrating undogmatic empirical research into the required theoretical frameworks.[98] However, in the majority of cases the bread is too thick, and the filling difficult to locate. Most studies,

---

[94] Cf. *Marxist Historiography in Transformation*, ed. Iggers, 16.
[95] Rosenfeld, 345.
[96] Christa Wolf, 'Überlegungen zum 1. September 1939: Rede in der Akademie der Künste, Berlin', in *Im Dialog*, 70–6 (70–1).
[97] Fulbrook, *German National Identity*, 138.   [98] Ibid. 132.

even from the late 1980s, confirm Georgi Verbeeck's contention that
it was only after 1989 that East German scholars were able to distance themselves from 'Marxist "mumbo-jumbo-history"', which had
reduced the history of National Socialism to another moment in the
historical process of social transformation, as well as from abstract generalizations about the primacy of economics and class conflicts'.[99]

The fact that *Kindheitsmuster* and the other 1970s critical literature
about the German past had little impact on the way GDR historians
approached the National Socialist past is testimony to the increasing
gulf between historiography and public debate in the GDR. As this
chapter has shown, Wolf's novel provoked important and belated discussion of the fascist past and the way it had been treated hitherto in
the GDR, amongst literary critics and readers. It was also instrumental in opening a space for other writers, women in particular, to explore
their own relationships to the fascist past. Dennis Tate has rightly
criticized the popular idea that *Kindheitsmuster* marks the culmination of
the process of *Vergangenheitsbewältigung* in GDR literature.[100] A brief
survey of works by women published after 1976 will show, rather,
that *Kindheitsmuster* initiated a new, more critical, and more gender-
conscious stage in the development of a literary discourse about fascism.

In the course of the 1980s a number of GDR women writers
responded to Wolf's appeal to readers to re-enact her narrator's processes of remembering for themselves, and produced texts tracing their
own 'Kindheitsmuster'. Vera Friedländer's *Späte Notizen* of 1982 is a
more transparently autobiographical text than *Kindheitsmuster*.[101]
Friedländer recalls the stories of members of her large Jewish family,
most of whom died in the concentration camps. Her perspective on the
National Socialist era is thus a very different one from Wolf's, but the
narrative structure and thematic focus of the work are clearly indebted
to *Kindheitsmuster*. The narrator, like Wolf's, reflects on the processes
of remembering a past she has partially suppressed and writing about
it (*Späte Notizen*, 5–7). She reports conversations with her husband
and fifteen-year-old son as she writes, and defines the purpose of her

[99] Georgi Verbeeck, 'Confronting the Nazi Experience in the GDR', in *Germany after Unification: Coming to Terms with the Recent Past*, ed. Gert-Joachim Glaeßner, GM 37 (Amsterdam and Atlanta: Rodopi, 1996), 67–85 (75). This impression is supported by the pro-
ceedings of a forum held by the Historische Kommission des SPD-Vorstandes in Bonn in Mar. 1987 to enable dialogue between East and West German historians. See *Erben deutscher Geschichte: DDR–BRD: Protokolle einer historischen Begegnung*, ed. Susanne Miller and Malte Ristau (Reinbek: Rowohlt, 1988).
[100] Tate, 'Writing in the Shadow of Auschwitz', 122.
[101] Vera Friedländer, *Späte Notizen* (Berlin: Verlag Neues Leben, 1982).

project in terms—reminiscent of Wolf's work in general—of keeping
the memory of her relatives alive for future generations:

> Es soll weder Aquarell noch Leuchter sein. Die Menschen, die meine Familie
> waren, sind tot. Ich will ihrer nicht gedenken mit Blumen oder Steinchen. Mir
> widerstrebt der Gedanke an Kerzen vor schwarz umrahmten Bildern.
>   Ich erinnere mich an die Lebenden.
>   Damit die Erinnerung nicht vergeht, habe ich sie notiert. Es ist niemand
> mehr da, der es könnte und wollte, also schrieb ich die Notizen. Sie sind nicht
> Poesie, nur ein Bericht.
>   Ich übergebe sie meinen Kindern und bitte, sie zu bewahren. Man muß
> wissen, was war und wie es war. (*Späte Notizen*, 271)

Elisabeth Schulz-Semrau's *Suche nach Karalautschi: Report einer Kindheit*
of 1984 also bears a number of striking similarities to *Kindheitsmuster*.[102]
The text presents the narrator's attempt to remember and come to
terms with the events of her childhood in Königsberg under National
Socialist rule, in order to attain greater self-understanding in the present (*Suche*, 42). Like Wolf's Nelly, she was not entirely immune to the
attractions of the fascist regime, her perspective on it being the highly
personal one of a child, rather than one based on considered ideological and moral judgement. Like *Kindheitsmuster*, Schulz-Semrau's novel
offers a specifically female perspective on the experience of National
Socialism and the war. The narrator focuses closely on the gender relations within her family. While her relationship to her elderly and disci-
plinarian father was a distanced one, it is the relationships with her
mother and aunt, each problematic in its own way, which are presented with most prominence.

Schulz-Semrau continues the taboo-breaking critique of the traditional GDR treatment of the fascist past which Wolf initiated with
Kindheitsmuster. She touches on problematic aspects of history, such as
the widespread rape of German women by Soviet soldiers in the immediate post-war era, and criticizes the official refusal to acknowledge
these elements of the past. The narrator deeply regrets her own earlier
dogmatic responses to her unconventional aunt Ella's experiences:

> Als wir über ihre Nachkriegserlebnisse sprachen, hatte die Tante ein paarmal,
> da ich für alles ein ideologisches Trostpflaster parat hatte, wie außer sich zu
> schreien angefangen, hatte mir jegliche Reife, jenes zu begreifen, abge-
> sprochen.
>   Das war, als ich an die Stelle geriet, wo ihr infolge des Krieges als Frau

[102] Elisabeth Schulz-Semrau, *Suche nach Karalautschi: Report einer Kindheit* (Halle and Leipzig:
Mitteldeutscher Verlag, 1984).

Schäden zugefügt worden waren, die schwerer heilten als männliche Verwundungen. Wenn ich auch damals Erklärungen und Entschuldigungen gefunden hatte, habe ich doch mit diesen Erlebnissen meiner Tante bis in die Gegenwart zu kämpfen gehabt. (*Suche*, 134)

When the narrator reads from the unfinished manuscript of the novel and listens to the responses of young people—presumably an incident reflecting the author's own experience—she becomes aware of the broader effects which such attempts to explain the past in terms of abstract and dogmatic formulas have had in the GDR:

Ich bin erstaunt, ein wenig enttäuscht auch, was sie heraushören. Ja, sagen sie, das gerade wollen wir wissen: Die großen historischen Zusammenhänge haben wir im Geschichtsunterricht gehört, den faschistischen Krieg in Filmen gesehen, über den Widerstandskampf in Büchern gelesen, aber wie seid ihr damit täglich umgegangen? Wieso habt ihr euch von *so was* erfassen lassen? (*Suche*, 139)

Schulz-Semrau's aim of broadening the discourse about the German past by presenting individual experiences as a complement to the broad, abstract explanations offered by historiography is one shared by Ursula Höntsch-Harendt, whose novel *Wir Flüchtlingskinder* appeared in 1985.[103] Höntsch-Harendt, too, is concerned to challenge the taboos resulting from an ideologically dogmatic approach to the past. Her novel tells the story of the Hönow family, forced to leave their home in Silesia when it becomes Polish territory in 1945. A first-person retrospective narrative organized around a series of diary entries written at the time, the work covers the period from 1944 to 1950. The narrator, Marianne Hönow, intersperses her memories and present reflections with a considerable amount of documentary material relating to the historical period. This material—which includes extracts from a speech by Himmler, the diaries of the Breslau priest Paul Peikert, articles from the *Schlesische Zeitung*, and the 1945 Potsdam Conference's decrees concerning the Polish-German border—serves to explain the historical background of the narrative and gives the work a rather pedagogical tone. The representative status of the narrator's family is emphasized:

Vierzig Jahre ist das her! Was damals geschah und damals schmerzte, ist überwunden, aber nicht vergessen. Weil ein Krieg sich nicht vergessen läßt.

[103] Ursula Höntsch-Harendt, *Wir Flüchtlingskinder: Roman* (Halle and Leipzig: Mitteldeutscher Verlag, 1985; repr. 1991).

Wovon ich erzählen will, ist auch ein Stück Geschichte meines Volkes, das gute und schlechte Tage hatte, wie die Hönows, wie wir alle. (*Flüchtlingskinder*, 9)

The novel serves as a critique of the official GDR version of history, which insisted that the ceding of Silesia to Poland was historically justified, resulting in a denial of the experience of Silesian refugees who were bitter about the loss of their home and culture. The later sections of the text, set in the Soviet Zone of Occupation and the early GDR, highlight the new authorities' lack of understanding for these people's predicament. At a Christmas party in 1945 the dogmatic new *Bürgermeister* forbids the refugees' singing of a traditional song, because of the line 'Riesengebirge, deutsches Gebirge' (*Flüchtlingskinder*, 188). While Marianne is able to integrate herself into the newly formed GDR society, her parents remain isolated and bitter, mourning the death of their native culture (*Flüchtlingskinder*, 212–13).

In a review of the work, the GDR literary critic Elke Mehnert framed her textual discussion with comparisons to Wolf's *Kindheitsmuster* and Schütz's *Vorgeschichten*.[104] Mehnert complains that the genre designation 'Roman' is inappropriate for *Wir Flüchtlingskinder*, and reads it instead as documentary prose. However, it seems significant that Höntsch-Harendt, who had studied journalism and history, chose a fictional form for her treatment of a historical experience still surrounded by taboos in the mid-1980s. The novel form allows her to write with an ambiguity which would be difficult to achieve in a nonfictional genre. Mehnert herself unwittingly demonstrates this when, basing her interpretation on the narrator's identification with the newly founded GDR, she reads the work as an affirmation of the orthodox interpretation of this chapter in German history: 'Die neuen Grenzen im Osten sind gerecht, und sie haben den Frieden in Europa sicherer gemacht. *Wir Flüchtlingskinder* schafft Sätzen wie diesem Hinterland.'[105] The text can, however, just as easily be read as a challenge to the orthodox historical narrative. In a brief afterword to the 1991 edition of the work, Höntsch-Harendt highlights the intention of her work to challenge the exclusion of the Silesians' experience from GDR public discourse:

Ich wußte ja, daß die einstigen Flüchtlinge hierzulande im gesellschaftlichen Gedächtnis nie eine Rolle gespielt hatten und ihre Heimat als nicht existent erklärt worden war, als hätte sie nicht auch zur deutschen Vergangenheit

---

[104] Elke Mehnert, 'Ursula Höntsch-Harendt: Wir Flüchtlingskinder', *WB* 32 (1986), 12, 2071–9.
[105] Ibid. 2078.

gehört. Nicht einmal den Schmerz um die verlorene Heimat außerhalb der eigenen vier Wände anzusprechen war ihnen erlaubt.

Auch deshalb schrieb ich dieses Buch—spät zwar, aber doch auch nicht zu spät. (*Flüchtlingskinder*, 270)

The extracts from around fifty letters from enthusiastic and grateful readers which are included in this edition testify to the important function which literature of this kind fulfilled in the GDR, as a forum for the discussion of historical experience which defied the ideologically determined categories of the official discourse.

While Friedländer, Schulz-Semrau, and Höntsch-Harendt rework Wolf's project with regard to their own particular sets of circumstances, each presenting a female child's experience of National Socialism, two GDR women writers develop the topic in distinctly new directions in texts written in the late 1980s. Helga Königsdorf's *Respektloser Umgang* (1986) and *Ungelegener Befund* (1989), and Helga Schubert's *Judasfrauen* (1990) each, in their various ways, represent a move away from presenting experiences under National Socialism from a semi-autobiographical perspective.[106] Gender is a central concern in each of these texts, but instead of focusing on the ways in which fascist ideology pervaded everyday life in the domestic sphere to which women were traditionally confined, Königsdorf and Schubert explore more direct ways in which women and other social 'outsiders' supported Hitler's regime. These texts focus more explicitly than the earlier works on the relationship between the National Socialist past and the GDR present. In particular, they point up the inadequacies of the official discourse about the German past.

Respektloser Umgang and *Ungelegener Befund* both deal with scientists' potential complicity with the fascist state through their work. In the first work, the narrator's hallucinatory conversations with Lise Meitner prompt her to reflect on the ethics of scientific research and the scientist's responsibility to humankind in both past and present, as well as on her own Jewish grandmother's fate and her parents' behaviour in the Third Reich. Königsdorf rejects the notion—evident, for example, in *Kindheitsmuster*—that women, because of their relative outsider position in patriarchal society, have a stronger capacity for resistance to dominant ideologies than men. Instead, in Meitner she explores the

---

[106] Helga Königsdorf, *Respektloser Umgang: Erzählung* (Darmstadt: Luchterhand, 1986; repr. 1988), *Ungelegener Befund: Erzählung* (Berlin and Weimar: Aufbau, 1989; repr. Frankfurt am Main: Luchterhand, 1991); Helga Schubert, *Judasfrauen: Zehn Fallgeschichten weiblicher Denunziation im Dritten Reich* (Berlin: Aufbau, 1990; repr. Munich: Deutscher Taschenbuch Verlag, 1992).

conformist mentality of a figure who, as a female scientist and a Jew, was a twofold outsider.

The processes of reflection which the narrator's discussions with Meitner provoke demonstrate the continuing need for a more honest and thorough confrontation with Germany's past, even in the 1980s. As a member of a generation which did not directly experience National Socialism, born in 1938, Königsdorf's narrator is not faced with the problems of a repressed personal past which were central to the works by Wolf, Schulz-Semrau, and Höntsch-Harendt. Instead, the dominant GDR discourse has left her with a feeling of not being able to identify with the past:

Ich bin geschichtslos. Zu spät geboren, um mitschuldig zu werden. Zu betroffen, um Mitschuld nachträglich für möglich zu halten. Ohne Identifikation mit Vergangenheit.

Gewiß. Es gab Angebote. Berichte von Menschen, die widerstanden hatten. Sie erwiesen sich als die wahren Sieger der Geschichte, auch wenn man sie gemordet hatte. Nun wurden sie für das ramponierte Selbstwertgefühl eines Volkes dringend benötigt. Ich bewunderte sie. Ich verehrte sie. Nur als ihresgleichen konnte ich mich nicht verstehen. (*Umgang*, 20–1)

Because *Respektloser Umgang* brings together the various thematic strands of the present study, combining reflection on the National Socialist past, the presentation of a historical female figure, and fantastic elements, it will be discussed in greater detail in the third chapter.

Ungelegener Befund also explores the continuing legacy of National Socialism in the present and the ethical responsibility of scientists. It is an epistolary novel on two time levels. A series of letters between the biologist Dieter Jhanz and a variety of correspondents, written between September 1986 and September 1988, forms the framework of the text. The 'ungelegener Befund' of the title is a series of letters written during the Second World War, which forms the middle section of the work. They are attributed, albeit with no certainty, to Jhanz's father and a Professor Markus, although the addressee's and sender's names have been made illegible. These letters implicate Jhanz's father, acclaimed for his progressive work with mentally handicapped children after 1945, in National Socialist-inspired research on race during the war, in an attempt to further his career. In presenting Jhanz's confrontation with his father's potential complicity with Hitler's regime, the work raises issues such as the continuities between the fascist past and the GDR present, the continuing importance of scientists' ethical responsibility in their work, and the failings of GDR *Vergangenheits-bewältigung*. Like the narrator of *Respektloser Umgang*, Jhanz is prompted by his unsolicited confrontation with the past to reflect critically on his own behaviour in the present. He recognizes parallels between his own conformity and his father's: 'Was unterscheidet mich eigentlich von meinem Vater? Die Zeiten sind anders. Das ist viel. Aber es gibt mir kein Recht, mich zu überheben' (*Befund*, 95). Like his father, Jhanz is professionally ambitious, and his own research on genetics also has the potential for ethically dubious uses (*Befund*, 24, 30).

Jhanz is forced to confront not only the likelihood that his father collaborated with the National Socialists, but also the failure of his own society to deal with this past in any adequate way. When he tries to prevent a commemoration of his father by the children's home where he worked, he receives letters from a variety of GDR citizens eager to defend his father. Perhaps the most alarming is an anonymous letter from a young citizen whose boredom and lack of commitment to GDR society have resulted in a considerable sympathy for fascism:

Ihr Vater soll ein Fascho gewesen sein. Glauben Sie, daß es damals wirklich so schlimm war? Manchmal denke ich, vielleicht erzählen die uns das bloß, um von den Problemen heute abzulenken. [. . .] Es muß doch einen Grund gegeben haben, daß die Leute damals begeistert waren. Mir fiele nichts ein, wofür ich mich begeistern könnte. (*Befund*, 77–8)

Two of the hostile letters Jhanz receives are from women, the only two women whose voices are heard in the whole text. The Director of the children's home, Maria Weiß, defends Jhanz's father's character and his past behaviour with references to 'schlimme Zeiten': 'Manch einer ist in etwas hineingeraten, besten Glaubens oft, was ihm später leid getan hat' (*Befund*, 76). An eighty-year-old, Regina Roßwein, who knew Jhanz's father, goes further:

Ich denke, man sollte endlich aufhören, in den alten Geschichten herumzustochern, und zur Tagesordnung übergehen. [. . .] Und, wenn man schon über die damalige Zeit spricht, muß man gerecht sein. Es gab auch Positives. Nach dem Durcheinander mit den Sozis in der Systemzeit und im Vergleich zu heute. Jeder hatte Arbeit. Man konnte auf der Straße gehen, ohne um sein Leben fürchten zu müssen. Daß dann alles so kam, lag auch daran, daß die anderen neidisch auf unsere Erfolge waren. (*Befund*, 84)

Through this spectrum of opinions, Königsdorf is suggesting that there is a widespread refusal in GDR society to confront the events of the past and to acknowledge responsibility and guilt. Jhanz's comments on the letters he receives make it clear that, by reducing fascism to an abstract historical category, the official discourse about National Socialism has enabled this evasion of personal and collective responsibility:

Warum sind sie nicht wenigstens ein bißchen ratlos. Flüchten in immer gleiche Beruhigungsformeln, die sie in all den Jahren wie Beschwörungen vor sich hingetragen haben. Sie sind nicht bestürzt und nicht traurig. Mit ihnen hat es nie etwas zu tun gehabt. Entweder sie waren auf der richtigen Seite, oder sie kamen in der Geschichte nicht vor. Die Schuld blieb etwas Abstraktes, immer die von anderen. Nichts scheint mir so gefährlich wie mißbrauchte Wahrheit, weil sie der Lüge einen Tugendschein verleiht. (*Befund*, 80–1)

Significantly, the only female characters to figure in *Ungelegener Befund* do not represent positions of resistance to the dominant ideology, but share and defend the blind spots and failings of their society. Although Königsdorf's characters in this text are predominantly male, her interest in outsiders and the under-privileged in patriarchy continues: Dieter Jhanz is gay, a fact which he conceals from his homophobic society. Here, as in *Respektloser Umgang*, Königsdorf explores the propensity of 'outsiders'—whether women, Jews, or gays—to develop highly conformist patterns of behaviour. In an unsent confessional letter to his young lover Felix, Jhanz analyses the roots of his conformism in his childhood. He sees his homosexuality as an aggravating factor in an environment of dogmatism, prompting him to attempt to compensate for being different:

Als Junge lauschte ich begierig den großen Erzählungen vom bösen Wolf, von Jesus, von Mitschurin, von Stalin, von der guten Fee, von Hitler und vom Teufel. Ich verstand nichts von allem, war aber begabt genug zu spüren, welche Stellungnahme mir Beifall einbrachte. Ich lernte, mich zu verhalten. Auch mein Anderssein warf seinen Schatten. Ich war nicht wirklich zugehörig, ich mußte mich tarnen. Mein Verhalten wurde zum dauernden Manöver, in dem die Täuschung das Eigentliche war. (*Befund*, 98)

Like these two works by Königsdorf, Helga Schubert's *Judasfrauen* is a reaction to the idea that women occupy a position outside mainstream history and institutional power, and therefore have a stronger capacity than men for resistance to the dominant ideology. Schubert's text consists of ten case stories of women's denunciations in the Third Reich. Based on an examination of historical documents, the stories combine factual narration with occasional imaginative reconstructions of the historical figures' subjective experience, in the form of inner monologue. In an essay 'Judasfrauen', which precedes these narratives in the dtv edition, Schubert rejects what she terms 'die Frauenveredelung': 'So sensibel, so zart, so kooperativ, so mütterlich, so mitleidig, so kreativ, so authentisch sind wir nicht. Wir sind auch böse und auch gefährlich, auf unsere Weise' (*Judasfrauen*, 19). Gättens has discussed the problematic assumption here of 'a stable, trans-historical, universal identity of all women'.[107]

Schubert does not simply reverse a notion of women as innocent victims, to treat them instead as actively complicitous criminals. Rather, she problematizes the opposition between 'Opfer' and 'Täter', and aims to examine the conditions which led to these women's often fatal denunciations: 'Dabei interessier[t] mich besonders der Alltag der Diktatur und die spezifische Situation, ich vermute Ohnmacht, der Frau, die sie vielleicht zu diesem Verbrechen getrieben habe' (*Judasfrauen*, 21). She refrains from simple moral judgements of individuals, regarding the women themselves as 'Opfer der Diktatur' (*Judasfrauen*, 10). The individual women's motivations for their denunciations can rarely be ascertained with any certainty. At times Schubert reproduces the professional assessments of personalities and motives which were presented in post-war trials, or uses inner monologue to highlight the processes of imaginative invention involved in any attempt to understand why the women acted as they did (e.g. *Judasfrauen*, 44, 69–78). Gättens has shown that Schubert's statements in the essays preceding the case stories, about the specific characteristics of women's denunciation—that it was a response to powerlessness and a means, 'private Konflikte sozusagen mittels Staatsgewalt zu lösen' (*Judasfrauen*, 22)—do not do justice to the variety of ways in which the personal and the political intersect in the different cases.[108]

Like Königsdorf's works, *Judasfrauen* intensifies the critique of the official GDR discourse about the past which was beginning to emerge in *Kindheitsmuster*. In 'Judasfrauen', Schubert describes the bureaucracy and the ideological objections which she had to overcome in order to carry out her research in East and West Berlin. Even in the late 1980s, a 'negative' project of this kind encountered a considerable amount of opposition from historians and state authorities. Schubert is repeatedly advised to work on 'etwas historisch Relevanteres und Positiveres', and reminded of the SED's self-congratulatory insistence that the GDR

---

[107] Gättens, 125.
[108] See ibid. 121–48, for a more thorough analysis of *Judasfrauen*.

had dealt adequately with the past in its earliest years (*Judasfrauen*, 22, 29). The comments of an employee at an unspecified 'höheren Ort' of state authority make it clear that historical research on women will only find support if it serves to confirm the orthodox narrative of history:

Bitte widmen Sie sich dabei besonders dem Widerstand der Kommunistinnen. Unsere Analysen haben ergeben, daß wir ihnen im Vergleich zu ihren männlichen Genossen in der Literatur noch besser gerecht werden müßten. (*Judasfrauen*, 22)

Schubert's critique of the GDR is not restricted to the way it has dealt with the German past. In a preface to the paperback edition of *Judasfrauen* written in 1991, Schubert challenges the discourse of antifascism which underpinned the GDR, claiming that she wrote the text as a parable intended to highlight parallels between National Socialism and 'real existierender Sozialismus': 'Da die Machthaber in der SED-DDR all ihre Maßnahmen mit ihrem angeblichen Antifaschismus begründeten, war es ein Tabu, die Diktatur der Nazis mit ihrer Diktatur zu vergleichen' (*Judasfrauen*, 8). In her neglect of the significant differences between the two dictatorships Schubert comes close to the crude totalitarianism theories which have undergone a revival in post-1989 attempts to dismiss forty years of GDR history.[109] Furthermore, as Gättens has pointed out, the assumption of such parallels dehistoricizes, in so far as 'the present can be criticized only by identifying it with the past'.[110]

Gättens sees the relationship between *Judasfrauen* and *Kindheitsmuster* as one of opposition:

While the tenet that the GDR is based on principles of antifascism serves as a limit to Christa Wolf's critique of the GDR and its treatment of the past, it is at the very center of Schubert's critique. For Wolf the principle of antifascism, although ideologically exploited by those in power, is indeed rooted in the struggle against National Socialism by the antifascists and their subsequent construction of a socialist state; for Schubert the principle of antifascism has become solely an ideological justification for an undemocratic state.[111]

While it is undeniable that the two authors have fundamentally different attitudes to the socialist project, to set them in opposition in this way neglects the historical distance between the two works.

---

[109] Mary Fulbrook, *Anatomy of a Dictatorship: Inside the GDR 1949–1989* (Oxford: Oxford University Press, 1995), 284–6.
[110] Gättens, 126.   [111] Ibid. 122.

Criticizing Wolf for her narrator's blind spots concerning GDR antifascism means ignoring the constraints placed on the text by its historical context. Even thirteen years later, Schubert's text was not printed in the GDR until the Honecker government had fallen from power (*Judasfrauen*, 10). Furthermore, by 1989, Wolf was publicly criticizing the GDR's self-definition as 'Sieger der Geschichte', and speaking of her generation's eager exchange of one 'Heilslehre' for another.[112] Unlike Schubert, however, she never identified Stalinism with Nazism. Gättens's comparison plays down both the significance of Wolf's criticisms of GDR *Vergangenheitsbewältigung* in their 1976 context and the effects which *Kindheitsmuster* had in opening a space for more critical debates about the relationship between the GDR and the Third Reich. It is more appropriate to see the late 1980s texts by Königsdorf and Schubert as a historical continuation and diversification of a critical discourse about the past initiated in the 1970s, most prominently by Wolf. Despite their differences, both writers develop Wolf's critique of GDR historiography further, while reacting against her gender construction by offering more differentiated and less optimistically feminist perspectives on the complex relationship between gender and fascism. It is precisely this capacity for developments, diversity, and the rejection of earlier positions which most markedly distinguishes the GDR literary discourse about fascism in the 1970s and 1980s from a historiographical discourse still often obliged, even in the late 1980s, to defend positions established four decades earlier.

[112] Wolf, *Im Dialog*, 95, 74.

2

'IHRE GESCHICHTE WÄRE NOCH ZU SCHREIBEN': BIOGRAPHICAL FICTIONS ABOUT WOMEN

WOMEN'S LIVES AS A CHALLENGE TO ORTHODOX HISTORICAL NARRATIVES

The first chapter has shown how, from the 1970s onwards, a growing gulf separated the GDR literary discourse on National Socialism from historians' treatments of the topic. Whereas authors drew on their own subjective experience to challenge dogmatic interpretations of this era of the past, the works this chapter will examine deal with more distant periods of history. Although almost all of these texts present an individual figure, and so are concerned with a particular era in history, they are united not primarily by a concern with a single historical period, as in Chapter 1, but by an interest in a more general historiographical question: how do we approach the history of women's experience?

With the possible exception of Helga Schubert's *Judasfrauen*, all the texts discussed in Chapter 1 employed a broadly fictional literary form, into which the authors often incorporated autobiographical material. This chapter will look at a group of texts which occupy a wider range of positions between fiction and non-fiction, and which, like Wolf's *Kindheitsmuster*, often challenge the conventional generic boundary between the factual essay and literature. Sigrid Damm's 'Begegnung mit Caroline' (1979), Renate Feyl's *Der lautlose Aufbruch* (1981) and Christa Wolf's 'Der Schatten eines Traumes' (1978) share a non-fictional essay form.[1] 'Begegnung mit Caroline' served to introduce an edition of Caroline Schlegel-Schelling's letters, while 'Der Schatten

---

[1] Sigrid Damm, 'Begegnung mit Caroline', in *Begegnung mit Caroline: Briefe von Caroline Schlegel-Schelling* (Leipzig: Reclam, 1979; repr. 1984), 6–69; Renate Feyl, *Der lautlose Aufbruch: Frauen in der Wissenschaft* (Berlin: Verlag Neues Leben, 1981; repr. 1987); Christa Wolf, 'Der Schatten eines Traumes: Karoline von Günderrode—ein Entwurf', in *Die Dimension des Autors*, ii. 511–71.

eines Traumes' was the preface to a collection of Karoline von Günderrode's writings. Wolf's 'Nun ja! Das nächste Leben geht aber heute an' (1979)—written as an afterword to Bettine von Arnim's *Die Günderode*, though first published in *Sinn und Form* in 1980—takes the form of a letter.[2] Damm's *Cornelia Goethe* (1987) combines a non-fictional biographical form with imaginative elements.[3] Wolf's *Kein Ort. Nirgends* (1979) is fictional, but incorporates a large number of authentic quotations.[4] Brigitte Struzyk's *Caroline unterm Freiheitsbaum* (1988) fictionalizes Caroline Schlegel-Schelling's life, but includes the reflections of the authorial narrator at the end.[5] Feyl's *Idylle mit Professor* is a historical novel.[6]

During the 1970s a number of prominent GDR writers played a central role in reassessing the cultural heritage, prompting academics to re-evaluate previously problematic eras and figures, such as Romanticism, Kleist, Hölderlin, and E. T. A. Hoffmann.[7] They contributed to this discourse of reception not only with fictional works like Anna Seghers's 'Die Reisebegegnung' (1972) and Günter Kunert's *Ein anderer K.* (1977), but also with non-fictional essays (Kunert's 'Pamphlet für K.' of 1975), as well as works which combine factual and imaginative elements (Günter de Bruyn's *Leben des Jean Paul Friedrich Richter* of 1975, and Gerhard Wolf's *Der arme Hölderlin* of 1972). The more integral approach to history that entered GDR historiography with the debate about 'Erbe' and 'Tradition' in the 1970s was thus applied to literary history as well. The texts on which this chapter will focus bear a clear relation to the 1970s texts by Seghers, Kunert, de Bruyn, Gerhard

[2] Christa Wolf, 'Nun ja! Das nächste Leben geht aber heute an: Ein Brief über die Bettine', in *Die Dimension des Autors*, ii. 572–610.

[3] Sigrid Damm, *Cornelia Goethe* (Berlin and Weimar: Aufbau, 1987; repr. Frankfurt am Main: Insel, 1992).

[4] Christa Wolf, *Kein Ort. Nirgends* (Berlin and Weimar: Aufbau, 1979; repr. Frankfurt am Main: Luchterhand, 1981).

[5] Brigitte Struzyk, *Caroline unterm Freiheitsbaum: Ansichtssachen* (Berlin and Weimar: Aufbau, 1988).

[6] Renate Feyl, *Idylle mit Professor: Roman* (Berlin: Verlag Neues Leben, 1986; repr. Cologne: Kiepenheuer and Witsch, 1992).

[7] See Patricia Herminghouse, 'Die Wiederentdeckung der Romantik: Zur Funktion der Dichterfiguren in der neueren DDR-Literatur', in *DDR-Roman und Literaturgesellschaft*, ed. Jos Hoogeveen and Gerd Labroisse, ABNG 11/12 (Amsterdam: Rodopi, 1981), 217–48; Peter Uwe Hohendahl, 'Theorie und Praxis des Erbens: Untersuchungen zum Problem der literarischen Tradition in der DDR', in *Literatur der DDR in den siebziger Jahren*, ed. Hohendahl and Herminghouse, 13–52; Sonja Hilzinger, '"Avantgarde ohne Hinterland": Zur Wiederentdeckung des Romantischen in Prosa und Essayistik der DDR', in *Literatur in der DDR: Rückblicke*, ed. Heinz Ludwig Arnold and Frauke Meyer-Gosau (Munich: text + kritik, 1991), 93–100.

Wolf, and others, in that they too challenge orthodox narratives of history by reassessing figures who had previously been marginalized, overlooked, or excluded. However, the central focus is now on women's experience and the importance of gender.

Because of the taboo status of feminism in the GDR and the absence of an autonomous women's movement, historians could pursue studies on women only within the framework of the orthodox approach to history. This chapter will explore the rather different possibilities open to women writers not attached to institutions. Important points of contact emerge between these writers' projects and positions which have been adopted by western feminist historians during the development of feminist approaches to history since the 1970s. The debates and multiple perspectives of western feminist historical studies form a helpful contrast to the comparatively monolithic positions of GDR historians, and provide useful ways of conceptualizing the differences between the various texts by women writers. Challenging traditional, androcentric understandings of history by examining women's experience is a project which GDR women writers share with feminists internationally. Following the pattern of Chapter 1, I shall discuss academic approaches to women's history and biography, before proceeding to analyse the literary texts.

ACADEMIC WORK ON WOMEN'S HISTORY IN THE GDR AND FEMINIST DEBATES IN THE WEST

Both the achievements and the limitations of academic approaches to women's history in the GDR are demonstrated very clearly by a paper presented by two GDR historians, Petra Rantzsch and Erika Uitz, at an international conference on research in women's history, held in Bellagio, Italy, in July 1989.[8] Rantzsch and Uitz provide a summary of historical research on women's history in the GDR, listing the institutions which supported such research—most prominently a research group called Geschichte des Kampfes der Arbeiterklasse um die Befreiung der Frau, founded in 1966 at the Clara Zetkin College of Education in Leipzig[9]—and outlining the numerous contexts in which

---

[8] Petra Rantzsch and Erika Uitz, 'Historical Research on Women in the German Democratic Republic', in *Writing Women's History: International Perspectives*, ed. Karen Offen, Ruth Roach Pierson, and Jane Rendall (Basingstoke: Macmillan, 1991), 333–53.

[9] The research group was renamed 'Frauen in der Geschichte' in 1990.

historical studies focusing on women were produced.[10] These contexts clearly reveal the 'politically-motivated restrictions on research topics' which, as the authors concede when revising the paper for publication in December 1989, limited work on women's history in the GDR.[11]

From the 1960s onwards women featured prominently in medieval studies: work here concerned both women's role in marriage and the family, and outstanding female figures, such as Joan of Arc, Heloise, and Christine de Pizan. Research on more modern periods had a more overtly political focus: women were studied primarily in terms of their contribution to political movements regarded by the SED as progressive and therefore incorporated into the line of progress seen as leading to the foundation of the GDR. The lives of individual outstanding women in this context, such as Rosa Luxemburg and Clara Zetkin, were the subject of a mass of publications.[12] Similarly, women's contribution to the 1848 Revolution and the November Revolution of 1918, and the role of women in the antifascist resistance were the subjects of extensive historical research.[13] The proletarian women's movement was studied as part of the workers' movement, and studies of the international women's movement prior to 1945 focused on issues such as Comintern policies concerning women, and the histories of the International Women's League for Peace and Freedom and the International Democratic Women's Federation.

In the 1980s, as GDR historians began to overcome the restrictive search for progressive traditions in German history which had previously characterized their work, and as a broader reappraisal of the historical heritage as a whole became acceptable, studies of the bourgeois women's movement in early twentieth-century Germany were undertaken. Attention was also focused on the negative nature of National Socialist policies concerning women.[14] Rantzsch and Uitz regard this

[10] A more detailed account of 1980s GDR historical research dealing with women is offered by Hans-Jürgen Arendt, Petra Rantzsch, and Fritz Staude, 'Ergebnisse historischer Frauenforschung in der DDR 1980 bis 1990', *Mitteilungsblatt der Forschungsgemeinschaft 'Frauen in der Geschichte' an der Sektion Geschichte der Pädagogischen Hochschule 'Clara Zetkin' Leipzig* (1990), 2, 5–51.

[11] Rantzsch and Uitz, 334.

[12] Arendt, Rantzsch, and Staude claim that 'Lücken im Lebensbild Clara Zetkins sowie in der Untersuchung einzelner Aspekte ihres politischen Wirkens und theoretischen Schaffens konnten durch eine Vielzahl von Arbeiten geschlossen werden', and provide a lengthy list of such works. Arendt, Rantzsch, and Staude, 15–16, 45–7.

[13] See, for example, Sigrid Jacobeit and Lieselotte Thoms-Heinrich, *Kreuzweg Ravensbrück: Lebensbilder antifaschistischer Widerstandskämpferinnen* (Leipzig: Verlag für die Frau, 1987; repr. 1989).

[14] Such studies remained firmly within the orthodox interpretation of fascism which I discussed in Chapter 1. See Arendt, Rantzsch, and Staude, 12.

new, integral approach to history as valuable for women's studies because it also promoted biographies of 'wives of leading politicians and theorists of the workers' movement'.[15] Such biographies will form the focus of the third section of this chapter. Only in the late 1980s did topics relating to women begin to be studied with some degree of independence from the course of political history to which earlier studies had been strictly subordinated. Rantzsch and Uitz mention socio-historically oriented research on family history and projects on folklore and the history of culture. However, even here, the basic Marxist premiss that 'the relations between the sexes have to be seen as a result of particular social-economic conditions' remained in force, and women's position in past societies was examined in relation to their participation in paid labour.[16] An example of the kind of research which was possible within this framework by the late 1980s is Anneliese Neef's *Mühsal ein Leben lang: Zur Situation der Arbeiterfrauen um 1900* of 1988.[17] In her introduction Neef pays lip service to the orthodox view that class differences override gender difference, but then argues:

es ist bei aller objektiv angelegten Gleichartigkeit dennoch sinnvoll, die Situation der weiblichen Angehörigen der Arbeiterklasse gesondert zu beschreiben, weil das Leben der Frauen und der Männer von ganz und gar verschiedenen Anforderungen und Erfahrungen bestimmt wurde.[18]

What follows is a fascinating study of the history of everyday life, clearly indebted to the work of Jürgen Kuczynski. Neef deals not only with issues such as the nature of women's work and the economic conditions of their lives, but also with girls' education, the norms of sexual behaviour and the methods of contraception practised, relationships within the family, and the practicalities of childbirth.

Despite the broader range of topics studied in the 1980s, the ultimate aim of work on women's history, as of historical studies generally in the GDR, remained to legitimize the state as the realization of the ideals towards which all socially progressive movements in history were striving. The concluding chapter of Neef's work lists the achievements of the GDR regarding women's rights, but is unusual in also suggesting that further progress was necessary if the equality guaranteed by law

---

[15] Rantzsch and Uitz, 339.
[16] Ibid. 335–6, 339.
[17] Anneliese Neef, *Mühsal ein Leben lang: Zur Situation der Arbeiterfrauen um 1900* (Berlin: Dietz, 1988). Erika Uitz's study *Die Frau in der mittelalterlichen Stadt* (Leipzig: Edition Leipzig, 1988) adopts a similar emphasis on women's everyday experience.
[18] Ibid. 8.

was to become a reality in the private sphere as well.[19] The East German historian Susanne Schötz claims in an article of 1994 that research into women's history was directed towards providing 'evidence' for the notion that sexual equality had been achieved in the GDR, making any form of feminist movement superfluous. Quoting the East German sociologist Hildegard Maria Nickel, Schötz argues that women's studies in the GDR

hatten Anteil 'an den Mythenbildungen vom erfolgreichen Voranschreiten der Gleichberechtigung in der DDR, [. . .] an den Tabuisierungen der realen Lebensverhältnisse von Frauen, an der Verkümmerung des Frauenbewußtseins bzw. an der gesellschaftlichen Desensibilisierung in der Geschlechterfrage'.[20]

Considering that Rantzsch and Uitz revised their paper after the collapse of the SED regime, it is remarkable that they fail to criticize the methodology of historians who approached the writing of women's history purely as a task of assessing women's contribution to a pre-defined narrative. Rather than suggesting the need for alternative interpretative frameworks, they outline work still to be done on women's history as a process of filling in gaps left by GDR historians. In their 1990 summary of the achievements of GDR historiography concerning women, Arendt, Rantzsch, and Staude similarly list gaps in research, but also hint at the need for methodological changes:

Hier wird auch an Ergebnisse der internationalen historischen Frauenforschung angeknüpft werden müssen. Neben der Kategorie der Klasse bedarf die des Geschlechts und in diesem Zusammenhang auch der Patriarchats-Begriff verstärkte Aufmerksamkeit.[21]

It is clear from these two overviews that theoretical approaches to women's history in the GDR remained firmly within the tradition of Marxist thought right up to 1989. As Schötz argues, there was no attempt to unite Marx's theory of class and a theory of gender in a productive way.[22] Instead, the traditional Marxist subordination of gender

---

[19] Anneliese Neef, *Mühsal ein Leben lang*, 172–6.

[20] Susanne Schötz, 'Historische Frauenforschung in Ostdeutschland', in *Nach dem Erdbeben: (Re-) Konstruktion ostdeutscher Geschichte und Geschichtswissenschaft*, ed. Konrad H. Jarausch and Matthias Middell (Leipzig: Leipziger Universitätsverlag, 1994), 177–94 (181).

[21] Arendt, Rantzsch, and Staude, 17.

[22] Schötz, 178. Such attempts have, however, been undertaken by Marxist feminists in the West. See, for example, Heidi Hartmann, 'The Unhappy Marriage of Marxism and Feminism: Towards a More Progressive Union', in *Women and Revolution: A Discussion of the Unhappy Marriage of Marxism and Feminism*, ed. Lydia Sargent (Montreal: Black Rose Books, 1981), 1–41.

relations to class relations determined GDR historians' approaches to women's history, resulting in a focus on women of a particular class, that is, the working class, and a tendency to deny the heterogeneity of women as a social group. This led historians to overlook the need for differentiation when discussing 'women', and to regard terms such as 'women's emancipation' and 'women's interests' as unproblematic and self-explanatory.

Schötz attributes the failings of the GDR academy with regard to women's history to the lack of an autonomous women's movement to provoke an interest in women's studies, as occurred in the West, and to the SED's rejection of international feminism. Although GDR historians were influenced by developments in international women's studies, for example at conferences, the insights gained could be shared only in small discussion groups, and could achieve only minimal influence on published work and public debates on history. Schötz concludes that, although discussion of issues in women's history may have had a marginalized existence outside the institutional structures of the GDR academy, any public discourse on such issues was lacking:

Was grundsätzlich fehlte, das war die öffentliche, für alle nachlesbare Diskussion über den Stellenwert von Frauen- und Geschlechtergeschichte, über den Sinn einer eigenständigen historischen Frauenforschung, über die Herausforderungen der feministischen Geschichtswissenschaft für das Geschichtsbild, über prinzipielle Fragen der Geschichtstheorie und Wissenschaftsentwicklung also.[23]

In the West, where the politics of the 1970s women's movement initiated an interest in women's history, and where academic and public discourses were more tolerant of plurality, a marginalized discourse on women's history was able to emerge during the 1970s and 1980s, and to find a public forum which had no equivalent in the GDR. This feminist discourse was able to challenge conventional academic approaches in a way which was not possible for GDR work on women's history. The possibility for different perspectives to compete also enabled debates and developments within this discourse, while GDR studies remained bound to a single framework.

Interestingly, some of the earliest studies on women's history in the West resembled GDR work in their methodology. Gerda Lerner summarizes such studies in her essays 'New Approaches to the Study of Women in American History' of 1969 and 'Placing Women in History:

---

[23] Schötz, 183.

A 1975 Perspective'.[24] She shows how a 'middle-class, nativist, moralistic approach' resulted in a selective analysis of women's history aimed at supporting a particular view of history.[25] This approach, although different in content of course, bears striking similarities in its underlying principles to the approach which remained in force in the GDR until the 1980s. The significance of women's history was generally seen to lie in women's experience as an oppressed group and their struggle against oppression. The women's rights movement was a prominent topic in feminist studies, which often attributed inordinate significance to women's suffrage. Here again there are clear parallels with GDR research, which centred on the proletarian women's movement and the movement for women's rights within the workers' movement, and defined 'women's emancipation' essentially in terms of legally secured equality. Lerner shows how western historians wrote a 'compensatory history' of the achievements of 'notable women worthy of a place in history', and documented women's contribution to society, focusing in particular on their role in social movements such as abolition, reform, the Progressive movement, and the labour movement. These approaches to women's history shared the limitations of GDR work, in that, as Lerner shows, they 'applied questions from traditional history to women, and tried to fit women's past into the empty spaces of historical scholarship'.[26] Women's history was used to support, rather than challenge, accepted historical narratives, whether those of the West or those given authority in the GDR. However, in the West this approach was subsequently subjected to critical scrutiny and debate of a kind absent in the GDR, so that it was replaced by more refined methodologies.

During the 1970s a tension became apparent between the feminist aim of discovering evidence of women's unity through historical experience, and a growing recognition of the complex nature of women as a social group, requiring a differentiated approach to women's 'oppression'.[27] Reflection on how to conceptualize women as a group in history was accompanied by an increasing awareness of the

[24] Gerda Lerner, 'New Approaches to the Study of Women in American History', in *Liberating Women's History: Theoretical and Critical Essays*, ed. Berenice A. Carroll (Urbana, Ill.: University of Illinois Press, 1976), 349–56, 'Placing Women in History: A 1975 Perspective', in *Liberating Women's History*, 357–68.

[25] Lerner, 'New Approaches', 349.

[26] Lerner, 'Placing Women in History', 357–60.

[27] See Ann D. Gordon, Mari Jo Buhle, and Nancy Schrom Dye, 'The Problem of Women's History', in *Liberating Women's History*, ed. Carroll, 75–92 (84–8).

inadequacy of conventional historical categories for dealing with women. As Gayle Greene and Coppélia Kahn summarize the situation,

women present a special case for the historian: neither class nor caste nor minority, they are more closely allied to the men in their lives than they are to women of other classes and races, and so are more closely integrated with the dominant culture than is any other subordinate group.[28]

Lerner proposes a general rejection of male paradigms and categories, arguing that 'all conceptual models of history hitherto developed have only limited usefulness for women's history, since all are based on the silent assumptions of a patriarchal ordering of values'. She notes a progression in 1970s work on women's history towards a focus on 'the actual *experience* of women in the past'. This shift of emphasis led historians to use alternative sources which provide evidence of women's experience—rather than their contribution or role as defined by men —for example, women's letters, diaries, autobiographies, and oral history sources. Work on women's history now set out to establish new historical narratives structured according to female rather than male experience. The most significant constraint on GDR work on women's history, that is, the obligation to produce 'evidence' to support the accepted historical narrative, was precisely the approach to women's history which western feminist historians were beginning to challenge in the 1970s. Lerner calls not only for a new narrative of women's history structured by female-defined categories, but for an integration of the questions raised by this new narrative into general historical research, so that conventional interpretative frameworks and categories are questioned. Women's history is thus to problematize basic assumptions conventionally made by historians, by revealing 'the sexist bias which pervades the value system, the culture, and the very language within which they work'.[29]

Western developments in the study of women's history in the late 1980s reveal a shift away from the notion of a shared historical narrative unifying women, which was politically useful to feminists in the 1970s. The need for differentiation within the category of 'women',

---

[28] Gayle Greene and Coppélia Kahn, 'Feminist Scholarship and the Social Construction of Woman', in *Making a Difference: Feminist Literary Criticism*, ed. Gayle Greene and Coppélia Kahn (London and New York: Methuen, 1985; repr. Routledge, 1990), 1–36 (14). See also Hilda Smith, 'Feminism and the Methodology of Women's History', in *Liberating Women's History*, ed. Carroll, 368–84 (382–3).

[29] Lerner, 'Placing Women in History', 362–4.

already debated in the 1970s, became central to studies of the 1980s, and led to the recognition, voiced by the West German historian Gisela Bock, that 'the history of women can only be grasped in the plural, not in the singular'. Bock argues that women's history is not a 'special case' of history, subordinate to 'general history', but a history which 'resembles that of men in so far as it is just as rich and complicated, and that it is not linear, logical or coherent'.[30] The project of writing a separate narrative of women's experience, or 'herstory', gave way to a focus on gender history.

In her *Gender and the Politics of History* of 1988, Joan Wallach Scott summarizes the achievements of recent work on women's history which aimed 'to make women a focus of inquiry, a subject of the story, an agent of the narrative', and so attempted to alter conventional standards of historical significance.[31] She then outlines the limitations of this approach, arguing that it tends to isolate women as a special and separate topic of history, and that, while assuming that gender explains the different histories of women and men, it fails to theorize how gender operates historically. In her 1991 article 'The Evidence of Experience', Scott expresses a stronger critique of the 1970s shift towards taking women's experience as the focus of enquiry and as evidence for creating a narrative of women's history. Here she argues that by regarding women's experience (or that of any social group defined as 'other') as incontestable evidence of their history, historians take female identity as self-evident and thus naturalize difference rather than questioning how subjects are constituted as different.[32] Scott's project is rather to analyse 'the often silent and hidden operations of gender that are nonetheless present and defining forces in the organization of most societies'.[33] In Germany, Scott's work has been influential for feminist historians such as Ute Frevert, whose focus on women's history in her 1986 work, *Frauen-Geschichte: Zwischen bürgerlicher Verbesserung und neuer Weiblichkeit*, gave way to a concern with the historical construction of gender in her 1995 work, *'Mann und Weib, und Weib und Mann': Geschlechter-Differenzen in der Moderne*.[34]

[30] Gisela Bock, *History, Women's History, Gender History* (San Domenico: European University Institute, 1987), 5–6.

[31] Joan Wallach Scott, *Gender and the Politics of History* (New York: Columbia University Press, 1988), 17–20.

[32] Joan W. Scott, 'The Evidence of Experience', *Critical Inquiry*, 17 (1991), 4, 773–97 (779).

[33] Scott, *Gender and the Politics of History*, 27.

[34] Ute Frevert, *Frauen-Geschichte: Zwischen bürgerlicher Verbesserung und neuer Weiblichkeit* (Frankfurt am Main: Suhrkamp, 1986), *'Mann und Weib, und Weib und Mann': Geschlechter-Differenzen in der Moderne* (Munich: Beck, 1995).

These shifts in feminist approaches to history in the late 1980s share central features with those postmodernist and post-structuralist theories which were gaining broad intellectual influence at this time. Such theories are characterized by scepticism concerning meta-narratives and by a questioning of categories regarded in Enlightenment thinking as foundations for truth.[35] The foundational categories which feminist historians used to construct a women's history in the 1970s, such as gender, identity, and experience, now became themselves the objects of analysis. The aim of 'recovering' a lost female history was replaced by the idea that any coherent historical narrative is an ideologically motivated fiction, and by a focus instead on the constructed nature of such narratives. As Judith Bennett warns, there is a danger that such approaches result in intellectual abstraction from women's existence to a focus solely on impersonal social systems.[36] Recent work, however, has fruitfully recognized that women's history and gender history are complementary approaches which each have a valuable place in feminist work on history.[37]

WRITING A WOMAN'S LIFE

Writing the biography of an individual is a special form of historical study which raises many of the same methodological questions as other kinds of historical writing. Here, however, these questions are applied to a particular form of historical material, an individual's life. This means that biography conventionally focuses on the interrelations between narratives on two levels. Firstly, the narrative of an individual life with its own chronology and teleology is presented. The biographer's task of imposing a coherent narrative on a life is comparable to the historian's creation of a narrative linking social and political developments on a larger scale. Secondly, biography shows how this narrative of an individual life is related to broader historical narratives. This relationship generally defines the significance of the life.

In the 1980s a number of biographies of female subjects written by GDR historians were published. These works deal with women who,

[35] See *Postmodernism: A Reader*, ed. Patricia Waugh (London: Arnold, 1992), 5.

[36] Judith M. Bennett, 'Feminism and History', *Gender and History*, 1 (1989), 3, 251–72 (256).

[37] See, for example, Lynn Abrams and Elizabeth Harvey, 'Introduction: Gender and Gender Relations in German History', in *Gender Relations in German History: Power, Agency and Experience from the Sixteenth to the Twentieth Century*, ed. Abrams and Harvey (London: University College London Press, 1996), 1–37 (1).

either through their own actions or through their relationships with men, played a role in the development of socialism which the SED regarded as the prehistory of the GDR. I have already mentioned the attention devoted to the lives of more prominent women in this narrative of political history, such as Clara Zetkin and Rosa Luxemburg. Even when less prominent women were chosen as the subjects of biographies, they tended to be women who were associated with certain key individuals raised to heroic status by GDR historiography. Wolfgang Schröder writes the life of Wilhelm Liebknecht's first wife, Ernestine, while Petra Rantzsch and Ruth Kirsch present women who worked with, and were influenced by, Clara Zetkin: Helene Stöcker and Käte Duncker respectively.[38] The range of female lives covered by these biographies is therefore very narrow, comprising 'exemplary' cases of political activism. In accordance with the SED's emphasis on the collective, individual lives are shown to be part of a larger narrative, and nothing in the presentation of the individual life is allowed to challenge the validity of this authorized narrative. In particular, these women's lives are used to support the idea that gender considerations must be subordinated to the class struggle and are never to become the primary impulse for political action.

The distance between these female biographies and western feminism is particularly apparent in the case of Wolfgang Schröder's *Ernestine*. Schröder presents Ernestine as an 'ordinary' woman, whose achievements lay in her supporting role as wife and mother, rather than in any remarkable activity of her own. The value of her life, he suggests, derived solely from her relationship with Wilhelm Liebknecht. While it may be true that Ernestine lived a life in her husband's shadow, Schröder glorifies this role in a way which reinforces it as a female ideal:

Nicht mitreißende, aufsehenerregende Taten sind von ihr bekanntzumachen. Sie war vielmehr Heldin im tagtäglichen Lebenskampf. Insofern steht sie für viele Tausende von Proletarierfrauen, und sie könnte Amalie oder Wilhelmine, Anna oder Ottilie heißen, die sich ebenso wie sie als Frau und Mutter, als fürsorgende Hüterin der Familie in der unerbittlichen Sorge um das tägliche Stück Brot aufreiben mußten. Doch Ernestine wuchs über sie hinaus. Als Gefährtin Wilhelm Liebknechts, dessen wechselvolles Schicksal sie

[38] Wolfgang Schröder, *Ernestine: Vom ungewöhnlichen Leben der ersten Frau Wilhelm Liebknechts: Eine dokumentarische Erzählung* (Leipzig: Verlag für die Frau, 1987; repr. 1989); Petra Rantzsch, *Helene Stöcker (1869–1943): Zwischen Pazifismus und Revolution* (Berlin: Verlag Der Morgen, 1984); Ruth Kirsch, *Käte Duncker: Aus ihrem Leben* (Berlin: Dietz, 1982).

über 13 Jahre teilte, wurde sie einbezogen in jene damals noch winzig kleine Schar, die dieses millionenfache Schicksal der 'einfachen Leute' nicht als gottgegeben ansah, sondern antrat, es zu wenden.[39]

The life-story which Schröder then presents is not a new narrative of a female life, but the narrative of Wilhelm Liebknecht's life, in which Ernestine appears as an admiring and supportive companion and spectator. There may be some historical truth in this description of Ernestine's life, but Schröder unquestioningly presents Wilhelm's life as the more important and more interesting one, focusing primarily on the events in his life, only to intersperse it with occasional speculative descriptions of Ernestine's feelings. Schröder uncritically interprets Ernestine's and Wilhelm's relationship according to conventional gender stereotypes. He suggests that, while Wilhelm's primary concerns are political, loving a man is the entire content of Ernestine's life, and it is only through Wilhelm that she is able to escape the narrow confines and naïvety of her earlier life and become politically aware. The political sphere in which Wilhelm participates is unquestioningly presented as more valuable and worthy of attention than the private sphere, to which women's lives have typically been restricted:

Hatte Wilhelm aber mehr als nur ein Auge für Ernestine? Es war die Revolution, die ihn wie die anderen politischen Gefangenen befreit hatte! [. . .] Ernestines innere Beziehungen zur Revolution ergaben sich wohl vor allem daraus, daß diese ihren Wilhelm aus dem Gefängnis befreit und vor einer langen Kerkerstrafe bewahrt hatte. Ihre erste große Liebe erfüllte sie ganz. [. . .] Sie war keine 'Marianne', die die Fahne der Revolution ergriff, und sie konnte es nach ihrer ganzen Entwicklung und ihrem Herkommen auch gar nicht sein. Für sie war es schon sehr viel, daß sie sich mitreißen ließ, nicht skeptisch-abwartend oder abwehrend abseits stand. Sie schwamm im Strom der allgemeinen Begeisterung, ohne daß sie zu erkennen vermochte, wo dessen Quellen waren und wohin er zu fließen hatte.
Anders Wilhelm. [. . .] Er riß Ernestine heraus aus dem stillen Winkel, hinein in die bewegte Menge auf den Straßen, auf den Plätzen, in den Weinstuben.[40]

Petra Rantzsch's biography of Helene Stöcker, in contrast with Schröder's work, does present a narrative structured by Helene Stöcker's own life. As a woman who was politically active herself, Helene Stöcker's life is better documented than Ernestine Liebknecht's, and provides more material to present a narrative of female strength, achievement, and independence. However, despite her

---

[39] Schröder, 7.   [40] Ibid. 14–16.

choice of a bourgeois woman as subject, Rantzsch's narrative, like Schröder's, resists challenging the official history of socialism. Helene Stöcker's political development is presented as an exemplary learning process, in which flawed views, such as those of the bourgeois women's movement, are discarded, and the truth is discovered through involvement in the international workers' movement and the German Communist Party, and through meeting figures such as Clara Zetkin. This narrative structure, reminiscent of socialist realist fiction, is clearly manifested in the titles of the sections of Rantzsch's book, which summarize the stages in Helene Stöcker's life, from 'Kindheit, Jugend, Studium—das Finden einer Lebensaufgabe', through 'Für die Emanzipation der Frau und die Rechte von Mutter und Kind', 'Vom "Mutterschutz" zum "Menschenschutz"', and 'An der Seite der revolutionären Arbeiterbewegung', to 'Emigration—das Ende eines Kampfes?'.

Any 'subversive' potential in Helene Stöcker's life-story is diminished by a preface to the work, by Manfred Bogisch, which places the narrative firmly within a history of socialism and discredits any interpretation which might be tempted to see in Helene Stöcker's life a justification for regarding gender issues in isolation from class issues:

Wenn auch bei uns 'Emanzipations'-Tendenzen analog bürgerlichen Emanzipationsbestrebungen noch anzutreffen sein mögen (Emanzipation gegen den Mann und losgelöst von den gesellschaftlichen Umständen), so finden diese in dieser Schrift freilich keine Unterstützung. Die Studie führt vielmehr vor Augen, daß schon die Progressivität kleinbürgerlich-demokratischer Emanzipationsbestrebungen gerade darin bestand, die Benachteiligten, ob Mann oder Frau, gemeinsam in den Kampf für den Fortschritt zu führen, die Emanzipation als soziale und politische Aufgabe, keinesfalls aber als—noch dazu hauptsächlich sexuelle—'Befreiung' der Frau vom Manne zu begreifen.[41]

Bogisch describes the recent discussions of 'Erbe' and 'Tradition' as 'eine schöpferische Auseinandersetzung mit der deutschen Geschichte', and uses the new, broadened concept of 'Erbe' to justify Rantzsch's choice of subject:

Den Kern sozialistischen Nationalbewußtseins bildet revolutionäres Klassenbewußtsein; es umfaßt neben den revolutionären Traditionen auch das Erbe all jener geschichtlichen Kräfte, deren Wirken für unser Volk bedeutsam war. Zu diesen Kräften gehört Helene Stöcker.[42]

---

[41] Rantzsch, 5.   [42] Ibid. 6.

These biographies construct individual women's lives using narratives which claim to be transparent, merely reflecting a 'truth' about the individual which can be empirically discovered. This 'truth' is required to represent, in microcosm, the 'truth' of socialist history as defined by the SED. The interpretive processes involved in constructing the narrative of a life are concealed. Schröder, for example, states that the sources relating to Ernestine's life are sparse, yet claims that an accurate representation of her life can nevertheless be reconstructed:

Nur wenige Informationen und Dokumente geben Auskunft über sie. Vergangen—vergessen? Nein! Nicht alles gibt die Geschichte frei. Aber trotz vieler Lücken läßt sie das Lebensschicksal dieser bescheidenen, tapferen und aufopferungsvollen Frau skizzenhaft erstehen [. . .].[43]

His narrative then presents what, in the light of this introductory statement, can only be speculation, as the true facts of Ernestine's life. Schröder admits uncertainty about some events, for example, whether Ernestine witnessed the court scene when Wilhelm Liebknecht was freed from prison. However, the extent to which the presentation of her character is an interpretation from a particular ideological standpoint is not made clear.

Two western feminist models for writing women's biography provide alternative ways of approaching a woman's life without subordinating it to a narrative of political history determined predominantly by men's lives, as the GDR academic biographers do. The first is exemplified by the US Humanities Professor Carolyn Heilbrun's *Writing a Woman's Life* of 1988. Just as western feminist historians in the 1970s criticized the way women had been fitted into a male-determined course of history and set out to create a new narrative of women's experience, Heilbrun shows how biographies of women traditionally place a man at the centre of the woman's life and tell the story of her devotion to his needs. Thus, 'women have been deprived of the narratives, or the texts, plots, or examples, by which they might assume power over—take control of—their own lives'.[44] Heilbrun advocates a form of feminist biography which offers new, female-oriented, empowering narratives in the place of conventional ones. These, she suggests, will function as models for the readers of such biographies and so affect how they live their lives:

How can we find narratives of female plots, stories that will affect other stories and, eventually, lives, that will cause us neither to bury Shakespeare's sister

---

[43] Schröder, 7.
[44] Carolyn G. Heilbrun, *Writing a Woman's Life* (New York: Ballantine, 1988; repr. 1989), 17.

nor to throw up our hands in describing George Sand because we are unwilling to call her either a woman (under the old plot) or a man when she isn't one?[45]

A rather different feminist approach to biography is offered by the British sociologist Liz Stanley. Her work exemplifies the shift, apparent in 1980s developments in feminist work on history, towards a theoretical stance which questions the validity of coherent and objective narratives, and the existence of an essential, unitary self. Stanley argues that conventional biography is based on a realist fallacy, that is, it assumes that a text can be precisely referential in describing a person, and that the self in question is coherent, stable, and unitary. Stanley advocates an alternative form of biography which shares fundamental principles espoused by postmodernist theorists and central to modernist writing. Just as feminism aims to deconstruct essentialist views of sex and reveal the social construction of gender, this form of biography avoids essentializing the self. It focuses instead on the role of social processes in determining 'a self' and recognizes the complexity of views of 'the self'. Unlike conventional biography, it recognizes that a life cannot be 'reconstructed' in a narrative which transparently reflects reality. Instead, the biographer's perspective and the processes of construction and narration are to be incorporated visibly into the work.[46]

Both of these feminist approaches to biography are based on non-fictional writing in a western, democratic context. However, the central contrast which they bring into focus—between the creation of new, women-centred narratives and a fundamental suspicion of any coherent narrative as a means of explaining a life—provides a helpful means of differentiating between the texts by Wolf, Damm, Feyl, and Struzyk.

Kein Ort. Nirgends and, to a lesser extent, 'Der Schatten eines Traumes' and 'Nun ja! Das nächste Leben geht aber heute an' have been the focus of a considerable amount of attention, mainly within the contexts of studies on Wolf and work on GDR writers' renewed interest in Romanticism in the 1970s.[47] The texts by Damm, Feyl, and

[45] Carolyn G. Heilbrun, *Writing a Woman's Life*, 42.

[46] Liz Stanley, *The Auto/Biographical I: The Theory and Practice of Feminist Auto/Biography* (Manchester: Manchester University Press, 1992), especially 11, 127, 243.

[47] For example, Sonja Hilzinger, *Christa Wolf* (Stuttgart: Metzler, 1986), 106–29; Anna K. Kuhn, *Christa Wolf's Utopian Vision: From Marxism to Feminism* (Cambridge: Cambridge University Press, 1988), 138–77; Colin E. Smith, *Tradition, Art and Society: Christa Wolf's Prose* (Essen: Verlag Die blaue Eule, 1987), 201–45; Herminghouse, 'Die Wiederentdeckung der Romantik'; Hilzinger, '"Avantgarde ohne Hinterland"'.

Struzyk have attracted far less interest. Besides a number of brief reviews and articles on the individual texts,[48] three projects have offered comparative analyses of some of the works, in varying combinations. The most important of these is Stephanie Bird's *Recasting Historical Women: Female Identity in German Biographical Fiction*, which looks at *Kein Ort. Nirgends*, 'Der Schatten eines Traumes', *Caroline unterm Freiheitsbaum*, and *Cornelia Goethe*, alongside comparable works of biographical fiction by West German authors.[49] Doris Koller's *Biographisches Schreiben und Selbstreflexion: Frauen der Romantik in Lebensbeschreibungen von Schriftstellerinnen der DDR*, submitted as a *Magisterarbeit* at the University of Regensburg, compares the works by Wolf, Damm, and Struzyk.[50] Franziska Meyer's *Avantgarde im Hinterland: Caroline Schlegel-Schelling in der DDR-Literatur* is a study of 'Begegnung mit Caroline', *Caroline unterm Freiheitsbaum*, and works by Volker Ebersbach and Klaus Güntzel.[51]

Bird's *Recasting Historical Women* is concerned to assess the value of the works in question for a feminist discourse. The author relates each text to a context of western feminist theory, in order to establish whether it advocates a deconstruction of the notion of 'woman' or whether it is closer to Lacanian trends of psychoanalytical feminism.[52] Bird's primary interest is thus in how the texts construct female subjectivity. History is rendered subordinate to this concern: rather than examining the effects which both the author's and (the author's understanding of) the protagonist's historical context might have had on the

[48] Damm's *Cornelia Goethe* has received most attention. Reviews include Jürgen Grambow, 'Eine Vertraute seiner Kindheit, unbegreifliches Wesen, die Schwester', in *Kritik 88: Rezensionen zur DDR-Literatur*, ed. Eberhard Günther, Werner Liersch, and Klaus Walther (Halle and Leipzig: Mitteldeutscher Verlag, 1989), 62–5; Rulo Melchert, 'So könnte es gewesen sein', *NDL* 37 (1989), 4, 131–5; Christoph Parry, 'Zwischen Dekonstruktion, Rekonstruktion und Fiktion', *Ginkgobaum*, 11 (1992), 236–9; Kurt Sager, 'Der Schattenriß einer Frau', *Ginkgobaum*, 10 (1991), 155–62; Claudia Schepnitz, 'Sigrid Damm: Cornelia Goethe', *Deutschunterricht*, 42 (1989), 11, 559; Karin A. Wurst, 'Sigrid Damm: *Cornelia Goethe*', *GSR* 12 (1989), 1, 167–8. Very few responses to Feyl's and Struzyk's works have appeared. See Helga Meise, 'Frauen in der Wissenschaft: Renate Feyls "Der lautlose Aufbruch"', *Lesezeichen*, 6 (1983), 13; Dorothea Böck, 'Szenen einer Ehe', *NDL* 35 (1987), 2, 122–7; Dorothea Böck, 'Ein Weib von schärfstem Geist', *NDL* 37 (1989), 8, 150–4; Matthias Oehme, 'Ansichten von Caroline', *Temperamente* (1989), 2, 149–52.

[49] Bird, *Recasting Historical Women*.

[50] Doris Koller, *Biographisches Schreiben und Selbstreflexion: Frauen der Romantik in Lebensbeschreibungen von Schriftstellerinnen der DDR* (Regensburg: Regensburger Skripten zur Literaturwissenschaft, 1997).

[51] Franziska Meyer, *Avantgarde im Hinterland: Caroline Schlegel-Schelling in der DDR-Literatur* (New York: Lang, 1999).

[52] Bird, 5–16.

way the latter's subjectivity is constructed, Bird reads each text as a contribution to a contemporary debate about the nature of female subjectivity and how it should be represented. Different historiographical approaches are of interest primarily because they 'are instrumental in conveying specific understandings of gender identity'.

Bird is particularly interested in narrative technique and its implications for the construction of gender and the past. Her central criterion of judgement is the question of self-reflection. Arguing that all history is based on exclusions, her study aims 'to see how far the authors reflect upon their own use of the past, and how far they privilege their own interpretation by ignoring the exclusions they themselves have made'.[53] These issues are important in the present study as well, particularly since GDR historiography had a marked tendency to ignore its exclusions. However, Bird's relative lack of concern with the differences between the historical contexts of the GDR and West Germany often results in very different readings of the texts from those which will be offered here.

While Bird's introductory comment that women in both German states shared a dissatisfaction with patriarchal culture is undoubtedly true, her neglect of the particular conditions of cultural production in the GDR means that her criteria for judging texts cannot do justice to the ways they interacted with their immediate historical context. Her demand that women writers reflect on the exclusions in their constructions of history, for instance, ignores the special significance of such exclusions in a society where political taboos and state censorship made explicit discussion of certain topics impossible. Similarly, her discussion of the problem of identification between author and protagonist overlooks contextual factors which could add a further dimension to her readings of the GDR texts. She draws on Dominick LaCapra's work to argue that 'any dialogue occurs within a wider economic, social and political setting and it is necessary to be critically aware of how it is situated within that setting in order to acknowledge the difficulties of "transference"'.[54] However, her examination of this 'setting' rarely extends to the specific cultural and political context of the GDR, although this was particularly conducive to indirect explorations of taboo issues in the present through identification with past figures and eras.

Koller's *Biographisches Schreiben und Selbstreflexion* focuses on aspects of the texts and their context which are marginalized or neglected com-

[53] Bird, 25.   [54] Ibid. 20.

pletely in Bird's study. Koller precedes her textual analyses with brief discussions of the position of women in GDR Marxist theory and praxis, of Marxist historiography, GDR cultural policy, GDR work on Romanticism, and the recent popularity of biographical forms in both East and West. In her readings of the texts, she is concerned to highlight the extent to which Damm, Wolf, and Struzyk use historical figures to write indirectly about their own lives in the present. In relating the texts to their immediate GDR context, Koller's work shares the broad aim of this chapter. However, the scope of her project allows neither a detailed and differentiated presentation of GDR historiography, nor a thorough exploration of the ways in which the texts refer to their authors' present.

Meyer's work on Caroline Schlegel-Schelling in GDR literature examines the function which writers' construction of revolutionary romantic femininity fulfilled in GDR discourse. She shows how this resulted in revised approaches to the cultural heritage, and argues that Damm's, Struzyk's, Ebersbach's, and Güntzel's texts contributed to a reinstatement of reactionary eighteenth-century bourgeois concepts of womanhood in the later GDR. While I share Meyer's interest in the relationship between literary texts and GDR discourses, I consider her approach problematic for several reasons. Her implicit assumption that each literary text can be reduced to a coherent (and invariably objectionable) position on gender politics results in a suppression of the ambiguities of literature. Moreover, she plays down the differences between the four texts, in order to argue that they functionalize Caroline Schlegel-Schelling in the same way, and so form a unified discourse.

CHRISTA WOLF

Wolf's *Kein Ort. Nirgends*, 'Der Schatten eines Traumes', and 'Nun ja! Das nächste Leben geht aber heute an' have much in common with the earlier 1970s texts dealing with artist figures around 1800, and have often been read in this context.[55] Like Günter de Bruyn, Günter Kunert, and others, Wolf creates a dialogue between past and present. By exploring historical material, she aims to shed light on problems

---

[55] See, for example, Peter F. Teupe, *Christa Wolfs* Kein Ort. Nirgends *als Paradigma der DDR-Literatur der siebziger Jahre* (Frankfurt am Main: Lang, 1992), 196–224; Herminghouse, 'Die Wiederentdeckung der Romantik'; Hilzinger, '"Avantgarde ohne Hinterland"'.

and issues belonging to the present. She has commented that her impulse for writing was, as always, an autobiographical one. The dilemma facing her and other GDR writers after Wolf Biermann's expatriation prompted her to engage with historical lives:

1976 war ein Einschnitt in der kulturpolitischen Entwicklung bei uns, äußerlich markiert durch die Ausbürgerung von Biermann. Das hat zu einer Polarisierung der kulturell arbeitenden Menschen auf verschiedenen Gebieten, besonders in der Literatur, geführt: Eine Gruppe von Autoren wurde sich darüber klar, daß ihre direkte Mitarbeit in dem Sinne, wie sie sie selbst verantworten konnte und für richtig hielt, nicht mehr gebraucht wurde. Wir waren ja Sozialisten, wir lebten als Sozialisten in der DDR, weil wir dort uns einmischen, dort mitarbeiten wollten. Das reine Zurückgeworfensein auf die Literatur brachte den einzelnen in eine Krise; eine Krise, die existentiell war. Daraus ist bei mir unter anderem die Beschäftigung mit dem Material solcher Lebensläufe wie denen von Günderrode und Kleist entstanden. Das Problem am Gegenwartsmaterial zu bearbeiten, wäre mir gar nicht möglich gewesen, das wäre naturalistisch und banal geworden, platt.[56]

Rather than reducing the past to an allegory for the present, Wolf aims to create a productive dialogue which will illuminate both the past and the present and so lead to a deeper understanding of her own situation. Focusing on historical material is thus neither a way of escaping the present, nor an inferior substitute for talking directly about present issues, necessitated only by a desire to avoid censorship.

Kein Ort. Nirgends and the essays on Karoline von Günderrode and Bettine von Arnim employ different generic and narrative forms to approach broadly the same material. Many of the authentic quotations which Wolf places in the mouths of the fictional Kleist and Günderrode in *Kein Ort. Nirgends* form the basis of her argument and reflections in the essay and letter.[57] The three texts also share central thematic concerns, exploring issues such as the relationship between writer and state, the conditions of life and work for women writers around 1800, and the gender roles prevalent in German society at that time and their effects on individual identity. Each text uses a different narrative strategy to relate the past to the present. In the fictional work a shifting narrative voice blurs the boundaries between the interior monologues of the historical figures and the modern perspectives of narrator and reader. 'Der Schatten eines Traumes' offers more direct

---

[56] Christa Wolf, 'Projektionsraum Romantik: Gespräch mit Frauke Meyer-Gosau', in *Die Dimension des Autors*, ii. 878–95 (878, 882).

[57] For a comprehensive analysis of Wolf's use of quotations in *Kein Ort. Nirgends*, see Ute Brandes, *Zitat und Montage in der neueren DDR-Prosa* (Frankfurt am Main: Lang, 1984), 61–100.

reflection on the 'Verwandtschaft und Nähe' which make the historical material so fascinating for Wolf in the present ('Schatten', 512). The
letter form of 'Nun ja! Das nächste Leben geht aber heute an' places
the material of Bettine's life in the context of a communication in the
present.

Several ways of understanding the relationship between the fictional
text and the essays have been proposed. Hans-Georg Werner uses
'Der Schatten eines Traumes' as an interpretative aid for elucidating
the ideas of *Kein Ort. Nirgends*.[58] Sandra Frieden argues that Wolf uses
a conventional biographical form to present Günderrode's life in 'Der
Schatten eines Traumes', whereas the fictional work explores new
dimensions of the material through its more subversive form.[59] Bird
takes this criticism of the biographical essay further. She assumes an
absolute generic distinction between *Kein Ort. Nirgends*, as a work of
fiction where 'no historical truth claim is being made', and 'Der
Schatten eines Traumes', where 'the author Wolf is presenting historical material in order to establish just such a claim'.[60] This premiss,
accompanied by a marginalization of the specific autobiographical
experience which prompted Wolf to write both texts, leads Bird to
conclude that *Kein Ort. Nirgends* is complex and sophisticated in its
exploration of gender, while in 'Der Schatten eines Traumes' 'Wolf''s
constant recourse to generalization [. . .] condemns her study to
superficiality'. All the evidence of Wolf's career suggests that it is
counter to her own understanding of the texts to impose such a firm
boundary between fiction and non-fiction. It is interesting that Bird
pays no attention to 'Nun ja! Das nächste Leben geht aber heute an',
a text which, by using a letter form, casts doubt on the tenability of
a straightforward opposition between fiction and non-fictional essay.

My readings of the three texts will regard them as different and complementary approaches to the same historical material, which together
form a network comparable to the four lectures and narrative of
Wolf's later *Kassandra* project.[61] Rather than privileging the narrative
form of the fictional work and reading 'Der Schatten eines Traumes' as
a conventional historical essay, I shall highlight the extent to which the
two essays reflect on the different kinds of language characteristic of

---

[58] Hans-Georg Werner, 'Christa Wolfs Bild der Günderrode: Medium der
Selbstbesinnung', in *Christa Wolf in feministischer Sicht*, ed. Michel Vanhelleputte (Frankfurt am
Main: Lang, 1992), 43–53.
[59] Frieden, 135.
[60] Bird, 80.
[61] Cf. Werner Krogmann, *Christa Wolf: Konturen* (Frankfurt am Main: Lang, 1989), 263.

different genres and discourses. This feature, widely overlooked in the secondary literature hitherto, encourages an approach which does not see the generic differences between the texts as a signal to read them according to different (preconceived) criteria. Instead, they are much more fruitfully read as mutually supportive explorations, not only of the relationship between historical lives and the present, but also of new, more productive ways of writing about the past.

A New Model of History

Wolf's reasons for exploring historical lives are twofold. Not only does she seek historical parallels to the present, in order to gain a better understanding of her own situation, but she also hopes to find the origins of modern problems. The model of history which the texts construct by exploring these relations between past and present represents a considerable challenge to the orthodox GDR narrative of history based on progress culminating in the socialist state.[62]

Unlike *Kindheitsmuster*, *Kein Ort. Nirgends* provides little overt narratorial reflection on the relationship between the historical subject-matter of the work and the present in which it was written. However, a modern subjective consciousness is implied throughout the text by the framing paragraphs, which create historical distance between the present, and Kleist and Günderrode as 'Vorgänger' (*Kein Ort*, 5–6, 119). The constantly shifting narrative voice and frequent use of an undefined 'wir' serve to blur the boundaries between the perspectives of the historical figures, the narrator, and the reader.[63] This opens up the possibility that reflections and ideas in the text belong both to the past and to the present. Ute Brandes has shown how the quotations Wolf incorporates into the text 'weisen über sich hinaus und fassen Zeiten und politische Systeme in einem schwebenden Vergleich zusammen. Sie sehen die Gegenwart durch das Medium der Vergangenheit und durchforschen die vergangene Epoche mit heutigen Massstäben.'[64] *Kein Ort. Nirgends* is a text which demands a high degree of active interpretation and reflection from the reader in constructing a relationship between the historical material and the narrator's present. Wolf assumes the reader's familiarity with the context in which she wrote

[62] Cf. Michael Schenkel, *Fortschritts- und Modernitätskritik in der DDR-Literatur: Prosatexte der achtziger Jahre* (Tübingen: Stauffenburg, 1995), 204–31.

[63] Much has been written on Wolf's narrative technique in *Kein Ort. Nirgends*. See, for example, Bird, 61–5; Brandes, *Zitat und Montage*, 63–6; Hilzinger, *Christa Wolf*, 128–9.

[64] Brandes, *Zitat und Montage*, 80.

the text, incorporating details which subtly point to her concerns at the time of writing. Kleist, for example, reflects on a 'Zusammenbruch im November' (*Kein Ort*, 12). His own nervous breakdown in winter 1803–4 cannot be pinpointed to this month, unlike the Biermann affair in 1976.

The essays about Günderrode and Bettine offer more explicit reflection on the parallels between past and present.[65] However, these texts require the same active mode of reading, sensitive to the context in which Wolf was writing, as the more fictional work. In the Günderrode essay a broad parallel is constructed between two generations of intellectuals for whom the 'Zuversicht, Hoffnung [und] Lebensaufschwung', inspired by the French Revolution and the establishment of a socialist state respectively, have given way to 'schmerzliche Ernüchterung und Enttäuschung' and subjection to 'Fremdherrschaft' ('Schatten', 515–16). The image of 'eine volle Umdrehung des "Rades der Geschichte"' which Wolf evokes at the beginning of the essay negates any notion of progress in history ('Schatten', 512). The generalizations which Bird finds unacceptable in this essay have the function of drawing the attention of the alert reader, aware of the constraints imposed by the context in which the essay was written, to the fact that Wolf is not making a claim to objective historical truth. Instead, she is self-consciously interested in those aspects of Günderrode's generation's experience which are comparable to her own. A phrase like 'wie Generationen in Zwischenzeiten immer' can thus be read as a veiled signal of the extent to which her interpretation of historical lives is determined by her own situation and concerns in the present ('Schatten', 513). Bird's comment on *Kein Ort. Nirgends* is thus equally applicable to the two essays: 'what is important is not any truth claim for the depiction of [the] past, but the truths which emerge in imaginative dialogue with it.'[66]

Implicit parallels between the experience of women of Günderrode's generation and the present serve to undermine the GDR's claim to have achieved gender equality. Describing conditions in Germany after the French Revolution, Wolf comments, 'die Zeit hat mit ihren Losungen "Freiheit!", "Persönlichkeit!" auch Frauen erfaßt, die Konvention macht ihnen beinahe jeden selbständigen Schritt unmöglich'

---

[65] I follow Wolf's inconsistency in the use of surnames and Christian names to refer to these women. Throughout this chapter I refer to historical figures by the names which the GDR writers predominantly use for them in their works.

[66] Bird, 60.

('Schatten', 520–1). A similar discrepancy between the proclaimed ideal of equality and the resistance presented by traditional gender roles was responsible for the 'double burden' experienced by women in the GDR. Wolf goes on to reflect on a restrictive condition of nineteenth-century women's lives which would have had a broader resonance for a GDR reader; the impossibility of travel. She describes how, as young girls, Karoline and Bettine imagine travelling across Italy with the help of a map and later reconstruct their imaginary journeys:

Darauf angewiesen sein, sich an Erfindungen zu erinnern, eine Fiktion dem Gedächtnis als Wirklichkeit einzuverleiben—deutlicher könnte nichts die Grenzen markieren, auf die sie sich verwiesen sieht. Nur im Traum, in der Phantasie, im Gedicht kann sie sie überschreiten. ('Schatten', 521)

Here parallels become prominent between the conditions of women's lives at this time and the conditions of life for most GDR citizens, for whom travel was also impossible. Examining the restrictions imposed on women in history enables Wolf implicitly to question the achievements of a state whose citizens, like women for many centuries, were denied self-determination.

By the time Wolf wrote 'Nun ja! Das nächste Leben geht aber heute an' in 1979, new developments in the cultural life of the GDR had reinforced the sense of a system intolerant of constructive criticism. In response to the increasingly draconian measures adopted against writers who voiced any kind of criticism of the state, a group of writers wrote to Erich Honecker to protest about how public debate in the GDR was being stifled. Their communication of this action to the western media was used as a pretext for the expulsion of nine writers from the Berlin Schriftstellerverband in June 1979. Georgina Paul has offered a compelling account of the means by which Wolf highlights parallels between the repressive methods of the SED in the late 1970s and those of the Metternich era of restoration through which Bettine lived.[67] As in 'Der Schatten eines Traumes', the replacement of utopian ideals by a disappointing and repressive reality is a prominent idea. Here, though, Wolf paints a portrait of a historical society which corresponds in its details to specific failings of GDR socialism:

Das Land Utopia [. . .] geht unter in Demagogenverfolgung, Zensur und

---

[67] Georgina Paul, '"Ich meine nichts, was könnte gestrichen werden": Christa Wolf's "Brief über die Bettine"', in *Christa Wolf in Perspective*, ed. Ian Wallace, GM 30 (Amsterdam and Atlanta: Rodopi, 1994), 25–40.

Bespitzelung, in der zähen Fortdauer eines Gesellschaftswesens, welches unter monarchistischem Regiment auf bürgerliche Weise produzieren und seine eigenen Widersprüche nicht zur Kenntnis nehmen will [. . .] ('Brief', 577)

Whereas the Günderrode essay used generalizing formulations to hint at parallels between past and present, the letter about Bettine employs anachronistic, often GDR-specific vocabulary to refer to 1830s Germany.

The letter form of 'Nun ja! Das nächste Leben geht aber heute an' invites a mode of reading which is sensitive to the relevance of the historical material to the present. By directly addressing the recipient, Wolf is able to hint at a present context, without specifying the ways in which it resembles 1830s Germany: 'Sie wissen, wie und worüber die allgemeine Stimme heute mit uns spricht' ('Brief', 610). The letter does not imply a total identification of two historical eras, nor a mere projection of the present on to the past. Instead, Wolf uses Bettine's epistolary novel *Die Günderode* as a model for a productive dialogue between historical material and the present ('Brief', 590–1). She speaks of 'den Vorteil [. . .], den der historische Abstand uns bietet': it is the distance between the past and the present which enables the former to be made productive for the latter ('Brief', 572).

Wolf has described her turn to the era of Romanticism in terms of a search for the origins of contemporary problems: 'Mein Hauptinteresse war, zu untersuchen: wo hat sie eigentlich angefangen, diese entsetzliche Gespaltenheit der Menschen und der Gesellschaft?'[68] Her model of history is concordant with Marx's in so far as the division of labour is seen as a central determining factor in the creation of the conditions of the modern age. The gulf between manual workers and intellectuals is a recurrent idea in *Kein Ort. Nirgends*: both Kleist and Günderrode idealize the 'einfache Arbeit' of a carpenter as a mode of existence entirely other to their own (*Kein Ort*, 42, 82, 86).[69]

The Marxist notion of history as a teleological progression to overcome the alienation resulting from the division of labour, however, is not supported by Wolf's texts. The idea that scientific and technological progress will lead to increasingly idyllic conditions in human society is expressed with narrative irony in *Kein Ort. Nirgends* by Nees von Esenbeck, whose thinking is strongly criticized by Kleist as the result of 'zyklopische Einseitigkeit':

---

[68] Wolf, 'Projektionsraum Romantik', in *Die Dimension des Autors*, ii. 879–80.
[69] See also Wolf, 'Der Schatten eines Traumes', 570–1.

Er spricht nicht, er doziert: [. . .] Ich gäbe mein Alles dafür, wenn ich in ein, zwei Jahrhunderten noch einmal auf dieser Welt leben und an den paradiesischen Zuständigkeiten teilhaben dürfte, welche die Menschheit—dank der Entfaltung der Wissenschaften!—dann genießt. (*Kein Ort*, 80)

Wolf proposes instead a pessimistic model of history as a course which has been determined by a narrow and potentially destructive notion of 'progress'. The three texts show how the period of early industrialization in Germany, in the years following the French Revolution, saw the growing dominance of a new mode of thought based on binary oppositions. Reason was increasingly enthroned and instrumentalized, while non-quantifiable qualities such as imagination came to be seen as non-essential for society and outside the prevailing definition of 'reality'. As Wolf suggests in her reading of Günderrode's poem 'Vorzeit, und neue Zeit', the 'dürre[r] Rationalismus' of her age resulted in the debasement of Enlightenment ideas to 'pragmatische Vernünftelei' ('Schatten', 517–18). In 'Projektionsraum Romantik', Wolf implies that the history of the last two centuries has essentially been a worsening of this problem. The intellectuals associated with early Romanticism are of interest because of their clear-sighted perception of the implications of this development, even in its earliest stages:

Obwohl die Phänomene scheinbar noch gar nicht so brisant sind, registrieren die Romantiker sie ungeheuer scharf; und weil wir da wirklich Ähnlichkeiten spüren zu unserer eigenen Reaktion auf ungleich schwerwiegendere Prozesse und Erscheinungen, deshalb dieser sogenannte Rückgriff.[70]

The idea that contemporary problems can be traced back to their beginnings is, of course, largely a myth. However, it is one which is highly productive for Wolf, not only in the texts of the late 1970s, but also in *Kassandra*, where she turns to a much earlier period in her search for the point at which the history of western civilization took a wrong turn. As it became increasingly difficult to believe that GDR socialism was developing towards a utopian goal, the notion that social structures and modes of thought have identifiable origins could serve to keep alive some faith in the possibility of change which is central to Marxist thinking.

It is also valuable for feminists to regard the gender relations which have prevailed in recent history as the product of historical developments, and so neither inevitable nor permanent. Gender is central to

---

[70] Wolf, 'Projektionsraum Romantik', in *Die Dimension des Autors*, ii. 880.

Wolf's presentation of social changes at the beginning of the nineteenth century. As she explains in 'Projektionsraum Romantik', industrialization resulted in the marginalization of women and intellectuals: 'Das "weibliche Element" ist in den Industriegesellschaften sowenig vorhanden wie das "geistige Element": auf die lebenswichtigen Prozesse haben weder Frauen noch Intellektuelle Einfluß.'[71] Not only are women socially marginalized by the increasing division of labour, but, Wolf suggests, the newly dominant rationalism based on binary oppositions is a specifically masculine mode of thought. In *Kein Ort. Nirgends*, Günderrode describes Savigny in the following terms: 'Savigny hat für alles ein Entweder-Oder. Sie müssen wissen, Kleist, er hat einen männlichen Kopf. Er kennt nur eine Art Neugier: die Neugier auf das, was unanfechtbar, folgerichtig und lösbar ist' (*Kein Ort*, 81).

The texts suggest at several points that gender differences became particularly marked at this point in history because of the different kinds of work and social participation demanded of men and women respectively. Bird's contention that Wolf privileges the female 'as though there were something of essential value in woman' neglects the importance Wolf ascribes to these historical factors.[72] Talking to Kleist, Günderrode describes the effects which social differences have on the ways men and women think: 'Ihr werdet durch den Gang der Geschäfte, die euch obliegen, in Stücke zerteilt, die kaum miteinander zusammenhängen. Wir sind auf den ganzen Menschen aus und können ihn nicht finden' (*Kein Ort*, 94). In the Bettine letter Wolf argues that men are forced to conform to prevailing thought structures because of their need to work in the public sphere in order to earn a living ('Brief', 576). The idea that women occupy a privileged position of insight because of their marginalization by social structures, already implicit in *Kindheitsmuster*, is now formulated more fully and made central to Wolf's concerns. In the Günderrode essay she explains how it is no coincidence that it was women who recognized and wrote about 'die Übel der Zeit':

Die Tatsache, daß sie ökonomisch und sozial vollkommen abhängig sind, keine Stellung, kein Amt anstreben können, enthebt die geistig Freiesten unter ihnen der Mißlichkeit, um des Broterwerbs willen den Untertanen-Ungeist zu rechtfertigen. ('Schatten', 542)

Similar ideas are to be found in 'Berührung', Wolf's preface to Maxie

---

[71] Wolf, 'Projektionsraum Romantik', in *Die Dimension des Autors*, ii. 880   [72] Bird, 60.

Wander's *Guten Morgen, du Schöne*, which was completed during her work on Kleist and Günderrode:

Das dem herrschenden Selbstverständnis Unbewußte, das Unausgesprochene, Unaussprechliche findet sich immer bei den Unterprivilegierten, den Randfiguren, den für unmündig Erklärten und Ausgestoßenen; [. . .] Und eben, lange Zeit: bei den Frauen.[73]

Both Kleist and Günderrode are outsiders at Merten's tea party, and neither has adapted unproblematically to the prevailing thought structures. However, gender-determined differences between the two characters are emphasized throughout the text. The narrator first introduces them in such a way as to highlight the different conditions of their lives, contrasting Kleist's aimless travelling with the restrictions imposed on Günderrode, who is 'in den engen Zirkel gebannt' (*Kein Ort*, 6). Although Kleist is unable to conform to expectations of him, claiming he cannot divide the world 'in gut und böse [. . .] in zwei Zweige der Vernunft' (*Kein Ort*, 85), he has internalized the dominant mode of thought to a greater degree than Günderrode. He is threatened by Günderrode's failure to conform to conventional notions of femininity, preferring women, 'die im Rahmen bleiben' (*Kein Ort*, 21, 18).[74] He is reluctant to question the accepted construction of gender as a binary opposition, although he feels it to be a restriction (*Kein Ort*, 105).[75] As a result of her more marginalized position, Günderrode is freer from her society's blind spots, and so has a better insight into contemporary developments. Significantly, her understanding of Kleist is generally far superior to his understanding of her.[76] Whereas he attempts to impose conventional notions of femininity on her, her understanding of him is so astute that it threatens to reveal the blind spots in his self-perception (*Kein Ort*, 105, 108).

As critics have pointed out, the feminine ideal which Wolf constructs in Günderrode—as in Christa T. and Kassandra—is paradoxically one which cannot influence the course of history. These female figures are doomed to remain the victims of their societies, and all die premature deaths, having failed to change reality according to their ideals.[77] However, Wolf's shift of focus, after writing *Kein Ort. Nirgends*

---

[73] Wolf, 'Berührung', in *Die Dimension des Autors*, i. 201.

[74] Cf. Brandes, *Zitat und Montage*, 82.

[75] Cf. Myra N. Love, *Christa Wolf: Literature and the Conscience of History* (New York: Lang, 1991), 129–32.

[76] Cf. Bird, 72.

[77] See, for example, Werner, 52; Hilzinger, *Christa Wolf*, 112.

and 'Der Schatten eines Traumes', to a female figure who develops strategies of survival under difficult circumstances, suggests a temporal process of coming to terms with the newly restrictive cultural environment of the GDR after 1976. Whereas working on Kleist and Günderrode enabled Wolf to reflect on the social causes and the conditions of the crisis she and other GDR intellectuals were experiencing, her emphasis in the Bettine letter is on the tactical pragmatism of a woman who worked productively despite similarly repressive circumstances. Consequently, she focuses primarily on Bettine's productive later years, rather than the 'Verstrickung in Alltagsmühsal' of her years as wife and mother ('Brief', 578).

A New Approach to History

Wolf's interest in the victims of history, and in figures whose ideals were never translated into reality, is central to the approach to history which her texts advocate. She retains the basic Marxist idea that the past must be made productive for the present. However, whereas orthodox GDR historiography saw its task in delineating a progressive tradition of figures and movements which contributed to a positive historical development culminating in the GDR, Wolf is concerned to draw out of historical figures and events a productive potential which has not been realized by the course of history. An imagined meeting between two individuals, which in all likelihood never took place—'erwünschte Legende'—can reveal this potential and inspire hope better than the real events of history (*Kein Ort*, 6). As the Bettine letter makes clear, engaging with the past is to act as a vitally necessary spur to change in the present, and not as a mere affirmation of what has been achieved:

Und ich denke darüber nach, wie die unerledigten Einlagerungen in unserer Geschichte, die produktiven Ansätze, über die sie mit 'ehernem' oder bloß geschäftigem Schritt hinweggegangen ist, und unsere Selbstentfremdung miteinander zusammenhängen. Wir müßten unser Leben ändern. ('Brief', 599–600)

It is thus precisely in the lives of marginalized and victimized figures that alternative values to those which have shaped the course of history must be sought.

The brief period of transition between the French Revolution and the consolidation of a new industrialized society in Germany is of special interest to Wolf in her attempt to retrieve the buried potential of history. Wolf sees the Revolution as the source of ideals and longings, particularly for women, which the later course of history failed to fulfil: 'Ohne die Französische Republik, vor ihr hätte eine Frau wohl kaum begehren können, unabhängig und frei zu sein' ('Schatten', 528).[78] Bettine and Günderrode are thus representative of utopian values which could have provided the basis for a very different course of history. It is this glimpse of an alternative which Wolf wants to uncover for her own age. The women of Romanticism, she suggests, embodied a possibility of redemption for a society which was embarking on a course of destruction:

Diese jungen Frauen, die ersten weiblichen Intellektuellen, erleben die Anfänge des Industriezeitalters, der Vergöttung der Ratio und die fortschreitende Arbeitsteilung als eine Vergewaltigung ihrer Natur. [. . .] Die Welt ist krank, und sie merkt es nicht. Frauen, in diesen wenigen Jahren, einer Lücke zwischen zwei Zeitaltern, plötzlich aus alten Schablonen herausgefallen— auch aus den Schablonen, ihr Geschlecht betreffend—, schließen eine Art Bündnis, sie gesund zu machen. Die Zeichen, die sie geben, können erst jetzt wieder bemerkt, aufgenommen und gedeutet werden. ('Schatten', 541)

   In their 'Anspruch auf Ganzheit, Einheitlichkeit, Tiefe und Wahrhaftigkeit des Empfindens', Wolf suggests, these women kept alive the utopian spirit of Jena Romanticism long after this itself had disintegrated ('Schatten', 568; 'Brief', 575). She presents the friendships between these women as a model for a different, non-destructive form of human relationship, which had the potential, 'weibliche Elemente in eine patriarchalisch strukturierte Kultur einzubringen' ('Schatten', 541). Karoline's friendships with Lisette Nees von Esenbeck and with Bettine are shown to be productive in giving rise to '[Lebens-] Entwürfe, die denen der Männer nicht gleichen werden': 'denn diese beiden Frauen symphilosophieren über eine Religion der Lebensfreude, des Sinnengenusses und der Humanität' ('Schatten', 540; 'Brief', 603).
   In describing the productive potential of such friendships, Wolf repeatedly uses the terms 'Liebe', 'Leidenschaft', and 'Sehnsucht'. In suggesting that Wolf identifies with Günderrode's work as a poet, but disapproves of her involvement in 'mundane, banal love affairs', Bird overlooks the close connection which Wolf establishes between the two

---

[78] Brandes has shown how, in *Kein Ort. Nirgends*, Wolf's compression of quotations from Günderrode's letters into unified statements serves to highlight her function as a representative of this new female self-awareness. See Brandes, *Zitat und Montage*, 74–7.

activities: 'Dies, Schreiben und Lieben, sind die authentischsten Entäußerungen ihrer Natur' ('Schatten', 569).[79] Far from commenting disparagingly on the kind of romantic attachments traditionally seen as the central content of women's lives, Wolf is re-evaluating the notion of love as an essential quality with the potential to counteract the destructive tendencies of modern societies. As Sara Lennox has commented, 'for women like Günderrode and Bettine, love is a utopian image of human connection, [. . .] an encounter which permits the lovers to recognize, explore, and elaborate their deepest sensual, emotional, and intellectual needs'.[80] Wolf attributes the destructive nature of relations between the sexes to a discrepancy between women's capacity for 'ausschließliche Liebe', and men's inability to love resulting from their socially determined inner fragmentation ('Schatten', 549). Love is equally central to Wolf's analysis of contemporary gender relations in 'Berührung', where she comments on 'das unreife Liebesverlangen vieler Männer' in the GDR.[81] 'Liebe', as Wolf uses the term, is a form of human relationship which presupposes 'Menschlichkeit', as she defines it in 'Berührung': 'niemals, unter keinen Umständen einen anderen zum Mittel für eigene Zwecke zu machen'.[82] It is this quality which the three men Günderrode loves lack: 'Dreimal erfährt sie das Unleidlichste: Sie wird zum Objekt gemacht' ('Schatten', 529). However, love of the kind envisaged by Wolf—'eine andre Art Verbundenheit, eine andre Art Liebe'—does thrive between women ('Schatten', 540). Here, it is given a significance far beyond the purely personal, as the spur to a utopian way of thinking about the future, which does not involve abstraction away from the thinking subject, nor exclude emotion:

Miteinander denken aus Liebe und um der Liebe willen. Liebe, Sehnsucht als Mittel der Erkenntnis brauchen; denkend, erkennend nicht von sich selber absehn müssen; einander 'die Schläfe brennen' machen von 'heißem Eifer in die Zukunft'. ('Brief', 604)

Of particular interest to Wolf is the way these women used language to communicate. She likens their discourse to poetic language, and contrasts it with the dominant uses of language, both in the early nineteenth century and in the present: 'wir haben Gedichte, doch Poesie

[79] Bird, 84.
[80] Sara Lennox, 'Christa Wolf and the Women Romantics', in *Studies in GDR Culture and Society 2*, ed. Margy Gerber (Washington: University Press of America, 1982), 31–43 (36).
[81] Wolf, 'Berührung', in *Die Dimension des Autors*, i. 203.
[82] Ibid. 197.

als Umgangsform ist uns verwehrt' ('Brief', 600). Despite the contrast between Günderrode's conformity to the norms of masculine aesthetics and Bettine's rejection of these, Wolf finds in the writings of both a form of language which does not exclude subjectivity and the present experience of the writer. This language, she suggests, is able to facilitate insights where more abstract language merely obscures:

Welche Herausforderung an unsre verschüttete Fähigkeit, Wörter als Botschafter unsrer Sinne, auch unsrer Sinnlichkeit aufzunehmen, in Sätzen uns selbst hervorzubringen und unsre Sprache nicht zur Verhinderung von Einsichten, sondern als Instrument der Erkundung zu gebrauchen. Welche Gelegenheit auch, unsre eigne Lage zu begreifen. ('Schatten', 518–19)

The kind of language Wolf invokes here as the norm was exemplified in an extreme form by official GDR discourses, where the obligatory adherence to a series of abstract terms and categories obstructed communication and resulted in a language divorced from subjective experience.[83] The Günderrode essay and the Bettine letter contain frequent references to the failings of academic and public discourses in the GDR. When Wolf complains that the 'Literaturgeschichte der Deutschen' is 'orientiert an den retuschierten Kolossalgemälden ihrer Klassiker' and has neglected those figures regarded as 'unvollendet', it is clear that she is referring in the first instance to the GDR approach to literary history ('Schatten', 512). Not only has this academic discourse excluded Kleist, Günderrode, and Bettine, but its language is unable to capture the productive potential which Wolf perceives in their lives:

Vorwegnahme—wessen denn?
   Das Instrumentarium, das anzusetzen wir gewohnt sind, faßt es nicht. Literarische, historische, politische, ideologische, ökonomische Begriffe begreifen es nicht ganz. Der vulgäre Materialismus unsrer Zeit kann dem dürren Rationalismus ihrer Zeit nicht auf die Sprünge kommen, der rechthaberischen, alles erklärenden und nichts verstehenden Plattheit, gegen die die, von denen wir reden, sich ja grade zur Wehr setzen: gegen die eiskalte Abstraktion, diese ganze schauerliche Unbeirrbarkeit auf falsche, nicht mehr befragte Ziele hin [. . .] ('Schatten', 517)

Wolf defines her own engagement with historical figures in opposition

---

[83] Karin McPherson notes the importance of language and form in the Bettine letter, but does not relate Wolf's comments specifically to the GDR context. See Karin McPherson, 'Female Subjectivity as an Impulse for Renewal in Literature', in *Responses to Christa Wolf: Critical Essays*, ed. Marilyn Sibley Fries (Detroit: Wayne State University Press, 1989), 149–61 (158–60).

to the orthodox GDR approach to history, exemplified by 'die abgegriffene Formel der "Erbe-Pflege"' and the reduction of individuals to representatives of movements in a preconceived version of history: 'Das unklassifizierbar Bettinische, das in kein Raster paßt, auch in keine der Bewegungen, mit denen sie in ihrem langen Leben in Berührung kommt; [. . .] Sie eignet sich nicht als Objekt, irgendeine These zu demonstrieren' ('Brief', 599, 577).[84]

Wolf is attempting not only to uncover the productive potential contained in the lives of Günderrode and Bettine, but to follow their example in creating a discourse which reclaims language from its instrumentalization by a culture of rationalism. This is particularly evident in 'Nun ja! Das nächste Leben geht aber heute an', where Bettine's *Die Günderode* serves as a model of Wolf's own aims. Wolf is fascinated by the literary form which enabled Bettine to create a productive relationship between past and present, and to subvert the prevailing aesthetic and social structures: 'Die Bettine wittert, daß die Strukturen der ihr bekannten Ästhetik in irgendeinem wie immer vermittelten Sinn zusammenhängen müssen mit den hierarchischen Strukturen der Gesellschaft' ('Brief', 607–8). Unlike Günderrode, who conformed to masculine models of writing, Bettine rejected conventional aesthetic forms and found alternative ones, which Wolf understands as 'ein Ansatz zu einer anderen Ästhetik' ('Brief', 609).[85] The mixed form of the epistolary novel is able to do justice to the dynamic nature of a relationship and the contradictions inherent in an individual, whereas 'die geschlossene Romanform hätte reduzieren, beurteilen, einteilen und richten müssen' ('Brief', 601).[86] It is also able to create connections between past experience and the present. Wolf reads Bettine's work as a challenge to the prevailing notion of art as an autonomous realm, divorced from the subjectivity and historical circumstances of its creator:

[84] McPherson has read such views as a reassessment of Wolf's own earlier career as a literary critic. Ibid. 154.

[85] Wolf's complex relationships to the differing aesthetic models represented by Günderrode and Bettine have been the subject of much critical discussion. See Sigrid Weigel, 'Vom Sehen zur Seherin: Christa Wolfs Umdeutung des Mythos und die Spur der Bachmann-Rezeption in ihrer Literatur', in *Christa Wolf: Ein Arbeitsbuch*, ed. Drescher, 169–203 (170); Christiane Zehl Romero, '"Remembrance of Things Future": On Establishing a Female Tradition', in *Responses to Christa Wolf*, ed. Sibley Fries, 108–27 (120–1); McPherson, 159–60.

[86] Brandes has suggested that Wolf's use of authentic quotations in *Kein Ort. Nirgends* reproduces an open form of this kind, with the aim of eliminating the boundaries between life and art. Brandes, *Zitat und Montage*, 97.

Denn eine der Errungenschaften dieser Ästhetik, zur Zeit der Romantiker eben durch die Klassik ausgebaut und befestigt, ist ja die Methode, das 'Werk' von seinem Hervorbringer zu trennen und es, losgelöst von den Lebenszusammenhängen, aus denen heraus es entstand, in eine andre Sphäre, die der Kunst, entschweben zu lassen. ('Brief', 600–1)

In *Kein Ort. Nirgends* Wolf places similar ideas in the mouth of Savigny, who argues for a strict division between ideas and reality, and warns Kleist that any attempt to connect the two must lead to madness (*Kein Ort*, 50–1). Parallels are clear here with the experience of GDR intellectuals in the late 1970s, when it became apparent that the SED regime would not tolerate artists and thinkers who attempted to influence an increasingly disappointing reality. Wolf's three texts demand to be read as attempts to create an aesthetic based on a productive interaction between literature and its context. She shows how Bettine managed to incorporate reflection on the present into her work despite the repressive measures of Metternich's Europe. Stressing the need to read between the lines—'Viel Unausgesprochenes, absichtlich Zurückgehaltenes werden Sie vom Strom des Gesagten mitgetragen finden' ('Brief', 607)—she presents Bettine's writings as an exemplary illustration of the special potential of literary discourse in a society governed by censorship and prohibitions: 'Wie immer, wenn die öffentliche politische Diskussion unterdrückt wird, reiben sich die verschiedenen Meinungen und Parteien ersatzweise an der Literatur' ('Brief', 581).

Wolf's work on historical figures of the early nineteenth century challenges not only the orthodox narrative of history, but the nature of historical discourse in the GDR. Inverting the official optimistic model of history, she suggests that progressive ideals which might inspire hope in the present are to be sought only in the shadows of the course of destruction which is mainstream history or, in other words, in the female experience which has been increasingly marginalized by a patriarchal society. In order to retrieve these ideals and make them productive for the present, Wolf suggests, a historical discourse with distinctly literary qualities is needed. Her reflections on the contrast between the abstract language of GDR academic discourses and a more literary language which can incorporate a subjective present perspective on the past, and which can imply far more than it literally says, are highly pertinent to all the texts this chapter will examine.

SIGRID DAMM AND RENATE FEYL

The literary careers of Sigrid Damm and Renate Feyl display a number of parallels, which is why a comparative approach will be adopted here. Both had academic backgrounds, worked in literary criticism, and first pursued their interest in women's history in a non-fictional medium. In 1979 Damm published an edition of Caroline Schlegel-Schelling's letters, while two years later Feyl produced a volume of biographical portraits of women who made remarkable academic achievements, from the seventeenth to the early twentieth century. In the late 1980s both authors wrote full-length texts about the lives of individual historical women: Feyl's novel about Louise Adelgunde Viktorie Kulmus's marriage to Johann Christoph Gottsched, *Idylle mit Professor* (1986), and Damm's semi-fictional biography, *Cornelia Goethe* (1987). Since 1989 both have continued to pursue an interest in historical women, as well as publishing novels about individual women's experiences of GDR history: Damm's *Ich bin nicht Ottilie* and Feyl's *Ausharren im Paradies* (both 1992).[87]

'Begegnung mit Caroline' and Der lautlose Aufbruch

Damm's introduction to Caroline Schlegel-Schelling's letters and Feyl's introduction to her biographical volume are comparable as historical narratives in a non-fictional genre, written around the same time, by women who were not professional historians. However, Damm was a lecturer in German literature at the Friedrich Schiller University in Jena, while Feyl had been working freelance since 1970.[88] Both essays combine elements of the orthodox GDR approach to history with ideas which present a challenge to the official model, in particular, a focus on gender and the experience of women.

   Damm's 'Begegnung mit Caroline' opens by discussing reasons why Caroline is important and interesting, different ways of approaching

---

[87] Sigrid Damm, *Ich bin nicht Ottilie: Roman* (Frankfurt am Main: Insel, 1992), *Christiane und Goethe: Eine Recherche* (Frankfurt am Main and Leipzig: Insel, 1998); Renate Feyl, *Ausharren im Paradies: Roman* (Cologne: Kiepenheuer and Witsch, 1992; repr. 1997), *Die profanen Stunden des Glücks: Roman* (Cologne: Kiepenheuer and Witsch, 1996), *Das sanfte Joch der Vortrefflichkeit: Roman* (Cologne: Kiepenheuer and Witsch, 1999).

[88] See H. Jane Plenderleith, '"Der letzte DDR-Roman"? On the Interplay of the Personal and the Political in Sigrid Damm's *Ich bin nicht Ottilie*', in *The New Germany: Literature and Society after Unification*, ed. Osman Durrani, Colin Good, and Kevin Hilliard (Sheffield: Sheffield Academic Press, 1995), 337–48 (337). The cover of *Der lautlose Aufbruch* (Darmstadt and Neuwied: Luchterhand, 1983) offers biographical information about Feyl.

her life, and the aims of the essay, before presenting a detailed chronological account of her life. Damm outlines the various ways Caroline
has been understood in the past, and suggests that these have all been
inadequate ('Begegnung', 6-7). She proposes a new way of examining
Caroline's life, based on principles similar to those of western feminist
work on women's history in the 1970s. Firstly, she insists that she is
interested in Caroline, not because of her relationships with prominent
men, but for her own sake:

Nicht weil sie mit großen Männern, dem Philosophen Schelling, dem
Essayisten und Übersetzer August Wilhelm Schlegel, verheiratet war; nicht
weil historisch interessante Persönlichkeiten wie Georg Forster, Friedrich
Schlegel und Novalis ihre Freunde waren; nicht weil sie Goethe, Schiller und
Herder kannte, wenden wir uns ihr zu. Unsere Lesart zielt auf sie selbst, ihre
Beziehung und Auseinandersetzung mit der Welt und mit den Genannten.
('Begegnung', 7)

Secondly, Damm rejects an understanding and assessment of Caroline
based on her literary and theoretical writings. She associates this kind
of approach with a conventional form of historiography which she
aims to counter with a new form based on alternative criteria: 'All das
könnten wir tun, wir tun es aber nicht. Hieße es doch, Geschichte zu
beschreiben, wie es über Jahrhunderte üblich war und ist, nach Taten,
meßbaren Leistungen im Bereich der Politik, Ideologie, Kunst'
('Begegnung', 8). Like western feminists in the 1970s, Damm is suggesting that women's contribution to history cannot be measured by
the conventional criteria, tailored as they are to male lives. As we have
seen, such arguments have the potential to subvert the official GDR
discourse on history.

The degree to which Damm's essay fulfils the aims she outlines is
questionable.[89] The opening of the essay, far from suggesting a concern with Caroline for her own sake, positions her in relation to the
French Revolution and to Georg Forster. Damm quotes from a letter
in which Caroline expresses her excitement about the events in Paris,
then suggests that this was her motivation for moving to Mainz, 'dort-
hin, wo die Französische Revolution auf deutschen Boden übergreift'
('Begegnung', 6). (In fact, evidence from Caroline's letters suggests
very different reasons for her choice of Mainz.[90]) Damm then introduces Georg Forster as a determining influence on Caroline's personality:

---

[89] Cf. Koller, 126–7. [90] Damm, *Begegnung mit Caroline*, 128, 131.

Mit ihm, beeindruckt und beeinflußt durch seine große Persönlichkeit, erlebt diese Frau die Mainzer Republik. Die außergewöhnlichen zeitgeschichtlichen Umstände prägen in eigentümlicher Schärfe ihre Persönlichkeit, ihre Individualitätsauffassung und ihr Selbstwertgefühl. ('Begegnung', 6)

Later we are told that her 'schöpferische Rolle im Kreis der Jenaer Frühromantiker' would hardly have been thinkable without the influence of Forster and the years in Mainz ('Begegnung', 20).

Throughout the essay, Damm's apparently feminist programmatic assertions are never allowed to challenge the broad contours of the orthodox GDR narrative of history. This results in interesting tensions between different elements of the essay, particularly with regard to the way feminist ideas are presented. While Damm's stated intentions have much in common with western feminism, she is careful to construct Caroline in opposition to a notion of western feminism as it was commonly perceived in the GDR. She emphasizes that Caroline was 'keine Vertreterin der Emanzipation im engen Sinne des Begriffs, wie er damals und auch heute oft gebraucht wird', and 'entschieden für die Emanzipation, aber für die von Frau und Mann' ('Begegnung', 9–10). In order further to identify Caroline with the official GDR view of gender equality as an issue inseparable from the class struggle, Damm indirectly associates her with Clara Zetkin's writings. She describes how Caroline's personality is an inspiration for Friedrich Schlegel in his development of androgyny as an ideal, then associates these ideas with a quotation from Zetkin advocating women's participation in society:

Will Friedrich Schlegel, sich gegen die einseitige Sicht der Frau als Geschlechts-wesen wendend, nicht die Wertsumme der in ihr ruhenden geistigen und sittlichen Kräfte mobilisieren, in der Aufhebung der starren Rollenzuweisung die Emanzipation von Frau und Mann anstreben? So wie Clara Zetkin es im Jahre 1920 sieht: 'Freieste Mitarbeit der Frau auf allen Gebieten des gesells-chaftlichen Lebens bedeutet eine reichere, vielseitigere Qualität der Leist-ungen [...]' ('Begegnung', 11)

This rather poorly motivated association of two sets of ideas points to Damm's strategy in dealing with both Caroline and Friedrich Schlegel. This kind of reference to canonical historical figures raised to heroic status by the official GDR discourse was a tactic characteristic of academic historical writing, with the function of demonstrating a particular character's positive status within the national heritage. By emphasizing Georg Forster's role in Caroline's life and referring to

Clara Zetkin's writings, Damm is attempting to integrate Caroline—and early Jena Romanticism—into the GDR narrative of a progressive tradition.

Instead of questioning the orthodox model of history, Damm's suggestion that Caroline's achievements cannot be measured by conventional criteria serves to broaden the criteria according to which an individual's contribution to history can be defined, in order to allow Caroline a place within that same model. Furthermore, Damm's insistence that Caroline's importance lies not in her actions or her works, but 'in ihrem einfachen Dasein' effectively reinscribes the traditional stereotypes of creative male *Tun* and passive female *Sein*.[91] In examining 'welche inneren und äußeren Kräfte es sind, die sie befähigen, so selbstbewußt ihr Leben zu gestalten' ('Begegnung', 8), Damm constructs a notion of Caroline's essential self as the product of her political experiences, and so reduces her to a receptacle for the revolutionary ideas of her time:

Als Frau gezwungen, Zeitgeschichte und eigenes Dasein in enger Beziehung zu sehen, kommt sie in der Auseinandersetzung mit dem weltgeschichtlichen Gehalt der Französischen Revolution bei sich selbst an. ('Begegnung', 6)[92]

This interpretation of Caroline represents a fundamental continuity with the GDR historiographical tradition, whereby individual biographies were treated as concrete instances of broader historical forces, whether progressive ideals or reactionary impulses. Instead of questioning this approach to historical lives, Damm is suggesting a new, female-specific way in which individual lives might be related to broader historical movements. Women, excluded from participation in the public sphere, can thus contribute to history by being passively receptive to the political ideals which men are able to pursue more actively.

As a bearer of political ideals, Caroline serves to create a causal connection between the revolutionary events surrounding Georg Forster in Mainz, and Jena Romanticism. Damm implies that Caroline was the means by which Forster's political theory was translated into the practice of the Romantics. She presents Caroline as a passive recipient of Forster's ideas, who then—having undergone a model learning process reminiscent of socialist realist fiction—actively transmits these

---

[91] Cf. the title of Feyl's 1984 text, a compilation of quotations from German writers and intellectuals, relating to women's education. Renate Feyl, *Sein ist das Weib, Denken der Mann: Ansichten und Äußerungen für und wider die gelehrten Frauen* (Berlin: Union Verlag, 1984).
[92] See also 'Begegnung', p. 17.

ideas to the Jena circle: 'Hat Forster Carolines Begierde, zu wissen, zu erkennen, gefördert und gelenkt, so wird ihr im Zusammensein mit Friedrich [Schlegel] zum erstenmal das Glück zuteil, Anregende und Gebende zu sein' ('Begegnung', 36). Damm interprets the Jena circle as a utopian model of an intellectual community based on the ideals of the French Revolution, which society at large has failed to realize:

Was die Gesellschaft als Ganzes nicht verwirklicht, wie die jungen Leute im Taumel ihrer Revolutionsbegeisterung erhofften, wollen sie nun in der Praxis ihres eigenen Zusammenlebens realisieren und verstehen dies durchaus als Modell einer gesamtgesellschaftlichen Utopie. ('Begegnung', 49)

These ideas are similar to Wolf's interpretation of Jena Romanticism in 'Der Schatten eines Traumes' and 'Nun ja! Das nächste Leben geht aber heute an'.

As the title of Damm's essay suggests, the idea that Caroline is important for GDR society in the present is prominent. Damm evokes a dialogic model of the process of writing biography, as a meeting between a contemporary and an eighteenth-century woman. In relating Caroline's lifetime to the present, Damm challenges the orthodox GDR model of history by suggesting that, although some of the ideals which Caroline represents have been realized in socialist society, others have not:

Als Heutige begegnen wir ihr, treten mit ihr ins vertraute Gespräch, sehen Eigenes im Fremden, uns Erfülltes im Abstand der Zeit, in der gesellschaft-lichen Revolutionierung; Unerfülltes, wo Caroline durch ihr vorurteils-loses Handeln, ihr politisches und ästhetisches Feingefühl, ihre lebhafte Empfänglichkeit uns 'Maßstäbe für die Menschlichkeit' setzt. ('Begegnung', 7)

There are suggestions both here ('sehen Eigenes im Fremden') and at the end of the essay that Damm's intention is not only to create a place for Caroline within a progressive line of historical tradition. Caroline's life, she hints, can also be read as a model for the present. Like Wolf and other GDR authors from the 1970s onwards, Damm focuses on the aftermath of the French Revolution and emphasizes the painful disillusionment for intellectuals who had shared the political ideals of the Revolution. She describes how 'die praktische geschichtliche Bewegung beginnt von ihren Idealen abzufallen', resulting in a shift from 'Begeisterung' and 'Zukunftshoffnungen' to 'Zweifel und Ent-täuschung' ('Begegnung', 30). In view of the evident parallel between this situation and the increasing disillusionment of intellectuals with the results of the socialist 'revolution' by this stage in GDR history, Caroline and the Jena Romantic circle can be understood as a potentially valuable source of ideals for the present. They respond productively, Damm suggests, to the sense of disillusionment provoked by the shortcomings of the French Revolution. Recognizing the discrepancy 'zwischen verkündetem Ideal und realer gesellschaftlicher Situation', they remain faithful to their political ideals and attempt to initiate a 'geistige Revolution' ('Begegnung', 14, 46).

An underlying assumption of Damm's 'Begegnung mit Caroline' is that social and economic progress between the late eighteenth century and the GDR present has been such that figures and events whose utopian impulse was unable to achieve widespread social change two centuries previously can be made productive for the more progressive society of the GDR. Georg Forster's political isolation is described as 'die Einsamkeit des zu früh Gekommenen', suggesting a firm faith in the notion of progress characteristic of GDR historiography ('Begegnung', 29). This is strikingly different from Wolf's more pessimistic understanding of the course of history over the last two centuries.[93] Damm suggests that Caroline's ideal of a relationship based on equality was not realizable because of the social conditions of her time: 'Die unternommenen Versuche einer gleichberechtigten Entwicklung beider Partner scheitern [. . .] am grauen bürgerlichen Alltag mit seinen schwierigen materiellen Existenzbedingungen' ('Begegnung', 12). The swift disintegration of the Jena circle is similarly attributed to the 'Widersprüche [. . .] der neuen geschichtlichen Etappe' and the 'sozialökonomische Unsicherheit' of its members ('Begegnung', 53–4). Whereas Wolf emphasizes the unifying characteristics of all industrial societies, Damm's terminology here remains indebted to orthodox GDR historiography with its insistence on the fundamental differences between capitalism and socialism.

In 'Begegnung mit Caroline' Damm attempts to broaden the boundaries of GDR historical discourse, without calling into question the orthodox narrative at its centre. She uses new, female-specific criteria of historical significance in order to argue that Caroline Schlegel-Schelling deserves a place within this narrative. Similarly, she reassesses early Jena Romanticism, suggesting that its revolutionary roots and

---

[93] Damm's faith in the progress of socialism is reminiscent of Wolf's *Nachdenken über Christa T.*, where the narrator describes Christa T. in the following terms: 'deutlich fühlt sie, wie die Zeit für sie arbeitet, und muß sich doch sagen: Ich bin zu früh geboren' (*Nachdenken über Christa T.*, 180).

utopian ideals warrant its inclusion amongst the productive traditions of GDR prehistory. The most subversive element of the essay is the idea that not all of Caroline's ideals have been realized by socialist society, but this is judiciously balanced by a strong faith in the socio-economic progress represented by the GDR.

If Damm focuses on a woman who could be integrated into the GDR narrative of history as a link between a political and a cultural movement, Renate Feyl's *Der lautlose Aufbruch* is about the lives of women who had very little to do with the orthodox notions of political or cultural tradition. While GDR historians' work on women concentrated, if not on heroic, politically active individuals, then on proletarian female lives, Feyl's choice of subject matter—women's education—entails a potentially subversive focus on the lives and struggles of predominantly bourgeois women.[94]

In her introduction to the work, Feyl presents a broad historical narrative, for which the eleven biographical portraits then provide detailed evidence. The central principle of this narrative is gender. Feyl discusses the popular ideas about women which limited their opportunities for centuries, and shows how individual women managed to overcome these restrictions in their pursuit of knowledge, resulting in the gradual opening of the academic sphere to women. Whereas Damm's opening to 'Begegnung mit Caroline' situates her biographical subject in relation to a figure and an event prominent in the orthodox GDR account of history, Feyl's opening paragraphs present a cultural tradition of gender roles as the backdrop against which the women's lives explored here are to be understood:

Der Mann handelt. Die Frau liebt. Der Mann ist der Kopf. Die Frau ist das Herz. Er ist der Pflug, die rastlose Bewegung, und sie ist der Acker, die ruhende Erde. [...]
Was unter dem Zwang der Arbeitsteilung zur Gewohnheit wurde, erklärt man schließlich zur Natur: Nicht denken, erkunden oder wissen ist die Natur der Frau, sondern fühlen, erdulden, erfahren. (*Aufbruch*, 5)

Rather than situating her narrative firmly within the master narrative of GDR historiography as Damm does, Feyl hints at a more tangential relationship between the story she is telling and this master narrative. With her reference to the division of labour, she suggests that capitalist labour relations are at the root of the cultural history she is presenting, thus rendering her account compatible with, though not subordinate

---

[94] Compare, for example, Neef, *Mühsal ein Leben lang*; Luise Dornemann, *Alle Tage ihres Lebens: Frauengestalten aus zwei Jahrhunderten* (Berlin: Dietz, 1981).

to, the conventional narrative of economic and political history. As in Wolf's works, the division of labour is given a new significance as a determining factor in gender relations.

Feyl's history of women's education extends the boundaries of GDR historical discourse more radically than Damm's biography of Caroline Schlegel-Schelling because, rather than integrating women into the orthodox historical narrative, Feyl tells a different story which places women at its centre. She explores gender as a constraint whose effects override those of class, thus challenging the framework within which academic work on women's history was contained:

> Jene Frauen, die als erste an dem Bildungsprivileg der Männer zu rütteln wagen, sind zunächst meist selbst privilegiert: ausgestattet mit den Vorteilen eines vermögenden Elternhauses. Doch diese wenigen haben es von Anfang an schwerer als jeder durchschnittlich begabte Mann. (*Aufbruch*, 8)

Feyl traces a history of ideas about women deriving from influential thinkers, from Luther to Paul Möbius via Gottsched, Kant, Rousseau, Olympe de Gouges, Mary Wollstonecraft, Theodor Gottlieb von Hippel, and Nathusius. Against this background of intellectual debate about women's nature and capabilities, she shows how an increasing number of individual women succeeded in overcoming the restrictions imposed on them. Generalizing and idealizing tendencies are apparent in Feyl's characterization of these women. The individual portraits all serve to support the story told by the introduction; a story of a quiet, non-aggressive rebellion against convention, and a patient and courageous struggle against adversity:

> Ohne attackierende Forderungen, ohne fanatisches Eifern, ohne draufgängerischen Ehrgeiz, eher lautlos und aus der Stille heraus bahnen sich die Frauen weltweit den Weg in die Wissenschaft. Es ist ein langes, behutsames Sichvorwärtstasten; ein verhaltenes Schweben zwischen gewohnter Unterwürfigkeit und verlockender Auflehnung; ein Suchen und Irren, Finden und Verlieren voll geduldiger Leidenschaft. Bewundert von den einen, belacht von den andern, gehen sie, gelassen und auf sich selbst vertrauend, ihren Weg durch das Dickicht von Intoleranz und Mißachtung, Beschränkung und Spott. (*Aufbruch*, 7)

Feyl neglects individual differences, contradictions, and complexities which do not fit this pattern, in order to present the women she has chosen as heroic historical role-models, paving the way for general female access to education at all levels. This approach bears some resemblance to early western work on women's history, in its quest for an inspirational narrative of women's persistent ability to resist oppression. Methodologically, it is also very similar to conventional GDR historiography: individual lives are idealized and simplified, so that they can serve as evidence for a broader historical narrative of progress, culminating in the present.

Although Feyl presents a new historical narrative centred on women, she highlights the points of intersection between this 'herstory' and the official GDR version of political history. Key events in the latter—the French Revolution and the revolutions of 1848 and 1918—are incorporated, as important milestones, into Feyl's narrative. Her presentation of the French Revolution contrasts sharply with Damm's. Instead of asking what role women played in the revolutionary movement, Feyl focuses on the impact which the Revolution had on notions of female nature and women's access to education. For Damm, the Revolution is the trigger for Caroline's self-realization; the value of Caroline's life lies in her 'Bereitschaft, die Ideen der Revolution aufzunehmen' ('Begegnung', 6, 17). The ideal of gender equality is, in Damm's account, a logical consequence of the Revolution ('Begegnung', 35, 37). Feyl, like Wolf, is more ambivalent about the Revolution, emphasizing its inherent contradictions with regard to the question of gender. She describes Jean-Jacques Rousseau as 'einer der geistigen Wegbereiter der Französischen Revolution', and interprets his thinking as an expression of the class struggle at that point in history: 'Sparen und speichern, fleißig schaffen und Werte erwirtschaften, jene praktischen Bürgertugenden, die gegen Luxus und Laster des genußsüchtigen Adels gerichtet sind, bestimmen das Rousseausche Frauenbild' (*Aufbruch*, 10–11). Rousseau's ideas may have been in accord with the direction of history according to Marx's model, but in Feyl's narrative he represents a regression to a view of women which had been partially overcome by the Enlightenment:

Das alte Hindernis stellt sich ihnen [den Frauen] von neuem in den Weg. Frauen sind im öffentlichen Bewußtsein wieder das, was sie immer waren: ein Etwas ohne Namen und Rechte; ein Geschlecht, das für das andere Geschlecht erzogen wird. (*Aufbruch*, 11)

The Revolution itself is presented with similar ambivalence: Feyl recognizes the gender specificity of its ideals, and suggests that it was only the critical responses of de Gouges and others which produced positive results for gender relations:

Neue Hoffnung bringt den 'weisen Weibern' die Französische Revolution. Als unter dem Jubel des Volkes die Menschenrechte proklamiert werden, erkennt

Olympe de Gouges, daß dies nur Männerrechte sind, und erlaubt sich, was in keinem Jahrhundert gestattet noch denkbar war: Sie verfaßt die *Erklärung der Rechte der Frau und Bürgerin* und formuliert hier jenen Satz, der männliche und weibliche Zeitgenossen außer Fassung bringt: Wenn die Frauen das Recht haben, das Schafott zu besteigen, müssen sie auch das Recht haben, auf einer Rednertribüne zu stehen. (*Aufbruch*, 11–12)

Damm mentions de Gouges only very briefly, in order to imply, rather negatively, that she—in contrast with Caroline—was a 'Vertreterin der Emanzipation im engen Sinne des Begriffs' ('Begegnung', 9).

The attempted revolutions of 1848 and 1918 are given more unambiguously positive roles in Feyl's account. She describes 1848 as a 'neue[r] Ausgangspunkt' for women's rebellion against their subordinate position (*Aufbruch*, 12). She sketches the increasing exploitation of women's labour in the late nineteenth century, showing how this led to the development of a 'weibliches Selbstbewußtsein', expressed in productive, characteristically socialist, political activity:

Es artikuliert sich in einem heftigen, unversöhnlichen Kampf um soziale Rechte, organisiert sich in Frauenvereinen und bildet eine starke Frauenbewegung, die die Forderung nach ökonomischer Gleichberechtigung auf ihre Fahnen schreibt. (*Aufbruch*, 13)

This glimpse of political history as it was conventionally written in the GDR is, however, quickly reduced to a backdrop for the story Feyl is telling: 'Vor diesem mutmachenden Hintergrund wagen nicht mehr nur einzelne, sondern nunmehr eine beträchtliche Anzahl von wissenschaftlich ambitionierten Frauen die ihnen verwehrten Früchte vom Baum der Erkenntnis zu pflücken' (*Aufbruch*, 13).

While the effects of the First World War on women's social position are not mentioned, the November revolution of 1918 is presented as a momentous leap forward in the history of women's education. Feyl identifies the workers' revolutionary movement with the movement for women's suffrage, and suggests that the revolution was directly responsible for women's gaining the right, in 1920, to become professors and give lectures at universities (*Aufbruch*, 21).

While positioning herself clearly within the GDR historical discourse, punctuated as it was by such landmark events, Feyl offers a new perspective on these events. Instead of focusing on women's contribution to this narrative of history, she assesses the role which each of these events played in the history of women's emancipation. This inversion of priorities, though, is balanced by two elements which *Der lautlose*

Aufbruch shares with the orthodox GDR discourse. Firstly, like Damm, Feyl voices clear opposition to the kind of women's 'emancipation' associated with western feminism. She stresses that the women of her study had little to do with the 'Emanzipationskampf', and argues that their silent academic work contributed to making 'Emanzipation' 'mehr als nur eine Phrase [. . .], deren sich mit Vorliebe leere Köpfe bedienen, um sie als zeitgemäßes Banner der eigenen Gedankenarmut voranzutragen' (*Aufbruch*, 22). She distances herself from western feminism as it was commonly perceived in the GDR, by emphasizing that these academic women wanted 'weder die Loslösung vom andern Geschlecht noch die Freiheit von sozialen und biologischen Bindungen' (*Aufbruch*, 22–3).

Secondly, Feyl's narrative shares the teleology of orthodox GDR accounts of history. Her story of women's long struggle against oppression culminates with the triumphant arrival in socialism, which represents the fulfilment of women's dreams of being able to participate fully in intellectual life:

Doch erst als die Frauen, unter ihnen die Wissenschaftlerinnen, erkennen, daß der Kampf gegen die Geschlechtsschranken wirkungslos bleibt ohne den Kampf gegen die Klassenschranken, erst als der Herrschaft der Besitzenden über die Besitzlosen ein Ende gesetzt, das Kapital, das 'Kommando über die unbezahlte Arbeit andrer', beseitigt und das Eigentum an den Produktionsmitteln in die Hände der Produzenten gelegt ist, erst von diesem Zeitpunkt an verwandelt sich das von Frauen tausendfach geträumte Anderssein endlich in ein geistiges Mitsein. (*Aufbruch*, 23–4)

Here, Feyl's narrative of women's history converges with the orthodox GDR model of history and, for the first time in the essay, the struggle for gender equality is subordinated to the class struggle. What distinguishes Feyl's conclusion from more orthodox historiography is her suggestion that, while socialism may provide 'jener sozialökonomische Nährboden' which is a condition of women's equality, there is still further progress to be made. She argues that traditional prejudices against women still hold force, and her final sentence implies that 'real existierender Sozialismus' is not the end of the story, but the beginning of a new one: 'Der lange Kampf um die Emanzipation, der jahrhundertealte Traum nach vorwärts, die Suche nach Identität, die Erwartungen und Sehnsüchte, all die verwirkten Hoffnungen und verwehrten Utopien haben einen neuen Anfang' (*Aufbruch*, 24).[95]

[95] These ideas are almost identical to those with which Neef concludes her 1988 study of proletarian women around 1900. Cf. Neef, 174–6.

Both Damm and Feyl succeed in broadening GDR historical discourse by introducing a concern with gender. However, in their non-fictional texts they signal a clear allegiance to this discourse, in order to subvert the official narrative of history from within. This orthodox narrative is more central to Damm's text than to Feyl's, perhaps because of Damm's institutional position as an academic. While Damm adjusts the parameters of the accepted narrative, Feyl tells a new story, but relates it to the official one. Unlike Wolf in her texts of the late 1970s, neither Damm nor Feyl challenges the teleological model of history as progress which was fundamental to orthodox GDR discourses.

Rewriting Women's Lives: Cornelia Goethe *and* Idylle mit Professor

By the time Damm wrote *Cornelia Goethe,* she had left her university post in Jena and had become, like Feyl, a freelance writer. While Feyl's *Idylle mit Professor* marks a shift to a fictional genre, *Cornelia Goethe* combines fictional elements with the style and form of an academic biography. In both cases, the move to a more fictional medium goes hand in hand with a greater degree of emancipation from the orthodox historical discourse.

Both Damm and Feyl tell the life-stories of eighteenth-century women associated with the literary world. Damm's narrator reconstructs the life of Goethe's sister chronologically from her birth in 1750 until her death at the age of twenty-six. Cornelia lived in her parents' house in Frankfurt am Main until 1773, when she married Johann Georg Schlosser, a lawyer eleven years older than herself. After a brief stay in Karlsruhe, the couple moved to Emmendingen, where Cornelia gave birth to a daughter in the autumn of 1774. The birth was followed by periods of illness and depression which prevented Cornelia from being able to care for her child herself. Two and a half years later she gave birth to a second daughter and died three weeks later.

Feyl's *Idylle mit Professor* follows the biography of Louise Adelgunde Viktorie Kulmus—referred to in the novel as Victoria—from her marriage to Johann Christoph Gottsched at the age of twenty-two in 1735 to her death in 1762. Unlike Cornelia Goethe, Victoria Gottsched bore no children, and achieved an unusual degree of success as a writer of dramatic comedies and a translator of literature and academic works. By 1749 she had achieved such a high reputation that the Austrian Empress Maria Theresa referred to her as 'die gelehrteste Frau von

Deutschland'.[96] However, like Cornelia Goethe she suffered from depressive illness and died prematurely.

The two works differ considerably in their narrative form. In *Cornelia Goethe* a prominent first-person narrator documents her engagement with historical source materials, combining analysis of these with imaginative speculation about aspects of Cornelia's life for which no evidence is available. Feyl uses a more conventional novel form, with a third-person omniscient narrator. She does not incorporate reflection on the processes of research and interpretation into the work, but presents instead an overtly fictional reconstruction of possible scenes in the Gottscheds' marriage. The inner worlds of Victoria and Gottsched are presented not as tentative speculation, but through a shifting narrative voice which conveys the *erlebte Rede* of the two figures in alternation. While Damm's narrator strives to uncover what she believes to be the truth about Cornelia, Feyl distances herself from any claim to present a definitively true and historically verifiable account of Victoria's life. One way in which this is achieved is the designation 'Roman'. Another is her use of the name 'Victoria' for Louise Gottsched. She is more commonly known either as 'Louise' or as 'Adelgunde', her second and favourite name.[97] Feyl is not ignorant of this preference: in her introduction to *Der lautlose Aufbruch*, she refers to her as 'Adelgunde Kulmus' (*Aufbruch*, 9). The decision to use the name 'Victoria' in the novel signals that the subject of the work is a fictional version of the historical figure.

Cornelia Goethe and *Idylle mit Professor* differ both from their authors' earlier, non-fictional works and from GDR historians' work on women, in that they reinterpret individual women's lives by contextualizing them within a broader historical narrative that has little to do with the orthodox history of progress. Both Damm and Feyl use an individual life-story to demonstrate the nature of gender relations and, in particular, the restrictions imposed on women in the eighteenth century. There is no attempt here to relate this history of oppression to the official narrative of the class struggle.

This shift in methodology is particularly apparent in Damm's *Cornelia Goethe*. Whereas 'Begegnung mit Caroline' had redefined criteria for measuring historical significance, in order to acknowledge Caroline Schlegel-Schelling's contribution to history, the later work

---

[96] See Veronica C. Richel, *Louise Gottsched: A Reconsideration* (Berne and Frankfurt am Main: Lang, 1973), 17.
[97] Ibid. 13.

rejects the notion that the only history worth telling is one of individuals and episodes which contributed positively to a line of progress. Damm focuses instead on an outwardly uneventful life:

> Ich wußte doch, daß das Leben dieser Frau gerade im Zuschütten ihrer Ursprünge und Fähigkeiten, im Nicht-Leben bestanden haben muß.
> Aber wie etwas beschreiben, was es nicht gab? Einem gestaltlosen, fast ungelebten Leben, ausschließlich im häuslichen Bereich, ereignislos, ohne Ortswechsel, ohne äußere Dramatik, Gestalt geben? Und warum? (*Cornelia*, 10)

Damm's understanding of women's place in history has undergone a fundamental shift. She is now aware of the problems of integrating women into mainstream history by finding ways in which they contributed to it, because women have generally been barred from the public sphere.[98] Cornelia's 'Nicht-Leben' prompts Damm to ask important new questions which challenge the premises of GDR historiography. Rather than demonstrating an individual's 'value' by elucidating her contribution to a predefined course of history, she asks what it was that prevented Cornelia from making any such contribution. Here, she works against a long tradition of interpretations which have attributed Cornelia's depression and premature death variously to the workings of fate, a poor constitution, personal failings, and an inability to fulfil the role expected of her in marriage because of her particularly intense relationship to her brother. The West German sociologist Ulrike Prokop, whose 1985 essay 'Die Melancholie der Cornelia Goethe' was an important source of information and ideas for Damm, summarizes earlier approaches to Cornelia's life, such as Heinrich Düntzer's of 1852, Georg Witkowski's of 1903, and Ernst Beutler's of 1960, claiming that 'ihre Arbeiten geraten unterschwellig zu einer Serie von Vorwürfen gegen eine Lebensunfähige'.[99]

Damm follows Prokop in approaching Cornelia's short life and her failure to find happiness and self-fulfilment by asking not what was wrong with Cornelia which prevented her from adapting successfully to her society's expectations of her, but instead which roles were available to her and how the constraints which eighteenth-century society

---

[98] The West German literary historian Silvia Bovenschen takes this 'Geschichte der weiblichen Geschichtslosigkeit' as the starting-point for her 1979 work, *Die imaginierte Weiblichkeit: Exemplarische Untersuchungen zu kulturgeschichtlichen und literarischen Präsentationsformen des Weiblichen* (Frankfurt am Main: Suhrkamp, 1979), 10.

[99] Ulrike Prokop, 'Die Melancholie der Cornelia Goethe', in *Schwestern berühmter Männer: Zwölf biographische Portraits*, ed. Luise F. Pusch (Frankfurt am Main: Insel, 1985), 49–122 (58).

placed on women interacted with Cornelia's personal background and disposition to render self-fulfilment impossible. By setting the course of Cornelia's individual psychological development within the context of contemporary intellectual ideas about women and the experiences of other women at that time, Damm's narrator presents Cornelia's life as a case study which sheds light on the social structures determining women's existence in late eighteenth-century Germany. The question which the narrator invokes as the impulse for her work is why Cornelia lived a life characterized by 'fortwährende Fremdbestimmung' by men: first her father, then her brother, and finally her husband (*Cornelia*, 10).

In attempting to find answers to this question, the narrator considers Cornelia's life in terms of the possibilities open to her at each stage. She shows how a tension arose between the opportunities Cornelia had in childhood and the social requirements of her as an adult. As a child Cornelia received an education which was unusually broad and intensive for a girl at that time: her father made little distinction between her and her brothers with regard to their education, thus to some extent masking the very different opportunities available to men and women in the public sphere. Basing her interpretation on imaginative empathy with Cornelia, the narrator conveys the growing sense of the pointlessness of this education. When Cornelia's older brother leaves home to go to university, the gender-based distinctions which her childhood had enabled her to overlook now make themselves felt:

Die kindlich-naïve Illusion einer immerwährenden Gemeinschaft gerät ins Wanken. Was wird sie, das Mädchen, tun? Wozu hat sie eigentlich das alles gelernt, sich geplagt und gemüht über so viele Jahre? Bestürzend, erschreckend wird die Frage vor ihr stehen. (*Cornelia*, 45)

For Cornelia adolescence brings the harsh realization that her education has no value or application in the public sphere, and that the role for which she must now prepare herself, that is, marriage, demands very different qualities. An important source for Damm is Cornelia's diary, sent as a series of secret letters to her friend Katharina Fabricius between October 1768 and August 1769.[100] Damm reproduces Prokop's analysis of this diary as a means of exploring in literary form the female roles offered by her society. According to this interpretation of the diary, Cornelia stylizes her own experience of her society, drawing on contemporary literary models, particularly the

[100] Cornelia Goethe, *Briefe und Correspondance secrète, 1767–1769*, ed. and trans. Melanie Baumann *et al.* (Freiburg: Kore, 1990).

novels of Samuel Richardson which formed her favourite reading. The very act of writing, Damm suggests, is an attempt to distance herself from the roles which she is expected to play, and to gain self-realization 'außerhalb des "weiblichen Schicksals"' (*Cornelia*, 81). However, like Cornelia's education, this writing experiment has a function only at a private level, never becoming literature for a broader public. The last diary-letters are marked by a growing apathy and boredom with the banalities of social interaction, and the diary ends, in the narrator's words, 'mit der Selbstabtötung der Heldin, mit stummer Verneinung' (*Cornelia*, 82).

The narrator explains how the institution of marriage was changing during Cornelia's lifetime. As the individual came to be seen as an autonomous being with certain rights, the old model of marriage as a social contract between families, which had still been in force for Cornelia's parents, was gradually replaced by the notion of marriage as a matter of individual choice. The narrator reads Cornelia's diary as an exploration of this new ideal of marriage based on love. She offers a somewhat simplified version of Prokop's analysis of Richardson's novels as one important source of this ideal for Cornelia:

Das Modell Jäger und Gejagte, Käufer und Gekaufte ist außer Kraft. Das Ideal der Gleichheit taucht auf, die Ehe aus Liebe. Aus Sympathie und Übereinstimmung erwächst Neigung und Leidenschaft—und führt zur Heirat. Ein völlig neuer Gedanke. (*Cornelia*, 83–4)[101]

The narrator suggests that Cornelia analyses both the opportunities for limited power open to women within this new model and the difficult situation of women who, like Cornelia herself, were excluded from this power because they lacked the means necessary to exercise it, that is, physical beauty as defined by their society. Cornelia contrasts her own situation with that of her friend Lisette Runckel: while Cornelia's intellectual accomplishments have no value in this society, Lisette is able to gain what she wants by attracting the right man with her beauty (*Cornelia*, 94). Despite Cornelia's rational rejection of this value system in which external qualities are the key to power, and of the superficiality and rivalry amongst women which it causes, it is a social code which she has internalized, and on which her future remains dependent: 'In diesem Widerspruch zwischen rationaler Abwehr und emotionaler Verinnerlichung [. . .] reibt Cornelia sich auf' (*Cornelia*, 99).

---

[101] See Prokop, 78–9.

The narrator confesses ignorance about the circumstances of Cornelia's early acquaintance with her future husband Schlosser and how her feelings for him related to her ideals. Whether Cornelia married on the basis of love or rational considerations, married life proves to mean increasing isolation for her in Emmendingen society and a reduction of earlier possibilities to one rather restrictive role: 'Endete das phantastische Rollenspiel auf dem Papier des Tagebuches mit der Ablehnung jeglicher Rolle, mit Verweigerung, Rückzug, so legt die Wirklichkeit sie nun auf eine fest: Ehefrau und Mutter' (*Cornelia*, 168). Following Prokop, Damm's narrator interprets the melancholic illness which recurs throughout Cornelia's short married life as the only form of rebellion against her feminine role available to her.

By interpreting Cornelia's life in relation to contemporary ideas about women, Damm generalizes her experience and makes it representative of women's lives at that time. She discusses the definitions of femininity offered by Rousseau, Herder and the *Sturm und Drang* movement, Schiller, and Goethe (*Cornelia*, 219–22). She also relates Cornelia's experience to that of other women at the same time: a parallel is drawn between Cornelia and Anna Maria Mozart, while Damm uses evidence from the lives of Caroline Schlegel-Schelling, Bettine Brentano, Sophie Laroche, Karoline von Günderrode, Mary Lamb, Dorothy Wordsworth, and Alice James to support her arguments about Cornelia (*Cornelia*, 45–7, 77–8, 107–8, 182–5, 195, 215–18, 225, 256):

Nicht ihr allein geht das so. Frauen, die in Kindheit und Jugend durch Väter oder Brüder geistig geweckt wurden, die begabt sind, verlieren die Fähigkeit, sich erfolgreich weiblich anzupassen—einzig lebbare Alternative. (*Cornelia*, 255)

Damm has been criticized for this historical generalization, and for the notion of women as inevitable victims which it entails. Bird argues persuasively that 'the narrator reconstructs Cornelia's fate as a typical one, and unites women under the generalized experience of oppression'.[102] Indeed, Damm's emphasis throughout the text is on Cornelia's suffering as a victim of a patriarchally structured society and, more specifically, of her brother's patronizing and possessive attitude towards her. Cornelia's life is presented as a series of passive responses to other people's demands, and Damm denies the idea that Cornelia

[102] Bird, 120.

could have had any autonomy over, or responsibility for, her 'fate', by suggesting that it followed an inevitable pattern:

Was wird aus ihrem Leben, ihrer Zukunft? Ewig im väterlichen Haus. Entfliehen, wohin? Sie hat keine Alternative. Der Bruder wird sie nicht bieten. Also illusionslose Vernunftehe, Heirat—das ist der einzige Weg, vorgezeichnet, von allen gegangen. (*Cornelia*, 77)

Damm's narrator's identification with Cornelia as a victim—an aspect of the text which the next section will discuss in greater detail—is reminiscent of some of the earliest feminist work on history in the West.[103]

Criticisms of *Cornelia Goethe* are certainly not without justification. Quite apart from her tendency to generalize and victimize Cornelia, Damm's arguments are at times unconvincing. Her analysis of the diary as a female equivalent of *Die Leiden des jungen Werther*, for example, exaggerates its literary qualities and simplifies the relationship between two very different kinds of text (*Cornelia*, 82). However, despite its weaknesses when read from a twenty-first-century western perspective, *Cornelia Goethe* represented an important development in approaches to women's history, both in Damm's personal career, and within the GDR historiographical tradition. The work was very popular when it first appeared in the GDR, and the first impression quickly sold out.[104] It provided a valuable complement to academic work on women's history in the GDR by focusing on the conditions which prevented women from contributing to the public sphere. Damm understands Cornelia's life in terms of certain topics which have been central to studies on women's history in the West, such as the separation between a male public sphere and a female private sphere, women's education, and the institution of marriage and its potentially oppressive consequences for women. She understands gender as the result of socialization and conformity to certain historically determined roles available in a particular society. Her work thus shows an awareness of the need to problematize notions of gender and to use new criteria to investigate the history of women's experience, notably absent from GDR academic historical studies.

Like *Cornelia Goethe*, Feyl's *Idylle mit Professor* contextualizes its subject

---

[103] Cf. Arlette Farge's critique of such work, in 'Praxis und Wirkung der Frauengeschichtsschreibung', in *Geschlecht und Geschichte: Ist eine weibliche Geschichtsschreibung möglich?*, ed. Michelle Perrot, trans. Wolfgang Kaiser (Frankfurt am Main: Fischer, 1989), 29–45 (33).

[104] Schepnitz, 559.

within a historical narrative of roles available to women and philosophical thought about femininity. Born almost four decades before Cornelia Goethe, Victoria Gottsched lived at a time when the early Enlightenment was enabling a minority of women to gain an education, before learned women increasingly became the target of ridicule, as Rousseau's notion of naturally determined femininity became influential.[105] Bovenschen describes the conditions which increased the popular acceptability of women's education for this brief period in the first half of the eighteenth century:

In dieser Interimsphase waren die traditionellen Legitimationen für die Unterwerfung der Frauen unzweifelhaft brüchig geworden, doch die neuen Geschlechtsideologien, die jene Eigenschaften, die die Frauen durch die Anbindung an das ihnen zugewiesene Aufgabenfeld bis zu einem gewissen Grade tatsächlich ausgebildet haben mögen, zum 'naturgewollten' Substrat des weiblichen Charakters verklärte, fungierten noch nicht als Rechtfertigungsmuster der Herrschaft der Männer über die Frauen.[106]

Feyl presents Victoria and Gottsched as representatives of their society's understanding of women, so that the fictional Victoria's experiences demonstrate the interaction between theoretical notions of femininity and women's lived experience.

The central theme of *Idylle mit Professor* is women's education and intellectual activity. The research which Feyl presented in *Der lautlose Aufbruch* thus becomes the basis for a fictional reconstruction of past lives in the novel. In her characterization of Gottsched, Feyl explores the contradictions inherent in early Enlightenment thought on women. Women were included in proclamations of the perfectibility of human beings through reason and education, yet, at the same time, strict limitations were imposed on their participation in intellectual life in practice. Bovenschen analyses this 'nie ganz verdeckte Diskrepanz zwischen der Exklusivität des Gelehrsamkeitsprinzips und den Anforderungen der Realität' with respect to Gottsched.[107] She shows how the 'moralische Wochenschriften', such as Gottsched's *Die vernünftigen Tadlerinnen*, are characterized by 'ein ständiges Schwanken zwischen egalitären Ansätzen einerseits und der Ausrichtung auf häusliche Funktionen andererseits'.[108]

In her introduction to *Der lautlose Aufbruch*, Feyl had presented Gottsched as a progressive thinker with regard to women, showing how his advocacy of education for women contributed to a foundation on

---

[105] See Frevert, *Frauen-Geschichte*, 21.   [106] Bovenschen, 149.
[107] Ibid. 138.   [108] Ibid. 141.

which women's intellectual ambitions could be realized (*Aufbruch*, 8–9). In *Idylle mit Professor*, by contrast, she exposes the ambivalence of his position, as highlighted by Bovenschen. The novel opens with a 'lehrreiche Unterweisung' which Victoria receives from Gottsched immediately after their wedding. Gottsched claims that 'Bildung und Wissen sind für eine Frau unerläßlich', but only because they enable the woman to be an ideal wife, always able to fascinate her husband. Anticipating later, Rousseauean concepts of femininity, he argues that nature has given women a different form of reason from men's, one which, unlike men's, is not suited to penetrate 'zu den Tiefen der Erkenntnis' (*Idylle*, 5). In outlining woman's role as her husband's assistant, Gottsched employs a rhetoric which implies that men's and women's respective roles, although different, are of equal value and equally able to ensure self-fulfilment: 'Arbeitet sie [. . .] an ihrer eigenen Vervollkommnung, ein innerlich reicher, erfüllter Mensch und damit ihm ebenbürtig zu werden, so hat er die ideale Frau gefunden' (*Idylle*, 5–6). He confines women's influence to the domestic sphere, where they are to represent 'das andere' for men, namely 'Ruhe, Freude, Anmut, Harmonie' (*Idylle*, 5). Bovenschen analyses this model of femininity, borrowing Hedwig Dohm's term, 'Ergänzungstheorie':

Die Frauen sollen die Männer 'ergänzen', allerdings nicht in dem Sinne, daß sie ihren Interessen und Lebenszusammenhängen adäquate Inhalte und Formen in das öffentliche Leben einbringen, sondern indem sie das einzelne männliche Individuum stützen, abschirmen, indem sie 'drinnen walten' und bestimmte Sektoren—speziell den des Hauses—so strukturieren, daß der Mann zur materiellen und geistigen Produktion freigesetzt ist.[109]

Feyl makes it clear that Gottsched advocates women's education only within this model. The different significance attached to his and Victoria's work respectively is conveyed by a contrast in their working conditions. While Gottsched's study is ostentatiously furnished to provide every comfort for his work and to endow it with a sense of grandeur and importance, he shows Victoria her room 'mit der Geste eines hochherzigen Gönners':

Ihr ureigenstes Reich wird das Toilettenzimmer sein. Es ist nicht groß, aber für ihre Zwecke wie geschaffen. Hier, wo die Frau des Hauses sich aufhält, liegt für ihn das eigentliche Zentrum einer Wohnung. Hierher zieht es die vertrauteren Freunde der Familie, für die nicht immer gleich der Salon her-

[109] Ibid. 26.

gerichtet werden muß, und hier wird auch er seine Stunden mit ihr verbringen [. . .] (*Idylle*, 14–15)

The lack of a 'room of her own', which Gottsched presents to Victoria here in the guise of a privilege, is coupled with a lack of freedom to use her time for her own ends. Having educated her to a level where she can be of use to him, Gottsched demands her assistance with the menial tasks involved in his work, so that he can devote himself to higher matters. This leaves Victoria with only a few hours in the late afternoon for her own writing.

Gottsched is threatened by Victoria's intellectual independence and tries to maintain at least the appearance and the belief that she is an extension of him, and that her accomplishments are both due to his help and subordinated to his own achievements. When the translation of Bayle's *Historical and Critical Dictionary*, on which they have worked together for some years, appears, Victoria is disappointed to see that her name is not included in the list of contributors. Gottsched responds to her complaint by arguing that 'ihr Name ist in seinem aufgehoben' and that it is proper for him to represent her in public (*Idylle*, 110). At this point she recognizes the discrepancy between Gottsched's public advocacy of women's education and his demand that she remains 'nur sein Beistand und seine Gehilfin' in her intellectual activities (*Idylle*, 109).

By showing how Victoria's work as a writer has serious consequences for her sense of identity as a woman, Feyl makes her individual experience indicative of her society's construction of gender. However, by allowing her fictionalized character to reflect on the roles available to her, Feyl attributes to Victoria a degree of autonomy which Damm's Cornelia does not have. Whereas Damm assumes a straightforward causal relationship between contemporary notions of femininity and Cornelia's subjectivity, Victoria is shown constructing her subjectivity in relation to, and in differentiation from, such notions. The novel makes it clear that Victoria's society defines femininity in physical terms and in opposition to intellectual activity. Victoria's failure to produce a child induces in her the 'Gefühl, als Frau nur etwas Halbes, Hüllenhaftes zu bleiben' (*Idylle*, 82). Furthermore, this failure is attributed by others to her devotion to learning and writing. Gottsched cruelly accuses her of depriving him of the pleasures of fatherhood:

Das größte Glück auf Erden, das Vaterglück, geht an ihm vorbei und warum?

Weil er eine Frau hat, die ehrgeizig und auf Ruhm erpicht ist und sich Tag und Nacht in die Knechtschaft des Wortes begibt, statt sich mehr den Freuden des Leibes zu widmen. (*Idylle*, 153)

The polar relationship between intellectual activity and sensuality implied here is central to the social construction of femininity in relation to which Victoria defines her own sense of identity. She contrasts two forms of female being, comparing her own life as a 'gelehrtes Geschöpf' to that of a 'schönes Sinnenwesen' (*Idylle*, 84–5). Her marriage to Gottsched allows her to exercise her intellectual powers, but deprives her of any sense of value in her existence as a physical being. During the course of the novel she oscillates between gratitude for her unusual opportunities and disappointment at not being able to fulfil both her intellectual and her physical needs.

Like Damm's *Cornelia Goethe*, Feyl's work is an important complement to the GDR historiographical tradition. In focusing on the problems facing a bourgeois eighteenth-century woman privileged enough to receive a thorough education and attain significant scholarly achievements, *Idylle mit Professor* explores topics in women's history which were neglected by GDR historiography in its prioritization of the working class and non-intellectual work. Feyl also demonstrates a more sophisticated and differentiated approach to women's identities than many GDR historians. Instead of treating the term 'women' as an unproblematic universal category and regarding theories about women as simple reflections of women's experienced reality, she shows how theoretical models relate to lived experience, and how individual gender identity is dependent on, though not identical to, socially constructed notions of 'femininity' and 'masculinity'. She explores how the gender roles prevailing in Victoria's society create contradictions between her intellectual and physical needs, rather than treating 'women's needs' as a self-explanatory term reducible ultimately to economic requirements.

Like Damm, Feyl uses an individual life-story to demonstrate the oppressive conditions for women in eighteenth-century Germany. However, she does not present Victoria as a passive victim of her circumstances. Feyl fictionalizes the historical Louise Gottsched in order to show an inner development towards autonomy for which there is little historical evidence. Unlike *Cornelia Goethe*, *Idylle mit Professor* does not incorporate its author's processes of research into the text. However, the novel demonstrates Feyl's thorough engagement with both historical evidence and previous accounts of Louise

Gottsched's life. Feyl offers a similar interpretation of the Gottscheds' marriage to that of Veronica Richel in her study, *Louise Gottsched: A Reconsideration*. Richel, basing her account on Louise Gottsched's letters, writes of her sadness at not having children, her dislike of ostentation in contrast with her husband, her view that it is unfeminine to appear learned, the unhappiness of her married life, her friendship with Dorothea Henriette von Runckel, the intensification of her sufferings during the Seven Years' War, and her poor health towards the end of her life.[110] All of these feature in Feyl's novel. Richel ends her biographical account with the ironic contrast between Gottsched's proclaimed grief for his wife in his biographical sketch of her, and his remarriage, shortly afterwards, to a much younger woman. Feyl concludes her novel on the same ironic note, with the curt sentence, 'Die Trauer vergeht, der Kummer weicht, und er heiratet die neunzehnjährige Susanna Katharina Neueneß' (*Idylle*, 245).

The most significant difference between Richel's factual presentation of Louise Gottsched and Feyl's characterization of Victoria is that the fictional Victoria responds to the conditions of her life with a more modern and a more feminist consciousness than her historical counterpart. Richel stresses Louise Gottsched's modesty and shows how she perceived her academic lifestyle as an exceptional one which was not to be recommended to other women. She disapproved of women being awarded doctorates and believed strongly in the limitations of women's intellects.

Louise Gottsched has generally been understood to be a woman who shared her husband's views and translated his dramatic theories into literary practice.[111] Feyl presents a considerable challenge to such understandings of Louise Gottsched. The novel charts Victoria's gradual inner emancipation from her husband's demands, as she replaces his ideals and the desire to please him with her own ideals and criteria of success. Feyl's characterization of Victoria can be understood in two ways. Firstly, she is presenting Victoria's private thoughts, feelings, and opinions, for which there is no historical evidence. Within the novel Feyl shows how Victoria is obliged to display devotion and loyalty to her husband in public, and how she has to be cautious about writing openly to Dorothea Runckel, knowing that their letters are intercepted not only by Gottsched, but by Prussian soldiers during the Seven Years' War (*Idylle*, 224, 227). Feyl is thus recon-

---

[110] Richel, 16–19.
[111] See, for example, Bovenschen, 136–7. For an alternative interpretation, see Richel, 7.

structing a possible version of aspects of Victoria's experience which would have left no traces. Secondly, Feyl's speculative reconstruction of Victoria's personality and her attitude to the conditions of her life displays a clear feminist motivation which could be said to override any concern for a historically accurate portrayal.

Both these elements are evident in Feyl's use of her main source, Dorothea Runckel's collection of Louise Gottsched's letters. Many of the central events in the novel have a factual basis recorded in the letters.[112] Feyl frequently bases incidents in the novel on details in the letters, reading between the lines and imaginatively complementing the documentary evidence to reconstruct stories and opinions which could not have been included in the letters.[113] Feyl's portrayal of Gottsched as a selfish and insecure man with an inflexible faith in order based on rational rules and a greed for power both over his wife and in the public sphere certainly has a basis in Louise Gottsched's depiction of him.[114] The development in Victoria's attitude towards Gottsched and her marriage which structures *Idylle mit Professor* also corresponds quite closely to a development evident in Louise Gottsched's letters. While Feyl bases her portrayal of Victoria's personal development from willing submissiveness to unhappiness and disillusion on historical evidence, she couples this with a political development for which there is less evidence. In the novel, Victoria's discontent with her own situation induces in her a consciousness of the injustice of the limitations generally imposed on women's lives. She expresses sympathy for 'jene Frauen, die den Inhalt ihres Lebens einzig und allein in ihrem Gemahl sehen und das Glück, ihm dienen zu dürfen und die Stunden zu versüßen, als ihre ureigenste Bestimmung betrachten', particularly since this role requires qualities which fade later in a woman's life. For this reason Victoria advocates women's access to education and angrily criticizes her society:

Nur die Landestöchter dürfen nicht zuviel lernen, keine Universität besuchen, keine akademische Ausbildung bekommen, um nicht zu tief den Dingen auf den Grund zu gehen und ihre sinnlichen Talente als höchste Erfüllung ihres Daseins etwa in Frage zu stellen. Denkt Victoria an dieses schreiende Unrecht, tröstet sie nicht einmal die Gewißheit, daß wenigstens sie zu den Ausnahmen gehört, die damit gebrochen haben. (*Idylle*, 119)

---

[112] *Briefe der Frau Louise Adelgunde Viktorie Gottsched geborene Kulmus*, ed. Dorothee Henriette von Runckel, 3 vols. (Dresden: Harpeter, 1771).

[113] Compare, for example, ibid. i. 349 and *Idylle mit Professor*, 60–3.

[114] See, for example, *Briefe der Frau Louise Adelgunde Viktorie Gottsched geborene Kulmus*, ed. von Runckel, ii. 134, 153, 167.

The thoughts which the narrator attributes to Victoria by using *erlebte Rede* represent a late twentieth-century interpretation of Louise Gottsched's life. Feyl thus incorporates a modern perspective on history into her novel, not by allowing her narrator to reflect explicitly on the relationship between the past and the present, but by using a modern narrative voice to articulate a response to the experiences of a woman in the eighteenth century. Rather like Wolf's *Kein Ort. Nirgends, Idylle mit Professor* combines historical evidence with fictional elements in order to present an encounter between historical figures' experience and a modern narratorial perspective. However, whereas Wolf highlights parallels between past and present but maintains a sense of historical distance, Feyl projects modern views on to a historical character.

The Relationship between Past and Present

Both *Cornelia Goethe* and *Idylle mit Professor* differ from GDR historiography in relating individual lives to a history of gender notions and female oppression, rather than to a narrative of social progress. This is not the only way in which they present a challenge to the orthodox discourse. As earlier sections of this study have shown, the primary function of GDR historiography was to use the past to legitimize the state in the present. In these texts, however, Damm and Feyl relate past lives to the present in such a way as to criticize the achievements of 'real existierender Sozialismus'.

Because both *Cornelia Goethe* and *Idylle mit Professor* focus on women who lived prior to the French Revolution, political parallels between a post-revolutionary era and the GDR, of the kind central to *Kein Ort. Nirgends* and the accompanying essays, as well as 'Begegnung mit Caroline', are absent from these works. However, the two later works share a broad plot structure with these earlier works, determined by a similar development from hopes and ideals to disappointment and discontent. This process of disillusionment is now expressed through gender relations in the private sphere. Cornelia and Victoria suffer disappointment not in their revolutionary social ideals, but in their hopes of egalitarian and fulfilling relationships with men, an idea already prominent in 'Der Schatten eines Traumes'.[115] A narrative of an indi-

---

[115] I explore this idea in relation to Damm's *Cornelia Goethe* and Johanna Hoffmann's *Charlotte von Stein* in 'Biographical Fiction by GDR Women Writers: Reassessing the Cultural Heritage', in *Travellers in Time and Space: The German Historical Novel*, ed. Osman Durrani and Julian Preece, ABNG, 51 (Amsterdam and Atlanta: Rodopi, 2001), 155–65.

vidual woman's disillusionment provides the basis also for novels published by both Damm and Feyl after 1989. Damm's *Ich bin nicht Ottilie* and Feyl's *Ausharren im Paradies*, however, tell the life-stories of GDR women of the authors' own generation. Gender relations continue to be a prominent theme, but the shift from optimism to disillusion is presented here also as a political development in response to the consolidation and stagnation of 'real existierender Sozialismus'. The recurrence of this basic plot structure, and the close relationship established in the post-1989 novels between the protagonists' personal disillusionment and the course of GDR history, support a reading of the earlier texts which is sensitive to the ways Damm and Feyl use historical material to explore issues pertaining to the GDR present as well.

Cornelia Goethe relates the past to the present more explicitly than *Idylle mit Professor* because of Damm's prominent, reflecting narrator. As in 'Begegnung mit Caroline', a first-person voice serves to create a dialogue between a past life and the present. Whereas in the earlier essay history was a teleological progression, even if some ideals remained unrealized in the present, in the later work the basis of the dialogue is an identity between past and present. Although the text as a whole offers a historically specific study of eighteenth-century German society, the narrator's reflections emphasize an underlying continuity between Cornelia's lifetime and the present. She associates Cornelia's 'fortwährende Fremdbestimmung' with a quotation from Ingeborg Bachmann's *Der Fall Franza*, in order to evoke a sense of a universal female experience of oppression:

'Er hat mir meine Güter genommen. Mein Lachen, meine Zärtlichkeit, mein Freuenkönnen, mein Mitleiden, Helfenkönnen, meine Animalität, mein Strahlen, er hat jedes einzelne Aufkommen von all dem ausgetreten, bis es nicht mehr aufgekommen ist. Aber warum tut das jemand, das versteh ich nicht . . .' Ingeborg Bachmann schreibt das in 'Der Fall Franza'. Cornelias Schicksal, immer wieder durchlebt, an keine Zeit und Umwelt gebunden. (*Cornelia*, 11)

The act of quoting Bachmann signals Damm's new critical stance towards the GDR. In 'Begegnung mit Caroline' she associated her protagonist with Clara Zetkin in order to position her within the orthodox discourse; here, her frame of reference has become western feminism. Furthermore, the argument that all historical eras, including the present, have in common a patriarchal structure which allows men to oppress women, is a clear indictment of the GDR with its claim to have achieved gender equality.

Damm's narrator's emphasis on the parallels between the past and the present—'der Abstand der Jahrhunderte und die Nähe zum Jetzt, zu dem, was ich bin, die andere neben mir ist' (*Cornelia*, 255)—also suggests that the work, like much historical fiction of the GDR, is concerned not with the past for its own sake, but with the potential of historical material to shed light on the present. There are a number of ways in which both *Cornelia Goethe* and *Idylle mit Professor* can be read allegorically as models of developments in the GDR.

Firstly, a very general parallel can be seen between the situation of women in the eighteenth century and that of GDR citizens. As Emmerich puts it, the SED conceived of the GDR reading public as 'ein durchaus noch unmündiges, gleichsam dauerhaft minderjähriges'.[116] The term 'unmündig', frequently used as a metaphor to describe the conditions of life for GDR citizens, has been used similarly to describe women's lives in history.[117] Like Wolf, both Damm and Feyl highlight aspects of eighteenth-century women's lives which could apply equally to life in the GDR. Cornelia Goethe and Victoria Gottsched are shown to live within narrow boundaries. For them, as for GDR citizens, travel is impossible, and reading and writing take on an enhanced significance as substitutes for experiencing the world (*Cornelia*, 46; *Idylle*, 122).

In both works, the relationship between men and women can be read as a critique of the GDR authorities. Cornelia and Victoria are shown to be subject to an authoritarian form of male pedagogy—represented by Cornelia's father and brother, and by Gottsched—which bears striking parallels to the SED's exercising of power, particularly in the cultural sphere. Both Goethe and Gottsched make aesthetic prescriptions which Cornelia and Victoria are obliged to follow. In his early letters to his sister, Goethe attempts to mould her to his will by instructing her on what to read and how to write (*Cornelia*, 59–62). Damm's work has been criticized for its focus on Goethe: Bird argues that 'the narrator allows Goethe to dominate the text, reduces the relationship [between him and Cornelia] to a simplistic active/ passive duality, and thereby deprives Cornelia of what little autonomy or responsibility she may have had'.[118] This may be a valid criticism,

---

[116] Emmerich, *Kleine Literaturgeschichte*, 46.
[117] See, for example, Barbara Becker-Cantarino, *Der lange Weg zur Mündigkeit: Frauen und Literatur in Deutschland von 1500 bis 1800* (Stuttgart: Metzler, 1987).   [118] Bird, 129.

but Bird does not take into account the particular values attached to Goethe in the GDR and the consequent significance of presenting him negatively in this context. For the SED, Goethe was not only a dominant figure in cultural history as in the West (Bird relates Damm's text to this context), but an embodiment of protosocialist values, whose ideals had allegedly been realized by the socialist state, and whose aesthetic tastes and judgements were taken as a basis for GDR cultural policy. Damm's criticisms of Goethe can thus, like those voiced by Günter Kunert and Günter de Bruyn in the 1970s, be read as an indirect comment on the values underlying the GDR.[119] This reading is supported by Damm's comments in 'Unruhe', her speech on accepting the Lion Feuchtwanger Prize in 1987, for her work on another figure who lived in Goethe's shadow, Lenz. She explains her interest in Lenz by drawing parallels with her own generation: 'Die Erfahrung meiner Generation, nicht mit den Eigenschaften gebraucht zu werden, die uns wichtig waren, unsere Kräfte nicht gefordert zu sehen. [. . .] Wir Unmündige, die von Vorschriften lebten.'[120] In *Cornelia Goethe*, on which Damm was working when she gave the speech, these ideas are manifested in gender relations.

Gottsched did not have such a high status in official GDR discourse, but a number of parallels with GDR cultural policy are prominent in Feyl's presentation of him. If Victoria shares the 'Unmündigkeit' of GDR citizens, Gottsched takes on the role which the SED attributed to authors, aiming to become an 'Erzieher der Nation' (*Idylle*, 9).[121] Like the SED, he sees literature as a didactic means with a political function. He claims that 'Poesie soll erziehen und bilden' and aims to create a national identity by directing the development of the German language and literature (*Idylle*, 23–4). He regards literature as an 'erlernbare Wissenschaft' and believes that good literature can be created by following certain rules and using prescribed literary forms (*Idylle*, 42). These ideas bear a clear similarity to the theory of socialist realism and the policies of the Bitterfeld Conferences. Like Goethe in Damm's text, Feyl's Gottsched tries to keep Victoria in the role of his pupil and is reluctant to grant her the capacity for independent thought and speech associated with adulthood (*Idylle*, 114). He allows her to read only literature of which he approves, and he reads her mail before giving it to her (*Idylle*, 67, 158).

[119] Cf. Günter Kunert, 'Pamphlet für K.', *SF* 27 (1975), 5, 1091–4; Günter de Bruyn, *Das Leben des Jean Paul Friedrich Richter: Eine Biographie* (Halle: Mitteldeutscher Verlag, 1975).
[120] Sigrid Damm, 'Unruhe: Anläßlich der Verleihung des Lion-Feuchtwanger-Preises 1987', *SF* 40 (1988), 1, 244–8 (247).   [121] Cf. Emmerich, *Kleine Literaturgeschichte*, 46.

It is not only his views on literature which associate Feyl's Gottsched with the GDR authorities. The discrepancy between his proclaimed ideal of education for women and his own practice with regard to Victoria is comparable to the increasing gap between the way GDR socialism was officially presented and the way it was popularly experienced. Likewise, the contradiction for Victoria between private disagreement with Gottsched and the obligation to support his views in public resembles the conditions of life for many in the GDR.

An interesting aspect of *Idylle mit Professor* is its presentation of Prussia.[122] Gottsched fled his native Königsberg in order to avoid being conscripted into the Prussian army, and because of Frederick Wilhelm I's contempt for intellectuals (*Idylle*, 10–12). However, when the Seven Years' War breaks out and Frederick II visits Leipzig, Gottsched changes his attitude. Scorning Victoria's abhorrence at the misery caused by the Prussians' invasion, he boasts of his Prussian roots and expresses his admiration for the Prussian values of order and discipline (*Idylle*, 204–9). When he accepts gifts from both Frederick and Maria Theresa, Victoria is horrified at his opportunism (*Idylle*, 213). Feyl is clearly voicing a veiled judgement of GDR heritage policy, suggesting that the sudden re-evaluation of Prussian history and the restoration of Frederick the Great's statue to Unter den Linden in 1980 merely revealed the hollowness of the values on which the official understanding of history was ostensibly based.[123]

In their late 1980s texts both Damm and Feyl significantly expand the boundaries of the GDR discourse on history, which their texts at the beginning of the decade had been careful not to transgress. By hinting at parallels between individual lives in the eighteenth century and the course of GDR history, *Cornelia Goethe* and *Idylle mit Professor* criticize the idea that the socialist German state represented the culmination of progressive traditions in history. They share with Wolf's works of the late 1970s both this critique of history as progress and an interest in women's experience. However, whereas Wolf's three texts use a variety of techniques to highlight the relevance of the historical material for the present, the relationship between past and present remains sketchy and implicit in Damm's and Feyl's works. This might be because comparatively little-known writers could voice criticisms of the regime only through even more indirect methods than a prominent writer like Wolf, an argument which seems convincing in light of

---

[122] Cf. Reid, *Writing Without Taboos*, 188–9.
[123] See ibid. 176–7.

the extensive and overt criticisms of the GDR contained in Damm's and Feyl's post-1989 novels. Working within a tradition of GDR writers' engagement with historical figures which was well established by the late 1980s, Damm and Feyl could undoubtedly be confident that readers familiar with works like Wolf's essays on Günderrode and Bettine would be receptive to hidden references to present conditions. The relationship between past and present is in any case far less central to Damm's and Feyl's works than to Wolf's. Whereas Wolf aimed primarily to make the past productive for the present, Damm and Feyl display a greater interest in women's history for its own sake. While all three authors focus on female experience and thus construct new narratives of history, the nature of these narratives differs markedly. Wolf rewrites the history of modern industrialized society as a negative development, in which gender relations play a vital role, and female experience is privileged as the source of redemptive alternative values. If this bears some resemblance to western studies of gender history, in their attempt to analyse how gender operates historically, then Damm and Feyl adopt an approach very similar to the 'herstory' project pursued by western feminist historians in the 1970s and early 1980s. They contextualize their female subjects within a narrative of women's experience and conditions of life.

While Wolf offers a more detailed cultural critique of the past two centuries than Damm and Feyl, a correlative of this critique is that the socialist discourse about history remains a prominent reference point of her texts. Her model of history maintains central tenets of Marxism, notably the key roles attributed to the industrial revolution and the division of labour, as well as the conviction that ideals expressed in the past must be made productive in the present, in order to enable future progress. Although Damm and Feyl make considerable concessions to GDR historical discourse in their non-fictional essays, in their more fictional works of the late 1980s they construct new narratives of history with no reference to orthodox Marxist ideas. This may be indicative of a general pessimism and lack of identification with socialism by the late 1980s, when the GDR seemed to have stagnated. It may also point to generational differences.[124] The striking ideological contrast between Damm's and Feyl's non-fictional texts and their later full-length imaginative works suggests that their adherence to state discourses in the former was to a large degree a requirement of the genres in which they were working. When they gained positions of greater

[124] Damm and Feyl were born in 1940 and 1944 respectively.

freedom as freelance writers of fiction, they found it much easier to dismiss socialist ideology in its entirety than an older writer like Wolf.

BRIGITTE STRUZYK

Struzyk had produced two volumes of poetry before publishing her first prose work in 1988. *Caroline unterm Freiheitsbaum* shares Wolf's and Damm's interest in a woman who lived through the aftermath of the French Revolution, Caroline Schlegel-Schelling. However, Struzyk's text differs considerably from most of the other works I have discussed. In stark contrast to Damm's 'Begegnung mit Caroline', *Caroline unterm Freiheitsbaum* does not provide the reader with an informative introduction to either Caroline's life or her times, but rather, like Wolf's *Kein Ort. Nirgends*, presupposes familiarity with these. However, whereas Wolf's work covers only a few hours in its protagonists' lives, Struzyk's follows Caroline from childhood to the final years of her life.

A Challenge to Historical and Biographical Narratives

Caroline Schlegel-Schelling's extraordinary life offers plentiful material for those who wish to interpret her significance within the context of either political or literary history. In her study of Caroline's contribution to German literature, Caroline Knowles shows how previous biographers have used her life as an example of broader movements in history and have displayed 'the tendency to classify and assess her as either a "Romantic woman", an emancipated woman, a product of the Enlightenment, a domestic member of the circle at Jena or an intellectual'.[125] Damm's account of her life is typical of such biographies in its focus on Caroline's significance within a history of revolutionary political and cultural movements.

Struyzk's *Caroline unterm Freiheitsbaum* is remarkable because Caroline's life is not explicitly placed within such a narrative, whether the GDR historical narrative of revolutionary progression, as in Damm's essay, or a history of the conditions determining women's lives, as in *Cornelia Goethe* and *Idylle mit Professor*.[126] Both formal and thematic fea-

---

[125] Caroline Knowles, 'Caroline Michaelis-Böhmer-Schlegel-Schelling's (1763–1809) Contribution to German Literature' (unpublished M.Litt. thesis, University of Oxford, 1992), 7.

[126] Indeed, Struzyk has expressed suspicion of gendered narratives of history which

tures of Struzyk's work ensure that Caroline's life is not contextualized within a narrative of this kind. The narrator also avoids presenting a coherent and causal narrative of Caroline's life itself. The major events in Caroline's life, whether in the public or in the private sphere, form the background of Struzyk's presentation, rather than its focus. A brief factual account of Caroline's life is provided by Franz Muncker's 1890 contribution to the *Allgemeine Deutsche Biographie*, which is reproduced on the inside covers of the book. Struzyk treats the events outlined there as a given context, within which she focuses on moments in Caroline's everyday life. The work consists of a series of scenes which have a dramatic quality, resulting from a lack of introduction, explanation, and comment from the narrator, as well as from the consistent use of the present tense. Characterization is achieved through the presentation of dialogue and actions, with comparatively little explanation of thoughts or motivations. The episodes presented are neither causally related nor explicitly interpreted by the narrator. In order to understand what is happening in each chapter, the reader has to construct a narrative to fill in the unexplained gaps between episodes. After the chapter 'Entbindung' has ended with Böhmer's death, for example, the next chapter, 'Die bunten Teppiche verblassen', opens with a scene from which the reader must deduce that Caroline is now living with her parents again:

'Komm, Väterchen, wir sehen Bücher an!'
    Der alte Michaelis schaut stumm aus dem Fenster. Die Tochter zupft an seinem Ärmel. (*Caroline*, 39)

Struzyk's text presents a challenge to the conventional—in Hayden White's terminology, 'narrativizing'—modes of storytelling in both historiography and fiction.[127] However, throughout most of the work she does not use a prominent, reflecting narrator, such as Wolf's in *Nachdenken über Christa T.* or Damm's in *Cornelia Goethe*, to produce a biographical discourse which openly reflects on its own perspective and its inevitable exclusions. Rather, she shows a version of historical reality which is a self-conscious textual construction, and which neither claims completeness nor imposes a coherent narrative on reality to endow it with a meaningful plot. She presents a series of episodes which are open-ended, incomplete, and discontinuous. The act of link-

privilege women as a positive 'other' to men's aggression. Christa Schuenke, 'Viel verlangen: Gespräch mit Brigitte Struzyk', *Temperamente*, 1986, 4, 79–82 (79).
    [127] Cf. White, 2.

ing these episodes to form a continuous narrative with plot features is performed not within the text, but by the reader in attempting to make sense of the work. It is in her selection of episodes from Caroline's life, rather than in any explicit comment, that the narrator conveys her own interpretation of her. The manifest incompleteness of the episodes included in the text serves to highlight this process of selection.

The high degree of freedom the work allows the reader in interpreting the material presented is confirmed by the markedly different readings offered by Bird and Meyer. Bird presents a thorough and convincing analysis of the narrative form and technique of the work, and focuses on its thematization of democratic ideals and on parallels between Struzyk's treatment of gender and Kristeva's model.[128] She concludes that the work is 'successful and enjoyable' in many respects, applauding a narrative technique which signals the constructed nature of the presentation. Her chief criticism is that, read in relation to Kristeva's construction of gender, the work does not seem to allow for the possibility of change in gender relations. Meyer, by contrast, is extremely critical of the text, arguing that it serves to reinforce conventional gender roles. She pays no attention to the open narrative technique, attempting instead to fix the meaning of the text 'in der spezifischen Erzählperspektive und Blicklenkung auf die so unterschiedenen Figuren'.[129]

The characterization of Therese Forster is central to both Bird's and Meyer's analyses. Meyer reduces Struzyk's presentation of the relationship between Caroline and Therese to a simple opposition between a positively valued notion of traditional, domestic femininity and a negative form of transgressive femininity.[130] While Bird acknowledges that Struzyk's narrator identifies with Caroline and that Therese is presented at times negatively, she shows that the characterization of the two women is actually more differentiated.[131] The open narrative form of the work allows Bird to present a reading of Therese as a potentially positive embodiment of resistance to the dominant social order from a position of marginality.

Bird is right to take issue with readings of the text which impose clear-cut judgements on the characters.[132] Struzyk's characterization is striking for its non-judgemental quality. Her text rejects simple black-

---

[128] Bird, 87–113.   [129] Meyer, 49.   [130] Ibid. 51–2.   [131] Bird, 107–10.
[132] Besides Meyer, Matthias Oehme has criticized Struzyk's portrayal of Therese Forster and Dorothea Veit. See Oehme, 151; Bird, 106–8.

and-white notions of character, characteristic of the orthodox GDR approach to historical figures and evident to a certain extent, in a new feminist form, in Damm's and Feyl's texts. Rather than constructing individual personalities as intrinsic and independent entities which can be subjected to moral or political assessment, her focus is on human relationships and behaviour. All of the relationships presented in the work undergo shifts over the course of time, and when hostility arises it is usually due to a complex mixture of factors which frustrates, and renders inappropriate, attempts to apportion blame. When characters are presented negatively, explanations for their behaviour are usually offered by other characters. Caroline finds her brother Fritz impossible to live with, but attributes his pedantic intolerance to his traumatic experiences in the American War of Independence (*Caroline*, 45). Schelling explains Huber's attack on the *Athenäum* in similarly psychological terms: 'Da ist ein Mann bemüht, sich radikal von der Vergangenheit zu trennen' (*Caroline*, 121). Caroline herself is at times motivated by jealousy and thoughtlessness (*Caroline*, 26, 130), while Struzyk's Georg Forster is far from the hero of Damm's 'Begegnung mit Caroline'. Unable to recognize the connections between the political and the personal, he is reduced to sympathy-seeking misery by Therese's adultery, though again the narrator refrains from explicit judgement, allowing for a range of reader responses (*Caroline*, 69, 51). Struzyk's work can be read as a rejection of the tendencies of some historical discourses, whether GDR socialist or feminist, to reduce personalities to heroes and villains. She highlights instead the contradictions within characters, the dependency of individual behaviour on circumstances and the behaviour of others, and the complexities of human relationships.

Bird shows how Struzyk's treatment of gender is central to the text, despite the absence of any feminist intention.[133] She discusses how the work reveals 'the conditioned roles of male and female with the varying expectations and opportunities which were attached', and how 'the ubiquitous limitations imposed upon women are strongly felt'. It is true that certain incidents in the text demonstrate such gender issues. As a child, Caroline finds her father's world of interesting guests exciting, and rejects her mother's domestic sphere: 'Sie will ins Vaterland. Dort riecht es besser. Von der neuen Schwester, vom Wochenbett der Mutter hat sie schon die Nase voll' (*Caroline*, 9). As Bird comments, Caroline is under pressure as a young woman to control her sexuality

[133] Bird, 102–3.

and direct it towards marriage: she protects her virginity from both the student living in her father's house and Meyer (*Caroline*, 12, 24). When she and Goethe discuss the idea of bathing naked in the River Ilm, his freedom to act is contrasted with her ability, as a woman, only to desire (*Caroline*, 104). I would argue, however, that Struzyk's interest in the gender roles prevalent during Caroline's lifetime is surprisingly marginal to the text. These examples of the different expectations of men and women are small textual details which convey neither a historically specific nor a comprehensive picture of gender construction. The pressure to remain a virgin until marriage, and restrictions on certain activities, such as bathing naked in public, were conditions of women's lives until relatively recently.

In her presentation of Caroline, Struzyk minimalizes the sense that her experiences and behaviour were remarkable within her historical context. Caroline is comparable to Louise Gottsched in that she received an education far superior to that generally granted to girls in the eighteenth century.[134] However, whereas Feyl makes women's education a central theme of her work and explores the consequences an education had for one particular woman, in Struzyk's text the only hint that Caroline's education was unusual consists in her mother's attitude to her early love of books such as *Geschichte der entarteten Menschheit*: 'Zu früher und zu häufiger Genuß von Lesemitteln, die den Horizont kindlicher Begriffe überschreiten, wirkt sich auf Seele und Gesicht aus. Der Teint muß leiden' (*Caroline*, 13). Similarly, Struzyk does not focus on conflicts between Caroline's desire for independence and self-determination, and social expectations of her, for which there is historical evidence. When she refused to remarry after her first husband's death, for example, the reactions from friends such as Friedrich Wilhelm Gotter indicate the extent to which her behaviour differed from the role women were expected to play in her society.[135] In Struzyk's presentation, Caroline's brother hints that she should remarry, with the words 'du bekommst sehr viele Briefe. Ist da vielleicht der Mann fürs Leben drunter?' (*Caroline*, 45). This is clearly a modernization of the situation, which detracts from the historically specific expectations imposed on the real Caroline. Whereas Feyl modernized Victoria's consciousness in order to highlight the gender inequalities of her age, Struzyk's modernization has the opposite effect.

At other points in the text, contemporary expectations of women can be seen to have an impact on Caroline, but there is no overt

---

[134] See Knowles, 13–14.   [135] See Damm, 'Begegnung mit Caroline', 18.

thematization of these expectations. Instead, Struzyk assumes the reader's familiarity with the historical conditions of Caroline's life. When she is engaged to Böhmer, for example, there is no explanation of, or reflection on, marriage as a social pact organized by families, such as that provided by Damm in *Cornelia Goethe* (*Cornelia*, 17, 83–4). Instead, Caroline's disappointment, anger, and jealousy of Therese are portrayed: 'Die kriegt den Forster, und ich muß Böhmer nehmen!' (*Caroline*, 26).

Struzyk's presentation of the public and private spheres, too, prevents Caroline's life from being interpreted as a contribution to any broader narrative of political or literary history. Struzyk reverses the respective degrees of importance conventionally attributed to these spheres: instead of contextualizing an individual life by relating it to events and figures in the public arena, she presents these only in so far as they affect the individual's everyday life. This means that traditional criteria of 'historical significance' are replaced by far more personal criteria, determined by an individual's life lived primarily in the private sphere. A focus on historical events and movements from the perspective of an individual life with its own developments at a personal level is humorously suggested by the section entitled 'Das Zeitalter der Aufklärung', in which a student lodging in Caroline's father's house introduces her to the facts of life (*Caroline*, 11–12). Throughout the work, events traditionally regarded as historically significant are presented from an unexpected personal perspective, usually in a domestic setting. A conversation between Caroline and Georg Forster in March 1793 shifts from the latest political developments in Mainz to Caroline's passionate love affair with the Frenchman Dubois-Crancé (*Caroline*, 79). Goethe visits Caroline and they share tea and cake, then he has to return, realizing that he has left a package containing the completed manuscript of *Wilhelm Meister* on the chair: ' "Mein Wilhelm Meister! Von mir aus kann er liegenbleiben. Das ist der wahre Schluß, Madame. Was könnte meinem Helden Besseres passieren, als daß Sie auf ihm sitzen?" ' (*Caroline*, 105).

Struzyk's presentation of the relationship between the public and private spheres forms an interesting comparison to Damm's and Feyl's treatment of it in their works of the late 1980s. Both the latter focus on the gendered polarity constructed between the public and private spheres. By presenting Cornelia's and Victoria's lives in the private sphere, they reveal a history of women's experience which highlights the difficulties encountered by women attempting to participate in public life. Struzyk, in contrast, does not thematize this dichotomy of public and private. Like Damm and Feyl, she privileges the private in her presentation, but the public sphere is presented not as a separate realm which is difficult for women to enter, but as a part of private life, which is of equal importance to, and inextricably interconnected with, more personal aspects of life.[136]

Bird shows how Struzyk's 'dissolution of the strict dichotomy between public and private is one which is closely allied to feminist concerns'.[137] The feminist historians Abrams and Harvey discuss the nature of this dichotomy as a gendered construct and show how, 'for feminist theorists and historians [. . .] undertaking a critique of the public/private dichotomy has been an important way of exploring how different spheres of action for men and for women have been defined, enforced and challenged in the past and present'.[138] It is in enacting such a critique, rather than in any overt reflection on women's position in a historical society, that *Caroline unterm Freiheitsbaum* represents a feminist approach to history. Struzyk focuses on a number of aspects of life conventionally neglected by historical discourses, in order to undermine gendered dichotomies which attribute greater value to men's experience than to women's. Presenting political events and intellectual debates within the context of domestic scenes is one way this is achieved. Women's work, often of a practical nature, is as much the focus of the work's attention as events which have entered the history books. In the midst of political turmoil in Mainz, Caroline is shown attending to practical household chores in preparation for a visit from Goethe: 'Die Fenster müssen geputzt werden, auch wenn sich scheinbar alles ändert' (*Caroline*, 58).

Struzyk also challenges the traditional dichotomy between the intellectual and the physical, whereby the former is valued above the latter. Events in Caroline's life are presented in physical and practical terms where conventional historiography would use abstractions which detract from these elements of experience. The work treats sexuality, for example, as an undeniably physical phenomenon: Caroline's sex education consists in watching a man masturbating, and her attraction to Meyer is conveyed through descriptions of physical experience (*Caroline*, 11–12, 23–4). Her first pregnancy is signalled by physical symptoms: 'Beim Abwasch wird ihr übel. Sonderbar. Und in der Brust

---

[136] Cf. Bird's discussion of the relationship between politics and the erotic in the text. Bird, 92–6.

[137] Ibid. 110.   [138] Abrams and Harvey, 17.

ein Ziehen. Natürlich!' (*Caroline*, 33). When Böhmer dies, the practical aspects of the incident are highlighted: 'Doch Böhmer wacht nicht wieder auf. Sie ist ganz starr vor Schreck. Was macht man denn mit einer Leiche? Wo lernt man das im Leben? Auf jeden Fall die Augen zu' (*Caroline*, 38). While imprisoned at Königstein, Caroline is shown treating calluses on her feet; at Bad Bocklet just before Auguste's death, she and Caroline joke about constipation; when Caroline is distressed, her digestive problems reflect her anxiety (*Caroline*, 84, 134, 139–40).

The body, its functions, and its ailments are thus not excluded from the text. The course and conditions of history find expression in Caroline's bodily experience. Recent work by feminist historians has recognized the importance of examining conceptions of the body and bodily experience in order to understand how gender is constructed historically.[139] However, rather than highlighting the historical 'instability of notions of corporeal reality', Struzyk's text is curiously ambivalent in its approach to the body and history.[140] While physical ailments and even death are often presented as the result of historical and social conditions—Böhmer dies as an indirect consequence of laws which allow miners to be exposed to poisonous substances (*Caroline*, 37)—at the same time the focus on physical experiences detracts from the historical context of Caroline's life. Her experiences of sexuality, pregnancy, physical ailments, and death have an aura of timelessness, and help to underline common elements between Caroline's life and modern women's lives.

While Struzyk's text challenges conventional notions of what constitutes 'history' by privileging the private sphere and physical experience, the author's refusal throughout the main part of the text explicitly to contextualize Caroline's life within a larger historical narrative of any kind results in a seemingly ahistorical presentation of many aspects of her experience. Up to this point I have left out of consideration the final two chapters of the work, where the narrator approaches her historical material from a rather different perspective.

The Importance of Caroline for the Present

The narrator of *Caroline unterm Freiheitsbaum*, identifiable with Struzyk herself as a figure collecting and presenting material, becomes an

---

[139] See, for example, Abrams and Harvey, 9–16; Catherine Fouquet, 'Führt der Weg der Frauengeschichte über die Geschichte des weiblichen Körpers?', in *Geschlecht und Geschichte*, ed. Perrot, 47–61. [140] Abrams and Harvey, 10.

explicit presence in the text only in the last two chapters, where she presents her engagement with Caroline's life and the sources which provide the only access to it. She describes her research as a form of personal identification with Caroline and suggests that the text she has written is as much about her own experiences as about Caroline's:

Ich habe jahrelang mit Caroline vertrauten Umgang gehabt. So ganz all-täglich. Da ein Fetzen, hier ein Schlag ins Wasser, dort eine Naht. Da kommt schon was zusammen, wenn wir zusammenkommen.
Ich kann nur davon schreiben, was ich kenne. (*Caroline*, 179)

Although based on historical evidence, the text is thus a personal inter-pretation of a life, which makes no claim to truth. Struzyk signals the subjective nature of her interpretation with both the subtitle, 'Ansichtssachen', and the lines preceding the main text: 'Es ist alles frei gefunden, | Quellen fließen am angegebenen Ort . . .' (*Caroline*, 6).

As Bird shows, the narrator's ironic and witty style throughout the work has the effect of highlighting 'her role as the creating agent'.[141] Little attempt is made to reconstruct personalities with historical accuracy. The text thus conveys an awareness that a past reality can be neither reconstructed nor represented directly and transparently in writing. Such a problematization of historical representation is central to western developments in historiographical theory in the 1980s, and informs both Hayden White's work on narrative and Liz Stanley's model of biography. Struzyk's characters function as projections of the narrator's personality, displaying her wit and sense of humour. The narrator does not aim for historical realism, instead placing modern colloquial dialogue in the mouths of her characters. When Tatter visits Caroline's father with two English princes, for example, the narrator says that the princes 'finden merry old England eigentlich zum Kotzen' (*Caroline*, 40). The narrator's delight in wordplay and the poetic qualities of language similarly draws attention to the con-structed nature of the text and confounds any expectation of a trans-parently realist presentation.

The narrator's presence in the text clearly has the effect of refuting any suggestion that the work is concerned with the past for its own sake. In the final chapters she adopts a new perspective on the histori-cal matter she has presented, marked by a switch from the present to the past tense. It is only here that the narrator makes her historical situation clear and explicitly offers a retrospective interpretation of the

---

[141] Bird, 100.

past. She contextualizes her material in a larger historical narrative in a way which has been notably avoided in the rest of the text. She situates Caroline's life in relation to events which dominate traditional historical accounts of this period, such as the Seven Years' War, the American War of Independence, the French Revolution, and the Napoleonic Wars (*Caroline*, 185–6). She then contrasts this historical perspective on the time with a contemporaneous perception, such as that which she has attempted to construct, where events of this kind constitute 'den alltäglichen Hintergrund'. She describes the political conditions which affected the lives of her characters as 'die eine Seite der Medaille, auf deren Rückseite die großen Lebensversuche und Entwürfe eingeprägt sind, deren Alltagskonturen ich aufzuspüren gewillt war' (*Caroline*, 186). This image emphasizes the inseparability of historical conditions determined by political events and individual lives and ideals, but it also highlights Struzyk's focus on the everyday lives of her characters and the need to translate grand political ideals into practical action, particularly in the private sphere.

One way in which a historical view of events and figures differs from a contemporaneous view, Struzyk suggests, is that periodization is a form of narrative imposed retrospectively: 'Sie kannten sich alle, ohne Rücksicht auf die Etiketten, die wir jetzt auf die Fächer kleben: Aufklärung, Sturm und Drang, Klassik (frühhochspät), Frühromantik, Jakobinismus' (*Caroline*, 186). *Caroline unterm Freiheitsbaum* attempts to undo the divisions imposed on lives, between public role and private experience, between movements and periods, and to present life as a totality where such distinctions are not easily perceptible, which is closer to how it is actually experienced. It becomes clear in the final paragraphs of the text that this aim is intimately connected with the significance which Struzyk perceives in Caroline and the early Romantics. The narrator shows how holistic ways of thinking were central to these figures' democratic ideals: 'Schelling wollte Poesie und Physik miteinander verbinden—er hat das als einen Weg zur Erkenntnis gesehen, der die disziplinären Schranken überwindet und den Menschen als Ziel nicht vergißt' (*Caroline*, 187). Caroline herself is significant for her role in connecting a network of different people and ideas: 'Und Caroline war nicht nur eine anregende Person, sie knüpfte die Fäden.' (*Caroline*, 186).

The narrator rejects a retrospective interpretation of history which regards the early Romantics' ideas as a failure because historical developments did not produce a realization of them. Responding to

Johann Georg Müller's statement of 1793, 'Ich traue den Schwimmern in Empfindung, den Fliegern in Ideen immer weniger. Es ist nur Rauch, nicht Feuer, es ist Samkorn auf Felsen', she suggests that history is valuable as a source of utopian ideals which, although never realized in the past, can provide an impetus for change in the present: 'Aber ohne dieses Fliegen und Schwimmen gibt es keine Bewegung, und die zukunftsgreifenden Pläne dieser Demokraten sind Angebote für die Gegenwart' (*Caroline*, 187).

A clear parallel is evident between Struzyk's ideas here, and Wolf's and Damm's approaches to figures of the same era. All three authors regard early Romanticism as a source of progressive ideals which are valuable for the present.[142] For both Wolf and Struzyk, these ideals involve replacing divisive polarities with ways of thinking based on wholeness; 'nicht in starren Antinomien, sondern in fließenden Übergängen'.[143] Struzyk's work, however, does not construct a historical narrative to link the era of Romanticism with the present in the way Wolf's texts do. The narrator does not explain why the ideals of Caroline and her contemporaries are 'Angebote für die Gegenwart', stressing instead a personal and subjective interest in the historical figure (*Caroline*, 179, 187). However, her insistence throughout the text on the interconnection of the personal and the political points to the unspoken relevance of Caroline's political ideals for a state claiming to be heir to all democratic traditions in history.

The form of the text can be seen as an enactment of the democratic ideals and holistic ways of thinking which inspire the narrator's interest in the early Romantics. While the work avoids presenting Caroline's life as a closed totality by requiring the reader to discover background information excluded from the text, conventional criteria of selection are not applied in the presentation of the moments which are included, so that an impression of life in its immediacy and totality is created. In juxtaposing well-known historical figures and events with seemingly insignificant details of everyday life, the narrator does not impose traditional, hierarchical notions of 'historical importance' on the past reality she presents. This has the consequence that areas of experience traditionally belonging to women receive the attention they have been denied in conventional accounts of history. The text avoids reducing the complexity of a woman's life and its relevance for the present to a single, coherent interpretative narrative, instead pre-

---

[142] Wolf, 'Projektionsraum Romantik', in *Die Dimension des Autors*, ii. 882.
[143] Ibid. 895.

senting the reader with a selection of episodes which can only offer starting-points for historical interpretation and judgement. Western feminist historians' work in the 1980s was characterized by a similar recognition of complexity and plurality. *Caroline unterm Freiheitsbaum* can be seen as a literary expression of Gisela Bock's statement that women's history is 'not linear, logical or coherent' and Liz Stanley's suggestion that feminist biography should not attempt to protect readers from complexity by seeking to present a seamless 'truth' about its subject.[144] Struzyk perhaps comes closest to the aim voiced by Wolf in her Bettine letter, of not reducing an individual's life to material used to support a hypothesis.[145]

The clear sense of a chronological development of a critical literary discourse about National Socialism which emerged in Chapter 1 finds no equivalent in the texts of this chapter. Instead, marked contrasts have emerged between Wolf's career and the careers of less established women writers of a younger generation. The more fragmentary nature of the 'tradition' this chapter has traced probably has several reasons. The works about National Socialism were responding to a long-established and prominent discourse which served as a central ideological underpinning of the state. They were, for all their differences of interpretation and emphasis, united by an interest in one particular historical period, and by a desire to criticize, and overcome the limitations of, the orthodox GDR discourse about that period. The texts about historical women, by contrast, were not part of such a prominent cultural and historiographical tradition, nor did they share such specific interests and aims. The new perspectives on the fascist past which a work like *Kindheitsmuster* opened up, provoked extensive public debate in mainstream journals, and so lifted taboos for later works, as well as encouraging other writers to respond with their own new perspectives on the subject. In comparison, presenting eighteenth-century women's lives was uncontroversial and of relatively marginal interest to the public. Wolf's *Kein Ort. Nirgends* and biographical essays attracted a number of reviews.[146] These voiced a range of

[144] G. Bock, 6; Stanley, 11.

[145] Cf. Wolf, 'Brief', 577.

[146] Karin Hirdina, 'Begegnung zwischen den Zeiten', *SF* 31 (1979), 2, 1099–1104; Jürgen Engler, 'Herrschaft der Analogie', *NDL* 27 (1979), 7, 128–33; Ursula Püschel, 'Zutrauen kein Unding, Liebe kein Phantom', *NDL* 27 (1979), 7, 134–9; Sigrid Bock, 'Christa Wolf: Kein Ort. Nirgends', *WB* 26 (1980), 5, 145–57; Gabriele Lindner, 'Natürlich geht das nächste Leben heute an: Wortmeldung zu Christa Wolfs Brief über die Bettine', *WB* 28 (1982), 9, 166–71; Siegfried Streller, 'Christa Wolf: Kein Ort. Nirgends', *WB* 29 (1983), 2, 359–62.

opinions, from Siegfried Streller's high praise to Gabriele Lindner's rejection of Wolf's cultural critique. However, a debate of the kind sparked by *Kindheitsmuster* did not occur. The most controversial aspect of Wolf's dialogue with history—the implicit critique of the GDR in the present—was ignored by GDR critics. The texts by Damm, Feyl, and Struzyk received minimal attention from literary critics, though the few reviews which did appear tended to agree that the project of recovering historical women's lives made a valuable contribution to GDR literature.[147] It was not by provoking debate about controversial issues in history that the texts of this chapter made an impact on the public sphere. Rather, their main effect—in both East and West—was to help create a public interest in the lives and writings of women such as Karoline von Günderrode and Caroline Schlegel-Schelling, previously widely neglected by literary history.

---

[147] Melchert; Böck, 'Szenen einer Ehe', 'Ein Weib von schärfstem Geist'; Oehme.

3

'DIE WELT DER UNENDLICHEN MÖGLICHKEITEN NEBEN DIESER EINEN REALITÄT': FANTASTIC APPROACHES TO HISTORY IN LITERATURE OF THE 1970S AND 1980S

LITERARY TREATMENTS OF MYTH IN THE GDR

The 1970s and 1980s saw the publication in the GDR of a number of major works of literature which incorporate, reflect on, and revise fantastic figures and stories belonging to the cultural traditions of western civilization, in order to challenge orthodox views of history. This chapter will start with an analysis of two texts which employ fantastic motifs and plot structures to relate women's historical experience to the requirements of the present: Irmtraud Morgner's *Leben und Abenteuer der Trobadora Beatriz nach Zeugnissen ihrer Spielfrau Laura* of 1974 and Helga Königsdorf's *Respektloser Umgang* of 1986.[1] These texts, particularly Morgner's, belong to an aesthetic tradition of fantasy and humour which contrasts sharply with the serious, realistic approaches to history which have been central to this study so far, represented most prominently by Wolf and the notion of subjective authenticity. A comparison between *Trobadora Beatriz* and *Respektloser Umgang* will highlight shifts in the way history was understood over the course of the 1970s and 1980s. In the main part of this chapter I will then compare two works in which mythological material and forms are central elements in the authors' responses to the sense of global crisis ensuing from the escalation of East–West tension in the early 1980s: Morgner's *Amanda* and Christa Wolf's *Kassandra* project.[2]

---

[1] Irmtraud Morgner, *Leben und Abenteuer der Trobadora Beatriz nach Zeugnissen ihrer Spielfrau Laura: Roman in dreizehn Büchern und sieben Intermezzos* (Berlin and Weimar: Aufbau, 1974; repr. Hamburg and Zurich: Luchterhand, 1991); Königsdorf, *Respektloser Umgang*.

[2] Irmtraud Morgner, *Amanda: Ein Hexenroman* (Darmstadt and Neuwied: Luchterhand, 1983; repr. 1984); Christa Wolf, *Kassandra: Erzählung* (Darmstadt: Luchterhand, 1983; repr. Frankfurt am Main: Luchterhand, 1989), *Voraussetzungen einer Erzählung: Kassandra: Frankfurter*

Much has been written about the relationship between myth and gender in German literature, as well as in women's writing of other nations, and it is often in this context that some of the texts by GDR authors have been discussed. Feminist work has looked at 'revisionary' rewritings of myths which aim to challenge the patriarchal values at the heart of traditional mythological stories. Rachel Blau DuPlessis distinguishes between two kinds of revision; rewriting a myth from a new, female perspective, so that 'the other side of the story' is heard, and a more radical delegitimation of the story, 'a critique even unto sequences and priorities of narrative'.[3] Sigrid Weigel proposes a rather different distinction. She stresses the ambivalence of myths, which are both open to variation—in their content—and closed in their structure, 'insofern sie als Bild für eine historische Erfahrung diese vereindeutigen, festlegen'. The crucial question for her is how texts respond to this ambivalence,

ob sie—um die beiden Pole der Möglichkeiten zu nennen—die Produktion von Bildern fortsetzen, indem sie der Serie von Mythen neue, wenn auch veränderte, möglicherweise aktualisierte Mythen oder auch Gegenmythen hinzufügen und damit der Struktur des Imaginären folgen und sie fortschreiben, oder ob sie die Funktionsweise der Mythen für unser Gedächtnis mitreflektieren und die Strukturierung unserer Wahrnehmungen, Erinnerungen, Ängste und Hoffnungen durch Muster des Imaginären als Voraussetzung in den Text aufnehmen und in eine Bewegung überführen. Man könnte diese Unterscheidung auch als Differenz zwischen einer geschlossenen, auratisierenden Schreibweise und einer offenen, mythenreflektierenden Schreibweise kennzeichnen.[4]

Neither Blau DuPlessis's nor Weigel's distinction seems to me fully adequate for conceptualizing the differences between the various authors' approaches to myth to be examined here.

Two studies of recent German women's writing, by Dorothe Schuscheng and Jutta Rosenkranz-Kaiser, assess the value of literary revisions of myth for feminism.[5] Schuscheng discusses *Kassandra*

Poetik-Vorlesungen (Darmstadt: Luchterhand, 1983; repr. Frankfurt am Main: Luchterhand, 1988).

[3] Rachel Blau DuPlessis, *Writing Beyond the Ending: Narrative Strategies of Twentieth Century Women Writers* (Bloomington, Ind.: Indiana University Press, 1985), 107–8.

[4] Sigrid Weigel, *Die Stimme der Medusa: Schreibweisen in der Gegenwartsliteratur von Frauen* (Reinbek: Rowohlt, 1989), 279–80.

[5] Dorothe Schuscheng, *Arbeit am Mythos Frau: Weiblichkeit und Autonomie in der literarischen Mythenrezeption Ingeborg Bachmanns, Christa Wolfs und Gertrud Leuteneggers* (Frankfurt am Main: Lang, 1987); Jutta Rosenkranz-Kaiser, *Feminismus und Mythos: Tendenzen in Literatur und Theorie der achtziger Jahre* (Münster and New York: Waxmann, 1995).

alongside texts by Ingeborg Bachmann and Gertrud Leutenegger, while Rosenkranz-Kaiser examines *Amanda* and works by Christa Reinig, Barbara Frischmuth, and Elfriede Jelinek, as well as a variety of theoretical feminist texts. Schuscheng examines ways in which the treatment of myth in each text promotes or opposes women's autonomy. Rosenkranz-Kaiser's work is more sophisticated. Its strength lies in its critical assessment of the unacknowledged myths at the centre of several strands of feminist theory. Its main weakness, however, is the author's assessment of both theory and literature according to the same criteria. Her demand for enlightened demythologization in literature as well as in theory means that she cannot appreciate the productive potential of myth as a form of fantasy, nor distinguish between myth as a kind of false 'truth' and myth as an imaginative literary model. Both Schuscheng and Rosenkranz-Kaiser bring to the texts prescriptive criteria which define myth as either potentially productive for feminism (Schuscheng) or negative (Rosenkranz-Kaiser). Sigrid Weigel has highlighted the limitations of approaches of this kind: 'In einer Rede *für* und *wider* den Mythos wird der alte Streit zwischen Mythos und Logos reproduziert, der in dieser Konstellation (für und wider, entweder—oder) schon immer an der Sache vorbei führte.'[6]

Petra Waschescio adopts a more fruitful approach in her study, which sees the recent popularity of myth with authors in both East and West as a response to a broad sense of cultural crisis.[7] Waschescio recognizes that the terms 'myth' and 'femininity' are not stable, timeless notions, but are defined in opposition to ideas which dominate in modern culture: 'reason' and 'masculinity'. She understands writers' interest in both myth and a notion of the feminine as a response to a widespread modern loss of faith in reason and patriarchy. She analyses *Amanda*, as well as works by Heiner Müller, Botho Strauß, and Gisela von Wysocki, asking to what extent the texts go beyond the binary oppositions otherwise perpetuated by both pairs of fixed categories.

Obviously the relationship between rewriting myth and feminist concerns will be central to my readings of texts. However, my specific focus is on the ways in which women writers employed myth to voice a critique of history, and on the significance of such a project in the GDR context. By the 1970s literary treatments of ancient myth already had

---

[6] Weigel, *Die Stimme der Medusa*, 267.

[7] Petra Waschescio, *Vernunftkritik und Patriarchatskritik: Mythische Modelle in der deutschen Gegenwartsliteratur; Heiner Müller, Irmtraud Morgner, Botho Strauß, Gisela von Wysocki* (Bielefeld: Aisthesis, 1994).

a long tradition in the GDR. However, a significant shift in the purposes for which myth was employed by writers occurred in the 1970s and 1980s. In official SED discourse, myth was rejected as a primitive mode of thought with no relevance for a socialist society or its literature. A GDR *Kulturpolitisches Wörterbuch* of 1978 claims that,

sinnbildhafte Bedeutungen, die mit dem mythologischen Ursprung von Gestalten und Konflikten verbunden sind, kaum mehr in der Gegenwart lebendig sind. Sie können wohl aufgrund entsprechender wissenschaftlicher Informationen rational begriffen, aber kaum mehr ästhetisch erlebt werden.[8]

In reducing myth to an object for rational analysis and denying it any power over the modern subject's imagination and any role in modern experience, this definition draws on Marx's understanding of myth. For him, myth was historically confined to the ancient world and had no function in the modern world, where science and technology enable mankind to exert control over nature, in reality as well as in the imagination.[9] A more pragmatic reason for the SED's dismissal of myth was the close association perceived between myth and the irrationality and barbarism exhibited by the National Socialist regime. The need to legitimize the state as the antithesis of its fascist predecessor provided a practical motivation for the idea that Marxism, as a scientific theory of historical progress, and myth, as a primitive mode of thought, were mutually exclusive opposites.[10] These negative connotations of myth, as well as a cultural policy determined by Lukács's predilection for classical realism, meant that in the early years of the GDR taboos surrounded myth as a source of material for literature.[11] Marxist literature, as defined by GDR cultural policy in the 1950s and 1960s, was to portray contemporary everyday life in a realist mode diametrically opposed to fantastic forms such as myth. There were several discrepancies, however, between this theory and the realities of both SED propaganda and GDR literary practice.

Myth proved to be particularly pertinent to the GDR context in various and shifting ways. While claiming that myth had no place in a socialist society and rejecting classical mythology as material for

---

[8]   Quoted in Michael von Engelhardt and Michael Rohrwasser, 'Kassandra—Odysseus—Prometheus: Modelle der Mythosrezeption in der DDR-Literatur', *L'80*, 34 (1985), 46–76 (46).

[9]   See Karl Marx, 'Einleitung [zu den *Grundrissen der Kritik der politischen Ökonomie*]', in *Ausgewählte Werke*, ii. 466–97 (496–7).

[10]   See Wolfgang Emmerich, 'Antike Mythen auf dem Theater: Geschichte und Poesie, Vernunft und Terror', in *Die andere deutsche Literatur*, 79–114 (79).

[11]   See Engelhardt and Rohrwasser, 46.

modern literature, the SED created narratives which, in their persua-
sive claim to truth and their self-legitimizing motivation, can be seen as
modern myths and legends. As Mary Fulbrook suggests, 'myths are
clearly a major and important element in [. . .] identity construction:
the tales that are told about a nation's past are crucial to embodying an
almost anthropomorphic sense of that nation's history as biography'.[12]
The narrative structures which were prescribed for socialist realist
fiction, for example, have much in common with myth. The first chapter of this study showed how literature of the early decades after 1945
was required to support the antifascist foundation myth which served
to legitimize the state. Novels were to provide variations on a small
number of plot structures and archetypal characters, with the aim of
consolidating a sense of the GDR's roots in antifascist resistance to
Hitler. Literature dealing with the present was similarly required to
inspire faith in the positive direction of history towards communism by
creating legends of heroic socialist achievements. Eduard Claudius's
1951 novel, *Menschen an unsrer Seite*, based on the Berlin bricklayer Hans
Garbe's success in repairing part of a factory furnace while it continued
to burn at 1,000°C, exemplifies this process.[13] Fulbrook identifies three
kinds of official myth in the GDR: 'myths of creation; myths of heroes
and villains; and myths of a glorious future'.[14]

Despite the official hostility towards the notion of myth, Greek
mythology became an increasingly popular source of material and
motifs in GDR literature from the 1950s (in poetry) and 1960s (in prose
and drama) onwards.[15] However, prior to the 1970s classical mythology
was generally employed not with the intention of subverting official
cultural policy, but instead in support of the orthodox socialist view of
history. As Emmerich has pointed out, literature of the 1950s and
1960s—such as Georg Maurer's poetry and Peter Hacks's drama
adaptations—transformed material from Greek mythology into 'von
antagonistischen Widersprüchen freie, utopische Zukunftsbilder [. . .]
Die griechische Mythologie war zuallererst eine Vorratskammer für

[12] Mary Fulbrook, 'Myth-Making and National Identity: The Case of the GDR', in *Myths
and Nationhood*, ed. Geoffrey Hosking and George Schöpflin (London: Hurst, 1997), 72–87 (73).
See also the contributions to that volume by Overing and Schöpflin for more detailed discussions of the function of myths in creating and sustaining national identities.

[13] Eduard Claudius, *Menschen an unsrer Seite: Roman* (Halle: Mitteldeutscher Verlag, 1965).
See also Emmerich, *Kleine Literaturgeschichte*, 138–9.

[14] Fulbrook, 'Myth-Making and National Identity', 74–86.

[15] See Volker Riedel, *Antikerezeption in der Literatur der Deutschen Demokratischen Republik*
(Berlin: Akademie der Künste, 1984), 1.

Lehrbeispiele optimistisch-prometheischen Veränderungsdenkens'.[16] Greek mythology thus proved a valuable source of powerful images and figures which could serve well as embodiments of socialist ideals, and provide models of historical progress towards communism. Prometheus became a key figure, embodying the potentially socialist qualities of initiative and revolutionary rebellion against an oppressive order.[17]

In their quest for images, stories, and characters to inspire faith in the socialist state and hope for a utopian future, writers of the early GDR were able to draw on traditional mythology as a powerful form of support and historical legitimization for the socialist principles in which they believed. Appropriating ancient myths for the socialist cause could lend an aura of timeless truth to SED ideology in a way which could not be achieved by the creation of modern legends. As Fulbrook establishes, SED myth-making failed because the official myths propagated were too incongruent with collective memories and current experiences to achieve true popular resonance.[18] After writers had demonstrated the potential of myth as a form of ideological support for the official discourse, the academic literary world gradually responded to this development in literature, so that a delayed recognition of the value of myth was achieved by the 1970s. Conferences on the relation of ancient mythology to socialism and aesthetic realism were held in Jena in 1969 and in Leipzig in 1972.[19] In the early 1980s, two important works on myth in GDR literature were published, by Rüdiger Bernhardt and Volker Riedel.[20]

Ironically, by the time academics acknowledged the value of myth in literature and legitimized it by arguing that it was wholly compatible with Marxist theory, literature was beginning to use myth for very different, subversive purposes. As writers began, from the late 1960s onwards, to question the orthodox SED world view and to experiment

[16] Wolfgang Emmerich, 'Zu-Ende-denken: Griechische Mythologie und neuere DDR-Literatur', in *Kontroversen, alte und neue*, ed. Albrecht Schöne (Tübingen: Niemeyer, 1986), 216–24 (216). There are notable exceptions to this generalization. Müller's *Philoktet*, for example, published in *Sinn und Form* in 1968, anticipated the use of myth for broad cultural criticism which became popular in the 1980s.

[17] See Hans-Dietrich Dahnke, *Erbe und Tradition in der Literatur* (Leipzig: Bibliographisches Institut Leipzig, 1977; repr. 1981), 41–55.

[18] Fulbrook, 'Myth-Making and National Identity', 72–4.

[19] See Emmerich, 'Antike Mythen auf dem Theater', 80.

[20] Rüdiger Bernhardt, *Odysseus' Tod—Prometheus' Leben: Antike Mythen in der Literatur der DDR* (Halle and Leipzig: Mitteldeutscher Verlag, 1983); Riedel, *Antikerezeption in der Literatur der Deutschen Demokratischen Republik*.

with new, more modernist literary forms, myth proved to be a particularly attractive mode in which to question the certainties of official GDR discourse and to construct alternative models of history. There are two main reasons for this. Firstly, a growing disillusionment with 'real existierender Sozialismus' meant that the myths of the early years were now widely recognized as such. By reflecting on the nature and functioning of myth and legend, and exposing their deceptive qualities, literature was thus able to voice a critique of the socialist state. Secondly, myth is a form of discourse which is open to multiple interpretations and plural versions of a particular story. The ease with which Greek myths were incorporated into early GDR literature as embodiments of socialist values is itself evidence of this quality. In allowing contradictions within characters and situations, and in validating several versions of a story, myth represented an extremely apt literary form for challenging an ideology which authorized only one version of events and which understood the world in terms of the simple binary oppositions of socialist realism.

FANTASTIC APPROACHES TO HISTORY: MORGNER'S *TROBADORA BEATRIZ* AND KÖNIGSDORF'S *RESPEKTLOSER UMGANG*

Although published more than a decade apart and very different in length, scope, narrative structure, and tone, Morgner's *Trobadora Beatriz* and Königsdorf's *Respektloser Umgang* share central characteristics which warrant a comparison of the two works.[21] Patricia Herminghouse has compared them as contributions to a feminist critique of

---

[21] My brief analysis here cannot do justice to the complexities of both these texts. For discussions of aspects which are not my concern here, see, among others, Silke von der Emde, 'Irmtraud Morgner's Postmodern Feminism: A Question of Politics', in *WIGY 10*, ed. Jeanette Clausen and Sara Friedrichsmeyer (Lincoln, Neb., and London: University of Nebraska Press, 1995), 117–42; Patricia Herminghouse, 'Die Frau und das Phantastische in der neueren DDR-Literatur: Der Fall Irmtraud Morgner', in *Die Frau als Heldin und Autorin: Neue kritische Ansätze zur Deutschen Literatur*, ed. Wolfgang Paulsen (Berne and Munich: Francke, 1979), 248–66; Linklater, '*Und immer zügelloser wird die Lust*', 71–130; Biddy Martin, 'Irmtraud Morgner's *Leben und Abenteuer der Trobadora Beatriz*', in *Beyond the Eternal Feminine: Critical Essays on Women and German Literature*, ed. Susan L. Cocalis and Kay Goodmann (Stuttgart: Heinz, 1982), 421–39; Petra Reuffer, *Die unwahrscheinlichen Gewänder der anderen Wahrheit: Zur Wiederentdeckung des Wunderbaren bei Günter Grass und Irmtraud Morgner* (Essen: Verlag Die blaue Eule, 1988); Gabriela Scherer, *Zwischen 'Bitterfeld' und 'Orplid': Zum literarischen Werk Irmtraud Morgners* (Berne: Lang, 1992); Jeanette Clausen, 'Resisting Objectification: Helga Königsdorf's Lise Meitner', in *Studies in GDR Culture and Society 10*,

science. While her article draws out important parallels between
the two works, Herminghouse neglects differences between the two
authors' aesthetics and ideas, in order to argue that Morgner, Königsdorf, and Wolf explore 'Alternativen zum herrschenden Wirklichkeits-
begriff' in essentially the same way, aiming to voice 'eine feministische
Kritik in phantastischer Form'.[22]

Both works present encounters between a modern GDR woman
and a historical woman of the past, although in Morgner's work the
historical figure is endowed with legendary qualities.[23] Whereas in
the texts discussed in the previous chapter 'dialogues' of this kind
remained metaphorical, resulting from the narrator's or author's
research into, and identification with, the past, Morgner and Königsdorf use fantasy to bring historical figures into the present. The conversations between Königsdorf's narrator and Lise Meitner are given
a rational explanation, as hallucinations resulting from the drugs the
narrator has to take (*Umgang*, 9). In Morgner's novel, however, the
fantastic elements are not contained within a realistic framework of
this kind. In Rosemary Jackson's terms, borrowed from Todorov,
Königsdorf's work belongs in the category of the uncanny, where all
strangeness is explained by natural forces. Morgner's novel, meanwhile, could be seen as a variation of the fantastic, combining elements
of the marvellous, where events are subject to supernatural forces, with
a mimetically realistic world.[24] The twelfth-century female troubadour's transportation to the twentieth-century present obeys only the
laws of a supernatural world of myth and fairy tale. Beatriz is granted
eight hundred and ten years of sleep by Persephone in return for
promising to work for her and Demeter in their efforts to reinstate
matriarchy (*Beatriz*, 20). While the causal explanation derives from

---

ed. Margy Gerber (Lanham, Md.: University Press of America, 1991), 165–80; Brigid Haines,
'"Botschaft aus einem seltsamen Land": Helga Königsdorf and her Critics', in *Geist und
Macht*, ed. Goodbody and Tate, 140–50; Nancy A. Lauckner, 'The Treatment of the Past and
Future in Helga Königsdorf's *Respektloser Umgang*: "Sich der Erinnerung weihen oder für die
Zukunft antreten? Mit der Vergangenheit im Bunde"', in *Studies in GDR Culture and Society 10*,
ed. Gerber, 151–63.

[22] Patricia Herminghouse, 'Phantasie oder Fanatismus? Zur feministischen
Wissenschaftskritik in der Literatur der DDR', in *Zwischen gestern und morgen*, ed. Brandes,
69–94 (93).

[23] Agnès Cardinal describes her as 'half myth, half history'. Agnès Cardinal, '"Be
Realistic: Demand the Impossible": On Irmtraud Morgner's Salman Trilogy', in *Socialism
and the Literary Imagination: Essays on East German Writers*, ed. Martin Kane (New York and
Oxford: Berg, 1991), 147–61 (153).

[24] Rosemary Jackson, *Fantasy: The Literature of Subversion* (London and New York: Methuen,
1981; repr. Routledge, 1998), 24–37.

myth, the details of the process draw on fairy tale motifs: like the Sleeping Beauty's, Beatriz's long sleep is induced by a spindle prick (*Beatriz*, 11). Because of her recourse to fantasy, Morgner has been associated with the reception of Romanticism in the GDR, suggesting a close relationship between her work and presentations of the lives of figures from the Romantic period such as those discussed in Chapter 2. However, Morgner's approach to the past is markedly different from that of most of the authors there. Her aesthetic is based on a sense of humour and a love of the fantastic which could hardly be further from Wolf's and Damm's earnest attempts to reach a subjective truth about the past. Commenting on this difference, Hanne Castein speaks of Morgner's 'anti-museale Haltung zum kulturellen Erbe', and describes her view of past culture as material to be selected, re-assembled, digested, and made productive in creating something new for the present.[25]

Bringing a historical character from the past into a fictional present has two main purposes in these works. Firstly, a historical figure's out-sider perspective on the present provides a means of assessing the achievements of a society in the present and measuring historical progress. Secondly, the direct interaction between a historical and a contemporary figure allows the authors to explore the ways in which the past is valuable for the present. The works of biographical fiction which formed the focus of the previous chapter imaginatively recon-structed historical lives in order to present possibilities in place of the gaps in historical documentation. Morgner and Königsdorf are more consciously concerned with the value which the fantastic possibilities of history, as opposed to what actually occurred, can have for the present.

Morgner's Beatriz de Dia enables the GDR to be measured against the Marxist narratives of social progress—or myths—which formed its ideological basis. Assuming history to be a course of ongoing progress of this kind, Beatriz decides to leave 'die mittelalterliche Welt der Männer' which allows women a place only as objects, in order to re-enter history as a subject after the demise of patriarchy which she feels must surely have come with social progress: 'Ich bin aus der Historie ausgetreten, weil ich in die Historie eintreten wollte. Mir Natur

---

[25] Hanne Castein, 'Wundersame Reisen im gelobten Land: Zur Romantikrezeption im Werk Irmtraud Morgners', in *Neue Ansichten: The Reception of Romanticism in the Literature of the GDR*, ed. Howard Gaskill, Karin McPherson, and Andrew Barker, GDR Monitor, 6 (Amsterdam and Atlanta: Rodopi, 1990), 114–25 (115–16).

aneignen' (*Beatriz*, 11, 113).[26] Morgner ironically highlights the discrepancy between the GDR's claims concerning its achievements—as exemplified by Uwe Parnitzke's description of the state to Beatriz (*Beatriz*, 69–71)—and the disappointing reality of this 'gelobtes Land'. When required to give her grounds for immigrating to the GDR, Beatriz's response, 'Ansiedlung im Paradies', meets with a characteristically humourless concern for bureaucratic matters from the border policeman: 'Er mahnte Beatriz, dem Ernst des Vorgangs entsprechende präzise Antworten zu erteilen, die Deutsche Demokratische Republik wäre kein Paradies, sondern ein sozialistischer Staat' (*Beatriz*, 90). Beatriz is filled with despair on discovering that, despite legislation ensuring sexual equality in almost every area of life, personal relations between men and women in the GDR continue to follow traditional patriarchal patterns, making the concept of a female troubadour as logically impossible as it was in the twelfth century:

> Ich habe achthundertacht Jahre umsonst verschlafen, ich begreif plötzlich, daß ich meine Berufung nach wie vor verleugnen muß: mich. Kein Wunder, daß ich keine ordentliche Anstellung finde. Die Sitten erlauben keine, man kann nicht finden, was es nicht gibt. Ein passiver Trobador, ein Objekt, das ein Subjekt besingt, ist logischerweise undenkbar. Paradox. (*Beatriz*, 112)

Trobadora Beatriz may point up the discrepancy between ideal and reality in the GDR, and voice criticisms of the limited extent to which progress along Marxist lines has been achieved, but the notion of history as progress is not fundamentally questioned. After travelling in western Europe, Beatriz comes to the conclusion that the GDR has at least reached a more advanced stage in the process of overcoming patriarchy than its capitalist neighbours: 'die DDR wäre für Frauen tatsächlich das gelobte Land' (*Beatriz*, 335). Furthermore, the GDR is shown in the novel to be moving towards ever greater freedom for women. The new legislation of 1972 legalizing abortion is greeted as a momentous step in the direction of equality not only in law, but in everyday life:

> Zuzüglich aller frauenfreundlichen Maßnahmen und Gesetze vorher ist mit dem neuen Gesetz in unserem Staat die rechtliche Gleichberechtigung verwirklicht. Auf der allein die sittliche Chancen hat zu wachsen, verordnen kann man sie nicht. (*Beatriz*, 336)

---

[26] Marx defines production—as the basis of history—in terms of 'Aneignung der Natur von seiten des Individuums innerhalb und vermittelst einer bestimmten Gesellschaftsform'. See Marx, 'Einleitung [zu den *Grundrissen der Kritik der politischen Ökonomie*]', in *Ausgewählte Werke*, ii. 471.

Historical optimism of this kind is absent from the 1980s texts which this chapter will discuss. For the narrator of Königsdorf's *Respektloser Umgang*, for example, history is not a positive progression which needs to be accelerated, but a development towards crisis in the present. In this respect, it is similar to Wolf's works from the late 1970s onwards. The text explores the consequences of a loss of future prospects at both a personal and a global level: just as the narrator's life is threatened by a terminal illness, the future of humanity is threatened by the destructive potential of nuclear physics. Reflecting on her personal situation leads the narrator to consider this much broader sense of crisis:

Dieses sinnlose Aufbegehren: Warum gerade ich! In den verschiedenen Krankenstationen klang es mir entgegen. Geübt im Ursache-Wirkungs-Denken, sind wir überrascht, wenn uns ein Schicksal ereilt. Das gibt es also noch. Man muß doch etwas tun können. Man konnte schließlich stets etwas tun. Ich bin noch nicht darauf eingestellt. Es kann doch nicht einfach so zu Ende gehen. Und ehe wir es begreifen, sind wir schon tot. Im Kleinen wie im Großen. Wir haben keinerlei Erfahrung mit Bedrohung, die der ganzen Menschheit gilt. (*Umgang*, 52)

Like Morgner, Königsdorf uses a character from the past in order to question certain aspects of the present. However, important differences are evident, and Königsdorf's aims in this respect are less straightforward than Morgner's. Whereas Beatriz's expectations of the present function as a projection of an ideal course of historical progress against which the reality can be measured, there is no sense of such an ideal in *Respektloser Umgang*. In contrast with the sisterly sense of solidarity and shared ideals which characterize Beatriz's and Laura's meeting (*Beatriz*, 108), Königsdorf's narrator's conversations with Lise Meitner bear the tensions of a conflict between two very different ways of seeing the world. While the narrator identifies with Meitner as a female scientist whose career was cut short—as a Jew, Meitner was forced to leave Germany for Sweden in 1938—she finds herself unable to empathize with her understanding of her role. In contrast with Beatriz de Dia's highly progressive notions of gender, Königsdorf's Lise Meitner voices opinions which disturb and frustrate the narrator by their failure to challenge the status quo. The narrator is only too aware of the continuing social disadvantages of being a woman in the GDR, and imagines the situation to have been a great deal worse in the 1930s. Yet, instead of criticizing a society which only allowed women scientists as exceptions to the rule and which made the pursuit of such

a career incompatible with marriage and motherhood, Meitner claims
to have been fully content with her life:

Die Biologie ist schon in Ordnung. Die ja. Als soziales Wesen wäre ich [the
narrator] lieber ein Mann. Das ist wahr. Sozial fühle ich mich unvollständig.
   Sie habe sich stets komplett gefühlt. Diese Lust des Denkens. Diese kleinen
Siege. Diese Überlegenheit.
   Sie lügt. Das sind Lügen von der Art, die man zum Überleben braucht.
(*Umgang*, 22)

Meitner's criteria for assessing the achievements of the GDR are not
presented as ideals which highlight its failings, but as a series of questions which the narrator finds inappropriate and rather embarrassing.
For her, the success of a society is not measured in terms of the number
of Nobel prize winners it produces or the availability of household
servants to take responsibility for childcare (*Umgang*, 57–8).

   By offering a different historical perspective on the present, Königsdorf's Meitner serves as a provocation to the narrator, prompting her
to question her own ways of thinking. Meitner's sense of certainty,
grounded as it may be in a dissatisfaction she has repressed, causes the
narrator to recognize her own lack of certainty. When she quotes Max
Planck to Meitner, to the effect that a woman scientist can only be an
exceptional case, she is surprised and dismayed by Meitner's response:

Wissen Sie, wer das geschrieben hat? Frage ich.
   Nein.
   Max Planck.
   Sehr gut.
   Was, rufe ich, und Sie selbst?
   Ich bin die Ausnahme. Erwidert Lise Meitner.
   Und ich? Was bin ich? (*Umgang*, 25)

   Whereas Morgner uses a historical figure to reinforce a contemporary set of ideals concerning gender equality, Königsdorf employs
a figure from a much more recent historical era to relativize and disturb the modern narrator's understanding of herself and her society.
This contrast reflects a difference in the two authors' approaches to
women's history. *Trobadora Beatriz* shares certain assumptions with
works like 'Der Schatten eines Traumes' and *Cornelia Goethe*. Women
are seen as the victims of history, marginalized and oppressed by
society, and excluded from the historical record. While Wolf, Struzyk,
Damm, and Feyl imaginatively reconstruct female lives which were
not adequately recorded by history, Morgner takes a historical female

figure as the basis for a fantastic projection. In all of these cases, the woman chosen is presented as an exemplary figure of identification, and in some cases sympathy. Engaging with a historical woman is shown to help women in the present to understand both women's oppression and the strategies which women have developed to challenge it. Königsdorf's text can be read as a reaction to these somewhat idealizing approaches to women's history. For her narrator, identification with Lise Meitner comes only as the result of an uncomfortable struggle. Königsdorf's Meitner fights any suggestion that she was a victim of oppression. Her central role in a discovery which was to shape twentieth-century history offers a challenge to the notion that women are necessarily marginalized from the course of history. Königsdorf's narrator counters this assumption, which she finds expressed in Wolf's *Voraussetzungen einer Erzählung: Kassandra* and which disturbs her in its fatalism. She is offended by the idea that women are the passive victims of patriarchy, and suggests rather that women have the power to assert their autonomy as subjects in the face of objectifying mechanisms of oppression:

Bei diesem Geschehen gibt es immer zwei Seiten. Die eine, die den Angriff, das Objektemachen, als Machtmittel inszeniert, und die andere, die als Subjekt ihre Autonomie bewahrt. Oder auch nicht. Sind die Mechanismen tatsächlich so effektiv, daß es kein Entrinnen gibt?

Lise Meitner etwa? (*Umgang*, 54)

Meitner is also one of the women Feyl presents in *Der lautlose Aufbruch*. Here, Meitner is idealized as a patient, uncomplaining victim who quietly struggles to overcome adversity and heroically makes her mark on scientific history despite all odds (*Aufbruch*, 178–91). Feyl's opening sentence is calculated to provoke sympathy for Meitner as a victim of patriarchy: 'Ihre Arbeit ist gekrönt worden mit dem Nobelpreis für Otto Hahn' (*Aufbruch*, 178). No mention is made of the destructive ends to which this work was later put. Jeanette Clausen has commented that Königsdorf's interpretation of Meitner 'contradicts Feyl's in nearly every way'.[27] As Clausen concludes, Königsdorf is rejecting attempts 'to construct unambiguously positive examples based on the lives of historical figures', and is concerned rather to highlight the ambiguities inherent in historical figures and events.[28] Her narrator's dialogue with history is not a simple process of straightforward identification, but a discomforting struggle constantly requiring her to differentiate in her

----

[27] See Clausen, 168–70.   [28] Ibid. 179.

understanding of the past. This can be read as a reaction not only to feminist attempts to find identificatory figures in history, but also to the GDR appropriation of 'progressive' traditions, which functioned essentially by projecting contemporary values on to figures and events in the past.

Despite these differences in the way a historical woman is presented, both *Trobadora Beatriz* and *Respektloser Umgang* suggest that a certain kind of interaction with the past, as represented by these figures, is essential in the present if history is to take a more positive course in the future. Morgner suggests in *Trobadora Beatriz* that the endurance of patriarchal structures at the level of personal relationships, despite legal provisions for gender equality, is due to women's lack of a historical consciousness. As Beatriz puts it, 'ein Zusammenhang besteht zwischen Geschichtsbewußtsein und Selbstbewußtsein. Weshalb es nicht genügen kann, den Expropriierten nur ihr materielles Eigentum zurückzugeben' (*Beatriz*, 107). Beatriz hears similar views from Bele H., whom she encounters in Split. Complaining that 'nur die Geschichte der Mächtigen steht in den Büchern verzeichnet', Bele H. develops further the principle of Brecht's 'Fragen eines lesenden Arbeiters' to highlight the status of women under patriarchy, as a class even less acknowledged than the working classes under capitalism: '["]Ich warte auf den Dichter, der eine lesende Arbeiterin fragen lassen könnte", sagte Bele H. "Nach den Sklaven der Sklaven, die keinerlei sichtbare Spuren ihrer Fähigkeiten hinterlassen konnten"' (*Beatriz*, 193–4). Morgner's novel, like many of the texts in Chapter 2, could be regarded as a response to this call. The sixth tapestry in the Musée de Cluny in Paris has a central role in the text as a rare example of women's work which did leave visible traces. Laura interprets the picture as an expression of a specifically female utopian yearning for peace and harmony in the form of a world devoid of male aggression: 'Ein aus Verzweiflung gewachsenes Sehnsuchtsbild also—extreme Zustände bringen extreme Utopien hervor' (*Beatriz*, 27). In taking up a utopian impulse produced by women's experience in the past and attempting to make it productive for the present, Morgner's work is creating an inspirational sense of a female tradition, in the way Bele H. believes necessary:

Niemand, der sich müht, etwas Größeres zu wollen, kann den Beistand der Geschichte entbehren. Diese Gewißheit der Verwurzelung. Selbstbewußtsein schaffendes Traditionsbewußtsein. Stolz. Ein Adliger, der sich an einen

Stammbaum lehnen kann, ist beispielsweise gegenüber Arbeitern und Frauen, die allein zu stehen glauben, im Vorteil. (*Beatriz*, 194)

Because women's past is largely excluded from the history books, if such a sense of history is to be created for women then women's documented past must be complemented by a fantastic construction of a past. As Uwe Parnitzke says immediately before inviting Beatriz to the GDR, 'Wir müssen ein legendäres Geschichtsbewußtsein schaffen' (*Beatriz*, 68). It is this function which Beatriz is to fulfil in the modern GDR: Laura expresses gratitude to Beatriz for personally bringing to her and similar women 'die ungeschriebene Geschichte, die nicht von Männern gemacht wurde' (*Beatriz*, 181). As a historical figure, Beatriz de Dia represents a paradox: at a time when women were the objects of history, she was a troubadour, a role which conventionally required a male subject to address an objectified female representative of virtue. Morgner builds on this historical basis to transform Beatriz into a legendary embodiment of women's ability to transcend the restrictions imposed on them by patriarchy. As Laura argues in a fictional dialogue with Morgner herself, Beatriz thus represents a utopian principle of undisillusioned hope for the future:

Aber wer von uns hat nicht in jungen Jahren oder Augenblicken die Historie verlassen, dieses männliche Meer von Egoismus, wer ging nicht, als er noch ungebrochen war von Erfahrungen, mit dem Kopf durch die Wand, die dieses Meer trennt von der Zukunft. (*Beatriz*, 26)

Beatriz's status between history and fantasy is made clear by this exchange between Laura and Morgner. Laura counters Morgner's view that Beatriz is 'ein Wunschbild' with the insistence that she is 'eine historische Erscheinung'. Morgner then concludes, 'Also ein typischer Fall von Legendenbildung mittels Geschichtskorrektur' (*Beatriz*, 28). Beatriz can indeed be seen as a legendary correction to, or compensation for, history. In the place of women's history of oppression, she offers an inspirational example of women's determination to become subjects of history.

Beatriz's historical existence is shown in the novel to be subject to the laws of a fantastic world combining elements of traditional myths, fairy tales, and legends. As a framework for the novel, however, this world remains sketchy compared with the mythological worlds of the later *Amanda*. Its plot consists broadly of a conflict between two parties attempting to overthrow the male gods of patriarchy. While Persephone and Demeter want to reinstate matriarchy, Melusine's oppositional faction represents a third order, 'die weder patriarchalisch noch matriarchalisch sein sollte, sondern menschlich' (*Beatriz*, 20). Persephone and Demeter are imprisoned in a bunker because of a conspiratorial agreement between Zeus, now fallen from power, and God. The campaigners for their liberation, now dominated by Melusine's Opposition, meet at King Arthur's Round Table, 'zwischen Kaerllion am Usk und der Zukunft, aber etwas näher an Kaerllion' (*Beatriz*, 60, 445). Morgner's sympathies clearly lie with the Oppositional aims and strategies. Laura is co-opted to the Round Table at the end of the novel (*Beatriz*, 446). Persephone and Demeter, by contrast, are described as reactionary and associated with historical stagnation. In the eight hundred and eight years of Beatriz's sleep they have made no progress, continuing to behave in exactly the same way:

> Aber ebenso wie vor achthundertacht Jahren fiel ihr plötzlich ein Bunker vor die Füße. [. . .] Persephone und Demeter beschrieben tatsächlich noch immer in den gleichen Rache- und Zukunftsgesängen die Wiedereinführung des Matriarchats. Auf denselben Strohsäcken? (*Beatriz*, 19)

Morgner's novel suggests that fantasy is a highly positive force, enabling women to transgress historical boundaries: it is the goddesses' capacity for miracles which allows Beatriz to enter the twentieth century. However, most of the characters belonging to the fantastic realm are subjected to mockery. Persephone's and Demeter's solemn faith in their matriarchal principles is ridiculed:

> Den letzten Satz ['Der Himmel ist für Frauen da.'] wiederholten Persephone und ihre Mutter Demeter anschließend siebenundzwanzigmal in einem Kanon. Dabei landeten zwei Engel exerziermäßig. Sie schlossen die Tür, legten die Stangen vor und schlugen an Eisenösen, die aus Betonwänden ragten, vier Taue. Dann hob ein Engel schneidig den rechten Arm, und der Bunker entschwebte. (*Beatriz*, 20)

Penthesilea's brief appearance is similarly humorous:

> Die Frau nannte sich Penthesilea. Laura entsann sich, den Namen in Büchern gelesen zu haben. 'Hat sich ein gewisser Achill nicht mal in Sie verliebt?' fragte Laura scherzhaft. 'Nachdem er mich im Zweikampf zerhackt hatte', antwortete Penthesilea ebenfalls scherzhaft, setzte Daumen und Zeigefinger der rechten Hand an ihre Zähne und zog einen Kaugummifaden armlang. (*Beatriz*, 213)

When Melusine visits Laura, a comic discrepancy is created between the profane everyday reality of the GDR and a world of fantasy.

Melusine, like her sister-in-law Beatriz, has historical roots in medieval France. Her name and her body—half-woman, half-dragon—derive from fairy tale, yet her form of existence, like Beatriz's, is dependent on the powers of the goddesses. As a politician, she is granted permission to leave the patriarchal medieval world in return for actively support-ing Persephone's and Demeter's cause (*Beatriz*, 20). Despite her espousal of views on gender equality similar to Morgner's own, she is presented with an irony which makes her hard to take seriously. In contrast to Laura's and Beatriz's harmonious first meeting, Melusine's nocturnal visit to Laura is marked by a comic clash of two worlds. Laura tries to integrate the sphinx figure in her living room into every-day reality, first by attributing the vision to the lentils she has eaten, and then by asking whether Melusine has a resident's permit (*Beatriz*, 181–2). Melusine responds to this question with a lengthy abstract account of cybernetic theory which is humorously inappropriate in the context, however valuable its ideas might otherwise be.

These examples of the meeting points between reality and fantasy in *Trobadora Beatriz* suggest that Alison Lewis's claim that 'the nether-world of Greek Goddesses and medieval legends seldom interferes in Laura's life, and yet when it does the divine intervention is always of momentous significance' might be apt for *Amanda*, but is far less appro-priate for the earlier novel.[29] Here, the comic quality of these episodes serves primarily to point up the need for a greater imaginative input into daily life in the GDR. Fantasy is presented as a productive and urgently needed force, yet utopian hopes are associated not with the mythical and fairy tale figures themselves, but rather with Beatriz, a historical figure who gains the assistance of fantastic powers in order to transcend historical boundaries. As Ingeborg Nordmann has sug-gested, the tragic deaths of Beatriz and Vera Hill, both of whom lose their balance, point to the importance of 'das richtige Verhältnis zwischen Phantasie und Realität'.[30]

Despite the less optimistic understanding of history underlying Königsdorf's *Respektloser Umgang*, an engagement with the past is shown to be valuable in enabling productive responses to the crisis in the present. Rather like Laura Salman, Königsdorf's narrator lacks a sense of history as a past which belongs to her. However, this is not

[29] Alison Lewis, *Subverting Patriarchy: Feminism and Fantasy in the Works of Irmtraud Morgner* (Oxford and Washington: Berg, 1995), 44.

[30] Ingeborg Nordmann, 'Die halbierte Geschichtsfähigkeit der Frau: Zu Irmtraud Morgners Roman *Leben und Abenteuer der Trobadora Beatriz nach Zeugnissen ihrer Spielfrau Laura*', in *DDR-Roman und Literaturgesellschaft*, ed. Hoogeveen and Labroisse, 419–62 (443).

primarily because of her gender, as in Morgner's novel. Instead, as I mentioned in Chapter 1, Königsdorf suggests that the way the GDR has dealt with Germany's past has resulted in difficulties for individuals of Königsdorf's (and her narrator's) generation in identifying personally with history: 'Geschichte blieb ein von Heldensagen umrankter ökonomischer Prozeß, der mit mir wenig zu tun hatte' (*Umgang*, 21). Her choice of the word 'Heldensagen' indicates her awareness of the processes of mythologizing which were involved in the GDR's version of its history.

The fantasy conversations with Lise Meitner serve to provide the personal engagement with history which the narrator has always lacked. Meitner provokes the narrator to rethink her relation to the past on several levels. Meitner's experiences as a Jew in Nazi Germany prompt the narrator to consider her own family history. She dwells on the fate of her Jewish grandmother, who died in a euthanasia clinic because of alleged insanity, and concludes, 'Nein, meine Großmutter war nicht verrückt' (*Umgang*, 38). She also begins to question her parents' behaviour during this time. Initially angry at their apparent naïvety and willingness to compromise with the National Socialists, she grows to realize that there might be ways, however small, in which they offered resistance. Thus she reinterprets her own conception:

Lange habe ich mit dem Bewußtsein gelebt, meine Existenz politischer Unbedarftheit zu verdanken. Wenn ich jetzt überlege, will es mir scheinen, meine Zeugung war auch eine Art persönlichen Widerstandes. Ein Stück Selbstbehauptung. Das Bestreben meines Vaters, sich nicht zum Objekt machen zu lassen. (*Umgang*, 53)

As a physicist involved in the discovery of nuclear fission, Meitner also prompts the narrator to explore the roots in scientific history of the present global crisis. The narrator sees the moral issues involved in Meitner's contribution towards a discovery which was then put to destructive effect as particularly pertinent to the contemporary world. When Meitner suggests that it is always possible to do something to resist oppression, the narrator reacts indignantly:

Ich bin nicht bereit, mir moralisierende Reden anzuhören. Vor allem nicht von jemandem, der sich ein Jahr nach Hiroshima von der amerikanischen Presse zur Frau des Jahres küren ließ. Welch zweifelhafte Ehre. Heute mehr denn je. (*Umgang*, 31)

She frequently draws parallels between the need for resistance under Hitler's regime and the need to act against the more sophisticated application of science to destructive ends in the present and future: 'In-zwischen arbeitet man an hochwirksamen, rassenspezifischen Giften. Gaskammern erübrigen sich in Zukunft' (*Umgang*, 70).

The narrator's exploration of the past is shown to be productive in two main ways. Firstly, finding lines of continuity in history and discovering the roots of present problems help her to see her own existence within a broader perspective, and so to begin to accept her bleak future prospects:

Der Verlust an Zukunftsträumen schafft den Erinnerungen Raum. Sehnsucht nach einer größeren Kontinuität. Verantwortung für das, was kommen wird. Aber auch die Erkundung des Ursprungs. Der Wurzeln. Nur durch die Relativierung des Ichs ist die eigene Existenz noch ertragbar. (*Umgang*, 27)

Secondly, as she suggests here, discovering opportunities for positive action in the past makes her aware of the need to take responsibility for the future. At first, the narrator scorns Meitner's suggestion that she has a historical mission: 'Soweit habe ich meinen Marxismus kapiert: Dazu braucht man die historische Chance. Sonst ist das weiter nichts als dumme Selbstüberschätzung' (*Umgang*, 85). However, her attitude is changed by a pivotal fantasy scene in which she is put on trial, surrounded by her ancestors, both genetic and intellectual (*Umgang*, 87). This scene can be read as a symbolically compressed and heightened demonstration of the function which the narrator's engagement with the past has in the work as a whole. Anticipating the judgement of her ancestors, the narrator finds herself surrounded by mirrors and is forced to confront her image. Seeing her face as a physical expression of her past, she concludes, 'Ich liebe mein Bild nicht' (*Umgang*, 88–9). This discovery prompts an honest acknowledgement of the faults in her past behaviour:

Wieviel kleinlicher Ehrgeiz und wieviel Geltungssucht bestimmten mein Leben! Habe ich nicht Menschen benutzt und weggeworfen, wie es mir gut dünkte! Wenn hier vom Objektemachen die Rede ist: Ich war hervorragend auf dieser Strecke! Meinmann. Meinsohn. Meinmitarbeiter. Haben mich nicht Selbstmitleid und Zynismus wechselweise beherrscht. Ging es mir wirklich jemals um den Zustand der Welt, oder immer nur um mich? (*Umgang*, 89)

Through this experience she gains a sense of historical purpose. She feels she has been the recipient of a message which she can pass on to her daughter and her son, who is studying to become a physicist and likes to see the world in purely quantifiable terms. The essence of her message is that responsibility must accompany scientific research in future if destruction on a hitherto unknown scale is to be avoided:

Von der Würde des Menschen werde ich sprechen, die nicht aus naturwis-senschaftlicher Kalkulation folgt. Von der Verantwortung, die er überneh-men muß, weil es zwischen Verantwortung und Mitschuld in Zukunft nichts mehr gibt. Mitschuld am Mißbrauch von Erkenntnis. Mitschuld am Abstempeln zu Untermenschen. Zu Objekten. Zu Megatoten. (*Umgang*, 94)

By passing this message on to the next generation, the narrator feels she is creating a continuity which transcends her individual life: 'Unsterblich sind wir, solange diesem Leben Kontinuität beschieden ist' (*Umgang*, 116).

The narrator's repeated questions concerning what Lise Meitner and her own father could have done to resist fascism, and what she her-self would have done in those circumstances, find a response at the end of the text. Meitner tells her that she deliberately led her colleagues astray by espousing false theories, in order to delay the discovery of nuclear energy, as she foresaw its potential for destruction (*Umgang*, 111–14). Although this possibility is not incompatible with the evidence, the narrator is reluctant to believe her. However, Meitner suggests that it is not in its relation to truth that her story has its value for the present: 'Ist es wirklich so wichtig. Ich meine, ob es den Tatsachen entspricht oder nicht. Ist nicht lediglich von Bedeutung, daß es wahr sein könnte' (*Umgang*, 114). The text thus suggests that it is not just the real events of history which can be made productive for the present, but also events which could have taken place, but (probably) did not. The narrator's sense of a mission in the present is consolidated by a story of what Meitner could have done in the past.

Like *Trobadora Beatriz*, *Respektloser Umgang* proposes an approach to history which takes figures and events from the past as the basis for legends which, regardless of their relation to truth, are able to inspire positive action in the present and so change society for the better in the future. Like Beatriz de Dia, Lise Meitner is associated with a fantastic principle which contrasts sharply with the contemporary protagonist's way of thinking. As a product of the narrator's imagination, Meitner represents forms of knowledge which the narrator has excluded from her rational, scientifically grounded view of the world. At the begin-ning of the text, the narrator attempts to explain her hallucinations rationally and to maintain control over them, keeping 'Realität' and 'Scheinwelt' separate (*Umgang*, 9). However, it is no coincidence that she uses a motif from fairy tale to describe the temptation of turning round when she senses that Meitner has appeared behind her: 'Die Verlockung des verbotenen Zimmers. Habe ich das Verbot nicht immer als Zumutung empfunden' (*Umgang*, 8). One of the ways in which Meitner unsettles the narrator in her habitual way of thinking is by suggesting the value of fantasy for the present world. When Meitner suggests that the salvation of humanity can only come from 'dem Bereich der Überwelt', the narrator anticipates 'die abgenutzte Himmelslitanei' and reacts with scornful impatience. However, a Christian notion of heaven is far from what Meitner has in mind:

Keineswegs. Nur—zwischen Himmel und Erde läge so manches. Die Welt der Vorstellungen, Erinnerungen, Bilder, Träume, Erfahrungen. Von Generation zu Generation überliefert. Die Welt der unendlichen Möglichkeiten neben dieser einen Realität. Die Welt der Mythen und Märchen. (*Umgang*, 48)

Again, the narrator is not convinced, refusing to believe that the cultural imaginary outlined here can have any practical relevance for the contemporary world: 'Das ist ja fast noch schlimmer. Das Märchen vom Hans im Glück mit der Neutronenbombe unterm Arm. Ich lache. Obgleich es eigentlich zum Heulen ist' (*Umgang*, 48).

Over the course of the text, however, the narrator's attitude to traditional stories of this kind changes drastically. Her engagement with Meitner results in a recognition that myths and fairy tales can provide valuable models for attempting to understand the present global crisis. In particular, the Prometheus myth proves fruitful. The narrator compares the discovery of atomic energy with the gift of fire:

Wieder einmal wird dem Menschen Feuer in die Hand gegeben. Noch war keine Zeit für Mythen. Noch steht der moderne Prometheus in seiner ganzen Blöße vor uns. Ist er nicht zu winzig, um die Verantwortung für die Folgen seines Tuns allein zu tragen. Ja, überhaupt allein zu erkennen. Ihn zur Strafe an einen Felsen zu schmieden und von einem Adler zerfleischen zu lassen, hat schon beim ersten Male nichts genützt. Sein Geschenk kann Wohltat oder Vernichtung bringen. Bisher hat der Mensch stets beides in Szene gesetzt. Warum sollte es diesmal anders sein? (*Umgang*, 78)

A similar reading of this myth against the grain of traditional GDR interpretations is given greater prominence and detail in Morgner's *Amanda*. *Respektloser Umgang*, like *Trobadora Beatriz*, combines mythological references with an emphasis on fantasy as a vital complement to modern rational thought, but does not integrate mythological plots into its narrative to the same degree as the texts which form the focus of the next section.

MYTH AS HISTORY AND HISTORY AS MYTH: WOLF'S *KASSANDRA* AND MORGNER'S *AMANDA*

Two works of the early 1980s—Irmtraud Morgner's *Amanda* and Christa Wolf's *Kassandra* project—engage much more deeply with myth than *Trobadora Beatriz* and *Respektloser Umgang*. These texts present fully developed theories of myth in relation to history, and use it to express a specifically feminist critique of western patriarchal society. This part of the chapter will show how, by relating myth both to history and to literature, these texts create models, not only of the course of history, but also of the interaction between history and literature.

The similarities between the two works, both of which appeared in 1983, have been the focus of much critical attention. Both are concerned with the one-sidedness of the values which have determined the course of history and led to a situation of global destruction. Rather than aiming to integrate women into history, which was presented as a vital goal in *Trobadora Beatriz*, *Kassandra* and *Amanda* voice critiques of the history of western civilization from a feminist perspective. Both analyse the exclusive concentration on scientific and technological progress as an end in itself, seeing this as characteristic of patriarchal society and intrinsically related to the suppression of women and of principles associated with femininity. Both use myth in their exploration of these ideas and their attempt to re-create a balanced unity of principles regarded as masculine and those seen as feminine. J. H. Reid focuses on 'the similarity of themes and ideas in the two works', and asserts that Wolf and Morgner are 'both using and revising traditional myths and creating their own as Utopian models for future behaviour'.[31] While the broad parallels between the two works are undeniable, significant differences in the two authors' views of myth and its relation to history are evident, but have been largely neglected by critics. Alison Lewis does go beyond a recognition of the similarities, to contrast the two projects in a number of ways. She rightly sees Morgner's use of myth as less concerned than Wolf's with questions of

---

[31] J. H. Reid, 'Woman, Myth and Magic: On Christa Wolf's *Kassandra* and Irmtraud Morgner's *Amanda*', in *Honecker's Germany*, ed. David Childs (London: Allen Unwin, 1985), 97–117 (98).

historical conditions and origins, but her assertion that Morgner's myths are therefore 'more purely utopian' is an over-simplification of the complex set of parallels and divergences between the two works.[32] Both Wolf and Morgner use myth to create utopian models, and both are concerned essentially with history and the origins of contemporary problems, though they approach these topics differently. Although they both use myth to contribute to a feminist understanding of history, they focus on different aspects of history and propose contrasting models of literature as a means of gaining such an understanding.

Wolf's *Kassandra* project was originally presented at the University of Frankfurt am Main in 1982 as a series of five lectures on poetics. In the first four lectures, Wolf offers an account of a visit to Greece, a working diary charting her thoughts about the Kassandra figure and developments in her ideas as she works on the project, and reflections on Homer and Aeschylus, the origins of western civilization, myth, literary form, the threat of nuclear war, and the relationship between gender and the history of the western world. The fifth and final lecture, published as a separate volume in the Federal Republic, consists of Kassandra's inner monologue as she awaits her death in Mycenae, having been brought there as a prisoner by Agamemnon after the fall of Troy. Her memories, narrated in isolation and shared with nobody, constitute a perspective on the Trojan War not found in the canonical accounts by male authors.

Like *Trobadora Beatriz, Amanda* is a montage novel, consisting of short and relatively self-contained sections of text. Although marked by a greater degree of narrative coherence than the earlier novel, it is a highly complex work, in which a variety of plot strands, some set in a recognizable historical reality and others based in myth, intertwine and different time levels are juxtaposed. One strand of the novel follows the life of Laura Salman in the 1970s, as a single mother forced to work night shifts as a driver on the Berlin S-Bahn. In a characteristic meeting of the real and the mythical plots, Laura is divided in two by the chief devil Kolbuk. Her other half, the witch Amanda, is confined in a brothel in the Hörselberg. Laura, weakened by this division, embarks on a quest for wholeness which introduces one of the main thematic concerns of the work. Another plot strand, set in 1980, involves the rebirth of Beatriz de Dia as a siren, in response to the threat posed to the earth by environmental destruction and the nuclear arms race. Accompanied by Arke, a snake with seven-mile wings,

[32] Lewis, 231.

Beatriz lives in a cage in the zoo in East Berlin. Having had her tongue stolen by unknown enemies, she is unable to sing to save the world, so writes instead, producing the novel itself. Two other mythological plot strands are prominent in the novel. The first is a feminist revision of the stories of Pandora and Prometheus. The second centres on the Brocken mountain and combines elements of Christian mythology with a positive re-evaluation of the witch figure; it is to this realm that Amanda belongs.

Both *Amanda* and the *Kassandra* project combine theoretical reflection on the nature and functions of myth with the reworking or creation of myths. Because of their self-reflective character, the texts are able to convey relations between myth and history at several levels. Firstly, Morgner and Wolf regard ancient myth as a historical phenomenon and, by situating it at a certain point in the course of history, create a particular model of history. Secondly, they express ideas about history through the content of the myths they present. Finally, they explore how myth, as a form of discourse, relates to both reality and literature. This enables them to establish the role which myth plays in historical processes, as well as the potential of ancient myth and literature to represent history and enhance historical understanding.[33] Before discussing in detail how the texts use myth, I shall make a brief excursus into the theory of myth.

The Nature of Myth and its Place in History

There exists a vast body of academic work on myth. Debate on the subject has been marked by an underlying, yet generally unacknowledged disagreement about the range of phenomena covered by the term 'myth'. Contributions to our understanding of the term have been made by a wide and disparate range of writers and theorists, from Roland Barthes to Franz Fühmann, and from Claude Lévi-Strauss to Hans Blumenberg. A corresponding breadth characterizes the term's sphere of reference. Fulbrook offers a particularly broad definition of the term:

At their most basic, myths are stories which are not necessarily true, nor even believed to be true, but which have symbolic power. They are constantly repeated, often re-enacted. Myths are, in other words, essentially propagated for their effect rather than their truth value. The extent to which they embody

---

[33] See also my 'Myth and History in Irmtraud Morgner's *Amanda*', *GLL* 51 (1998), 4, 483–95.

claims to truth varies greatly, from those stories which are widely held to be true and are only revealed as myths when 'exploded' by new 'revelations', to narratives which are of particular exemplary value and may be repeatedly retold or re-enacted as symbolic expressions of important values (the Christian myths of the virgin birth or the Resurrection, for example) irrespective of a general collusion in the knowledge that 'this could not have taken place in this way', in other words, a willing suspension of disbelief.[34]

This broad definition encompasses forms of narrative which could be seen as opposed to each other, although both can be categorized as 'myth'. Such contradictions between different manifestations of myth become clear when narrower definitions are adopted. When Barthes defines myth as 'a type of speech' which 'has the task of giving an historical intention a natural justification, and making contingency appear eternal', he seems to have in mind something very different from the 'myth' which Fühmann defines as a 'Gleichnis für die Verschränkung dessen, was sowohl draußen wie drinnen ist, von historisch-sozialen wie von psychischen Realitäten'.[35] Barthes claims that myth 'abolishes the complexity of human acts' and 'organizes a world which is without contradictions because it is without depth', while Fühmann asserts precisely the opposite: 'Der Mythos gibt den Widerspruch wieder, das Märchen aber schafft ihn weg.'[36] The diversity—and at times incompatibility—of the phenomena which have been termed 'myth' has received little attention in secondary literature on this aspect of Wolf's and Morgner's works.[37] Instead the tendency has been to assume a basic consensus about what myth is, and either to adopt narrow definitions which cannot do justice to the complexities of these literary texts, or to juxtapose different theories of myth, as though they merely represented different approaches to an unproblematic, predefined object. Herbert A. Arnold, for example, attempts to conflate Barthes's and Blumenberg's models in order to analyse *Kassandra* and Heiner Müller's *Philoktet*, apparently unaware of the problems of relating these very different kinds of myth.[38] The Classicist Katharina Glau, in her study of Wolf's work as a reception of

---

[34] Fulbrook, 'Myth-Making and National Identity', 73.
[35] Roland Barthes, 'Myth Today', in *Mythologies*, trans. Annette Lavers (London: Paladin, 1973), 117–74 (117, 155); Franz Fühmann, 'Das mythische Element in der Literatur', in *Essays. Gespräche. Aufsätze 1964–1981* (Rostock: Hinstorff, 1993), 82–140 (124).
[36] Barthes, *Mythologies*, 156; Fühmann, 'Das mythische Element', 95.
[37] Petra Waschescio's study is an exception.
[38] Herbert A. Arnold, 'On Myth and Marxism: The Case of Heiner Müller and Christa Wolf', *CG* 21 (1988), 1, 58–69.

Aeschylus's *Oresteia*, discusses a wide variety of approaches to myth, but seems to assume that 'myth' itself is a constant. Her proposal that it is necessary to distinguish between the mythical and the literary—'zwischen dem (anonymen) griechischen Mythos als mündlich tradiertem Sagenkreis und dem Mythos als Produkt einer literarischen Verarbeitung'—is undoubtedly of great importance in understanding Wolf's approach to ancient myth, but these categories cannot account for Wolf's use of the term 'myth'—in Barthes's sense—to refer also to much more modern phenomena.[39]

It is not my aim to measure Morgner and Wolf against developments in academic work on myth and to infer—as Jutta Rosenkranz-Kaiser has in the case of Morgner—that the GDR context was an unfortunate hindrance to the absorption into their works of the latest trends in thinking about myth.[40] Instead this study is concerned with the ways *Kassandra* and *Amanda* construct myth in order to voice critiques of history and historiography. To this end it is necessary to distinguish between the different concepts of myth which play a role in the two works. Firstly, both Wolf and Morgner understand myth to be a particular kind of narrative associated primarily with the ancient Greek world and its literature. This kind of myth is exemplified by the collections of stories which the modern world has inherited from ancient cultures, and whose contents provide explanations of the world which usually involve supernatural beings. Ancient myth is thus defined by its content, but it is also a particular form of discourse. Both Morgner and Wolf also explore a rather different notion of myth, as a form of false belief which is usually ideologically motivated, has an influential impact on a particular population, and is by no means restricted to ancient societies. This kind of myth cannot be defined according to its content, but must be regarded instead as a process, a means of representing a set of ideas about reality. It is the kind of myth which, according to Roland Barthes, 'cannot possibly be an object, a concept, or an idea; it is a mode of signification, a form'.[41] It deceptively claims to be a direct representation of reality, and it offers a mono-

[39] Katharina Glau, *Christa Wolfs 'Kassandra' und Aischylos' 'Orestie': Zur Rezeption der griechischen Tragödie in der deutschen Literatur der Gegenwart* (Heidelberg: Winter, 1996), 41. See, for example, Wolf, *Voraussetzungen einer Erzählung: Kassandra*, 104.

[40] 'In diesem Zitat [from *Amanda*] spiegelt sich die konventionelle Entgegensetzung von Mythos und Logos wider, in der dem Mythos das Attribut "bildhaft" und dem Logos "rational" bzw. "abstrakt" zugeordnet ist. Die moderne Mythosforschung geht über diese einfache Dichotomie hinaus. Zu bedenken ist bei Morgner selbstverständlich der literarische Kontext.' Rosenkranz-Kaiser, 105.

[41] Barthes, *Mythologies*, 117.

lithic story, denying the validity of all others. In order to elucidate the different ways in which Wolf and Morgner relate these notions of myth to each other, I shall distinguish between two opposing forms of myth; between myth as an open discourse and myth as a closed discourse.[42] As my analysis will show, Wolf and Morgner position ancient myth differently in relation to this dichotomy. However, both authors are attempting ultimately to overcome and expose closed myths of the kind which abounded in GDR society—and, they suggest, abound in western civilization as a whole—and to make productive the potential of myth as an open literary discourse of the kind Fühmann outlines.

Both Wolf and Morgner work with a model of history which assumes a contrast between prehistory, which is associated with ancient myth, and later history. The two writers focus on different aspects of this contrast. Morgner understands it as a transition in ways of thinking, whereby ancient myth contrasts with the rational and objective discourses of science and other academic disciplines which succeeded it (*Amanda*, 220, 373–5). This understanding of myth bears a great resemblance to that of the GDR Classicist Fritz Jürß, who asserts that mythological thought differs from later rational thought in that it interprets the world 'nicht durch Begriffe, sondern durch Bilder, nicht durch Sachen, [. . .] sondern durch Personen (Götter)'. He contrasts ancient myth and the modern, rational discourses of science and philosophy, showing how 'das Nebeneinander widersprüchlicher Auffassungen', which is 'im Mythos häufig und nicht anstößig', becomes impossible in the latter.[43] Morgner shares this notion of ancient myth as an open and plural discourse. Wolf draws instead on Johann Jakob Bachofen and the feminist literature inspired by his work, in order to postulate a social transition from prehistorical matriarchy to modern patriarchy. Both the idea of a historical progression from *mythos* to *logos*, and the theory of a prehistorical matriarchal society have been contested by recent scholarship, but this is of little import in assessing the contribution which Wolf and Morgner made to GDR discourses by offering new, critical accounts of history.[44] Both authors draw on

---

[42] This is a slightly different distinction from Weigel's differentiation between open and closed literary approaches to myth. My categories allow for the presence of contrasting kinds of myth in a single text. Cf. Weigel, *Die Stimme der Medusa*, 280.

[43] Fritz Jürß, *Vom Mythos der alten Griechen: Deutungen und Erzählungen* (Leipzig: Reclam, 1988), 8.

[44] See, for example, Hans Blumenberg, *Arbeit am Mythos* (Frankfurt am Main: Suhrkamp, 1979; repr. 1986), 18, 34; Beate Wagner-Hasel, '"Das Private wird politisch": Die Perspektive "Geschlecht" in der Altertumswissenschaft', in *Weiblichkeit in geschichtlicher Perspektive:*

several different models of history, in order to place ancient myth in a historical framework in such a way that it becomes a valuable complement to modern thought.

In her study of myth in recent German literature, Petra Waschescio suggests that there are two contrasting ways in which myth can be defined: firstly as a phenomenon which is fundamentally other to modern thought based on reason, and is thus outside history, being either prehistorical or ahistorical; and secondly as a form of thought which exists in a dialectical relationship with reason, and is therefore present in the modern world.[45] Both of these definitions are necessary for a full understanding of myth in *Amanda* and *Kassandra*.

Marx's view of myth, which formed the basis of the official understanding of myth in the GDR, is typical of Waschescio's first definition. Associating myth with the 'geschichtliche Kindheit der Menschheit', he views it as a prehistorical mode of thought which has become redundant in the modern world:

> Wo bleibt Vulkan gegen Roberts et Co., Jupiter gegen den Blitzableiter und Hermes gegen den Crédit mobilier? Alle Mythologie überwindet und beherrscht und gestaltet die Naturkräfte in der Einbildung und durch die Einbildung: verschwindet also mit der wirklichen Herrschaft über dieselben.[46]

By the 1980s the ecological and military threats posed by advanced science and technology meant that faith in a form of progress based on controlling nature was no longer possible. Wolf and Morgner adopt the historical framework of Marx's view, but attach a different value to ancient myth. They draw on western feminist research such as that of Heide Göttner-Abendroth to associate ancient myth and prehistory with a matriarchal society, and thus view them not as an inferior substitute for later history and science, but instead as a valuable source of alternatives to the patriarchal values which have determined and dominated history.[47] In *Amanda*, for example, prehistory is associated with a feminine principle which can complement the masculine bias of a history determined by conflict: Laura decides to study ancient history in an attempt to discover 'was die Mutter aller Dinge ist', consciously countering Heraclitus' claim, 'Der Streit ist der Vater aller Dinge'

Fallstudien und Reflexionen zu Grundproblemen der historischen Frauenforschung, ed. Ursula A. J. Becher and Jörn Rüsen (Frankfurt am Main: Suhrkamp, 1988), 11–50 (24–5).

[45] Waschescio, 13–20.

[46] Marx, 'Einleitung [zu den *Grundrissen der Kritik der politischen Ökonomie*]', in *Ausgewählte Werke*, ii. 496–7.

[47] See Heide Göttner-Abendroth, *Die Göttin und ihr Heros* (Munich: Frauenoffensive, 1982).

(*Amanda*, 114). Kassandra is of special interest to Wolf because her life is historically situated 'an einer Nahtstelle' between a matriarchal and a patriarchal society (*Voraussetzungen*, 144). Wolf rejects Marx's dismissive view of the ancient Greeks as children, suggesting that modern archaeology has provided us with information vital for understanding their culture and myths which was not available to Marx. However, in rediscovering positive values in this society and mythology, Wolf is wary of the danger of idealizing a historical era which was not without deep inequalities and violence (*Voraussetzungen*, 95, 60–1).

At the same time as regarding ancient myth as a positive other, Wolf and Morgner work with a dialectical model of the relationship between myth and reason, such as that outlined by Horkheimer and Adorno in *Dialektik der Aufklärung*, and typical of Waschescio's second definition of myth.[48] The two texts show how ancient myths can provide valuable insights, and suggest that much supposedly rational thinking in the modern world is founded on unquestioned ideologically motivated myths. They thereby challenge Marx's model of modern history as a positive progression based on fundamentally different principles from those of prehistory. *Amanda* and *Kassandra* are important expressions of the paradigm shift in GDR intellectuals' ways of thinking about history which Emmerich has discerned in works from the late 1970s onwards.[49] Around this time, he suggests, faith in the Marxist model of historical progress facilitated by the enlightenment values underlying science and technology gave way to a recognition of the dialectical relationship between enlightenment and myth, according to which 'schon der Mythos ist Aufklärung, und Aufklärung schlägt in Mythologie zurück'.[50] A recognition of this dialectic was already implicit in *Kein Ort. Nirgends*, where Wolf allowed Kleist to reflect on the fallacy underlying Nees von Esenbeck's optimistic faith in progress as a linear development based on the expansion of knowledge:

Der Mensch hat ein unwiderstehliches Bedürfnis, sich aufzuklären, da er ohne Aufklärung nicht viel mehr ist als ein Tier. Doch sobald wir in das Reich des Wissens treten, scheint ein böser Zauber die Anwendung, die wir von unsern Kenntnissen machen, gegen uns zu kehren. (*Kein Ort*, 81)

---

[48] Max Horkheimer and Theodor W. Adorno, *Dialektik der Aufklärung: Philosophische Fragmente* (New York: Social Studies Association, 1944; repr. Frankfurt am Main: Fischer, 1995).
[49] Wolfgang Emmerich, '"Dialektik der Aufklärung" in der jüngeren DDR-Literatur', in *Die andere deutsche Literatur*, 115–28.
[50] Horkheimer and Adorno, 6.

By the early 1980s, the fact that enlightenment thinking with its emphasis on instrumental reason seemed to have brought the world to the brink of catastrophe prompted Wolf and Morgner to explore the relationship between enlightenment and myth as a matter of urgency.

The Content of Myth as a Critique of History

Both *Amanda* and the *Kassandra* narrative use the form and content of ancient myth to expose the closed ideological myths which have been influential in the historical development of modern conditions of existence. They thereby criticize the course of history, and offer alternative interpretations of it. Both writers base their critiques on the idea that the patriarchal principles underlying western society and thought have resulted in the suppression of certain qualities necessary for the peaceful development of mankind, and both work to expose the ideological myths which present this historically determined order as a natural one. However, they use ancient myth in quite different ways to achieve this.

Morgner constructs mythical realms which sometimes borrow elements of the content of ancient myth and, more importantly, share what she sees as the form of ancient myth. The three realms presented in the novel—one the setting for the story of Pandora and Prometheus, another centred on the Brocken, and the third concerning the rebirth of sirens and their task—offer broad models of the sociological and philosophical history of western civilization, exposing the myths on which western thought is founded. In contrast with the writing of history as Morgner understands it, and with myth as a closed discourse, the mythical realms in *Amanda* do not explicitly assert a single interpretation of events as authoritative. Individually, they present a series of unexplained and often relatively unconnected events, and thus initiate a search for possible meanings, which is pursued within the novel by Beatriz and Arke, and at an extratextual level by the reader. Collectively, they epitomize plurality by offering a variety of models of the way the modern world originated. In their refusal to fix meanings by denying contradictions and ambiguities, they resemble Fühmann's notion of myth as a mode of discourse which does not separate contradictory elements into distinct, opposable entities, but instead 'gibt den Widerspruch wieder'.[51] Morgner's myths function as

---

[51] Fühmann, 'Das mythische Element', 95.

an alternative, fantastic discourse on history which, in its use of images and personifications instead of abstractions, corresponds to the 'bild-liche Aneignung der Welt' which Girgana outlines in the 'Blocksberg-Vorlesung' chapter (*Amanda*, 375). These mythical realms represent an attempt to re-create the quality of ancient myth as a form of the quali-tative and subjective 'konkrete Zwiesprache' which Girgana sees as an essential complement to the quantitative and objective 'abstrakte Zwiesprache' which has become the exclusive principle in modern western thought (*Amanda*, 373). Alison Lewis fails to recognize the essential qualitative difference between the myths Morgner decon-structs and those she creates, when she claims that 'what Morgner is attempting is [. . .] a refeminization of myth via the process of demythologizing patriarchal myths and resurrecting matriarchal or feminine equivalents'.[52] A more serious misconception of the work's achievements is to be found in Rosenkranz-Kaiser's concluding com-ments. Implicitly applying a monolithic notion of myth as a negative phenomenon to the text, Rosenkranz-Kaiser is able to applaud only Morgner's demythologizing intent, regarding her creation of myths as a failing:

Mit dem Ziel der Entlarvung vermeintlich patriarchaler Interpretationen und ideologischer Vereinnahmungen von Mythen sollte eine feministische Ent-mythisierung stattfinden. In diesem Sinne und durch den Einsatz ihres satirischen Stils hat Morgner die Struktur des Mythischen durchbrochen. Bei der Aktualisierung von Mythologemen war ihr das nicht immer geglückt, viel-mehr unterstützte sie so die Begründung von feministischen Gegenmythen.[53]

This view of the text is, like Lewis's comment, based on the assumption that Morgner's mythical realms and the ideological myths she exposes are equivalents, marked by a simple reversal of gender relations. The idea that the two forms of myth represent contrasting kinds of dis-course is central to my argument.

In an interview with Eva Kaufmann in 1984 Morgner discusses the contemporary need for 'eine Überlebensstrategie gegen die Angst', which motivated her interest in prehistory and its myths:

Für diese Überlebensstrategie ist Ermutigung unentbehrlich. Woher nehmen? Aus dem, was man Geschichte nennt, kaum. Da könnte man nur sehen: Kriege hat es immer gegeben. Der Verdacht könnte entstehen, sie entsprächen der Natur des Menschen. Die Suche nach Menschheitsepochen,

---

[52] Lewis, 233.   [53] Rosenkranz-Kaiser, 167.

die ihre Auseinandersetzungen nicht kriegerisch bewältigt haben, führte zu einem Interesse für das, was wir Vorgeschichte nennen.[54]

This comment highlights one of the functions of the mythical realms in *Amanda*. By reworking the content and the form of prehistorical myth, they serve to create a perspective outside the patriarchal value systems of the modern world, and so have the potential to inspire hope in a way history is unable to do, by positing the possibility of a utopian solution to contemporary world problems.

The 'Parnaß-Mythologie' chapter demonstrates the development of a tradition of male violence, power seeking, and conflict which prevents humans from living harmoniously with each other and with the earth (*Amanda*, 63–8). Zeus is presented here not as the greatest of all gods, but as a personification of the principles which are shown in the novel to have determined history and which are responsible for the destructive behaviour of mankind as manifested in wars and ecological damage. He exists in conflict with Gaja [Morgner's spelling], who embodies the needs of the earth, which have been increasingly neglected by mankind in the course of history.

In contrast with these personifications of abstract and unambiguously evaluated principles, Prometheus and Pandora can be seen as embodying more ambivalent human qualities. Morgner's treatment of these figures is thus very close to Fühmann's analysis of mythical characters as embodiments of inner contradictions.[55] Prometheus has those characteristics regarded by society as masculine and valued by patriarchy: his ambitious nature and urge for progress can have both positive and negative consequences, as demonstrated by the benevolent and destructive uses to which the fire which he gains for humanity can be put (*Amanda*, 66). However, the masculinist bias of Prometheus' exclusively male human race results in a 'Mangel an Liebesfähigkeit' which leads to the predominance of the negative, destructive application of his qualities. In an attempt to achieve her harmonious ideal, Gaja introduces Pandora to balance the bias of this human race. This produces the potential for love and the creation of further human beings through love, which should ensure that Prometheus' qualities are used positively to peaceful ends. The idea, presented as the truth in Hesiod's version, that Pandora is the bringer of 'alle Übel der Welt' and a gift from Zeus to hinder mankind's progress ('Prometheus und

---

[54] 'Der weibliche Ketzer heißt Hexe: Gespräch mit Eva Kaufmann', in *Irmtraud Morgner: Texte, Daten, Bilder*, ed. Gerhardt, 42–69 (47).
[55] Fühmann, 'Das mythische Element', 94–5.

seinem Werk zum Verderben bestimmt'), is reduced here to the status of a rumour spread by Zeus to prevent this potential from being fulfilled (*Amanda*, 66). This misogynist version of events is thus exposed as an ideologically motivated and inaccurate presentation, reflecting the patriarchal values which Hesiod imposed on the myth in his interpretation.

The fact that Pandora's box, as the meaning of her name suggests, contains all human qualities, both those regarded as masculine (the 'Luftgestalten') and those regarded as feminine (the 'Güter mit Fittichen'), reflects the androgyny of the ideal she represents and the conviction on which the novel is based, that it is the union of masculine and feminine values which is to be achieved, rather than the replacement of masculine by feminine values. The fact that the qualities from Pandora's box are referred to as 'Zukunftsbilder' indicates that Pandora and the ideal she embodies are to be understood as a model of a potential utopian future, in contrast with humanity at present, as represented by Prometheus. This humanity values only the goods represented by the 'Luftgestalten', disregarding the 'Güter mit Fittichen', with the result that it becomes increasingly destructive (*Amanda*, 67).

The union in love of Pandora and Prometheus which is prevented in this mythological realm is presented in the narrative framework of the novel and in the world of the Brocken witches as an event which must be achieved: the Oracle of Delphi defines Beatriz's task as helping to bring about this union, while the witches shout 'Holt Pandora heim' at Walpurgisnacht (*Amanda*, 9, 332).

The second mythological sphere in *Amanda*, established in the chapter 'Brockenmythologie', is presented as a parallel to the first: this chapter, like 'Parnaß-Mythologie', concerns a creation myth and is presented orally to Beatriz, this time by Arke (*Amanda*, 88–95). Although elements of this Germanic mythology are based on traditional ideas, such as the legendary association of the Brocken with witches, unlike the 'Parnaß-Mythologie', the 'Brockenmythologie' as a whole does not have a traditional basis. Like the 'Parnaß-Mythologie', it can be seen as a model of the development of the principles on which the patriarchal world is based: it focuses particularly on the ideas of division and subordination through which patriarchy operates, and demonstrates the effects of these on women. History is presented here as a series of divisions creating polarities whereby one pole either gains dominance over the other or is given positive value while the other is devalued. The original polarity is presented as that between Mother

Earth and the air. These elements represent respectively the concrete and visible concerns of the world, as exemplified by care for the earth, and abstract and intangible (or invisible) ideas.[56] Whereas Mother Earth is presented as the source of life, air is presented as the source of conflict (*Amanda*, 88–9). Air's outwitting and imprisoning of earth thus represents the dominance of abstract thought over concrete concerns which has developed in patriarchal society and which, as the novel suggests, underlies contemporary world problems.

Morgner undermines the opposition between Good and Evil, embodied by God and the devil, which forms the basis of Christianity, and exposes it as a myth by presenting God and the devil as the two halves of an originally united being, which therefore have the same function, status, motivations, and insubstantial origin. Created for the purpose of allowing dispute, they are dependent on each other for their existence and meaning (*Amanda*, 89). An opposition regarded as absolute in western thought is thus subordinated to a further opposition, in which God and the devil are both representative of the same patriarchal principle and abstract mode of thought, and are together opposed to the concrete concerns embodied by Mother Earth.

The patriarchal order by which men are given control over women is, in this mythological world, introduced by God and the devil, in freeing Mother Earth's sons, dividing each into an 'Oberengel' and an 'Oberteufel', and giving them 'die Ehre, als Kerkermeister der Schwestern zu wirken' (*Amanda*, 91). The principles of division and specialization underlying the formation of this religion, and vital for its perpetuation, are shown to represent a way of thinking which, because of their respective social roles, men eagerly accept but women are reluctant to adopt. It is characteristic of Morgner's Marxist form of feminism that the division of labour, seen in Marxist theory as a root cause of inequalities in capitalism, is here analysed as an important element in the rise of patriarchy: 'Den Frauen, mit Ackerbau und Kindern beschäftigt und so im Umgang mit Ganzheiten, fiel teilen schwer. Die Männer spezialisierten sich zuerst' (*Amanda*, 91). The order created by God and the devil is imitated by humanity in the polarization of men and women, and the attachment of values to each, such that men are positive, or good, and women are negative, or evil. Furthermore, women are not defined in their own right, but as a negative pole to give meaning to men as 'Fachmänner für das Gute'

---

[56] Cf. Reid, 'Woman, Myth and Magic', 106.

(*Amanda*, 92).[57] The development of a patriarchal order is thus presented as parallel to the development of western religion, reflecting the collaboration of the latter in oppressing women.

'Magic mountains', exemplified in Germany by the Brocken, are introduced here as places outside the order of society, where it is possible to think about utopian future possibilities conflicting with this order: 'In Ordnung ist das Mögliche von heute und morgen denkbar. Unmögliches, das heißt, das Mögliche von übermorgen, wird ordentlich als Unordnung empfunden und ist nur auf Bergen denkbar' (*Amanda*, 93). The witches and heretics who gather on such mountains are thus given positive significance as people who refuse to conform to an unjust and oppressive regime and who seek an alternative order: alchemy becomes a metaphor for the attempt to create such an order. The way the men gain dominance over the women in these activities, until they have sole control in them—the women being imprisoned in the Hörselberg—reflects the way men and values regarded as masculine have historically become dominant in attempts to improve society. The red and the white magic stones represent two different forms of progress: the red stone represents a form based on the ideal of acquiring wealth and power, while the white stone represents a form based on the ideal of regaining wholeness (*Amanda*, 94). As is reflected by the activities of the ravens, western society has neglected the latter in concentrating on the former:

Als der weiße Zauberstein nicht gelingen wollte, versuchten sie, den roten nachzubauen.
Und dieses Streben faszinierte sie so, daß sie nichts anderes mehr denken konnten. (*Amanda*, 95)

This bias can be seen as the consequence of the valuing of abstract thought above concrete concerns, which is presented critically throughout the novel. Most of the characters in the plot centring on Laura's biography suffer from divisions which either result from the impossibility of fulfilling all aspects of their personality in society, or are forcibly imposed and deprive them of the strength needed to cope with everyday life. Their society, however, has little interest in solving the immediate and concrete problems of these people: the 'Philosophie [. . .] für Nichtfachleute. Über täglich zu bewältigende, unabweisbare, elementare Lebensereignisse' which Laura desires does not exist

---

[57] Here Morgner's mythology echoes the idea that patriarchal society constructs women as men's Other, which is central to modern feminism. Compare, for example, Simone de Beauvoir, *The Second Sex*, trans. H. M. Parshley (Harmondsworth: Penguin, 1972).

(*Amanda*, 124). Instead humanity is, as Arke and Konrad Tenner recognize, trapped by the myth of eternal economic, scientific, and technical expansion which has made the present state of the world possible (*Amanda*, 290, 217–18). Historically, society's ideals concerning the future have thus moved away from any idea of changing the polarizing patriarchal order, to ambitions of endless growth based on principles central to this order. This historical phenomenon is reflected mythologically in the way the Brocken, as the site where ideals for the future are constructed, is no longer used to search for an alternative social order, but is occupied by a regime representing the same order as that of society, which works towards its ideals by expanding the analytical sciences.

The attempts of women with alternative ideals to use the Brocken for their own purposes lead Kolbuk to introduce 'teuflische Teilung' in order to maintain the ravens' monopoly in the use of the Brocken (*Amanda*, 95). This division of women whose non-conformist elements are not destroyed by society (that is, by 'sittliche Teilung') and the diversion of the 'unusable' witch halves of these women to the Hörselberg brothel form a model of society's channelling of women's energy and creativity (and indeed those of all dissidents) into activities which do not disrupt, but support the existing order. This principle is demonstrated by the historical example of the execution of Damiens, where the discontent and aggressive energy of the oppressed masses are channelled into enthusiastic support for society's brutal punishment of a dissident (*Amanda*, 74–7). In a similar way, Kolbuk attempts to divert the energies of the creative and non-conformist sides of women, embodied in this mythology by witches, into support for the patriarchal raven regime at the Blocksberg.

In contrast with the myth of Pandora and Prometheus, which remains in the realm of theory, on which Beatriz and Arke can draw as a model of their aims, the sphere of the Brocken mythology is the setting of a plot which is narrated directly by Beatriz. This plot is integrated with the story concerning Laura and Berlin, so that a fictive and even fantastic, but historically grounded, 'reality' merges with myth here. The integration of the Brocken sphere and the Berlin sphere demonstrates what the Brocken mythology, presented theoretically, means in terms of historical reality. The 'teuflische Teilung' which Laura undergoes is thus related to the specific context of the GDR. Its effects in removing her non-conformist and potentially rebellious side, and halving her energy, can at a more realistic level be seen as the natural consequences of social conditions in the GDR, where the double burden of career and household duties left women with little energy to contemplate ways of changing the situation, and where any form of rebellion against the system was not tolerated by the authorities. This element of the Brocken mythology may therefore be read as a metaphor for the reduction of women's energy and the elimination of their non-conformist sides by conditions in the GDR if these have not already been effected by social and cultural expectations of women ('sittliche Teilung').

The ideal of gaining wholeness represented by the liquid silver, presented in the mythology as a global and social necessity, is presented at a personal level in the Berlin plot: for Laura and the other women, witchcraft and alchemy represent the only possible means of finding the energy to perform the daily tasks required of them. The failure of Laura's and Konrad Tenner's attempts to gain the liquid silver demonstrates, however, that any successful solution to the problems of the present situation must be found at a collective, rather than a personal, level.

The three factions amongst the Hörselberg witches represent different strategies which can be adopted by women in an attempt to overcome patriarchy. The hope associated with Amanda's androgynous owl faction contrasts with criticism of Isebel's 'Rotrock-Fraktion', which 'schätzt die von Männern entwickelte Kriegskunst für ihre Zwecke und ist männerfeindlich' and of Hulle's 'Grünröcke', who 'wissen nur, was sie nicht wollen, nämlich: wie Männer sein' (*Amanda*, 329–30). Morgner's hopes for an improved future in reality clearly lie in the creation of a balance between masculine and feminine principles, and not in militant feminism or a celebration of a vague concept of femininity. The achievement of change in the mythological sphere, in the witches' conquering of the Blocksberg between the time level of the Berlin plot and that of the narrative framework, provides hope for similar progress in the practical sphere of historical reality.

The mythological world of the Brocken is also related to historical reality within the novel through the roles played by its central symbol, the Brocken mountain, in each realm. It has mythological significance as a magic mountain on which utopian future orders can be conceived and later as the home of the ravens, and historical significance as an area bordering West Germany and therefore made inaccessible to civilians by the GDR authorities. The two spheres are comically integrated in the novel: the ravens are forced to evacuate the Brocken because it is needed by the GDR military, and in the chapter 'Wette auf dem Blocksberg', the meeting of Zacharias and Kolbuk is mediated by Colonel Manfred Fakal of the GDR *Volksarmee* (*Amanda*, 365–71). Furthermore, the witches' ultimate aim, beyond conquering Schloß Blocksberg, is to bring about 'Weltzustände [. . .], die Grenzbewachung und Militär überflüssig werden ließen', that is, to end the East–West conflict which is the subject of much concern in the narrative framework (*Amanda*, 231). Parallels can be seen between the historical and mythological situations centred on the Brocken: in each case, the Brocken is the meeting point of opposing forces in conflict. The meeting of Zacharias and Kolbuk from above and below is paralleled by the meeting of two opposed power blocs from East and West. Since the opposition between Zacharias and Kolbuk is exposed by the mythology as an ideological construct and both are shown to represent the same principle of conflict, this parallel implies that the opposition perceived between eastern and western bloc countries is similarly constructed for ideological purposes and to enable conflict. This opposition, it is suggested, denies the underlying identity of the two political systems, both of which are based on patriarchal principles, and neither of which values peace or the earth sufficiently.

The third mythological sphere, featuring sirens, is restricted to the narrative framework, and provides both the plot of this layer of the novel, and the purpose for the fictive writing of the novel within this layer. As in her reworking of the Pandora myth, Morgner reverses the values conventionally attached to the sirens. The fatal danger traditionally ascribed to these creatures, as embodiments of female beauty with the power to lure men—as represented by Odysseus—away from their ordered existence and to destruction, is exposed here as an ideological myth with a psychological basis. As Arke explains to Beatriz, demonizing the sirens served to counter the threats posed by sexual attraction for a male subject constituted by repression:

Wer heimlich begehre, was er öffentlich verachte, brauche diesen Trick. Die frauenverachtenden Kulturen brauchten ihn seit Jahrtausenden. Er verschaffe eine besondere Art von Lust. Die Lust des Verbotenen. Um sich eine Frau verächtlich zu machen, genüge, ihr Wesen als dumm zu deuten. Um eine weise Frau verächtlich zu machen, wäre erforderlich, ihr Wesen wenigstens als mörderisch zu deuten. [. . .] Vor Mördern [fürchtete sich Odysseus] nicht, aber vor sich. Die sagenhaften Gesänge der Sirenen hätten in ihm ausgraben können, was zugeschüttet war ... (*Amanda*, 41)[58]

---

[58] Cf. Horkheimer and Adorno, 50–87; Inge Stephan, *Musen und Medusen: Mythos und Geschlecht in der Literatur des 20. Jahrhunderts* (Cologne: Böhlau, 1997), 122–9.

Morgner re-evaluates the effects of the sirens on men as a positive ability to threaten patriarchal value systems and so draw humanity away from the destructive course it has taken: 'Schlachtenmut, Eroberungswille, Siegesgier: Dieser Tugendsockel, worauf Odysseus' Leben gründete, würde unterm Gesang von Sirenen zerstieben' (*Amanda*, 11). This interpretation of sirens links them to the other meaning of the word, as creatures who warn of dangerous situations (*Amanda*, 78). Due to the increasing frequency of the wars which have formed patriarchal history, the original powers of the sirens have been lost: it is the task of Beatriz and the other sirens reborn in response to the desperate situation of the world, to regain the ability to sing and thereby warn humanity of the approaching catastrophe. As the reincarnations of wise women—Catherine the Great, Sappho, and Yetunde, transported as a slave from Benin to Brazil in the sixteenth century, besides Beatriz herself—Morgner's sirens serve to translate women's historical experience into a mythical reserve of power which, although crippled by the present patriarchal world, has the potential to change the future course of history. While hope in *Trobadora Beatriz* was associated with a historical woman's ability to transcend boundaries, the greater severity of present problems means that in *Amanda* only a power outside—and above—history can provide hope for the future. The siren mythology reflects the historical need both for a warning which humanity will take seriously and for a means of diverting mankind from the aggression which has become the determining factor in its behaviour. The fact that Beatriz has to resort to using her 'schriftliche Sirenenstimme' points to the lack, in reality, of a truly effective means of warning and overcoming aggression, and to the function of literature as an available, but less effective means (*Amanda*, 243).

Christa Wolf uses ancient myth to present a critique of history in very different ways. Unlike Morgner, whose myths offer broad models of long-term developments in western society, Wolf uses the Kassandra myth to focus closely on the psychological development of one individual, and on the political and social developments at one particular point in history. The implications of this myth for understanding history more broadly arise from the connections between the myth and the contemporary world which are suggested by the accompanying lectures. One way in which Wolf uses the mythical story is to reconstruct a potential historical reality at a time which she understands as a crucial turning-point in the history of the western world. In the third lecture accompanying the narrative, she proposes a conception of history as a series of crossroads—at which humanity had alternative choices to the one actually taken—which has determined the development of society into its present form:

Gab es Kreuz- und Wendepunkte, an denen die Menschheit, will sagen: die europäische und nordamerikanische Menschheit, Erfinder und Träger der technischen Zivilisation, andere Entscheidungen hätten treffen können, deren Verlauf nicht selbstzerstörerisch gewesen wäre? (*Voraussetzungen*, 107)

Wolf is using the myth to explore the roots of later historical developments in the earliest of these historical turning-points for which evidence still exists. Kassandra's life-story is intended to demonstrate the beginnings of the patriarchal social order and its accompanying modes of thought, which Wolf regards as the central determinants in the history of western civilization:

Aber eben diesen Weg ist doch, vereinfacht gesagt, das abendländische Denken gegangen, den Weg der Sonderung, der Analyse, des Verzichts auf die Mannigfaltigkeit der Erscheinungen zugunsten des Dualismus, des Monismus, zugunsten der Geschlossenheit von Weltbildern und Systemen; des Verzichts auf Subjektivität zugunsten gesicherter 'Objektivität'. (*Voraussetzungen*, 139)

Wolf is rejecting the Marxist view of history as a law-determined and teleological progression from one stage to the next, more advanced stage, in favour of a model which posits various possible courses of further development at each stage in history, and thus allows the notion that history could have been, and even should have been, different.

A second way in which the Kassandra myth is related to later history is through its capacity as an allegorical model of the contemporary East–West tensions in Europe. The third Frankfurt lecture juxtaposes developments in international politics of the early 1980s with reflections on the myth, in such a way as to highlight both the parallel principles underlying the Trojan War and the Cold War, and the marked differences with regard to the respective states of technology and the corresponding potentials for destruction: 'In Troia aber, das glaube ich sicher, waren die Leute nicht anders, als wir es sind. Ihre Götter sind unsre Götter, die falschen. Nur sind unsre Mittel nicht ihre Mittel gewesen' (*Voraussetzungen*, 95). David Jenkinson has provided a detailed reading of the narrative as a *Schlüsselerzählung*, showing how

Kassandra's position in Troy can be seen as a cipher for the position of writers in the GDR in the early 1980s.[59]

Like *Amanda*, *Kassandra* exposes closed ideological myths, showing how they are used as tools of power in determining people's consciousness. In the *Voraussetzungen* essays, Wolf emphasizes her aim of demythologizing the myth: 'Mein Anliegen bei der Kassandra-Figur: Rückführung aus dem Mythos in die (gedachten) sozialen und historischen Koordinaten' (*Voraussetzungen*, 111). The narrative accordingly exposes the instances of divine intervention central to the traditional Kassandra story as ideological myths masking political motives. Instead, Wolf subjects the story to the laws of historical and psychological causality. The story of Paris's abduction of Helen after being promised the most beautiful woman in the world by Aphrodite is thus rejected as the cause of the Trojan War. Instead it is presented as an ideological myth deliberately created by human beings to induce the belief that the war is in accordance with divine intentions, and so beyond human responsibility (*Kassandra*, 79–82). With a characteristically Marxist emphasis, Wolf exposes economic and ideological factors which she believes to be the real causes of the war: competition for the rights to sea passages important for trade, and a developing mentality of aggression which begins to regard war as an end in itself (*Voraussetzungen*, 19).

Similarly, Wolf rejects the mythical explanation of Kassandra's gift of prophecy as bestowed by Apollo. This story is reduced, in the narrative, to the status of a dream, which may have psychological and metaphorical truth but is not literally true as a real cause (*Kassandra*, 19–20). The dream and Marpessa's interpretation of it are shown to be significant for Kassandra because of their value in explaining her life more generally: she claims that Marpessa has given her 'den Schlüssel für meinen Traum und für mein Leben'. Marpessa's suggestion that she has the gift to foretell the future, but will not be believed, gains its resonance for Kassandra from the fact that she has long desired this gift. In Wolf's formulation of her reaction to Marpessa, it is very clear that the ability to prophesy is to be seen not as a gift imposed on Kassandra from outside, but as something originating within Kassandra herself: 'Die Sehergabe. Das war sie. Ein heißer Schreck. Ich hatte sie mir erträumt' (*Kassandra*, 29). Wolf demystifies the nature

---

[59] See David Jenkinson, 'Loyalty and its Limits: Christa Wolf's *Kassandra* as a "Schlüsselerzählung"', in *Literature on the Threshold: The German Novel in the 1980s*, ed. Arthur Williams, Stuart Parkes, and Roland Smith (New York: Berg, 1990), 235–52.

of Kassandra's activities as a seer, rejecting any suggestion of supernatural or mysterious powers and regarding her ability instead as one of psychological understanding. She interprets dreams as the expression of latent human thoughts which evidently have a determining influence on the future (*Voraussetzungen*, 32). The true reason for Kassandra's ability, Wolf suggests in the third lecture, lies in her clearsightedness in perceiving present conditions: 'Sie "sieht" die Zukunft, weil sie den Mut hat, die wirklichen Verhältnisse der Gegenwart zu sehen' (*Voraussetzungen*, 96). It is through renouncing her privileged position within the increasingly patriarchal hierarchies of her society and gaining contact with people outside these social structures, that Wolf's Kassandra attains the ability to escape sharing the blind spots of her culture. The fact that her prophecies are not believed is likewise explained not as a punishment by Apollo for refusing his advances, but in social and historical terms. In revealing the blind spots of the ideology developing in Troy and thereby threatening it, and in doing so as a woman in an atmosphere of increasing hostility towards women, Kassandra must be disbelieved and branded as mad by representatives of the new patriarchal mentality, eager to uphold their new way of thinking.

Wolf thus uses the Kassandra myth as a model of how myth functions as a closed discourse. Like Morgner, she reworks the myth in such a way as to expose the ideological myths which, in her view, have determined traditional interpretations of the central characters. However, whereas Morgner explicitly creates new myths which—in stark contrast to the closed form of myth—function by opening possibilities of meaning, the status of Wolf's narrative in relation to myth is far less clear. Although her version of Kassandra's story subjects the myth to the laws of historical and psychological causality, it retains mythical qualities, and cannot be regarded as a total demythologization to produce a narrative of a different order.

Wolf presents her version of Kassandra's story as a model of processes which she sees as generally applicable to female experience throughout the modern age: 'In Kassandra ist eine der ersten Frauengestalten überliefert, deren Schicksal vorformt, was dann, dreitausend Jahre lang, den Frauen geschehen soll: daß sie zum Objekt gemacht werden' (*Voraussetzungen*, 86). Wolf's professed aim to free Kassandra from myth and establish a historically plausible account of her life exists in tension with a desire to create a story which can serve as a model for the origins of the modern world and for experiences shared by women throughout the last three thousand years. As an allegorical model of origins, the narrative retains one of the central functions of ancient myth.

The utopian elements of the story, too, suggest that Wolf is demythologizing the traditional story in order to create her own, alternative myth of Kassandra. After divesting the traditional version of those elements Wolf sees as distorting ideological myths, the remaining, historically governed story has little utopian potential. Georgina Paul has pointed out that Kassandra, like the later Medea, can remain an innocent ideal embodying a redemptive notion of femininity only by failing to act in the course of history and adopting instead a position of impotence in the face of history.[60] As Sigrid Weigel has observed, Wolf counterbalances her historical aims concerning the Kassandra figure with a psychologization which is able to inspire hope where the historical events are unable to do so:

Erzählerisch kommt dieses Ergebnis dadurch zustande, daß die Autorin aus der deprimierenden historischen Wahrheit, die aus ihrem Konzept der Historisierung des Mythos folgt, sich mit der Psychologisierung der mythischen Figur einen Ausweg geschaffen hat.[61]

Thus, although Kassandra cannot have any influence on the course of history, her psychological development becomes a model of a woman's 'Ringen um Autonomie' (*Voraussetzungen*, 118). By focusing on Kassandra's inner development as a potentially utopian element in what would otherwise appear a hopeless historical situation, Wolf's myth attempts to inspire hope in a similar way to Morgner's mythical realms, in their utopian aspects. In the lectures, Wolf expresses an awareness of the tension between her historicizing and her utopian intentions concerning the Kassandra material. She confesses to an 'Übertragung eines gegenwärtigen Wunschbildes auf eine mythologische Figur, die so nicht gewesen sein *kann*', and admits that her conception of Kassandra's story as an inner 'Befreiungsprozeß' is 'eine utopische Sicht, nicht eine historische' (*Voraussetzungen*, 46, 90).

The 'Gegenwelt' of the cave community at the foot of Mount Ida, as a space outside the course of history, is an element in the narrative which has a particularly clear status as myth (*Kassandra*, 58). It is a world in which matriarchal myth, as a way of thinking belonging to the

---

[60] Georgina Paul, 'Schwierigkeiten mit der Dialektik: Zu Christa Wolfs *Medea: Stimmen*', *GLL* 50 (1997), 2, 227–40 (236).
[61] Weigel, 'Vom Sehen zur Seherin', 181–2.

prehistoric society which is gradually being replaced in Troy by one organized patriarchally and based on instrumental reason, is kept alive. It functions within the narrative as a utopian realm exemplifying a holistic way of life, humane human interaction, and equality between men and women. Although demonstrating the possibility of a non-aggressive way of life in a truly communist society, it proves to be powerless to change the course of history in any way.

Although Morgner and Wolf are using ancient myth to construct very similar models of history as a progression towards an increasingly one-sided way of thinking based on the exclusion of everything associated with the feminine, striking differences are apparent in the ways they employ myth to express a critique of this history. Morgner sees the pluralistic and non-authoritarian discourse of ancient myth as a valuable means of offering new perspectives on the course of history. Her myths provide open-ended models of how the contemporary world problems developed, as well as suggesting utopian possibilities for their resolution. Wolf, by contrast, reworks the story of an individual mythical figure in an attempt to tell history from a new, feminist perspective. This project is problematic because she defines her intentions primarily in terms of demythologizing, and offers no clear reflection on the potential of myth as a productive medium—for the construction of utopian models, for example. Although professing to replace myth with history, Wolf's narrative introduces new myths about Kassandra —for instance, her exemplary inner progress towards autonomy and her participation in the cave community.

For both Wolf and Morgner, ancient myth—in Weigel's sense, as 'gesellschaftlich Imaginäres'[62]—serves as a reservoir of constructions of femininity which, when read against the grain of traditional interpretations, can provide powerful images of the potential which both writers attribute to the feminine as a redemptive alternative to the destructive course of western history. However, the nature of this feminine ideal and its relationship to history are different in the two texts. Morgner's mythical models demonstrate how female sexuality in particular has been suppressed by western civilization, either through demonization based on fear—in the cases of Pandora and the sirens— or through control and exploitation by men, as in the case of the Hörselberg witches. In these mythical realms, the potential for a utopian future course of history is associated with the reassertion of female sexuality: Pandora's return is required for the creation of a

---

[62] Weigel, *Die Stimme der Medusa*, 269.

human race through sexual love, the goal in the Brocken world is to reunite divided women with their more libidinous witch halves, and the sirens are to regain their original powers to exert sexual temptation on men. Wolf's Kassandra represents a very different form of feminine ideal. Her model status derives from her attainment of subjective autonomy based on a profound insight into herself and others. Within the narrative, this ideal is shown to be impotent to influence the course of history, instead serving as a compensation for historical events by creating a utopian space of female autonomy outside history. In telling Kassandra's story, however, Wolf is attempting to make this ideal productive for the present, just as she aimed, in *Kein Ort. Nirgends* and the accompanying essays, to inspire change by retrieving the ideals contained in historical women's lives.

Constructing the Relationship between Myth and Historical Reality

Both *Amanda* and the *Kassandra* project relate the ancient mythical narratives which they present to a notion of historical reality constructed within the ultimately fictional world of the literary work. Morgner sets up a contrast between a historically realistic plot centred on the life of Laura Salman in Berlin, and a series of fantastic mythical plots which, although located in a recognizable historical and geographical setting, are not subject to the laws of reality. This contrast is then undermined in several ways. The historical and mythical plots interact with each other, so that the conventional opposition between historical realism and fantastic myth is challenged. Laura's apparently realistic existence is shown to be subject to the laws of the fantastic Brocken world: her other half, Amanda, is captive in the Hörselberg brothel. Furthermore, the ultimate 'reality' within the world of the novel, that is, the narrative level at which the process of writing the work itself is fictionally documented, is mythical. Beatriz and Arke are fantastic mythical beings, and the sources from which the novel is, within this fiction, being written, derive from the mythical Blocksberg archive. This is a significant difference from *Trobadora Beatriz*, where fantasy is contained within a realistic, historical framework: that novel is written, within the fiction, by Laura and then revised by Morgner herself.

In contrast with Morgner, who creates an opposition between fantasy and realism, in order then to show myth and history interacting in unexpected ways, Wolf does not make the status of the *Kassandra* narrative as myth explicit. The *Voraussetzungen* and the *Erzählung* are

presented in a relationship of continuity, rather than qualitative difference: any sense of a discursive break is diminished by the opening
of the narrative, where Kassandra's monologue is introduced as
the product of the authorial narrator's thoughts, resulting from her
experiences at Mycenae which she outlined in the first two lectures.
Through a process of empathy with Kassandra, the first-person pro-
noun gradually shifts its reference from the narrator to Kassandra herself: 'Hier war es. Da stand sie. Diese steinernen Löwen, jetzt kopflos,
haben sie angeblickt. [. . .] Mit der Erzählung geh ich in den Tod'
(*Kassandra*, 5). Any contrast which might be perceived between the aims
of the narrator of the lectures, in attaining historical truth concerning
Kassandra, and those of the narrative, in creating an alternative mythical model from the material, is suppressed, in order to emphasize the
unity of the lectures and narrative as a project which incorporates
various approaches to the myth.

It thus appears that Wolf and Morgner are relating ancient myth to
reality in diametrically opposite ways: while mythical narratives in
Amanda are presented in a fantastic mode which contrasts with historically realistic narratives within the work, in order then to interact with
these, the *Kassandra* project is an attempt to overcome any opposition
between myth and historical discourse by presenting both in the same
realistic mode. However, these very different relationships between
myth and the concepts of reality constructed by the two works actually
have the function of proposing a similar kind of relationship between
myth and history.

Both works present a critique of the way reality is defined by western
society, and show how this definition has been instrumental in creating
a particular notion of what constitutes history. In *Amanda*, Arke associates the standard concept of history with the origins of patriarchy:
'Dann übernahmen die Männer die Herrschaft und führten ein, was
die Menschen heute Geschichte nennen: Privateigentum, Klassen-
trennung, Ausbeutung, Staatsgewalt, Kriege' (*Amanda*, 12). This
suggests that the term 'history' as it is generally understood applies not
to the entire course of events in human society from its beginnings
to the present, but instead only to certain aspects of this course, which
are selected according to the prevailing value systems. This idea is
reinforced by Vilma's rejection of history as a 'queen' because of the
masculinist bias in writing history. She implies that an alternative form
of historiography, based on alternative values and principles of selection, is possible: 'Denn die Geschichtsschreibung hat die Frauen his-

torisch expropriiert. Und die nicht als aufschreibenswürdig erachtete Geschichte ist eine Geschichte von Verbrechen am weiblichen Geschlecht' (*Amanda*, 184).

Wolf voices the same critique of a concept of history based on a definition of reality according to which 'die ganze bisherige Existenz der Frau war unrealistisch' (*Voraussetzungen*, 115). Furthermore, she highlights the role of present values and concerns in the creation of 'eine dann "historisch" genannte Wahrheit', showing how empirical archaeological evidence is forced into preconceived historical schemas, and how ideas about the ancient world were for a long time determined by the contemporary western world's image 'von jener Kultur, aus der es die seine gerne entwickelt hätte' (*Voraussetzungen*, 116, 58).

Both works thus challenge any form of history which claims to be an objective and definitive documentation of the events of the past. The official writing of history in the GDR was, of course, a prime example of this kind of history. In transgressing the boundary between history and myth, Morgner comes close to recent western ideas about the narrative status of history, challenging what she perceives as society's way of classifying particular narratives as historical or mythical. Sigrid Weigel has offered a theoretical analysis of this process. She describes how myth is associated with 'dem Uneindeutigen oder Vieldeutigen, dem Nicht-Realen', while the concept of history makes claims to 'Eindeutigkeit, Authentizität oder wahre Beschreibung der Wirklichkeit':

Solcher Gegensatz verkennt aber die Dialektik von Mythischem und Historischem, denn *die* Geschichte, d.h. unser Bild von der Geschichte, entsteht aus den vielen Geschichten als Abstraktion und Vergessen und sie wird—hat sich eine Version einmal etabliert—in der Form von Legenden, als Mythos tradiert. Während aber im Begriff des Mythos die Differenz zwischen der Darstellung und dem Geschehen, auf das die Darstellung Bezug nimmt, offenbar ist, so wird im Begriff der Geschichte diese Differenz oft verkannt.[63]

The narrative framework of *Amanda*, in which Beatriz writes Laura's life-story, can be understood as a model of the processes by which reality is transformed into written history. The conditions which Isebel imposes on Beatriz's work are particularly reminiscent of the ideological constraints on writers of both history and literature in the GDR, highlighting the fact that Isebel's militant form of feminism functions in essentially the same way as a patriarchal and totalitarian regime.

[63] Ibid. 270.

Beatriz is told to regard herself as a 'Hofhistoriographin', that is, the writer of a version of history officially sanctioned by a particular society (*Amanda*, 51). The documents which form her sources betray a clear ideological bias and function, carrying the title, 'Historie von Amanda der Großen'. The fact that 'ohne Isebels Genehmigung darf am geformten Material nichts geändert werden', as well as the checks to which Beatriz's work is subjected, form a model of a censorship system attempting to ensure that written history is an interpretation of reality according to a particular ideology (*Amanda*, 42). Using a mythical narrative to demonstrate how official history functions, Morgner thus suggests that history contains the fictional elements usually associated with myth. She presents instead models of history which have an explicitly mythical status (as an open discourse) and involve fictional and fantastic elements yet, the novel suggests, convey a truer and more productive representation of the course of modern history.

Kassandra, in contrast, reworks a traditional myth and presents it as a form of historical reality. However, the very concept of historical truth towards which the whole project appears to be striving is simultaneously undermined, within the work, by the idea that objectivity in understanding the past exists only as an ideological myth masking the interests and values determining the practice of history. The narrator of the *Voraussetzungen* openly acknowledges both the subjective element in her understanding of the Kassandra figure, which takes a personal identification as its starting-point, and the present concerns which determine the way she reconstructs Kassandra's historical existence (*Voraussetzungen*, 10, 106–8). Any form of historical truth which the *Voraussetzungen* appear to claim for the *Erzählung* can thus be regarded as a self-consciously fictional construct, which has a function in subverting traditional conceptions of historical truth by questioning the masculinist values on which they are based and proposing an alternative, feminine set of values. It makes no claims to authenticity outside the fiction of the project. As Judith Ryan persuasively suggests, Wolf is demythologizing the Kassandra story to produce not a true historical account, but a utopian model for a new understanding of history:

Restructuring myth to reveal its psychological underpinnings is to transform it from a primitive, archetypal version of what history presents in a more complex guise into a forward-looking model for an eventual rethinking of history. What was myth becomes utopia.[64]

---

[64] Judith Ryan, 'Twilight Zones: Myth, Fairy Tale, and Utopia in *No Place on Earth* and *Cassandra*', in *Responses to Christa Wolf*, ed. Sibley Fries, 312–25 (322).

Amanda and the *Kassandra* project each focus on a different aspect of the same idea about how ancient myth and history are related. In *Amanda*, history is presented as myth: Morgner uses ancient myth as a form of discourse for representing the history of western society from an alternative perspective. In *Kassandra*, conversely, an ancient myth is presented as history: the narrative conforms to a standard of historical truth constructed within the work, however fictional that may ultimately be. Both are thus proposing an interactive relationship between myth, in both forms, and history. History is exposed as a closed ideological myth, while ancient myth is presented as a productive alternative mode in which to explore and represent history.

The Role of Literature in Relation to Myth and History

Wolf's and Morgner's constructions of the relationship between myth and history involve literature in two ways. Firstly, it is the form in which ancient myths are available to the modern world. Secondly, literature is the medium in which these writers are creating or reworking ancient myth. The manner in which they relate myth to history within the texts has important implications for a model of literature as a means of understanding and influencing history.

Much of the reflection in Wolf's *Voraussetzungen einer Erzählung* presupposes a distinction between a form of ancient myth which is 'alive' as a way of understanding reality, as was the case in ancient societies, and myth as a later process of imposing layers of interpretation on the original mythical stories. This dual use of the term 'myth' is very clear in a comment Wolf makes, concerning the aims of her project:

Zu zeigen, wie die historische Kassandra, von der ich ausgehe, und ihre historische Umgebung durch Ritual, Kult, Glauben und Mythos gelenkt werden, während für uns das *gesamte* Material 'mythisch' ist. (*Voraussetzungen*, 119)

In focusing on the reception of ancient myth, Wolf is adopting a historical model of myth's development which closely resembles that proposed by Hans Blumenberg in *Arbeit am Mythos* (1979). Rainer Koch usefully summarizes Blumenberg's arguments, describing a historical point of transition in ancient Greece, when writing takes over the role of earlier oral narrative, that is, the work *of* myth comes to an end and work *on* myth begins:

In der griechischen Antike wird der Mythos durch Herausbildung der Schrift aus erzählerischer Überlieferung herausgelöst und einer literarischen

Tradierung überantwortet. Damit verbunden ist ein Verlust seiner an den Zuhörerkontext gebundenen Freiheit zu parallel variierender Stoffentwicklung und zu spontaner innerer Modifikation.[65]

Wolf posits precisely such a transition, from an ancient society presumed to be matriarchal, to the early stages of modern western patriarchal culture, based on writing. The contrast between oral and written narrative, on which Blumenberg's model is based, is also a central idea in Wolf's project. The lectures imply a series of transformations of narrative material through time. First of all, Wolf postulates that historical reality is recorded in myth as an oral narrative: as Ulrich Klingmann observes, the aim of a 'Rückführung aus dem Mythos in die (gedachten) sozialen und historischen Koordinaten' presupposes that an original historical reality entered the myth (*Voraussetzungen*, 111).[66] The qualification by 'gedacht' in parentheses here implies Wolf's awareness that the actual original historical reality cannot be retrieved, and any reconstruction will necessarily be at least a partial fiction. This, however, does not invalidate the general historical model of how ancient myths originate and function which she is developing. Citing Fritz Schachermeyer, she adopts a theory of myth as a means by which oral cultures remember history through the narration of stories. According to a principle of 'Konzentration auf das für die dichterische Phantasie Wesentliche', this process involves a compression and simplification of the complex processes which constitute history (*Voraussetzungen*, 116–17). It is in this point that Wolf diverges significantly from Blumenberg's view of myth. He argues that the importance of myth lies purely in its form, as a means of gaining distance from a terrifying reality over which human beings have no control. He is not concerned with the relationship between the content of ancient myth and historical reality, so central to Wolf's model, and focuses instead on myth as a self-contained history of changing narrative forms:

Nicht in den Ursprüngen seiner Inhalte, nicht im Einzugsgebiet seiner Stoffe und Geschichten, liegt die Geschichtsmächtigkeit des Mythos begründet, sondern darin, daß er seinem Verfahren, seiner 'Form' nach etwas anderes *nicht mehr* ist.[67]

---

[65] Rainer Koch, *Geschichtskritik und ästhetische Wahrheit: Zur Produktivität des Mythos in moderner Literatur und Philosophie* (Bielefeld: Aisthesis, 1990), 67.

[66] Ulrich Klingmann, 'Entmythologisierter Mythos: Die Problematik des Wissens in Christa Wolfs *Kassandra*', *ZG* NS 1 (1991), 2, 270–9 (270).

[67] Blumenberg, 22.

The next stage in Wolf's model involves the transformation of myth, as an oral narrative, into the permanent form of literature. Like Blumenberg, Wolf sees the development of myth into a written form as a shift towards closure, involving a loss in the material's potential for plurality. She presents the origins of literature, in the form of the epic, as the ultimate stage in the process of compressing history into the highly symbolic narrative of myth: 'Bei diesem Konzentrations-prozeß—an dessen Ende im Glücksfall ein homerisches Epos stehn kann—[. . .]' (*Voraussetzungen*, 117). She sees the epic as situated 'auf der Grenze zwischen Mythos und Geschichtsschreibung', that is, between oral narrative as a means of remembering history and modern record-ings of history which claim objectivity (*Voraussetzungen*, 64). The con-ception of history 'als Heldengeschichte', which underlies oral myth, determines the linear form of the epic: 'Die Helden sind auswechsel-bar, das Muster bleibt. Auf diesem Muster entwickelte sich die Ästhetik' (*Voraussetzungen*, 117). The aesthetics based on the epic form which consequently developed do not, Wolf suggests, result in an objective and ideologically value-free representation of reality. Instead they endorse a view of reality which, through the creation of heroes as role-models and the objectification of women as heroines, reinforces patriarchy:

Das Epos, aus den Kämpfen um das Patriarchat entstanden, wird *durch seine Struktur* auch ein Instrument zu seiner Herausbildung und Befestigung. Vorbildwirkung wird dem Helden auferlegt [. . .]. Als Heroine kann die Frau nun Gegenstand der männlichen Erzählung werden. (*Voraussetzungen*, 147)

Myth and literature are thus, for Wolf, successive stages in the objec-tification of the living material of history into the dead—because closed—forms of art. The second half of this section will show how Wolf attempts to differentiate her own project from this traditional form of literature, by asking 'Fragen, die Kassandra aus Mythos und Literatur herauslösen können' (*Voraussetzungen*, 17).

Morgner's treatment of previous literary versions of the ancient myths which she is reworking in *Amanda* is quite different. She is con-cerned neither with the substance of myth before it entered literature, nor with the relation of the content of myth to some original historical reality. For her, ancient myth exists essentially as a model within literature. She explores different versions of the Pandora myth, for example, without the concern for its historical origins which marks the *Kassandra* project. As Morgner's treatment of Hesiod's misogynist version of the Parnassus mythology demonstrates, the quest for an 'original' form of the myth, preceding its patriarchal interpretations, takes place only within the fiction of the myth itself. Unlike Wolf's version of the Kassandra myth, Morgner's 'correction' of the myth is not authorized in relation to any standard of historical truth outside the myth itself. Early on in *Amanda* Beatriz rejects the idea of learning about mythology from books, and travels instead to Greece to seek it in a living form: 'Wo die Mythologie festgeschrieben war, erwartete ich kaum Aufschlüsse; wo sie gewachsen war, hoffte ich, den Schlüssel für die Entschlüsselung zu finden' (*Amanda*, 60). However, Chariklia is quick to challenge this view, alerting Beatriz to the value of literary reworkings of myth, in particular Goethe's *Pandora* (*Amanda*, 62). Beatriz's reflections on the different versions of the Pandora myth, in the chapter 'Deutungen', focus on the varying symbolic significances of the story, rather than on the extent to which each version relates to an original historical reality. Morgner sees the literary existence of ancient myth not as an inevitable petrification of living historical matter, but as an essentially plural phenomenon, where several contradictory versions of a story may fruitfully coexist. The idea that any one version is authoritatively binding is, as Beatriz discovers, a mistake (*Amanda*, 77). This is similar to Fühmann's concept of myth: he likens individual mythical stories to particular games, where the rules or central characters and events allow a large number of concrete manifestations, so that the essence of myth lies precisely in its plurality: 'Ein Mythos, das ist der Keim und all seine Entfaltung; gerade das Werden in stets neuer Gestaltung ist sein Leben [. . .]'.[68] As Beatriz's discussion of Goethe's version of the Pandora myth suggests, Morgner is aiming not to find the historical origins of an ancient myth, but to create a version of the myth which serves as a productive model of history. In this project, Goethe's reversal of the myth's meaning, although a relatively late reinterpretation, proves to be more relevant than the earlier versions available (*Amanda*, 78).

In her lack of regard for the idea that historical reality is somehow transformed into ancient myth, central to Wolf's project, Morgner's treatment of myth bears some resemblance to Blumenberg's theory of myth as a history of developing narrative forms which can never be traced back to an original story, whether historically real or already fictional. Waschescio relates Blumenberg's opposition between 'Geschichte' and 'Geschichtenerzählen' to Morgner's turn from history

[68] Fühmann, 'Das mythische Element', 105.

to ancient myth.[69] It is certainly true that Morgner rejects a notion of history as a singular and authoritative narrative, but telling stories is for her in no way opposed to an engagement with history. Both *Amanda* and *Kassandra* present ancient myth as a mode of storytelling which can offer alternative versions of history. A concept of history as a process of telling stories, and therefore comparable to myth, such as that outlined by Hayden White, is thus a more fruitful model for understanding how Wolf and Morgner are using ancient myth.[70]

Wolf and Morgner attribute quite different functions to literature in their explorations of ancient myth. In attempting to return the Kassandra figure to a social and historical context, however imaginary, Wolf is striving to undo the objectifying and petrifying effects of the literary 'Arbeit am Mythos' which determine all modern acquaintance with the figure: 'Wer war Kassandra, ehe man von ihr schrieb? (Da sie aber ein Geschöpf der Dichter ist; da sie nur durch sie spricht, nur in ihrer Sicht auf uns gekommen ist . . . [)]' (*Voraussetzungen*, 138). To attempt this in a literary work may appear paradoxical, since Wolf argues in her address introducing the lectures, that 'es gibt keine Poetik, und es kann keine geben, die verhindert, daß die lebendige Erfahrung ungezählter Subjekte in Kunst-Objekten ertötet und begraben wird' (*Voraussetzungen*, 8). However, the five lectures represent a search for an alternative form of art to that described and prescribed by traditional aesthetics, one which will present living subjects without fixing them in the permanence of artistic form. The closed form of the *Kassandra* narrative, which itself could be perceived as an alternative, but equally objectifying and static interpretation of the Kassandra figure, is countered by the four accompanying lectures. These open the project by posing questions which lead the enquiry concerning Kassandra in a variety of directions. They show the developments in Wolf's thinking as she works on the material, so that the narrative becomes the result of a temporal process, rather than a static object whose origins and process of creation are suppressed. Within the narrative itself, Wolf works to oppose the objectification which Kassandra has undergone in literature by men, by making her the subject of her own monologue, that is, by presenting 'ihre Geschichte' in the place of the familiar 'Geschichten von ihr, über sie' (*Voraussetzungen*, 145). Wolf's narrative answers Kassandra's own call, within the fiction, for a way of allowing her story to reach future generations, as an alternative history to the officially recorded one:

[69] Waschescio, 54.   [70] White, 26–57.

Schick mir einen Schreiber, oder, besser noch, eine junge Sklavin mit schar-
fem Gedächtnis und kraftvoller Stimme. Verfüge, daß sie, was sie von mir
hört, ihrer Tochter weitersagen darf. Die wieder ihrer Tochter, und so fort. So
daß neben dem Strom der Heldenlieder dies winzge [*sic*] Rinnsal, mühsam,
jene fernen, vielleicht glücklicheren Menschen, die einst leben werden, auch
erreichte. (*Kassandra*, 95–6)

In retrieving Kassandra from the objectifying effects of myth and literature, Wolf is thus creating a model for writing history from a female
perspective which has been ignored in traditional history: 'Es wäre
[. . .] die Geschichte einer der Kehrseiten unserer Kultur' (*Voraussetzungen*, 145). She summarizes this intention in a discussion at the
Ohio State University: 'Das war mein Prozeß der Entmythologisie-
rung: die Entfremdungssyndrome aufzulösen, die das Patriarchat auf
jede weibliche Stimme dieser Kultur gelegt hat.'[71]

   Myth, for Wolf, is primarily a form of ideological blind spot, as evident in modern society as in the early patriarchy depicted in *Kassandra*.
For her, ancient myth, as a process of fixing historical reality, is
very closely related to modern ideological myth: both are closed and
monolithic forms of discourse. Literature has traditionally continued
and intensified the work of myth in crystallizing history into a static
aesthetic form. Wolf, however, seeks to make literature useful in
enlightening society by exposing the myths determining its thinking
and creating an open discourse which can offer models for alternative
ways of thinking: 'Literatur ist auch dazu da, die "blinden Flecke" zu
verkleinern, sie aufzuhellen.'[72]

   Morgner clearly has no such archaeological aims in her exploration
of ancient myth. Unlike Wolf, she is not trying to retrieve myth from
the ossifying effects of literary form and trace it back to its origins in a
potential historical reality. Instead, she is seeking versions of ancient
myth within literature which, in their open-ended plurality, can provide valuable fantastic models to help contemporary society to understand its history and change its future.

   Both Wolf and Morgner are creating models of an interaction
between literature and history, but the subtle difference in how they
construct these models points to a significant contrast in their views of
how literature is to function as a tool for influencing reality. The blur-

[71] Christa Wolf, 'Aus einer Diskussion an der Ohio State University: Gespräch mit
Christa und Gerhard Wolf', in *Die Dimension des Autors*, ii. 896–911 (903).
   [72] Christa Wolf, 'Zum Erscheinen des Buches *Kassandra*: Gespräch mit Brigitte
Zimmermann und Ursula Fröhlich', in *Die Dimension des Autors*, ii. 929–40 (937).

ring of the boundaries between the realistic and the fantastic, or history and myth, in *Amanda* can be understood as a model for the interaction of literature and reality. The fantastic mythical realms in the novel are closely associated with literature, either as reworkings of literary models (the Parnassus mythology, for example), or as the world in which literature is written: Beatriz and the Brocken world are responsible for the fictional writing of *Amanda*. In the *Kassandra* project, on the other hand, the boundary between the literary work and reality outside it is blurred. In contrast with the fictional and fantastic narrative framework of *Amanda*, the equivalent level of self-reflective, 'authorial' commentary in the lectures accompanying the *Kassandra* narrative allows the fiction of the work to merge into reality, by presenting an apparently historically authentic narrative of the author of the whole project, identified with Wolf herself. This contrast points to the central difference between the two writers' aesthetics. Morgner is writing literature as a fantastic correlative to reality, which can challenge one-sidedly rational modes of thought and offer a radically different approach to history. Wolf, meanwhile, is attempting to create a form of literature which functions as a rational tool of enlightenment to expose ideological myths, and as an imaginative, but fundamentally realistic means of accessing the forgotten experienced realities of subjects who have been oppressed and objectified by history.

Both *Kassandra* and *Amanda* challenge the opposition between fact and fiction, or between history and myth. This can be seen as a specifically feminist attempt to regain a wholeness of thought outside the hierarchized binary oppositions of patriarchy.[73] In Wolf's *Voraussetzungen einer Erzählung*, she criticizes the concepts of reality which have force in the modern world and, quoting Ingeborg Bachmann's *Der Fall Franza*, proposes a broadening of the concept of reality, beyond concrete facts with a tangible existence: 'Denn die Tatsachen, die die Welt ausmachen—sie brauchen das Nichttatsächliche, um von ihm aus erkannt zu werden' (*Voraussetzungen*, 112, 126). Reading ancient myth, Wolf believes, is a way of discovering the 'anderen Inhalt des Begriffs "Wirklichkeit"', which she regards as an essential task for contemporary society (*Voraussetzungen*, 57). She reads the Kassandra myth as evidence of an alternative version of reality, based on female experience rather than the 'Linie männlichen Handelns' which structures the *Iliad* (*Voraussetzungen*, 91). In re-creating a wholeness of vision, Wolf thus

---

[73] Cf. Hélène Cixous, 'Sorties', in *New French Feminisms: An Anthology*, ed. Elaine Marks and Isabelle de Courtivron (New York: Harvester, 1981), 90–8 (90–1).

focuses on certain aspects of reality, particularly of women's reality, which have been suppressed by patriarchal society. She counters patriarchal history with a fictional version of history, which nevertheless remains obedient to the rational laws of reality.

Morgner's attempt to regain wholeness is more radical, in that she counters reality as it is understood in western society not just with an alternative form of reality, but with fantasy, as a mode which is fundamentally other to reality. For her, myth is not a means of approaching historical reality from an alternative perspective and writing a fictional history of women's experience to complement the traditional patriarchal documentation of history, but instead a fantastic mode which contains its own truth and can exert a formative influence on reality. Morgner's use of fantasy is subversive and transformative, sharing many of the features central to Jackson's analysis of the genre. It challenges patriarchal ideologies by opening up 'on to that which lies outside the law, that which is outside dominant value systems', and breaks the 'single, reductive "truths"' of Morgner's society, introducing in their place 'multiple, contradictory "truths"'.[74] Morgner's aesthetic may account for the fact that her novels, although at least as subversive of SED ideology as Wolf's, provoked far less controversy. Whereas Wolf's subjective authenticity articulated a clear and unified authorial position which was open to attack, Morgner's montage of realistic and fantastic elements created an often contradictory polyphony of voices which could not easily be reduced to a single meaning. While *Kassandra* provoked Wilhelm Girnus's wrath for suggesting that 'die Geschichte sei nicht in ihrem tiefsten Grunde der Kampf zwischen Ausbeutern und Ausgebeuteten, sondern zwischen Männern und Frauen, ja noch grotesker: zwischen "männlichem" und "weiblichem" Denken', Morgner's articulation of similar ideas went unremarked by GDR critics.[75] Nordmann has analysed the GDR reception of *Trobadora Beatriz*, showing how the subversive fantastic elements of the work were 'rückübersetzt in die präformierte Konzeption traditionellen Kunstverständnisses, das auf Geschlossenheit der Form und Eindeutigkeit des Sinns insistiert'.[76] Similarly, many of the more provocative implications of Morgner's use of myth in *Amanda* were 'muted by a tradition of literary criticism concerned with supporting establishment ideals

[74] Jackson, 4, 23. See also Lewis, especially 1–50.
[75] Wilhelm Girnus, 'Wer baute das siebentorige Theben? Kritische Bemerkungen zu Christa Wolfs Beitrag in Sinn und Form 1/83 S. 38ff.', *SF* 35 (1983), 2, 439–47 (442).
[76] Nordmann, 421.

rather than with subverting them', highlighting the relevance of Jackson's general analysis of fantastic literature to its role in the more specific context of the GDR.[77] Critics were able to integrate some aspects of the text into the accepted categories of Marxism–Leninism, while excusing others with the argument that 'Figurenmeinung' was not to be confused with 'Autorenmeinung'.[78]

Amanda and *Kassandra* might appear to bear comparatively little relation to GDR discourses. Both texts incorporate western ideas in their feminist critique of history. Like western theorists such as Hayden White, Wolf and Morgner regard history not as an objective representation of reality, but as a narrative which, like myth, involves fictional elements, and interprets the past from a particular ideological perspective in order to make it meaningful for a certain group of people in the present. However, although they are using western historical theory to present a critique of what they understand to be the long-term history of European civilization, this critique is most productively understood in relation to the GDR context in which the texts were written. By the 1980s, the idea that history is a narrative which imposes ultimately fictional interpretations on the past was widely accepted in the West. There remained little faith in the kind of history which Wolf's and Morgner's texts invoke and challenge: a naïve and monolithic history which narrativizes reality, claiming to be an objective representation of a story told by events themselves. Wolf and Morgner are reacting specifically to the historiographical tradition of the GDR, characterized as it was by an officially prescribed belief in a scientifically objective practice of history, existing in complete opposition to the fictions of both ancient and modern ideological (that is, in the SED's definition, capitalist) myth. Whereas the texts discussed in earlier chapters question certain aspects of the official GDR understanding of history and offer alternative approaches and interpretations, Wolf and Morgner use myth here to question the fundamental principles underlying this kind of historiography. All the texts this study has examined engage with, challenge, and rewrite myths about history which were current in the GDR public sphere. *Amanda* and *Kassandra* provide extensive reflection on these processes.

---

[77] Jackson, 173.

[78] Jürgen Engler, 'Die wahre Lüge der Kunst', *NDL* 31 (1983), 7, 135–44 (137). See also Klaus Kändler, 'Der Hexenroman "Amanda" von Irmtraud Morgner', in *DDR-Literatur '83 im Gespräch*, ed. Siegfried Rönisch (Berlin and Weimar: Aufbau, 1984), 155–62; Hermann Kähler, 'Widersprüchliches zu "Amanda"', *SF* 36 (1984), 1, 177–85.

CONCLUSION

Mary Fulbrook has described the difference between historical writing in the GDR and in western democratic states as 'not so much that history was politicized in the GDR, but rather that the state did not permit the plurality of voices and approaches, the clashes of opinion and open debate, characteristic of the West'.[1] Similarly, the preceding chapters of this study have shown that the relationship between historiography and literature within the GDR cannot be understood in terms of a simple opposition between 'politicized' historiography and politically 'liberated' literature. There is evidence in some historians' work of a shift away from the more dogmatic elements of the SED view of history, while certain Marxist categories and ideals remained central to the works of authors like Wolf, Morgner, and Königsdorf. The main differences between the two discourses are the greater plurality of positions articulated by literature, and its more self-reflective character. While mainstream historiography remained monolithic in its efforts to justify and support a preconceived model of history, and work which did pursue new approaches was produced only at the margins of the historical profession, literature of the 1970s and 1980s became a forum for the 'clashes of opinion and open debate' which Fulbrook associates with western historiography. While historians did not openly question the premises and categories of the SED's understanding of history, literature offered critical reflection not only on specific interpretations of events and figures, but on the broad frameworks within which such interpretations were produced. Both historians and writers retained the Marxist view of history as something which was to be made productive for the present. However, historical writing almost always used the past to legitimize conditions in the present, whereas literature increasingly explored historical topics in order to criticize the GDR, and to provoke change.

Rainer Eckert, who co-founded the Unabhängiger Historiker-Verband in 1990, has attributed the limitations of GDR historiography

---

[1] Fulbrook, *German National Identity*, 129.

to individuals' internalization of the requirements imposed on them, and to a system which rewarded conformity:

> So darf nicht vergessen werden, daß die Mehrzahl der Historiker in der DDR nicht zu einem Bekenntnis oder zur äußeren Loyalität gegenüber dem System gezwungen werden mußte, sondern daß sie dessen Überzeugungen und Zumutungen durchaus freiwillig angenommen, verinnerlicht und überzeugt, ja auch gläubig, vertreten und weitergetragen hatten. Niemand mußte platte Phrasen nachbeten, seine Arbeiten mit Zitaten der 'Klassiker' bis hin zu Honecker schmücken (auch nicht tarnen) oder sich auf der Karriereleiter nach oben kämpfen. Daß dies trotzdem geschah, lag in einem raffinierten Auswahlverfahren künftiger Sozial- und Geisteswissenschaftler, in einem Privilegien- und Überwachungssystem, in innerer und äußerer Zensur sowie in dem Wunsch nach persönlicher Erfüllung in einer Gesellschaft, die man für ewigwährend hielt, begründet.[2]

This explanation may account for some individuals' behaviour, and it indicates the different degrees to which historians and writers were dependent on institutions, as one factor in the divergence of their respective writings. However, as Bathrick has commented, writers too were 'situated institutionally very much *within* and dependent upon the official structures of the party public sphere', and subject to an 'absolutely coordinated system of publication, distribution, and evaluation'.[3] Indeed, after 1989 very similar criticisms were made of writers, who were accused of having produced 'eine autoritätsgläubige "Stillhalteliteratur" [. . .], die, trotz geringer Kritik im Detail, das System, den Staat und die undemokratische Gesellschaftsordnung stabilisierte'.[4] By looking at literature alongside historiography, this study has highlighted the remarkable degree of freedom which writers were able to gain from the official state discourse, as well as the more limited scope for debates in historical studies. However, since the respective relations of writers and historians to state institutions varied only in degree, an argument which explains the differences between their writings in terms of individual attitudes to the state threatens to degenerate into a superficial and inappropriate attempt to measure personal moral integrity, reminiscent of some contributions to the 'Literaturstreit'.

A more fruitful question to ask is why many writers were able to

---

[2] Rainer Eckert, 'Zwischen den Scherben einer zerbrochenen Welt: Hoffnung auf einen Neubeginn. Die Probleme der Historiker in den Neuen Bundesländern', in *Hure oder Muse?*, ed. Eckert, Kowalczuk, and Stark, 133–8 (134).

[3] Bathrick, 'The End of the Wall Before the End of the Wall', 304.

[4] '*Es geht nicht um Christa Wolf*', ed. Anz, 8.

articulate their ambivalence towards the state in their writings, while an enormous gulf divided many historians' private views from their conformist public statements.[5] This study has discussed a number of textual features which enabled literature to challenge and broaden the GDR discourse on history from within, while the different conventions of historical writing encouraged a much greater adherence to the boundaries imposed by the Party line. Since academic historiography conventionally relies on abstract categories of analysis, the subordination of all research to an ideological framework of Marxism–Leninism represented a fundamental continuity in a long historiographical tradition. It was not the use of abstract, and inevitably political, categories which marked GDR historiography as a special case, but rather, as Fulbrook suggests, the fact that the competition between different sets of categories usual in academic studies in democratic states was forcibly prevented.

The literary developments this study has traced could be defined as a series of challenges to the abstract categories which characterized GDR state and academic discourses. In December 1989, Wolf described her writing career as a shift away from academic 'theory' to subjective experience, a shift which applies more generally to the literature I have looked at:

Ich habe mich mit Mühe aus den Verstrickungen in Theorien losmachen können, in die ich in den fünfziger Jahren verwickelt war. [. . .] Es hat lange gedauert, bis ich mich befreit hatte von den ideologischen Konzepten, die damals das Literaturstudium beeinflußten; bis ich merkte, daß ich mich wohler fühle, wenn ich meine Sinne gebrauche.[6]

A recurring feature of the texts I have discussed is the use of subjective perspectives, in particular those of women, to question the authority of abstract categories as a means of understanding history. Writers counter Marxist socio-economic categories with personal experiences of the everyday life of women and children under National Socialism, with interpretations of historical and mythical female lives which are based on subjective identification, and with mythologies which can challenge abstract modes of thought (*Amanda*).

Besides literature's ability to highlight discrepancies between individual subjective experience and the conceptualization of that experience in the categories of SED discourse, writers use literary

---

[5] *Marxist Historiography in Transformation*, ed. Iggers, 8.
[6] Christa Wolf, 'Schreiben im Zeitbezug: Gespräch mit Aafke Steenhuis', in *Im Dialog*, 131–57 (142).

language and form to challenge the certainties at the heart of that discourse. While Iggers emphasizes the degree to which historians were able to move away from their early dogmatic positions despite the rigid terminology they were obliged to use, a comparison with literature reveals the extent to which historians' language imposed boundaries on their ideas. By arguing that 'once the ritualistic obeisance to the Marxist–Leninist phraseology was discounted, there remained [. . .] much solid scholarship', Iggers implies that the language of GDR historiography can be stripped away, revealing increasingly undogmatic analyses beneath.[7] However, this is to ignore the basic post-structuralist insights that 'meaning is constituted within language', and 'different languages and different discourses within the same language divide up the world and give it meaning in different ways'.[8] The present study has shown, rather, that the 'code' which became a convention for GDR historians played an important role in preventing intellectual enquiry which might have unsettled the central 'truths' of Marxism–Leninism.[9] Literature, with its traditions of subjective expression and storytelling, could not be bound to such a rigid ideological code so easily. The dominant gesture of the texts examined here is one of questioning: closed chapters of the past are opened up to enquiry, and certainties about history are replaced by a recognition of complexities and ambiguities which make final judgements problematic. This broad aim is shared by a variety of individual strategies: Schütz's narratives which never close and her narrator's reflections on the choices involved in telling a story; Wolf's emphasis in *Kindheitsmuster* on memory and writing as processes of self-exploration with no preconceived answers; her ambiguous, constantly shifting narrative voice in *Kein Ort. Nirgends*; Damm's presentation of possibilities where historical facts cannot be ascertained; Struzyk's and Morgner's use of montage, which precludes a single linear narrative and offers the reader questions, rather than answers; Morgner's open mythologies, which aim to replace abstractions with concrete images; Königsdorf's emphasis on the contradictions within Lise Meitner and refusal to provide a clear judgement on her characters.

The broadening of parameters for historical debate in literature had little impact on historiography, which was able to pursue new

---

[7] *Marxist Historiography in Transformation*, ed. Iggers, 35.

[8] Weedon, *Feminist Practice and Poststructuralist Theory*, 22.

[9] Cf. Wolf's insistence, on 31 Aug. 1989, that the process of overcoming stagnation in the GDR had to begin 'mit einer anderen, realitätsbezogenen Sprache in den Medien der DDR'. *Im Dialog*, 75.

approaches and gain limited freedom from the rigid categories of SED Marxism–Leninism only with the advent of *glasnost* in the late 1980s. However, changes in literature were able to reconfigure the boundaries within which literary criticism operated. Works containing critical elements provoked a wide range of responses. While some critics rejected works which did not correspond to their preconceived categories, others used such works to broaden the criteria according to which they assessed literature. Writers' increasing focus on individual experience which defied rigid abstract categories prompted literary critics to redefine the functions of literature and academic studies of history and society as different, but complementary. Literary critics thus occupied a mediating position between the theoretical framework of Marxism–Leninism, within which they were supposed to interpret texts, and a literature which increasingly resisted an understanding in such terms.

This study has presented not one narrative of literary history, but three interlocking histories, revealing a network of relations between the various texts. Chapter 1 established a broadly chronological development of a plural literary discourse about the German past, whereby authors' contributions at each point in time broadened the boundaries of the discussion for future works. Writers' explorations of the wider and more marginalized topic of historical women's lives revealed a much more fragmentary history, in which the position of an individual writer in GDR cultural life had a greater impact on her writing than the relationship between her work and previously published texts. By focusing on an alternative aesthetic tradition concurrent with the developments explored in Chapters 1 and 2, Chapter 3 highlighted a shift in writers' attitudes towards history over the course of the two decades, which applies to all the works I have discussed. Most of the 1970s texts, as well as Feyl's *Der lautlose Aufbruch*, maintain the faith in historical progress central to the GDR model of history, however significantly they transform the orthodox approach to the past. In Wolf's works of the late 1970s and in the 1980s texts, however, history is either a seemingly static state of affairs in which the parallels between different eras are more significant than any changes, or a negative development based on increasingly destructive ways of thinking.

A broad correlation is evident between critical reflection on the project of writing history and reflection on gender. Over the course of the 1970s and 1980s women writers develop several different approaches to the relationship between gender and history. Most of the works discussed here reject the strategy of integrating women into the authorized narrative of history, characteristic of historians' work on women and present to a degree in Damm's and Feyl's non-fictional essays. Schütz's texts and *Kindheitsmuster* rewrite the history of National Socialism by telling stories about the past from a female perspective, although the works provide little explicit reflection on gender as a historical category. In the works of Chapters 2 and 3, where writers explore broader questions of how to write about the past in general, Wolf, Damm, Feyl, and Morgner develop the idea of writing new, female-centred narratives of history into a conscious political programme. These narratives rewrite history in two ways. Firstly, writers focus on women's experience in order to produce an alternative 'herstory'. Secondly, some of the works, particulary those by Wolf and Morgner, rewrite mainstream history as a gendered course of events based on the marginalization and exclusion not only of women, but also of a set of principles associated with femininity.

These two approaches, often found together in a single work (for example, in *Trobadora Beatriz* and *Kassandra*), bear a close resemblance to the feminist ideas about history developed in the West in the 1970s and 1980s. In the GDR context, they are able to challenge the dogmatic SED understanding of history. However, they also risk creating a new dogma in their privileging of women and the feminine. In many of the texts I have discussed—Damm's *Cornelia Goethe* is a particularly striking example—sisterly identification between a modern narrator and a historical protagonist creates an idealized impression of a universally shared female experience of patriarchal oppression, resulting in women's solidarity with each other across the ages. In the works by Wolf and Morgner, women's experience, and qualities associated with the feminine, are endowed with the potential to redeem modern civilization by offering examples of alternative values to those which have determined the course of history. Three authors—Struzyk, Königsdorf, and Schubert—offer resistance to what they perceive as a new feminist master narrative which threatens to simplify history and reduce individual lives to 'evidence' in a way which parallels orthodox GDR historiography. Struzyk identifies with Caroline Schlegel-Schelling, but highlights the contradictions in her personality and attempts to avoid imposing a reductive interpretative narrative on her life. Königsdorf and Schubert, meanwhile, reject the idea that women necessarily occupy a position of resistance to prevailing value systems. Königsdorf's texts explore ways in which women and other 'outsiders' support the very regimes which oppress them. By exploring the contradictions in Lise Meitner's character, she exposes the falsifications involved in reducing a historical figure to a straightforward embodiment of ideals and an object of identification, whether by socialists or by feminists.

Feminism may have been taboo and officially superfluous in the GDR, but literature provided a forum for a broad spectrum of ideas about women and gender, comparable in many ways to those which formed the basis of debates amongst western feminists in the 1970s and 1980s. However, although GDR writers explored a diversity of approaches to gender which contrasted markedly with the state discourse, they shared a broadly socialist view of gender as the product of socio-historical conditions. None of the writers discussed here shares the tendency of much recent French psychoanalytic feminist theory 'towards general theories of the feminine, female sexuality and language which do not take account of historical difference'.[10] Similarly, mainstream writers showed no sympathy for the more radical factions of western feminism which promoted separatism from men as an ideal. As Herminghouse has shown, an area in which strong parallels did emerge between GDR women's writing and western feminist theory is the critique of science. Here, GDR literature was possibly even some years ahead of western theory.[11]

The writers I have discussed generally shared a hope of influencing social and political reality through their literature, as the basis of their aesthetic practice. A profound and lasting effect of GDR cultural policy was writers' understanding of their work as an instrument of change, even when their conceptions of the kind of change needed had shifted to a position of conflict with SED policy. The degree of faith in literature's potential varies widely between individuals and over the course of the two decades. While Schütz's aesthetic is based on presenting personal experience and concerns in such a way that others can relate to them,[12] Wolf and Morgner attribute a more ambitiously political function to literature. Morgner claimed in 1973, 'mein Antrieb wäre nicht, Kunst zu machen, mein Antrieb wäre, Welt zu machen', while Wolf demanded in 1980, 'Literatur heute muß Friedensforschung sein'.[13] However, by the mid-1980s even these

---

[10] Weedon, *Feminist Practice and Poststructuralist Theory*, 165.
[11] Herminghouse, 'Phantasie oder Fanatismus?', 72–3.
[12] See Walther, 107.
[13] Ibid. 54; Wolf, 'Von Büchner sprechen', in *Die Dimension des Autors*, ii. 623.

authors had little faith in the idea that literature could cause direct political change. In *Amanda*, writing is, for Beatriz, an inferior substitute to singing as a means of warning mankind of the imminent catastrophe.[14] In an interview after the publication of *Kassandra*, Wolf discusses the subtle ways in which she believes literature can function 'als Instrument für Veränderungen':

Ich glaube nicht, daß Literatur auf zentrale politische Entscheidungen einen wesentlichen Einfluß hat. [. . .] Meistens wirkt Literatur auf eine indirekte Art, indem sie das Weltbild des Lesers, seine Weltsicht, langsam differenziert und womöglich verändert.[15]

However sceptical writers became concerning the power of literature, it was never regarded as an autonomous realm, serving only as entertainment.

Within this shared notion of literature as a socially interactive force, several rather different aesthetic traditions developed. One is based on a conception of literature as a rational, serious, and essentially realistic tool of enlightenment. Literature of this kind questions the 'truths' about history, gender, and the present which were constructed by official GDR discourses, but maintains faith in a notion of truth, towards which literature can progress in a linear fashion. Wolf is the most prominent representative of this strategy, but it is shared by writers like Damm and Feyl. Damm's comments on history in an interview with Karlheinz Fingerhut exemplify an approach which regards truth as something complex, but ultimately an attainable goal of rational discourse. The false certainties of SED ideology are rejected, but new certainties are sought in their place:

Ich bin entschieden für die 'illusionszerstörende Wahrheit'. Das mag mit dem Verhältnis meiner Generation zur Geschichte zusammenhängen. Allzuoft wurde sie uns geboten ohne Widersprüche, Brüche, Abgründe. Mit Leerstellen. [. . .] Solche Erfahrungen haben mich, meine Generation, geprägt und, so glaube ich, etwas wie eine Gier nach der 'aktenmäßigen Wirklichkeit' erweckt, eine Sucht nach Geschichte, vor allem in ihren Umbruchphasen, wo Widersprüche und Abgründe besonders sichtbar werden.[16]

---

[14] Morgner, *Amanda*, 210.
[15] Wolf, 'Zum Erscheinen des Buches "Kassandra"', in *Die Dimension des Autors*, ii. 929–30. Compare also Wolf's comments to Hörnigk in 1987/8. *Im Dialog*, 60.
[16] Karlheinz Fingerhut, 'So könnte es gewesen sein—Angebote an die Vorstellungskraft: Gespräch mit Sigrid Damm über ihre dokumentarischen Roman-Biographien', *DD* 20 (1989), 313–17 (313–14).

This earnest pursuit of truth is countered by an alternative aesthetic tradition in GDR women's writing, which proposes a less straightforward relationship between the content of literature and truth. The quotation from Picasso which Morgner employs at the end of *Amanda* could serve as a motto for the literature of this tradition: 'Kunst ist nicht Wahrheit. Kunst ist eine Lüge, die die Wahrheit begreifen lehrt' (*Amanda*, 533). This aesthetic strategy, exemplified by Morgner's novels, is characterized by comic playfulness, fantastic elements, irony, and satire. Genia Schulz regards Wolf and Morgner as poles at either end of a spectrum of aesthetic possibilities explored by GDR women writers. She describes the contrast between the two aesthetics in the following terms:

Wolfs Ästhetik ist um die Identität zentriert; es geht ihr um das Subjektwerden des Menschen, der sich seiner eigenen Geschichte versichern muß. Der Zugang (der Autorin) zu fremdem Material erfolgt durch die Anverwandlung an die eigene Gefühlswelt, über Einfühlung, Identifikation, Herstellung von Nähe und (Seelen-) Verwandtschaft. Die 'subjektive Authentizität' ist Garant der ästhetischen Wahrheit.

Dagegen privilegiert Irmtraud Morgner die intellektuelle Verfügung über das fremde Material. [. . .] Sie spricht weniger das Einfühlungs- und Erinnerungsvermögen an, als die Kombinatorik, die Lust am Spielen nach verrückten Regeln mit allen Tricks der Ironie, des Witzes und der Satire.[17]

The authors I have discussed represent a range of positions between the poles established by Schulz. Schütz's works are comic montages of fragmentary pieces of text, and her narrative voice is characterized by ironic distance rather than subjective identification, but she is a fundamentally realistic writer. Königsdorf, meanwhile, employs fantastic elements in *Respektloser Umgang*, but incorporates them into a realistic framework with a reflecting narrator. Struzyk combines a deep subjective identification with her protagonist and a playful, ironic, and witty approach to historical material.

GERMAN REUNIFICATION AND THE TRANSFORMATION OF THE LITERARY FIELD

The cultural field which has been the subject of this study was revolutionized by the political events of 1989 and 1990. The democratization of the GDR and the subsequent unification process caused momentous

---

[17] Schulz, 222.

change in the conditions of life for East German women, the institutional structures of scholarship, the rules governing academic and critical discourses about history and literature, the role and expectations of writers as public figures and of literature itself, and the conditions for the production of literature. The sudden disappearance of a prescriptive master discourse released historians from the obligation to work within a particular teleological model of history, and literature was no longer officially required to support this understanding of history. This brought an abrupt end to the *Ersatzfunktion* literature had taken on, not only in relation to ideologically controlled media, but also in providing perspectives on history which were taboo in GDR historiography.

The material effects which reunification had on women as a social group resulted in a paradox which was also experienced, in different forms, by writers and academics in the former GDR: a gain in freedom was accompanied by a loss of rights, security, and status. However imperfect the gender equality which the SED claimed to have achieved may have been, the new Germany brought with it the loss of rights which women in the GDR had been able to regard as unquestionable, such as free access to abortion and excellent childcare provision. The mass unemployment afflicting the new *Bundesländer* has also resulted in more job losses for women than for men, threatening many women with an involuntary return to a traditional, house-bound female role.[18] However, whereas the GDR allowed no public opposition to the myth that gender equality had been achieved, women now gained the freedom to voice their discontent, and to form feminist groups in order to campaign publicly for women's rights. In the years following 1989, a variety of autonomous women's initiatives were founded, ranging from the politically campaigning Unabhängiger Frauenverband to numerous women's centres, health projects, and economic and professional advisory centres.[19] Meanwhile, feminist theory was gaining the attention of academics and other intellectuals. In December 1989 a Zentrum für interdisziplinäre Frauenforschung was founded at the

---

[18] See *Women and the* Wende: *Social Effects and Cultural Reflections of the German Unification Process*, ed. Elizabeth Boa and Janet Wharton, GM 31 (Amsterdam and Atlanta: Rodopi, 1994), in particular the contributions by Bergmann-Pohl, Einhorn, Alsop, Clements, Dodds, and Weedon.

[19] See Hanna Behrend, 'Keeping a Foot in the Door: East German Women's Academic, Political, Cultural, and Social Projects', in *Women and the* Wende, ed. Boa and Wharton, 64–79; *Aufbruch! Frauenbewegung in der DDR: Dokumentation*, ed. Cordula Kahlau (Munich: Frauenoffensive, 1990).

Humboldt University in Berlin. The centre supports a wide variety of projects concerned with feminist topics and gender theory, facilitates interdisciplinary contacts between students and academics working on such projects, and now co-ordinates a degree course in Gender Studies.[20]

Like all academic disciplines, the historical profession underwent momentous changes, both ideological and practical, after 1989. A chasm quickly developed between established Party historians, represented by the Historiker-Gesellschaft der DDR, and a smaller group of academics, mostly working at the Akademie der Wissenschaften, who founded the Unabhängiger Historiker-Verband in January 1990. The latter adopted as its agenda the 'Förderung der Freiheit von Geschichtsforschung und -lehre, des Theorie- und Methodenpluralismus und die Befreiung von jeder ideologischen Bevormundung'.[21] Although it gained little institutional influence, the group served to create debate in place of the comparatively monolithic consensus which had previously dominated GDR academic discourses. It voiced fundamental criticisms of the legitimizing function and ideologically determined methodology of GDR historiography, while many historians were responding to the events of 1989—as examples in Chapters 1 and 2 have shown—merely with lists of 'gaps' in research, which still needed to be filled.[22] With the dissolution of the Akademie der Wissenschaften and the restructuring of universities aimed at reducing staff numbers to a level comparable with West German institutions, as well as the dismissal of staff for political reasons, most historians who had worked in the GDR found themselves without a job in the years following 1989.[23]

The collapse of the SED regime had complex implications for the literary field, and since 1989 the role of writers and literature in the post-war Germanys and in the new Germany have been the subject of remarkably extensive and heated media debate. One of the most immediate effects of democratization in the autumn of 1989 was the emergence of new forums for open debate and critical discourse of a kind which had not been possible before. Writers played a prominent

[20] See Jähnert.
[21] Isolde Stark, 'Warum ein Unabhängiger Historiker-Verband', in *Hure oder Muse?*, ed. Eckert, Kowalczuk, and Stark, 11–20 (13).
[22] Cf. Bernd Florath, 'Zur Situation am Institut für deutsche Geschichte der Akademie der Wissenschaften (der DDR): Diskussionsbemerkungen auf der Mitgliederversammlung des UHV im Januar 1991', in *Hure oder Muse?*, ed. Eckert, Kowalczuk, and Stark, 120–2 (120).
[23] See Behrend, 64–5; Hörnigk, 'Contours of a New Academic Landscape', 175.

role in this development, using the new forums—demonstrations, new political groups, and democratic media—to express their views and appeal for popular support. The mass demonstration on the Alexanderplatz in Berlin on 4 November 1989 was organized by writers and artists. Similarly, writers—Christa Wolf, Stefan Heym, and Volker Braun—initiated the 'Für unser Land' proclamation of 26 November 1989, arguing for a sovereign, reformed GDR, and against a sell-out of values to the economically dominant Federal Republic. In both the former GDR and the Federal Republic, writers' voices were prominent in media discussions about the future of Germany in the final months of 1989 and the early part of 1990: Wolf, Königsdorf, Stefan Heym, Monika Maron, Wolf Biermann, Günter Grass, and Martin Walser were amongst those publishing contributions to the debate in newspapers and journals.[24] Struzyk was involved in the Neues Forum in its early days, and later worked for Bündnis 90.[25]

In their active and prominent participation in the political developments of autumn 1989, many GDR writers attempted to continue to play their accustomed roles as representatives of the people, or—in Bathrick's terms—as institutions for the articulation of social interests.[26] Both the content and the form of the most prominent writers' contributions to the new political debates suggest a broad continuity of intent with their function as producers of literature in the GDR. The 'Für unser Land' appeal, for example, criticized the 'vom Stalinismus geprägte Strukturen' of the SED state, but proposed 'eine sozialistische Alternative zur Bundesrepublik', 'eine solidarische Gesellschaft [. . .], in der Frieden und soziale Gerechtigkeit, Freiheit des einzelnen, Freizügigkeit aller und die Bewahrung der Umwelt gewährleistet sind'.[27] It thus measured the reality of the GDR against a utopian vision of socialism and retained faith in the values underlying that vision, just as a significant section of GDR literature had done in the

---

[24] Wolf and Königsdorf subsequently published their contributions, as well as the opinions of members of the public. Christa Wolf, *Im Dialog, Angepaßt oder mündig? Briefe an Christa Wolf im Herbst 1989*, ed. Petra Gruner (Frankfurt am Main: Luchterhand, 1990); Helga Königsdorf, *1989 oder Ein Moment Schönheit: Eine Collage aus Briefen, Gedichten, Texten* (Berlin and Weimar: Aufbau, 1990), *Aus dem Dilemma eine Chance machen: Aufsätze und Reden* (Hamburg and Zurich: Luchterhand, 1990; repr. 1991), *Adieu DDR: Protokolle eines Abschieds* (Reinbek: Rowohlt, 1990).

[25] Eva Kaufmann, 'Adieu Kassandra? Schriftstellerinnen aus der DDR vor, in und nach der Wende: Brigitte Burmeister, Helga Königsdorf, Helga Schütz, Brigitte Struzyk, Rosemarie Zeplin', in *Women and the* Wende, ed. Boa and Wharton, 216–25 (221).

[26] Cf. Bathrick, 'Kultur und Öffentlichkeit', 64.

[27] 'Für unser Land', in Wolf, *Im Dialog*, 170–1.

latter decades of the SED's rule. Quite apart from some of the most prominent writers' reluctance to surrender the socialist ideals which had informed their literature, their participation in the political debates of the *Wende* revealed a continuing expectation that their role in the changes would be one of moral and political authority, and that they were entitled to speak on behalf of the people. This is evident, for example, in the collective tone of Wolf's Alexanderplatz speech of 4 November 1989: 'Wir fürchten, benutzt zu werden. Und wir fürchten, ein ehrlich gemeintes Angebot auszuschlagen. In diesem Zwiespalt befindet sich nun das ganze Land.'[28] Elizabeth Mittman notes Wolf's frequent references to 'her role as mediator between the state and the newly vocal people', and suggests that, 'in effect, Wolf transfers her authority from the previously existing literary public sphere to newly emerging spaces'.[29]

For a brief period in the autumn of 1989, the kind of transformation of history which writers such as Wolf, Hermlin, Müller, and Braun had been hoping to achieve through their literature for the past two decades seemed to have become a reality. As Königsdorf wrote in December 1989, the peaceful revolution produced the temporary hope that it might be possible, 'daß Völker sich vom Objekt der Geschichte zum gestaltenden Subjekt erheben können'.[30] The extent to which writers who hoped for reform in accordance with socialist ideals were already out of touch with public opinion in the autumn of 1989 is debatable. Stephen Brockmann argues that there was initially widespread support within East Germany for the 'third way' proposed by prominent writers like Wolf and Königsdorf. He cites an opinion poll conducted by *Der Spiegel* and ZDF in early December 1989, according to which 71 per cent of the 1,032 respondents from all over East Germany were in favour of sovereignty for the GDR and only 27 per cent wanted reunification.[31] Brockmann sees the 4 November demonstration as 'a golden moment for writers when their dreams of a freer and more open public sphere appeared to have been achieved, but when writers had not yet lost the moral and political authority granted to East German writers only because of GDR authoritarian-

---

[28] Wolf, 'Sprache der Wende: Rede auf dem Alexanderplatz', in *Im Dialog*, 119–21 (120).
[29] Mittman, 27.
[30] Königsdorf, *1989 oder Ein Moment Schönheit*, 116. See also Konrad H. Jarausch, 'Kritische Perspektiven zur deutschen Vergangenheit: Folgen der Vereinigung für die Geschichtswissenschaft', in *Nach dem Erdbeben*, ed. Jarausch and Middell, 21–37 (21).
[31] Stephen Brockmann, *Literature and German Reunification* (Cambridge: Cambridge University Press, 1999), 54.

ism'.[32] However, a different interpretation is offered by the literary scholar Marianne Streisand, who attended the demonstration. From her position in the crowd, Streisand perceived a gulf between the writers making speeches at the front and the 'people':

What was being chanted about democratic socialism didn't interest them [the people in the crowd] in the slightest. They were there to express their protest against, their dislike of, the circumstances. They used this demonstration that was organized by artists and didn't organize one of their own. Their demonstration was to go to the west via Hungary. [. . .] I think that the idea of a democratic socialism was always the intellectuals' utopia.[33]

Whether or not writers were deluded in their confidence that they were representing the interests of a significant sector of the GDR population in the early days of the revolution, by the beginning of 1990 it had become undeniable that writers who argued for a 'third way' were seriously out of touch with popular opinion. By this stage, hopes for a reformed socialism had faded, and the CDU's landslide victory in the Volkskammer elections of 18 March confirmed that history was taking a very different direction from that which some of the most prominent writers of the GDR had envisaged. The process which Emmerich has described as 'das Ortloswerden der sozialistischen Vision im Prozeß der Wende' could not but result in a crisis of identity for those writers who had continued to believe in the reformability of socialism right up to and beyond November 1989.[34] The loss of socialism as a utopian vision and a philosophical framework within which to understand the world resulted in disorientation and a melancholy sense of loss for these writers. Volker Braun's poem 'Das Eigentum' captures this mood particularly effectively:

> Und unverständlich wird mein ganzer Text.
> Was ich niemals besaß, wird mir entrissen.
> Was ich nicht lebte, werd ich ewig missen.[35]

The enthusiasm with which writers had greeted the new forums and freedoms in November 1989 quickly subsided not only due to this loss of long-held hopes and values, but also because of a sudden decline

---

[32] Ibid. 50.

[33] *Literary Intellectuals and the Dissolution of the State: Professionalism and Conformity in the GDR*, ed. Robert von Hallberg, trans. Kenneth J. Northcott (Chicago and London: University of Chicago Press, 1996), 64–5.

[34] Emmerich, *Kleine Literaturgeschichte*, 457.

[35] *Neues Deutschland*, 4–5 Aug. 1990; repr. in *Grenzfallgedichte: Eine deutsche Anthologie*, ed. Anna Chiarloni and Helga Pankoke (Berlin and Weimar: Aufbau, 1991), 109.

in the importance attached to writers' views. In an interview with Gerhard Rein, broadcast on Deutschlandfunk on 8 October 1989, Wolf called for the GDR media to provide a space for open dialogue which until then had been possible only in cultural forums such as theatres.[36] Wolf did not seem to realize at this stage that the inevitable consequence of such a development would be a corrosion of her own authority. Königsdorf showed a greater awareness of the contradictions inherent in writers' calls for more democratic media:

Ich habe immer gewarnt, daß wir Schriftsteller mit unserer Forderung nach Glasnost uns selbst das Wasser abgraben. Was soll denn aus uns werden, wenn unsere Narrenfreiheit plötzlich für alle gilt? Und wenn die Leute schon mit dem Lesen von Zeitungen hinreichend zu tun haben.[37]

These fears proved prophetic. Not only did the media now take over one of the functions which literature had fulfilled in the GDR and provide a public sphere for a much wider audience, but writers were quickly forced to abandon the idea that they could represent the interests of the wider population and speak on the people's behalf. Democratization was accompanied by a backlash of public opinion against GDR intellectuals. As Jean E. Conacher has summarized the situation,

Within the space of only a few weeks the relationship of writer, journalist and reader had undergone a shift of loyalties. Readers now looked increasingly to the journalists for confirmation of their own interpretation of events around them, writers were seen more and more as members of a privileged élite holding on to a party and a system which no longer could nor should be spared.[38]

In their contributions to public debate, individual writers responded to the radically changed conditions and demands of the public sphere in a variety of ways. Of the writers discussed in this study, Wolf and Königsdorf were the most active participants in the debates of 1989 and 1990. Mittman has argued that, while Wolf constructs her identity around notions of identification and continues to regard herself as an institution, adopting an intensely moral tone, Königsdorf understands the public sphere as a space where her multiple and often conflicting identities enter into dialogue with each other.[39] It is undeniable that

---

[36] Wolf, 'Aufforderung zum Dialog: Gespräch mit Gerhard Rein', in *Im Dialog*, 77–89 (83).
[37] Königsdorf, *1989 oder Ein Moment Schönheit*, 79.
[38] Jean E. Conacher, 'Pressing for Change: The Case of Helga Königsdorf', in *Women and the* Wende, ed. Boa and Wharton, 164–76 (173).
[39] Mittman, 23–37.

Königsdorf responded to the changing demands of the public sphere with a flexibility which Wolf lacked. While Wolf publicly lamented the political and cultural developments following November 1989, looking back fondly to the 4 November demonstration, Königsdorf quickly came to welcome democratization and its impact on the cultural sphere:

Erst einmal sind wir vom Sockel gestürzt, auf dem wir zwar dem Wind ausgesetzt waren, auf dem es sich doch hochgemut stehen ließ. Und dieser Sturz ist gut. Für uns und für die, die uns stürzen. Was wären wir für Künstler, wenn wir die Wirkung unseres Kunstwerks bedauerten. Wenn wir unser Publikum in der Entmündigung belassen wollten.[40]

While Wolf continued to talk in an impersonally authoritative tone, and insisted on continuity in the function of literature, Königsdorf embarked on a process of intense self-questioning in the months following November 1989. Publicly acknowledging her complicity with a corrupt regime and documenting processes of self-criticism and personal development enabled Königsdorf to create a new public voice in response to the rapid changes around her. As Karoline von Oppen has pointed out, she showed herself to be adept at playing different roles in different media and for different audiences: '[Königsdorf] adapts to a dominant discourse in western newspapers, whilst restricting her critique and reform project to the pages of *Neues Deutschland.*'[41]

Despite her public rejection—especially in the West German press—of her earlier role and of the moral and political authority attached to writers and their literature in the GDR, there are underlying continuities in Königsdorf's position. Like Wolf, she does not renounce her conviction that literature should be politically critical and committed to the creation of a society based on respect for human dignity and for the earth. As Diana Alberghini has suggested, 'Königsdorf's idea of literature as a means of fostering critical culture becomes one which does not owe its validity to a specific political or cultural framework, and therefore can be sustained even after the earthquake which provoked the collapse of the GDR'.[42] Despite the painful loss of

---

[40] Königsdorf, *Aus dem Dilemma eine Chance machen*, 9. Cf. Wolf, *Im Dialog*, 132–3.

[41] Karoline von Oppen, *The Role of the Writer and the Press in the Unification of Germany, 1989–1990* (New York: Lang, 2000), 59.

[42] Diana Alberghini, 'Re-defining the Role of the Intellectual and the Function of Literature: The Example of Helga Königsdorf', in *East Germany: Continuity and Change*, ed. Paul Cooke and Jonathan Grix, GM 46 (Amsterdam and Atlanta: Rodopi, 2000), 32–41 (38).

a utopian vision, Königsdorf suggests that writers of committed litera-
ture will be needed in the new Germany, just as they were in the GDR:
'Wir werden gebraucht. Gebrauchtwerden deutet immer auf ein
Defizit. Sagen wir also: Wir werden wieder gebraucht werden.
Leider.'[43]

By mid-1990 it was clear that the entire cultural field, not only of the
GDR, but of West Germany too, was in a state of flux. The structure
and economy of the GDR literary field had collapsed, with the result
that many of the positions which had been available to writers and
critics prior to November 1989 now became untenable. For West
Germany too, the sudden disappearance of its 'ideological Other,
the specific location of its utopian hopes and its dystopian fears' meant
a destabilization of the cultural field as it had been organized there
until 1989.[44] The reception of Wolf's *Was bleibt* when it was published
in June 1990 was a very clear indication of the changed structure and
rules of the field. As Mittman has argued, although originally written
under GDR conditions, the text was not read as GDR literature by
or for a GDR public, but was inserted into a western journalistic discourse.[45] Instead of reading the work according to the criteria which
would have been valid before 1989, critics used it as a starting-point for
attempts to discredit writers who had remained in the GDR and
supported socialism, however critical they may have been of the SED
regime.[46] The 'Literaturstreit' which ensued was fundamentally a contest for the power to determine new cultural definitions and rules of
participation in the field. As Emmerich has commented, the debate
was 'kaum je ein Streit um ästhetische Fragen, sondern einer *um die kulturelle Definitionsmacht im Lande*'.[47] The contest was, significantly, played
out by West German intellectuals in West German newspapers. By
contesting the meaning and value of German literature of the past
forty years, critics attempted to determine cultural values for the
future. As Ulrich Greiner, one of the main participants, commented,
'wer bestimmt, was gewesen ist, der bestimmt auch, was sein wird. Der
Streit um die Vergangenheit ist ein Streit um die Zukunft'.[48]

Criticisms of GDR writers for strengthening the SED regime both

---

[43] Königsdorf, *Aus dem Dilemma eine Chance machen*, 11.

[44] Brockmann, 60.

[45] Mittman, 24.

[46] For more detailed accounts of the text's reception, see Brockmann, 64–70, and
Emmerich, *Kleine Literaturgeschichte*, 464–9.   [47] Ibid. 462.

[48] Greiner, 'Die deutsche Gesinnungsästhetik', in *'Es geht nicht um Christa Wolf'*, ed. Anz,
208.

through their fundamental support for socialism and by providing, in literature, an outlet for criticism and debate which did not threaten the regime's stability, quickly developed into rejections of post-war German literature in its entirety. The need to reassess the relationship between East and West German post-1945 literature became obvious with the collapse of Cold War dichotomies. However, critics such as Frank Schirrmacher and Karl Heinz Bohrer equated the two literatures in an undifferentiated and crude way, in order to condemn both on the grounds of their moral concerns, political commitment, and allegedly unhealthy obsession with Germany's past. As Brockmann has pointed out, such criticisms of left-liberal political engagement in West German literature were not new; Bohrer had attacked West German culture in the 1980s, but with little resonance. The changed and changing cultural field of 1990 offered a more favourable context for such views: 'the collapse of the GDR and the perceived failure of its literary intellectuals to effect democratic change provided an opportunity for critics inside West Germany who disliked the left-liberal political interventions of some writers.'[49] One of the ironies of the 'Literaturstreit' was that, despite calling for an aesthetically autonomous German literature, the participants overestimated the power of literature to cause social and political change, just as the SED regime had done with its highly politicized idea of literature. In accusing Wolf of stabilizing a corrupt regime and suggesting that *Was bleibt* could have damaged the Staatssicherheit if it had been published before the GDR's demise, Schirrmacher was attributing to literature a political power which is at odds with the artistic autonomy he later espoused as an ideal.[50] Similarly, his and Greiner's insistence on aesthetic autonomy contradicted the primarily moral and political judgements they themselves had pronounced on *Was bleibt*, and on GDR literature more generally.[51]

While ideas about what German literature should be and do were being debated, East German writers were more directly affected by material changes to the conditions of their working lives. The cultural field of the former GDR underwent a sudden currency change after November 1989. As an economy based on political prestige gave way to a market-led economy, ideological constraints were replaced by

[49] Brockmann, 71.
[50] Frank Schirrmacher, '"Dem Druck des härteren, strengeren Lebens standhalten": Auch eine Studie über den autoritären Charakter: Christa Wolfs Aufsätze, Reden und ihre jüngste Erzählung "Was bleibt"', in *'Es geht nicht um Christa Wolf'*, ed. Anz, 77–89 (78, 87).
[51] Cf. *'Es geht nicht um Christa Wolf'*, ed. Anz, 189, 194–5.

financial ones. The generous state funding of art—which had, for example, enabled Morgner to devote almost ten years to a single novel —disappeared, leaving writers subject to publishing houses' demands for regular and marketable works. All but the most successful writers now found it impossible to live on the income from literature alone.[52]

While the collapse of the SED regime resulted in drastic changes in conditions for literary production in East Germany, and in a radical rethinking of the role and function of literature and writers in Germany as a whole, the relative importance of 1989 as a caesura in literary history will only become apparent with greater historical distance. By the end of the century, new developments in German literature were beginning to emerge. Whereas the critics and authors contesting the past and future of German literature in the 'Literaturstreit' were almost exclusively men, women have played a far more significant role in actually shaping the literary field of reunified Germany through their writing. With the exception of Morgner, who died of cancer in May 1990, most of the writers who have formed the focus of this study produced works during the 1990s which displayed strong lines of continuity with their GDR works. However, the positions of these individuals within the literary field have inevitably changed as a result of the changes in the structure of the field as a whole.

Wolf's *Medea* is perhaps the most striking example of individual continuity in the face of change. Rather than making use of the new freedom to write directly about recent history, Wolf responds to a sense of crisis in the present as she had in the early 1980s, seeking analogies in Greek myth. The 1996 novel has rightly been read as a continuation and intensification of the concerns at the heart of *Kassandra*.[53] Both protagonists are situated at the point of a supposed historical shift between two value systems, and both embody a corrective to the reign of instrumental reason which has had increasingly destructive effects in the modern world. As Georgina Paul has pointed out, the Medea figure is 'eine gesteigerte Kassandra', an innocent victim whose lack of inner division ensures superior insight into herself and events around her.[54] The contrast between the Colchians and the Corinthians, like that between Trojans and Greeks in *Kassandra*, invites comparisons with contemporary East-West relations, problematic in new ways after the events of 1989–90.

---

[52] Emmerich, *Kleine Literaturgeschichte*, 448–9; Kaufmann, 'Adieu Kassandra?', 222.
[53] Christa Wolf, *Medea: Stimmen* (Gütersloh: Luchterhand, 1996). See Paul, 'Schwierigkeiten mit der Dialektik'. [54] Ibid. 231.

The most striking difference between the two works is not one of plot or theme, but one of form. The two voices of the *Kassandra* project—the authorial narrator of the *Voraussetzungen* and Kassandra herself—are replaced in *Medea* by six fictional voices and the narrator of the prologue. This polyphonic narrative form implies that truth is no longer located within an individual's memories, as in *Kassandra*, but somewhere between or beyond a number of complementary perspectives, each limited in its way. However, despite the plurality of perspective, the work actually promotes a single version of the events which supposedly underlie the myth in a very similar way to the earlier work. The perspectives and interpretations offered by some of the speakers may be unreliable, but the version of events which the reader is supposed to believe is always visible beneath the characters' self-delusions, and is never in question. As in a detective novel, the work suggests that a single truth can be discovered beneath the distorting perspectives offered by most of the characters. As a response to the transformation of the cultural field in 1989 and the hostile reassessments of Wolf's career following the publication of *Was bleibt*, this narrative strategy might be seen as a defensive attempt to reassert the authority in interpreting events which Wolf enjoyed prior to 1989.

While *Medea* responds to the sudden collapse of the political and cultural certainties of the post-war Germanys with an insistence on truth, its construction of history reflects the profound loss of meaning experienced by those who had maintained a socialist world view until the collapse of the GDR. As in *Kassandra*, the present in which Wolf is writing forms the starting-point for her exploration of the mythical material in *Medea*: 'Das Eingeständnis unserer Not, damit müßten wir anfangen' (*Medea*, 9). The idea of parallels between the two times remains prominent in the later work. In contrast with *Kassandra*, however, where the accompanying lectures offer extensive reflection on the relationship between the narrative and the present world situation, the relevance of Medea's story for the present is only hinted at by the narrative voice with which the work opens. Furthermore, the sense of a historical course of development leading from ancient times to the late twentieth century, which is central to the *Kassandra* project, is absent from the later work.[55] Although *Kassandra* expressed a pessimistic view of history as a negative course of destruction, it did present history as a coherent

---

[55] Such ideas are, however, explored by Wolf and a variety of critics, in *Christa Wolfs Medea: Voraussetzungen zu einem Text. Mythos und Bild*, ed. Marianne Hochgeschurz (Berlin: Janus Press, 1998).

and ongoing progression, in which continuity could be traced from ancient Greece to 1980s Europe. In *Medea* any sense that history has a meaningful shape has been lost. While the work is structured by the idea of parallels between two different eras, there is no sense of progression between them. History has been reduced to an unrelenting course of barbarity, in which there is no place for hope, either in the past or in the future.

If Wolf's *Medea* has elements of a detective novel, Königsdorf's 1992 narrative, *Gleich neben Afrika*, is more like a parody of a detective novel.[56] It contains mystery, crime, drama, and suspense, but lacks both narrative coherence and the gradual revelation of a truth at its centre. Set at the beginning of the 1990s, the work depicts the female narrator's attempt to adjust to the new social and economic conditions, her love relationship with Maria, and her confrontation with her past during a stay in the village where she grew up. The two women's quest for money culminates in their acquisition—by illegal, though unexplained means—of a large sum, and their consequent escape to an island off the coast of Africa. Throughout the text, reflections on the effects of reunification and accounts of individuals' experiences are juxtaposed with a series of mysterious occurrences. The reader's expectation that the mystery will be solved in the course of the text, however, remains frustrated: the narrator's comment that 'das wichtigste Geheimnis' in the GDR was 'daß es gar kein Geheimnis gab' seems to apply also to the work itself (*Afrika*, 43). The episodes which make up the text remain fragmentary, and no underlying plot emerges to unite them and make sense of the unexplained mysteries. The reader is left wondering whether much of the mystery is created by the narrator's need to dramatize events and create mystery where there is none. Her frequent admission of uncertainty about observations she has just reported suggests she has a tendency to leap to somewhat sensationalizing conclusions, perhaps as a result of her 'Überwachungsentzugssyndrom' (*Afrika*, 93), or perhaps because of a need to perceive in events around her all the elements of the bestseller which she has promised Maria she will write: 'Der Roman, um den es mir eigentlich ging, war das Leben' (*Afrika*, 13). Königsdorf's text captures and parodies a mood of ubiquitous suspicion and a sense that there are exciting secrets to be uncovered, whether those of the Staatssicherheit or those of western capitalism, which were widespread in Germany after 1989.

Königsdorf's 1993 novel, *Im Schatten des Regenbogens*, is a more con-

---

[56] Helga Königsdorf, *Gleich neben Afrika: Erzählung* (Berlin: Rowohlt, 1992).

ventional treatment of the same topic.[57] This work is about a group of single individuals who share a flat in East Berlin on a temporary basis in the early 1990s. Reviving characters from her early short stories, Königsdorf explores the effects of reunification on a variety of mature, highly qualified individuals who had a secure place in the GDR workforce, but become victims of the 'Abwicklung' of GDR structures. Three of the protagonists worked at a 'Zahlographisches Institut'; of these, significantly, only the man is able to gain a foothold in the new society. Despite the clear social criticism in the work, the tone is humorous, and the realistic problems faced by the characters are juxtaposed with unlikely events revealing the love of the absurd characteristic of Königsdorf's writing. One character is struck dead by lightning during a freak storm which is followed by a spectacular rainbow. Another apparently leaves the house with a hand grenade at the end of the novel. Dennis Tate has commented that the work continues to 'fulfil the old function of providing *Lebenshilfe* often associated with GDR literature':

It has been written in the conviction that the typical situations it depicts have *not* been adequately conveyed by other media and that the author is justified in presenting a clear moral perspective on the aftermath of unification, through the experiences of a group of protagonists whom she portrays sympathetically.[58]

Königsdorf's 1997 novel, *Die Entsorgung der Großmutter*, also clearly represents a continuity with the morally committed and socially critical tendencies of much GDR literature.[59] Although reunification and the GDR are not mentioned explicitly in this work, references to social changes in recent years, including a widespread loss of job security, suggest that the setting may be in the new *Bundesländer*. The novel depicts a society in which middle-class respectability, conformism, and material values have displaced compassion and respect for human dignity to such an extent that, rather than lose their house to pay care fees, a family abandons a grandmother who, suffering from Alzheimer's disease, has become a burden.

While Wolf's *Medea* provoked the criticism that the author had nothing new to offer, Königsdorf uses irony, satire, and humour to

---

[57] Helga Königsdorf, *Im Schatten des Regenbogens: Roman* (Berlin and Weimar: Aufbau, 1993).
[58] Dennis Tate, 'Trapped in the Past? The Identity Problems of East German Writers since the *Wende*', in *Germany in the 1990s*, ed. H. J. Hahn, GM 34 (Amsterdam and Atlanta: Rodopi, 1995), 1–16 (12–13).
[59] Helga Königsdorf, *Die Entsorgung der Großmutter: Roman* (Berlin: Aufbau, 1997).

treat the topic of German reunification and its effects in a variety of innovative ways in her 1990s novels.[60] This approach, which develops further the literary techniques she used before 1989, allows her to incorporate social criticism into her works, and to deal with the problems faced by individuals in the wake of reunification, without succumbing to the pessimism of Wolf's work. By the time *Medea* appeared in 1996, the 'Literaturstreit' and the revelation of Wolf's brief collaboration with the *Stasi* had done much to cement her position in the new literary field of reunified Germany, as the prime representative of GDR culture and its alleged failings. The continuity in ideas and approach between *Medea* and her earlier works could hardly challenge this new status. Königsdorf, lacking Wolf's prominence in the GDR, escaped the unwelcome new form of attention paid to Wolf in the early 1990s, and was able to maintain a position at the margins of the transformed literary field. The generational difference between the two writers is also an important factor in their different abilities to adapt to a radically changed set of conditions. Despite an age gap of only nine years, Wolf and Königsdorf belong, as writers, to different generations, whose careers were shaped by the GDR in different ways. Whereas Wolf began to write in the late 1950s, Königsdorf did not publish her first text until 1978. Eva Kaufmann has described the differences between these two generations in the following terms:

Während sich die Älteren im Laufe der sechziger Jahre mühsam aus den anfänglichen, den offiziellen Literaturmustern der fünfziger Jahre verpflichteten Schreibkonzepten herausarbeiteten, fingen die Jüngeren zehn oder zwanzig Jahre später auf einem anderen Niveau der Kunstreflexion an.[61]

The fact that her biography as a writer was less embedded in the history of the GDR may explain why Königsdorf, in contrast with Wolf, was able to experiment with a variety of new narrative strategies in the years following the *Wende*.

While Königsdorf, as a committed socialist, was forced to rethink her ideology and her identity as a writer in 1989–90, some writers of her age and younger lacked her commitment to the GDR and so did not experience such a disruption in their careers with the transition to the new Germany. Continuity has proved a successful strategy for Damm and Feyl, neither of whom attained any great degree of promi-

---

[60] See, for example, Andrea Köhler, 'Medea, Schwester: Christa Wolfs Voraussetzungen zu einem Roman', *Neue Zürcher Zeitung*, 2 Mar. 1996, 35.

[61] Eva Kaufmann, 'Adieu Kassandra?', 217.

nence in the literary field of the GDR. Both have gained a wide reader-ship throughout Germany since 1989. Both have continued to pursue their interest in historical women. Damm turned her attention to a second woman known because of her relationship with Goethe, Christiane Vulpius. *Christiane und Goethe*, released in advance of the 250th anniversary of Goethe's birth in 1999, became one of the best-selling non-fictional books of that year. Feyl has written historical novels about Sophie von La Roche and Caroline von Wolzogen, simi-lar to *Idylle mit Professor* in style and approach.[62] While neither achieved the popularity of *Christiane und Goethe*, both were more successful than Feyl's earlier works had been in their GDR context or in the Federal Republic before 1989. The fact that almost all of Damm's and Feyl's pre-1989 works have been published in new editions since 1989 indi-cates the more secure positions they have found in the literary field of reunified Germany.

As mentioned in Chapter 2, apart from their continuing work on historical women, both writers have also produced semi-autobiographical novels about life in the GDR, from its earliest years through to 1989 and beyond. *Ich bin nicht Ottilie* and *Ausharren im Paradies* tell stories of personal and political disillusionment over the course of GDR history, focusing in particular on women's experience. Both have a primarily documentary value, offering lengthy accounts of the ways individual histories were interwoven with the political history of the GDR. Aesthetically and thematically, they represent a con-tinuation of the authors' earlier works. Damm continues to portray women's suffering under patriarchy, both in the public sphere and in relationships with men, and to write in a predominantly paratactic style.[63] Feyl's ironic narrative technique and understanding of gender relations are so similar in *Ausharren im Paradies* and *Idylle mit Professor* that her characterization of Franz Kogler in the former is at times virtually indistinguishable from her presentation of Gottsched in the latter. Despite their shortcomings, these novels—particularly *Ausharren im Paradies*—did seem to meet a need in the literary market after 1989. Both were reissued by the Munich publishing house Heyne—pri-marily a publisher of popular literature—in 2000. Brigitte Struzyk's strongly autobiographical work of 1994, *In vollen Zügen: Rück-Sichten*, enjoyed no such success.[64] A much more demanding and poetic text, in

---

[62] Feyl, *Die profanen Stunden des Glücks, Das sanfte Joch der Vortrefflichkeit*.
[63] For a more detailed analysis, see Plenderleith.
[64] Brigitte Struzyk, *In vollen Zügen: Rück-Sichten* (Berlin and Weimar: Aufbau, 1994).

which a broad chronology is interrupted by sections dealing with the female narrator's present experiences in the 1990s, her memories of the GDR, and her dreams, this work was not aimed at a popular market. The Aufbau publishing house withdrew it from production shortly after its first appearance.

By the final years of the GDR, socialist ideology had become irrelevant to Damm's and Feyl's works. Neither was therefore faced with the difficulties of rethinking her position and her understanding of literature that writers like Wolf and Königsdorf had. Their blend of literary history, autobiography, and popular fiction has proved highly marketable under the new conditions. In other areas of the literary field too, some of the most interesting new contributions since reunification have been made by writers who have only come to prominence since 1990.

The literary treatments of the legacy of the GDR and the reunification process which have made the greatest impact in the new cultural field have been those written by East German writers who were barely known at the time of the GDR's collapse. These range from Thomas Brussig's hugely popular *Helden wie wir* and *Am kürzeren Ende der Sonnenallee*, which employ humour and farce in their presentation of everyday life in the GDR, to Wolfgang Hilbig's study of the world of a *Stasi* spy and the literary scene of Prenzlauer Berg, *'Ich'*. Jens Sparschuh's *Der Zimmerspringbrunnen* and Ingo Schulze's *Simple Storys: Ein Roman aus der ostdeutschen Provinz* both, in their different ways, deal with the consequences of reunification for East Germans. Sparschuh's comic-melancholic tale of one man's responses to crises in his personal and professional life contrasts with Schulze's network of intricately related short stories about a variety of characters. Both texts address experiences and problems which were widespread in the new *Bundesländer* in the wake of reunification, such as the need for individuals to change careers and undergo new training in order to be able to compete in the job market.

One of the most acclaimed texts by an East German woman writer to have appeared since 1990 is Brigitte Burmeister's *Unter dem Namen Norma*.[65] Set in 1992, the text is structured around the events of two days with strong historical resonances, 17 June and 14 July. The narrator

---

[65] Brigitte Burmeister, *Unter dem Namen Norma: Roman* (Stuttgart: Klett-Cotta, 1994). For a more detailed analysis of this text and a summary of its reception, see Volker Wehdeking, *Die deutsche Einheit und die Schriftsteller: Literarische Verarbeitung der Wende seit 1989* (Stuttgart: Kohlhammer, 1995), 76–89.

Marianne Arends's everyday life in an old block of flats in East Berlin and the breakdown of her marriage after her husband Johannes's move to the West are narrated alongside her memories of the GDR, and her reflections on the French revolutionary St Just as she translates a biography of him. Burmeister offers a highly differentiated picture of both reunified Germany and the GDR past. The presentation of the new Germany is sober: Marianne and her neighbours face problems such as unemployment, a crisis of identity, depression, and the breakdown of personal relationships in the wake of reunification. The GDR past, however, is treated without nostalgia. The East–West divide within the new Germany is shown to be reinforced by prejudices and stereotypical images on both sides which hamper mutual understanding. While Marianne's cliché-ridden account of her alleged past as a *Stasi* informant is not doubted by Johannes's guest because it corresponds to her image of East Germans, Marianne herself is quick to reject West Germans as 'diese aufgeblasenen Originale, für die der Osten bevölkert ist von Stereotypen' (*Norma*, 252). Although the process of reunification is clearly fraught with difficulties, hope is provided at the end of the novel in the form of friendship between women: Marianne and Norma, who met for the first time on 9 November 1989, propose a bond of friendship based on St Just's democratic ideals. As Beth Alldred has pointed out, this instance of female solidarity is quite different from the female friendships found in earlier GDR women's writing, in that it is not idealized, and tensions between the two women are made clear.[66]

While many East German writers still have a distinctly East German perspective to offer in their literature, and have taken up prominent positions in the new literary field with their treatments of the GDR past and the impact of reunification on East Germans, a new generation of German writers is now emerging, whose biographies have been less marked by the political divisions of the post-war period. In the last decade of the twentieth century a literary landscape which, in both East and West, had long been dominated by writers of older generations, was transformed by the first works of writers born in the late 1960s and the 1970s. Christian Kracht, Julia Franck, Benjamin von Stuckrad-Barre, Judith Hermann, Karen Duve, Tobias Hülswitt, Jenny Erpenbeck, and others have introduced to German literature prose works which leave behind the political commitment of much

---

[66] Beth Alldred, 'Two Contrasting Perspectives on German Unification: Helga Schubert and Brigitte Burmeister', *GLL* 50 (1997), 2, 165–81 (179).

post-war literature. As Martin Hielscher has commented, 'the individual methods and the particular literary backgrounds of these writers
are so different that they cannot be reduced to the common denomina-
tor of a homogeneous programme'. Attempting to summarize what is
new about their writings, he speaks of 'an intelligent and reflective,
but unideological and relaxed relationship to literature', and of 'the
insistence on narrative coherence'.[67]

In their refusal to subordinate literature to ideology, and their
respect for developments in other European and Anglo-American
literatures, these young writers and others who have come to prominence since 1990—Dagmar Leupold, Robert Menasse, Ingo Schulze,
and Jens Sparschuh, for example—might appear to answer the calls
for an autonomous and unpolitical literature along Anglo-American
lines made by Bohrer, Schirrmacher, and Greiner in the early 1990s.
However, the concern with the German past which Greiner saw as a
regrettable 'moralische Überlast' for post-war literature and declared
would come to an end with reunification, remains a prominent theme
in contemporary German literature.[68] Rather than creating a state of
'normality' and allowing the past to be laid to rest, reunification
arguably gave the past a new significance by recalling to mind German
national identity prior to 1945. As Brockmann comments,

German reunification seemed just as likely to prompt a renewed interest in
'coming to terms with' the common German past as to provide an excuse for
burying that past. [. . .] The double 'coming to terms with the past' now necessary with respect to Nazism and Stalinism might well mean not an erasure
but a heightening of historical sensitivity.[69]

This argument is borne out by the continuing popularity of historical
themes with writers of all ages. Besides the works by Königsdorf, Feyl,
Damm, Struzyk, Burmeister, Brussig, Schulze, and Hilbig, Helga
Schütz's *Vom Glanz der Elbe*, Monika Maron's *Stille Zeile Sechs* and *Animal
Triste*, Martin Walser's *Die Verteidigung der Kindheit*, Jurek Becker's
Amanda herzlos, Christoph Hein's *Von allem Anfang an*, Hans-Ulrich
Treichel's *Der Verlorene*, and Uwe Timms's *Die Entdeckung der Currywurst*
all deal with German history of the post-war period. New perspectives

[67] Martin Hielscher, 'The Return to Narrative and History: Some Thoughts on
Contemporary German-Language Literature', in *Literature, Markets and Media in Germany and
Austria Today*, ed. Arthur Williams, Stuart Parkes, and Julian Preece (Oxford: Lang, 2000),
295–309 (297).
[68] Greiner, 'Die deutsche Gesinnungsästhetik', in *'Es geht nicht um Christa Wolf'*, ed. Anz, 211.
[69] Brockmann, 162.

on the National Socialist past have been offered by Marcel Beyer's *Flughunde*, Bernhard Schlink's *Der Vorleser*, Gert Hofmann's *Der Kinoerzähler*, Judith Kuckart's *Die schöne Frau*, and Jens Sparschuh's *Der Schneemensch*, amongst others.

In a democratic public sphere where different interpretations of the past may compete, literary treatments of historical topics have a very different status from in the GDR, where they complemented, challenged, and undermined an ideologically controlled discourse on history. However, the demise of the GDR and the incorporation of its territory into a larger Federal Republic have given rise to a new teleological historical narrative, where socialism is seen as an unfortunate digression on the road to western capitalism. The attempts to discredit Christa Wolf and the GDR cultural and intellectual spheres she was taken to represent were symptomatic of wider efforts in the West German media to dismiss the socialist project in all its aspects, as a morally dubious experiment doomed to failure. As Chris Weedon has commented, 'unification has, in practice, implied attempts to obliterate anything that might have been good about the GDR from public consciousness. Forty years of history have been reduced to a single narrative of repression'.[70] Both writers and historians in the new Germany have challenged this popular understanding of GDR history by pursuing more differentiated approaches to the recent past.[71] Women writers continue to offer a distinct critical perspective on history. The dominant view that the transition from GDR socialism to western democracy represents unambiguous progress leaves out of consideration some of the more negative effects reunification has had on women. A text like Burmeister's *Unter dem Namen Norma* introduces a more differentiated view of the transition with all its contradictions.

The German literary field at the beginning of the twenty-first century is one in which different perspectives, aesthetic strategies, and understandings of literature fruitfully coexist. While post-war German literature was never as homogeneous as some of the contributions to the 'Literaturstreit' suggested, it is undeniable that the political prestige attached to literature, and the moral and political commitment of the most prominent authors were distinctive characteristics of German

---

[70] Chris Weedon, 'Reading Christa Wolf', in *Post-War Women's Writing in German: Feminist Critical Approaches*, ed. Chris Weedon (Providence, RI, and Oxford: Berghahn, 1997), 223–42 (224).

[71] Examples of historians' work include *Sozialgeschichte der DDR*, ed. Hartmut Kaelble, Jürgen Kocka, and Hartmut Zwahr (Stuttgart: Klett-Cotta, 1994); *Die DDR als Geschichte*, ed. Jürgen Kocka (Berlin: Akademie Verlag, 1994).

culture, particularly in the GDR, during this period. With the disappearance of the 'Leseland DDR' and the arrival of new media, as a result not only of democratization, but also of developing technologies, literature has lost the privileged status in relation to culture as a whole which it enjoyed—and under which it suffered—in the GDR. A broad consensus about the political function of literature and a philosophical framework within which to understand history have also been lost. Despite some critics' attempts to create a new consensus about what literature should be and do, literary developments since reunification indicate diversification, rather than an abrupt change of direction. The fact that it was literature which provided the context—and pretext—for a debate about the moral and political issues arising from the GDR's demise and the prospect of reunification is testimony to the continuing importance of literature in the German national consciousness. The changed structure of the field has resulted in radically different positions for individual writers, despite continuities in their own writings. However, within the field as a whole, literature which deals with historical topics, works through the past, and explores the present in relation to history, continues to occupy an important place. Helping to shape a society's understanding of its past—and so also of its present—is one of the functions of literature everywhere. The GDR's demise may have shaken faith in literature's ability to shape the future, but it is beyond doubt that in a nation with a history as remarkable as Germany's, literature will continue, amongst other things, to offer new perspectives on the past.

BIBLIOGRAPHY

This bibliography is divided into three sections: Primary Texts by GDR Writers and Historians; Secondary Texts about the GDR and GDR Authors; and Other Sources.

I. PRIMARY TEXTS BY GDR WRITERS AND HISTORIANS

ARENDT, HANS-JÜRGEN, RANTZSCH, PETRA, and STAUDE, FRITZ, 'Ergebnisse historischer Frauenforschung in der DDR 1980 bis 1990', *Mitteilungsblatt der Forschungsgemeinschaft 'Frauen in der Geschichte' an der Sektion Geschichte der Pädagogischen Hochschule 'Clara Zetkin' Leipzig* (1990), 2, 5–51.

DE BRUYN, GÜNTER, *Das Leben des Jean Paul Friedrich Richter: Eine Biographie* (Halle: Mitteldeutscher Verlag, 1975).

BURMEISTER, BRIGITTE, *Unter dem Namen Norma: Roman* (Stuttgart: Klett-Cotta, 1994).

CHIARLONI, ANNA, and PANKOKE, HELGA (eds.), *Grenzfallgedichte: Eine deutsche Anthologie* (Berlin and Weimar: Aufbau, 1991).

CLAUDIUS, EDUARD, *Menschen an unsrer Seite: Roman* (Halle: Mitteldeutscher Verlag, 1965).

DAMM, SIGRID (ed.), *Begegnung mit Caroline: Briefe von Caroline Schlegel-Schelling* (Leipzig: Reclam, 1979; repr. 1984).

——*Cornelia Goethe* (Berlin and Weimar: Aufbau, 1987; repr. Frankfurt am Main: Insel, 1992).

——'Unruhe: Anläßlich der Verleihung des Lion-Feuchtwanger-Preises 1987', *SF* 40 (1988), 1, 244–8.

——*Ich bin nicht Ottilie: Roman* (Frankfurt am Main: Insel, 1992).

——*Christiane und Goethe: Eine Recherche* (Frankfurt am Main and Leipzig: Insel, 1998).

DEHNE, HARALD, 'Have We Come Any Closer to *Alltag*? Everyday Reality and Workers' Lives as an Object of Historical Research in the German Democratic Republic', in *The History of Everyday Life: Reconstructing Historical Experiences and Ways of Life*, ed. Alf Lüdtke, trans. William Templer (Princeton: Princeton University Press, 1995), 116–48.

DORNEMANN, LUISE, *Alle Tage ihres Lebens: Frauengestalten aus zwei Jahrhunderten* (Berlin: Dietz, 1981).

ECKERT, RAINER, KOWALCZUK, ILKO-SASCHA, and STARK, ISOLDE (eds.), *Hure oder Muse? Klio in der DDR: Dokumente und Materialien des Unabhängigen Historiker-Verbandes* (Berlin: Gesellschaft für sozialwissenschaftliche Forschung und Publizistik, 1994).

EICHHOLTZ, DIETRICH, and PÄTZOLD, KURT (eds.), *Der Weg in den Krieg: Studien zur Geschichte der Vorkriegsjahre (1935/36 bis 1939)* (Berlin: Akademie Verlag, 1989; repr. Cologne: Pahl-Rugenstein, 1989).

FEYL, RENATE, *Der lautlose Aufbruch: Frauen in der Wissenschaft* (Berlin: Verlag Neues Leben, 1981; repr. 1987).

——*Sein ist das Weib, Denken der Mann: Ansichten und Äußerungen für und wider die gelehrten Frauen* (Berlin: Union Verlag, 1984).

——*Idylle mit Professor: Roman* (Berlin: Verlag Neues Leben, 1986; repr. Cologne: Kiepenheuer and Witsch, 1992).

——*Ausharren im Paradies: Roman* (Cologne: Kiepenheuer and Witsch, 1992; repr. 1997).

——*Die profanen Stunden des Glücks: Roman* (Cologne: Kiepenheuer and Witsch, 1996).

——*Das sanfte Joch der Vortrefflichkeit: Roman* (Cologne: Kiepenheuer and Witsch, 1999).

FRIEDLÄNDER, VERA, *Späte Notizen* (Berlin: Verlag Neues Leben, 1982).

FÜHMANN, FRANZ, *22 Tage oder Die Hälfte des Lebens* (Rostock: Hinstorff, 1973; repr. Frankfurt am Main: Suhrkamp, 1978).

——'Das mythische Element in der Literatur', in *Essays. Gespräche. Aufsätze 1964–1981* (Rostock: Hinstorff, 1993), 82–140.

GRUNER, PETRA (ed.), *Angepaßt oder mündig? Briefe an Christa Wolf im Herbst 1989* (Frankfurt am Main: Luchterhand, 1990).

HASS, GERHART, 'Krieg in Ost oder West? Zur Entscheidung über die Reihenfolge der faschistischen Aggressionen', in *Der Weg in den Krieg: Studien zur Geschichte der Vorkriegsjahre (1935/36 bis 1939)*, ed. Dietrich Eichholtz and Kurt Pätzold (Berlin: Akademie Verlag, 1989; repr. Cologne: Pahl-Rugenstein, 1989), 151–81.

HÖNTSCH-HARENDT, URSULA, *Wir Flüchtlingskinder: Roman* (Halle and Leipzig: Mitteldeutscher Verlag, 1985; repr. 1991).

JACOBEIT, SIGRID, 'Clothing in Nazi Germany', in *Marxist Historiography in Transformation: East German Social History in the 1980s*, ed. Georg Iggers, trans. Bruce Little (New York and Oxford: Berg, 1991), 227–45.

——and THOMS-HEINRICH, LIESELOTTE, *Kreuzweg Ravensbrück: Lebensbilder antifaschistischer Widerstandskämpferinnen* (Leipzig: Verlag für die Frau, 1987; repr. 1989).

KANT, HERMANN, *Der Aufenthalt: Roman* (Berlin: Rütten and Loening, 1977; repr. Aufbau, 1994).

——and WAGNER, FRANK, 'Die große Abrechnung: Probleme der Darstellung des Krieges in der deutschen Gegenwartsliteratur', *NDL* 5 (1957), 12, 124–39.

KIRSCH, RUTH, *Käte Duncker: Aus ihrem Leben* (Berlin: Dietz, 1982).

KÖNIGSDORF, HELGA, *Respektloser Umgang: Erzählung* (Darmstadt: Luchterhand, 1986; repr. 1988).

——*Ungelegener Befund: Erzählung* (Berlin and Weimar: Aufbau, 1989; repr. Frankfurt am Main: Luchterhand, 1991).

——*1989 oder Ein Moment Schönheit: Eine Collage aus Briefen, Gedichten, Texten* (Berlin and Weimar: Aufbau, 1990).

——*Adieu DDR: Protokolle eines Abschieds* (Reinbek: Rowohlt, 1990).

——*Aus dem Dilemma eine Chance machen: Aufsätze und Reden* (Hamburg and Zurich: Luchterhand, 1990; repr. 1991).

——*Gleich neben Afrika: Erzählung* (Berlin: Rowohlt, 1992).

——*Im Schatten des Regenbogens: Roman* (Berlin and Weimar: Aufbau, 1993).

——*Die Entsorgung der Großmutter: Roman* (Berlin: Aufbau, 1997).

KUCZYNSKI, JÜRGEN, *Geschichte des Alltags des deutschen Volkes*, 5 vols. (Berlin: Akademie Verlag, 1980–2).

KÜHNREICH, HEINZ, 'Der deutsch-sowjetische Nichtangriffsvertrag vom 23. August 1939 aus der zeitgenössischen Sicht der KPD', in *Der Weg in den Krieg: Studien zur Geschichte der Vorkriegsjahre (1935/36 bis 1939)*, ed. Dietrich Eichholtz and Kurt Pätzold (Berlin: Akademie Verlag, 1989; repr. Cologne: Pahl-Rugenstein, 1989), 517–51.

KUNERT, GÜNTER, 'Pamphlet für K', *SF* 27 (1975), 5, 1091–4.

MEIER, HELMUT, and SCHMIDT, WALTER (eds.), *Geschichtsbewußtsein und sozialistische Gesellschaft: Beiträge zur Rolle der Geschichtswissenschaft, des Geschichtsunterrichts und der Geschichtspropaganda bei der Entwicklung des sozialistischen Geschichtsbewußtseins* (Berlin: Dietz, 1970).

—— and ——(eds.), *Erbe und Tradition: Die Diskussion der Historiker* (Cologne: Pahl-Rugenstein, 1989).

—— and —— 'Zum marxistisch-leninistischen Traditionsverständnis in der DDR', in *Erbe und Tradition: Die Diskussion der Historiker*, ed. Helmut Meier and Walter Schmidt (Cologne: Pahl-Rugenstein, 1989), 27–57.

MITTENZWEI, INGRID, 'Die zwei Gesichter Preußens', *Forum*, 32 (1978), 19, 8–9; repr. in *Erbe und Tradition: Die Diskussion der Historiker*, ed. Helmut Meier and Walter Schmidt (Cologne: Pahl-Rugenstein, 1989), 72–8.

MORGNER, IRMTRAUD, *Leben und Abenteuer der Trobadora Beatriz nach Zeugnissen ihrer Spielfrau Laura: Roman in dreizehn Büchern und sieben Intermezzos* (Berlin and Weimar: Aufbau, 1974; repr. Hamburg and Zurich: Luchterhand, 1991).

——*Amanda: Ein Hexenroman* (Darmstadt and Neuwied: Luchterhand, 1983; repr. 1984).

MÜLLER, HEINER, 'Brief an die Redaktion', *Theater der Zeit*, 30 (1975), 8, 58–9.

NEEF, ANNELIESE, *Mühsal ein Leben lang: Zur Situation der Arbeiterfrauen um 1900* (Berlin: Dietz, 1988).

PÄTZOLD, KURT, *Faschismus. Rassenwahn. Judenverfolgung: Eine Studie zur politischen Strategie und Taktik des faschistischen deutschen Imperialismus (1933–1935)* (Berlin: Deutscher Verlag der Wissenschaften, 1975).

——'Hitlers fünfzigster Geburtstag am 20. April 1939', in *Der Weg in den Krieg: Studien zur Geschichte der Vorkriegsjahre (1935/36 bis 1939)*, ed. Dietrich Eichholtz and Kurt Pätzold (Berlin: Akademie Verlag, 1989; repr. Cologne: Pahl-Rugenstein, 1989), 308–43.

PETZOLD, JOACHIM, *Die Demagogie des Hitlerfaschismus: Die politische Funktion der Nazüdeologie auf dem Wege zur faschistischen Diktatur* (Berlin: Akademie Verlag, 1982).

RANTZSCH, PETRA, *Helene Stöcker (1869–1943): Zwischen Pazifismus und Revolution* (Berlin: Verlag Der Morgen, 1984).

——and UITZ, ERIKA, 'Historical Research on Women in the German Democratic Republic', in *Writing Women's History: International Perspectives*, ed. Karen Offen, Ruth Roach Pierson, and Jane Rendall (Basingstoke: Macmillan, 1991), 333–53.

ROSENFELD, GÜNTER, 'Die Sowjetunion und das faschistische Deutschland am Vorabend des zweiten Weltkrieges', in *Der Weg in den Krieg: Studien zur Geschichte der Vorkriegsjahre (1935/36 bis 1939)*, ed. Dietrich Eichholtz and Kurt Pätzold (Berlin: Akademie Verlag, 1989; repr. Cologne: Pahl-Rugenstein, 1989), 345–80.

SCHLESINGER, KLAUS, *Michael* (Rostock: Hinstorff, 1971).

SCHMIDT, WALTER, 'Geschichtsbewußtsein und sozialistische Persönlichkeit bei der Gestaltung der entwickelten sozialistischen Gesellschaft', in *Geschichtsbewußtsein und sozialistische Gesellschaft: Beiträge zur Rolle der Geschichtswissenschaft, des Geschichtsunterrichts und der Geschichtspropaganda bei der Entwicklung des sozialistischen Geschichtsbewußtseins*, ed. Helmut Meier and Walter Schmidt (Berlin: Dietz, 1970), 8–41.

SCHÖTZ, SUSANNE, 'Historische Frauenforschung in Ostdeutschland', in *Nach dem Erdbeben: (Re-) Konstruktion ostdeutscher Geschichte und Geschichtswissenschaft*, ed. Konrad H. Jarausch and Matthias Middell (Leipzig: Leipziger Universitätsverlag, 1994), 177–94.

SCHRÖDER, WOLFGANG, *Ernestine: Vom ungewöhnlichen Leben der ersten Frau Wilhelm Liebknechts: Eine dokumentarische Erzählung* (Leipzig: Verlag für die Frau, 1987; repr. 1989).

SCHUBERT, HELGA, *Judasfrauen: Zehn Fallgeschichten weiblicher Denunziation im Dritten Reich* (Berlin: Aufbau, 1990; repr. Munich: Deutscher Taschenbuch Verlag, 1992).

SCHULZ-SEMRAU, ELISABETH, *Suche nach Karalautschi: Report einer Kindheit* (Halle and Leipzig: Mitteldeutscher Verlag, 1984).

SCHÜTZ, HELGA, *Vorgeschichten oder Schöne Gegend Probstein* (Berlin and Weimar: Aufbau, 1970; repr. 1987).

——*Das Erdbeben bei Sangerhausen und andere Geschichten* (Berlin and Weimar: Aufbau, 1972).

——*Festbeleuchtung: Erzählung* (Berlin and Weimar: Aufbau, 1973; repr. Darmstadt: Luchterhand, 1982).

——*Jette in Dresden* (Berlin and Weimar: Aufbau, 1977; repr. Berlin: Aufbau, 1994).

——*Julia oder Erziehung zum Chorgesang* (Berlin and Weimar: Aufbau, 1980; repr. Darmstadt: Luchterhand, 1988).

——*Vom Glanz der Elbe: Roman* (Berlin: Aufbau, 1995).

STRUZYK, BRIGITTE, *Caroline unterm Freiheitsbaum: Ansichtssachen* (Berlin and Weimar: Aufbau, 1988).

——*In vollen Zügen: Rück-Sichten* (Berlin and Weimar: Aufbau, 1994).

UITZ, ERIKA, *Die Frau in der mittelalterlichen Stadt* (Leipzig: Edition Leipzig, 1988).

WEISSBECKER, MANFRED, and NOACK, GERT, ' "Die Partei als Rückgrat der inneren Front": Mobilmachungspläne der NSDAP für den Krieg (1937 bis 1939)', in *Der Weg in den Krieg: Studien zur Geschichte der Vorkriegsjahre (1935/36 bis 1939)*, ed. Dietrich Eichholtz and Kurt Pätzold (Berlin: Akademie Verlag, 1989; repr. Cologne: Pahl-Rugenstein, 1989), 67–90.

WOLF, CHRISTA, 'Vom Standpunkt des Schriftstellers und von der Form der Kunst', *NDL* 5 (1957), 12, 119–24.

——*Nachdenken über Christa T.* (Halle: Mitteldeutscher Verlag, 1968; repr. Frankfurt am Main: Luchterhand, 1991).

——*Kindheitsmuster: Roman* (Berlin and Weimar: Aufbau, 1976; repr. Frankfurt am Main: Luchterhand, 1988).

——*Kein Ort. Nirgends* (Berlin and Weimar: Aufbau, 1979; repr. Frankfurt am Main: Luchterhand, 1981).

——*Kassandra: Erzählung* (Darmstadt: Luchterhand, 1983; repr. Frankfurt am Main: Luchterhand, 1989).

——*Voraussetzungen einer Erzählung: Kassandra: Frankfurter Poetik-Vorlesungen* (Darmstadt: Luchterhand, 1983; repr. Frankfurt am Main: Luchterhand, 1988).

——*Die Dimension des Autors: Essays und Aufsätze, Reden und Gespräche 1959–1985*, 2 vols. (Frankfurt am Main: Luchterhand, 1987; repr. 1990).

——'Nun ja! Das nächste Leben geht aber heute an: Ein Brief über die Bettine', in *Die Dimension des Autors: Essays und Aufsätze, Reden und Gespräche 1959–1985* (Frankfurt am Main: Luchterhand, 1987; repr. 1990), ii. 572–610.

——'Der Schatten eines Traumes: Karoline von Günderrode—ein Entwurf', in *Die Dimension des Autors: Essays und Aufsätze, Reden und Gespräche 1959–1985* (Frankfurt am Main: Luchterhand, 1987; repr. 1990), ii. 511–71.

——*Im Dialog: Aktuelle Texte* (Frankfurt am Main: Luchterhand, 1990).

——*Was bleibt: Erzählung* (Berlin: Aufbau, 1990; repr. Hamburg and Zurich: Luchterhand, 1992).

——*Medea: Stimmen* (Gütersloh: Luchterhand, 1996).

2. SECONDARY TEXTS ABOUT THE GDR AND GDR AUTHORS

ALBERGHINI, DIANA, 'Re-defining the Role of the Intellectual and the Function of Literature: The Example of Helga Königsdorf', in *East Germany:*

Continuity and Change, ed. Paul Cooke and Jonathan Grix, GM 46 (Amsterdam and Atlanta: Rodopi, 2000), 32–41.

ALLDRED, BETH, 'Two Contrasting Perspectives on German Unification: Helga Schubert and Brigitte Burmeister', *GLL* 50 (1997), 2, 165–81.

ANZ, THOMAS (ed.), *'Es geht nicht um Christa Wolf': Der Literaturstreit im vereinigten Deutschland*, rev. edn. (Frankfurt am Main: Fischer, 1995).

ARNOLD, HEINZ LUDWIG, and MEYER-GOSAU, FRAUKE (eds.), *Literatur in der DDR: Rückblicke* (Munich: text + kritik, 1991).

ARNOLD, HERBERT A., 'On Myth and Marxism: The Case of Heiner Müller and Christa Wolf', *CG* 21 (1988), 1, 58–69.

AUER, ANNEMARIE, 'Gegenerinnerung', *SF* 29 (1977), 4, 847–78.

——— *et al.*, '*Respektloser Umgang* von Helga Königsdorf', *WB* 33 (1987), 8, 1338–57.

BAIER, LOTHAR, 'Wo habt ihr bloß alle gelebt: Christa Wolfs "Kindheitsmuster", 1994 wiedergelesen', in *Christa Wolf*, ed. Heinz Ludwig Arnold, Text + Kritik, 46, 4th rev. edn. (Munich: text + kritik, 1994), 59–67.

BATHRICK, DAVID, 'Kultur und Öffentlichkeit in der DDR', in *Literatur der DDR in den siebziger Jahren*, ed. P. U. Hohendahl and P. Herminghouse (Frankfurt am Main: Suhrkamp, 1983), 53–81.

——— 'The End of the Wall Before the End of the Wall', *GSR* 14 (1991), 2, 297–311.

——— *The Powers of Speech: The Politics of Culture in the GDR* (Lincoln, Neb., and London: University of Nebraska Press, 1995).

BEHREND, HANNA, 'Keeping a Foot in the Door: East German Women's Academic, Political, Cultural, and Social Projects', in *Women and the Wende: Social Effects and Cultural Reflections of the German Unification Process*, ed. Elizabeth Boa and Janet Wharton, GM 31 (Amsterdam and Atlanta: Rodopi, 1994), 64–79.

BERGER, CHRISTEL, *Gewissensfrage Antifaschismus: Traditionen der DDR-Literatur. Analysen—Interpretationen—Interviews* (Berlin: Dietz, 1990).

BERNHARDT, RÜDIGER, *Odysseus' Tod—Prometheus' Leben: Antike Mythen in der Literatur der DDR* (Halle and Leipzig: Mitteldeutscher Verlag, 1983).

BIALIK, WLODZIMIERZ, 'Christa Wolfs Abrechnung mit der Abrechnung', in *Christa Wolf: Ein Arbeitsbuch. Studien, Dokumente, Bibliographie*, ed. Angela Drescher (Berlin and Weimar: Aufbau, 1989; repr. Frankfurt am Main: Luchterhand, 1990), 78–90.

BIRD, STEPHANIE, *Recasting Historical Women: Female Identity in German Biographical Fiction* (Oxford and New York: Berg, 1998).

BOA, ELIZABETH, and WHARTON, JANET (eds.), *Women and the Wende: Social Effects and Cultural Reflections of the German Unification Process*, GM 31 (Amsterdam and Atlanta: Rodopi, 1994).

BÖCK, DOROTHEA, 'Ein janusköpfiger Epilog', *NDL* 30 (1982), 3, 146–52.

——— 'Szenen einer Ehe', *NDL* 35 (1987), 2, 122–7.

—— 'Ein Weib von schärfstem Geist', *NDL* 37 (1989), 8, 150–4.

BOCK, SIGRID, 'Christa Wolf: Kindheitsmuster', *WB* 23 (1977), 9, 102–30.

—— 'Christa Wolf: Kein Ort. Nirgends', *WB* 26 (1980), 5, 145–57.

BODEN, PETRA, 'Ornamente und Tabus: Antifaschismus als Herrschafts-diskurs', *WB* 41 (1995), 1, 104–19.

BRANDES, UTE, *Zitat und Montage in der neueren DDR-Prosa* (Frankfurt am Main: Lang, 1984).

—— (ed.), *Zwischen gestern und morgen: Schriftstellerinnen der DDR aus amerikanischer Sicht* (Berlin: Lang, 1992).

BRIDGE, HELEN, 'Myth and History in Irmtraud Morgner's *Amanda*', *GLL* 51 (1998), 483–95.

—— 'Biographical Fiction by GDR Women Writers: Reassessing the Cultural Heritage', in *Travellers in Time and Space: The German Historical Novel*, ed. Osman Durrani and Julian Preece, ABNG 51 (Amsterdam and New York: Rodopi, 2001), 155–65.

BROCKMANN, STEPHEN, *Literature and German Reunification* (Cambridge: Cambridge University Press, 1999).

CARDINAL, AGNÈS, '"Be Realistic: Demand the Impossible": On Irmtraud Morgner's Salman Trilogy', in *Socialism and the Literary Imagination: Essays on East German Writers*, ed. Martin Kane (New York and Oxford: Berg, 1991), 147–61.

CASTEIN, HANNE, 'Wundersame Reisen im gelobten Land: Zur Romantik-rezeption im Werk Irmtraud Morgners', in *Neue Ansichten: The Reception of Romanticism in the Literature of the GDR*, ed. Howard Gaskill, Karin McPherson, and Andrew Barker, GDR Monitor, 6 (Amsterdam and Atlanta: Rodopi, 1990), 114–25.

CLAUSEN, JEANETTE, 'Resisting Objectification: Helga Königsdorf's Lise Meitner', in *Studies in GDR Culture and Society 10*, ed. Margy Gerber (Lanham, Md.: University Press of America, 1991), 165–80.

CONACHER, JEAN E., 'Pressing for Change: The Case of Helga Königsdorf', in *Women and the* Wende: *Social Effects and Cultural Reflections of the German Unification Process*, ed. Elizabeth Boa and Janet Wharton, GM 31 (Amsterdam and Atlanta: Rodopi, 1994), 164–76.

CRICK, JOYCE, 'Dichtung und Wahrheit: Aspects of Christa Wolf's *Kindheitsmuster*', *LGS* 2 (1983), 168–83.

CWOJDRAK, GÜNTHER, 'Kindheitsmuster—ein Probestück', *Die Weltbühne*, 32 (1977), 18, 550–2; repr. in *Kritik 77: Rezensionen zur DDR-Literatur*, ed. Eberhard Günther, Werner Liersch, and Klaus Walther (Halle and Leipzig: Mitteldeutscher Verlag, 1978), 170–3.

DAHLKE, BIRGIT, *Papierboot: Autorinnen aus der DDR—inoffiziell publiziert* (Würzburg: Königshausen and Neumann, 1997).

DAHNKE, HANS-DIETRICH, *Erbe und Tradition in der Literatur* (Leipzig: Bibliographisches Institut Leipzig, 1977; repr. 1981).

DEIRITZ, KARL, and KRAUSS, HANNES (eds.), *Der deutsch-deutsche Literaturstreit oder 'Freunde, es spricht sich schlecht mit gebundener Zunge': Analysen und Materialien* (Hamburg and Zurich: Luchterhand, 1991).

DIDON, SYBILLE, *Kassandrarufe: Studien zu Vorkrieg und Krieg in Christa Wolfs Erzählungen* Kindheitsmuster *und* Kassandra (Stockholm: Almqvist and Wiksell, 1992).

DINTER, INGRID, *Unvollendete Trauerarbeit in der DDR-Literatur: Ein Studium der Vergangenheitsbewältigung* (New York: Lang, 1994).

DRESCHER, ANGELA (ed.), *Christa Wolf: Ein Arbeitsbuch. Studien, Dokumente, Bibliographie* (Berlin and Weimar: Aufbau, 1989; repr. Frankfurt am Main: Luchterhand, 1990).

DREWITZ, INGEBORG, 'Stil und Existenz gehören zusammen: Christa Wolfs "Kindheitsmuster" und "Kein Ort. Nirgends"', in *Christa Wolf*, ed. Heinz Ludwig Arnold, Text + Kritik, 46, 3rd rev. edn. (Munich: text + kritik, 1985), 60–6.

EIGLER, FRIEDERIKE, and PFEIFFER, PETER C. (eds.), *Cultural Transformations in the New Germany: American and German Perspectives* (Columbia, SC: Camden House, 1993).

EMDE, SILKE VON DER, 'Irmtraud Morgner's Postmodern Feminism: A Question of Politics', in *WIGY 10*, ed. Jeanette Clausen and Sara Friedrichsmeyer (Lincoln, Neb., and London: University of Nebraska Press, 1995), 117–42.

EMMERICH, WOLFGANG, 'Der Kampf um die Erinnerung: Laudatio auf Christa Wolf anläßlich der Verleihung des Bremer Literaturpreises 1977', in *Christa Wolf Materialienbuch*, ed. Klaus Sauer (Darmstadt and Neuwied: Luchterhand, 1979), 111–17.

——'Zu-Ende-denken: Griechische Mythologie und neuere DDR-Literatur', in *Kontroversen, alte und neue*, ed. Albrecht Schöne (Tübingen: Niemeyer, 1986), 216–24.

——*Die andere deutsche Literatur: Aufsätze zur Literatur aus der DDR* (Opladen: Westdeutscher Verlag, 1994).

——*Kleine Literaturgeschichte der DDR*, rev. edn. (Leipzig: Kiepenheuer, 1996).

ENGELHARDT, MICHAEL VON, and ROHRWASSER, MICHAEL, 'Kassandra—Odysseus—Prometheus: Modelle der Mythosrezeption in der DDR-Literatur', *L' 80*, 34 (1985), 46–76.

ENGLER, JÜRGEN, 'Herrschaft der Analogie', *NDL* 27 (1979), 7, 128–33.

——, 'Die wahre Lüge der Kunst', *NDL* 31 (1983), 7, 135–44.

FINGERHUT, KARLHEINZ, 'So könnte es gewesen sein—Angebote an die Vorstellungskraft: Gespräch mit Sigrid Damm über ihre dokumentarischen Roman-Biographien', *DD* 20 (1989), 313–17.

FISCHER, ALEXANDER, and HEYDEMANN, GÜNTHER (eds.), *Geschichtswissenschaft in der DDR*, 2 vols. (Berlin (FRG): Duncker and Humblot, 1988).

——and ——'Weg und Wandel der Geschichtswissenschaft und des

Geschichtsverständnisses in der SBZ/DDR seit 1945', in *Geschichtswissenschaft in der DDR*, ed. Alexander Fischer and Günther Heydemann (Berlin (FRG): Duncker and Humblot, 1988), i: *Historische Entwicklung, Theoriediskussion und Geschichtsdidaktik*, 3–30.

Fox, Thomas C., 'Germanistik and GDR Studies: (Re)Reading a Censored Literature', *MDU* 85 (1993), 3, 284–94.

Frieden, Sandra, '"Falls es strafbar ist, die Grenzen zu verwischen"': Autobiographie, Biographie und Christa Wolf', in *Christa Wolf: Ein Arbeitsbuch. Studien, Dokumente, Bibliographie*, ed. Angela Drescher (Berlin and Weimar: Aufbau, 1989; repr. Frankfurt am Main: Luchterhand, 1990), 121–39.

Fulbrook, Mary, *Anatomy of a Dictatorship: Inside the GDR 1949–1989* (Oxford: Oxford University Press, 1995).

—— 'Myth-Making and National Identity: The Case of the GDR', in *Myths and Nationhood*, ed. Geoffrey Hosking and George Schöpflin (London: Hurst, 1997), 72–87.

—— 'Reckoning with the Past: Heroes, Victims, and Villains in the History of the German Democratic Republic', in *Rewriting the German Past: History and Identity in the New Germany*, ed. Reinhard Alter and Peter Monteath (New Jersey: Humanities Press, 1997), 175–96.

—— *German National Identity after the Holocaust* (London: Polity, 1999).

Gaskill, Howard, McPherson, Karin, and Barker, Andrew (eds.), *Neue Ansichten: The Reception of Romanticism in the Literature of the GDR*, GDR Monitor, 6 (Amsterdam and Atlanta: Rodopi, 1990).

Gättens, Marie-Luise, *Women Writers and Fascism: Reconstructing History* (Gainesville, Fla.: University Press of Florida, 1995).

Geerdts, Hans Jürgen, 'Zur Thematik des Antifaschismus in der Geschichte der DDR-Prosa', *ZG* 1 (1980), 71–81.

Gerhardt, Marlis (ed.), *Irmtraud Morgner: Texte, Daten, Bilder* (Frankfurt am Main: Luchterhand, 1990).

Girnus, Wilhelm (ed.), 'Briefe an Annemarie Auer', *SF* 29 (1977), 6, 1311–22.

—— 'Wer baute das siebentorige Theben? Kritische Bemerkungen zu Christa Wolfs Beitrag in Sinn und Form 1/83 S. 38ff', *SF* 35 (1983), 2, 439–47.

Glaeßner, Gert-Joachim (ed.), *Germany after Unification: Coming to Terms with the Recent Past*, GM 37 (Amsterdam and Atlanta: Rodopi, 1996).

Glau, Katharina, *Christa Wolfs 'Kassandra' und Aischylos' 'Orestie': Zur Rezeption der griechischen Tragödie in der deutschen Literatur der Gegenwart* (Heidelberg: Winter, 1996).

Goodbody, Axel, and Tate, Dennis (eds.), *Geist und Macht: Writers and the State in the GDR*, GM 29 (Amsterdam and Atlanta: Rodopi, 1992).

Grambow, Jürgen, 'Eine Vertraute seiner Kindheit, unbegreifliches Wesen, die Schwester', in *Kritik 88: Rezensionen zur DDR-Literatur*, ed. Eberhard

Günther, Werner Liersch, and Klaus Walther (Halle and Leipzig: Mitteldeutscher Verlag, 1989), 62–5.

GREINER, BERNHARD, 'DDR-Literatur als Problem der Literaturwissenschaft', *Jahrbuch zur Literatur in der DDR*, 3 (1983), 233–54.

GRUNENBERG, ANTONIA, *Antifaschismus: Ein deutscher Mythos* (Reinbek: Rowohlt, 1993).

HAINES, BRIGID, '"Botschaft aus einem seltsamen Land"': Helga Königsdorf and her Critics', in *Geist und Macht: Writers and the State in the GDR*, ed. Axel Goodbody and Dennis Tate, GM 29 (Amsterdam and Atlanta: Rodopi, 1992), 140–50.

HALLBERG, ROBERT VON (ed.), *Literary Intellectuals and the Dissolution of the State: Professionalism and Conformity in the GDR*, trans. Kenneth J. Northcott (Chicago and London: University of Chicago Press, 1996).

HAMMER, KLAUS, 'Mobilisierung der Humanität', *NDL* 35 (1987), 8, 138–42.

HANNEMANN, JOACHIM, 'Ein Stück von der Wahrheit', *NDL* 26 (1978), 11, 150–2.

HARTMANN, KARL-HEINZ, 'Das Dritte Reich in der DDR-Literatur: Stationen erzählter Vergangenheit', in *Gegenwartsliteratur und Drittes Reich: Deutsche Autoren in der Auseinandersetzung mit der Vergangenheit*, ed. Hans Wagener (Stuttgart: Reclam, 1977), 307–28.

HAUSER, KORNELIA, *Patriarchat als Sozialismus: Soziologische Studien zu Literatur aus der DDR* (Hamburg: Argument-Verlag, 1994).

HELL, JULIA, *Post-Fascist Fantasies: Psychoanalysis, History, and the Literature of East Germany* (Durham, NC, and London: Duke University Press, 1997).

——'Critical Orthodoxies, Old and New, or The Fantasy of a Pure Voice: Christa Wolf', in *Contentious Memories: Looking Back at the GDR*, ed. Jost Hermand and Marc Silberman (New York: Lang, 1998), 65–101.

HELMECKE, MONIKA, 'Kindheitsmuster', *SF* 29 (1977), 3, 678–81.

HERMAND, JOST, and SILBERMAN, MARC (eds.), *Contentious Memories: Looking Back at the GDR* (New York: Lang, 1998).

HERMINGHOUSE, PATRICIA, 'Wunschbild, Vorbild oder Porträt? Zur Darstellung der Frau im Roman der DDR', in *Literatur und Literaturtheorie in der DDR*, ed. Peter Uwe Hohendahl and Patricia Herminghouse (Frankfurt am Main: Suhrkamp, 1976), 281–334.

——'Die Frau und das Phantastische in der neueren DDR-Literatur: Der Fall Irmtraud Morgner', in *Die Frau als Heldin und Autorin: Neue kritische Ansätze zur Deutschen Literatur*, ed. Wolfgang Paulsen (Berne and Munich: Francke, 1979), 248–66.

——'Die Wiederentdeckung der Romantik: Zur Funktion der Dichterfiguren in der neueren DDR-Literatur', in *DDR-Roman und Literaturgesellschaft*, ed. Jos Hoogeveen and Gerd Labroisse, ABNG 11/12 (Amsterdam: Rodopi, 1981), 217–48.

——'Vergangenheit als Problem der Gegenwart: Zur Darstellung des

Faschismus in der neueren DDR-Literatur', in *Literatur der DDR in den siebziger Jahren*, ed. P. U. Hohendahl and P. Herminghouse (Frankfurt am Main: Suhrkamp, 1983), 259–94.

——'"Der Autor nämlich ist ein wichtiger Mensch": Zur Prosa', in *Frauen Literatur Geschichte: Schreibende Frauen vom Mittelalter bis zur Gegenwart*, ed. Hiltrud Gnüg and Renate Möhrmann (Stuttgart: Metzler, 1985; repr. Frankfurt am Main: Suhrkamp, 1989), 338–53.

——'Confronting the "Blank Spots of History": GDR Culture and the Legacy of "Stalinism"', *GSR* 14 (1991), 2, 345–65.

——'Phantasie oder Fanatismus? Zur feministischen Wissenschaftskritik in der Literatur der DDR', in *Zwischen gestern und morgen: Schriftstellerinnen der DDR aus amerikanischer Sicht*, ed. Ute Brandes (Berlin: Lang, 1992), 69–94.

——'New Contexts for GDR Literature: An American Perspective', in *Cultural Transformations in the New Germany: American and German Perspectives*, ed. Friederike Eigler and Peter C. Pfeiffer (Columbia, SC: Camden House, 1993), 93–101.

HERRMANN, ANNE, *The Dialogic and Difference: 'An/other Woman' in Virginia Woolf and Christa Wolf* (New York: Columbia University Press, 1989).

HEUKENKAMP, URSULA, '*Eine* Geschichte oder *viele* Geschichten der deutschen Literatur seit 1945? Gründe und Gegengründe', *ZG* NS 5 (1995), 1, 22–37.

HIELSCHER, MARTIN, 'The Return to Narrative and History: Some Thoughts on Contemporary German-Language Literature', in *Literature, Markets and Media in Germany and Austria Today*, ed. Arthur Williams, Stuart Parkes, and Julian Preece (Oxford: Lang, 2000), 295–309.

HILZINGER, SONJA, '*Als ganzer Mensch zu leben . . .': Emanzipatorische Tendenzen in der neueren Frauen-Literatur der DDR* (Frankfurt am Main: Lang, 1985).

——*Christa Wolf* (Stuttgart: Metzler, 1986).

——'"Avantgarde ohne Hinterland": Zur Wiederentdeckung des Romantischen in Prosa und Essayistik der DDR', in *Literatur in der DDR: Rückblicke*, ed. Heinz Ludwig Arnold and Frauke Meyer-Gosau (Munich: text + kritik, 1991), 93–100.

HIRDINA, KARIN, 'Begegnung zwischen den Zeiten', *SF* 31 (1979), 2, 1099–1104.

HOCHGESCHURZ, MARIANNE (ed.), *Christa Wolfs Medea: Voraussetzungen zu einem Text. Mythos und Bild* (Berlin: Janus Press, 1998).

HOHENDAHL, PETER UWE, 'Theorie und Praxis des Erbens: Untersuchungen zum Problem der literarischen Tradition in der DDR', in *Literatur der DDR in den siebziger Jahren*, ed. P. U. Hohendahl and P. Herminghouse (Frankfurt am Main: Suhrkamp, 1983), 13–52.

——and HERMINGHOUSE, PATRICIA (eds.), *Literatur und Literaturtheorie in der DDR* (Frankfurt am Main: Suhrkamp, 1976).

——and ——(eds.), *Literatur der DDR in den siebziger Jahren* (Frankfurt am Main: Suhrkamp, 1983).

HOOGEVEEN, JOS, and LABROISSE, GERD (eds.), *DDR-Roman und Literaturgesellschaft*, ABNG 11/12 (Amsterdam: Rodopi, 1981).

HÖRNIGK, THERESE, 'Das Thema Krieg und Faschismus in der Geschichte der DDR-Literatur', *WB* 24 (1978), 5, 73–105.

——'Contours of a New Academic Landscape: Research Institutes and the University System in the New German States', in *Cultural Transformations in the New Germany: American and German Perspectives*, ed. Friederike Eigler and Peter C. Pfeiffer (Columbia, SC: Camden House, 1993), 172–9.

HUMBLE, MALCOLM, 'Pandora's Box: The Rehabilitation of the Siren and the Witch in *Amanda*', *FMLS* 28 (1992), 4, 335–48.

IGGERS, GEORG G. (ed.), *Marxist Historiography in Transformation: East German Social History in the 1980s*, trans. Bruce Little (New York and Oxford: Berg, 1991).

JÄHNERT, GABRIELE, 'Das Zentrum für interdisziplinäre Frauenforschung (ZiF) an der Humboldt-Universität zu Berlin', *ZG* NS 9 (1999), 1, 118–22.

JANKOWSKY, KAREN, 'Canons Crumble Just Like Walls: Discovering the Works of GDR Women Writers', in *Cultural Transformations in the New Germany: American and German Perspectives*, ed. Friederike Eigler and Peter C. Pfeiffer (Columbia, SC: Camden House, 1993), 102–16.

JARAUSCH, KONRAD H., 'The Failure of East German Antifascism: Some Ironies of History as Politics', *GSR* 14 (1991), 1, 85–102.

——(ed.), *Zwischen Parteilichkeit und Professionalität: Bilanz der Geschichtswissenschaft der DDR* (Berlin: Akademie Verlag, 1991).

——'Kritische Perspektiven zur deutschen Vergangenheit: Folgen der Vereinigung für die Geschichtswissenschaft', in *Nach dem Erdbeben: (Re-) Konstruktion ostdeutscher Geschichte und Geschichtswissenschaft*, ed. Konrad H. Jarausch and Matthias Middell (Leipzig: Leipziger Universitätsverlag, 1994), 21–37.

——and MIDDELL, MATTHIAS (eds.), *Nach dem Erdbeben: (Re-) Konstruktion ostdeutscher Geschichte und Geschichtswissenschaft* (Leipzig: Leipziger Universitätsverlag, 1994).

JENKINSON, DAVID, 'Loyalty and its Limits: Christa Wolf's *Kassandra* as a "Schlüsselerzählung"', in *Literature on the Threshold: The German Novel in the 1980s*, ed. Arthur Williams, Stuart Parkes, and Roland Smith (New York: Berg, 1990), 235–52.

JOHNSON, SHEILA K., 'A New Irmtraud Morgner: Humor, Fantasy, Structures, and Ideas in *Amanda: Ein Hexenroman*', in *Studies in GDR Culture and Society 4*, ed. Margy Gerber (Washington: University Press of America, 1984), 45–64.

KAELBLE, HARTMUT, KOCKA, JÜRGEN, and ZWAHR, HARTMUT (eds.), *Sozialgeschichte der DDR* (Stuttgart: Klett-Cotta, 1994).

KAHLAU, CORDULA (ed.), *Aufbruch! Frauenbewegung in der DDR: Dokumentation* (Munich: Frauenoffensive, 1990).

KÄHLER, HERMANN, 'Widersprüchliches zu "Amanda"', *SF* 36 (1984), 1, 177–85.

KÄNDLER, KLAUS, 'Der Hexenroman "Amanda" von Irmtraud Morgner', in *DDR-Literatur '83 im Gespräch*, ed. Siegfried Rönisch (Berlin and Weimar: Aufbau, 1984), 155–62.

KANE, MARTIN (ed.), *Socialism and the Literary Imagination: Essays on East German Writers* (New York and Oxford: Berg, 1991).

KANT, HERMANN, 'Kindheitsmuster', *Sonntag*, 31 (1977), 7, 5–6; repr. in *Kritik 77: Rezensionen zur DDR-Literatur*, ed. Eberhard Günther, Werner Liersch, and Klaus Walther (Halle and Leipzig: Mitteldeutscher Verlag, 1978), 174–82.

KAUFMANN, EVA, 'Irmtraud Morgner, Christa Wolf und andere: Feminismus in der DDR-Literatur', in *Literatur in der DDR: Rückblicke*, ed. Heinz Ludwig Arnold and Frauke Meyer-Gosau (Munich: text + kritik, 1991), 109–16.

——'Adieu Kassandra? Schriftstellerinnen aus der DDR vor, in und nach der Wende: Brigitte Burmeister, Helga Königsdorf, Helga Schütz, Brigitte Struzyk, Rosemarie Zeplin', in *Women and the Wende: Social Effects and Cultural Reflections of the German Unification Process*, ed. Elizabeth Boa and Janet Wharton, GM 31 (Amsterdam and Atlanta: Rodopi, 1994), 216–25.

KLINGMANN, ULRICH, 'Entmythologisierter Mythos: Die Problematik des Wissens in Christa Wolfs *Kassandra*', *ZG* NS 1 (1991), 2, 270–9.

KOCKA, JÜRGEN (ed.), *Die DDR als Geschichte* (Berlin: Akademie Verlag, 1994).

KÖHLER, ANDREA, 'Medea, Schwester: Christa Wolfs Voraussetzungen zu einem Roman', *Neue Zürcher Zeitung*, 2 Mar. 1996, 35.

KOLLER, DORIS, *Biographisches Schreiben und Selbstreflexion: Frauen der Romantik in Lebensbeschreibungen von Schriftstellerinnen der DDR* (Regensburg: Regensburger Skripten zur Literaturwissenschaft, 1997).

KOSTA, BARBARA, *Recasting Autobiography: Women's Counterfictions in Contemporary German Literature and Film* (Ithaca, NY, and London: Cornell University Press, 1994).

KRAUSS, HANNES, 'Die Kunst zu erben—zur romantischen Rezeption (nicht nur) romantischer Literatur: Über Sigrid Damm, Christa Moog und Brigitte Struzyk', in *Neue Ansichten: The Reception of Romanticism in the Literature of the GDR*, ed. Howard Gaskill, Karin McPherson, and Andrew Barker, GDR Monitor, 6 (Amsterdam and Atlanta: Rodopi, 1990), 41–52.

KRENZLIN, LEONORE, 'Helga Schütz' Erzählweise', *WB* 22 (1976), 2, 90–8.

——'Interview mit Helga Schütz', *WB* 22 (1976), 2, 77–89.

KRIEGER, GERD, 'Ein Buch im Streit der Meinungen: Untersuchungen literaturkritischer Reaktionen zu Christa Wolfs "Kindheitsmuster"', *WB* 31 (1985), 1, 56–75.

KROGMANN, WERNER, *Christa Wolf: Konturen* (Frankfurt am Main: Lang, 1989).

KUHN, ANNA K., *Christa Wolf's Utopian Vision: From Marxism to Feminism* (Cambridge: Cambridge University Press, 1988).

LAUCKNER, NANCY A., 'The Treatment of Holocaust Themes in GDR Fiction from the Late 1960s to the Mid-1970s: A Survey', in *Studies in GDR Culture and*

Society 6, ed. Margy Gerber (Washington: University Press of America, 1981), 141–54.

——'The Treatment of the Past and Future in Helga Königsdorf's *Respektloser Umgang*: "Sich der Erinnerung weihen oder für die Zukunft antreten? Mit der Vergangenheit im Bunde."', in *Studies in GDR Culture and Society 10*, ed. Margy Gerber (Lanham, Md.: University Press of America, 1991), 151–63.

LENNOX, SARA, 'Christa Wolf and the Women Romantics', in *Studies in GDR Culture and Society 2*, ed. Margy Gerber (Washington: University Press of America, 1982), 31–43.

——'"Nun ja! Das nächste Leben geht aber heute an": Prosa von Frauen und Frauenbefreiung in der DDR', in *Literatur der DDR in den siebziger Jahren*, ed. P. U. Hohendahl and P. Herminghouse (Frankfurt am Main: Suhrkamp, 1983), 224–58.

LEWIS, ALISON, *Subverting Patriarchy: Feminism and Fantasy in the Works of Irmtraud Morgner* (Oxford and Washington: Berg, 1995).

LINDNER, GABRIELE, 'Natürlich geht das nächste Leben heute an: Wortmeldung zu Christa Wolfs Brief über die Bettine', *WB* 28 (1982), 9, 166–71.

LINKLATER, BETH V., *'Und immer zügelloser wird die Lust': Constructions of Sexuality in East German Literatures. With Special Reference to Irmtraud Morgner and Gabriele Stötzer-Kachold* (Berne: Lang, 1998).

LOVE, MYRA N., *Christa Wolf: Literature and the Conscience of History* (New York: Lang, 1991).

LÜBBE, PETER, 'Zur Funktion der Geschichtswissenschaft im staatlich etablierten Sozialismus', *DS* 25 (1987), 292–300.

MCPHERSON, KARIN, 'Female Subjectivity as an Impulse for Renewal in Literature', in *Responses to Christa Wolf: Critical Essays*, ed. Marilyn Sibley Fries (Detroit: Wayne State University Press, 1989), 149–61.

MARTIN, BIDDY, 'Irmtraud Morgner's *Leben und Abenteuer der Trobadora Beatriz*', in *Beyond the Eternal Feminine: Critical Essays on Women and German Literature*, ed. Susan L. Cocalis and Kay Goodmann (Stuttgart: Heinz, 1982), 421–39.

MATHEJA-THEAKER, MECHTHILD M., *Alternative Emanzipationsvorstellungen in der DDR-Frauenliteratur (1971–1989): Ein Diskussionsbeitrag zur Situation der Frau* (Stuttgart: Heinz, 1996).

MEHNERT, ELKE, 'Ursula Höntsch-Harendt: Wir Flüchtlingskinder', *WB* 32 (1986), 12, 2071–9.

MEISE, HELGA, 'Frauen in der Wissenschaft: Renate Feyls "Der lautlose Aufbruch"', *Lesezeichen*, 6 (1983), 13.

MELCHERT, RULO, 'So könnte es gewesen sein', *NDL* 37 (1989), 4, 131–5.

MEYER, FRANZISKA, *Avantgarde im Hinterland: Caroline Schlegel-Schelling in der DDR-Literatur* (New York: Lang, 1999).

MILLER, SUSANNE, and RISTAU, MALTE (eds.), *Erben deutscher Geschichte: DDR–BRD: Protokolle einer historischen Begegnung* (Reinbek: Rowohlt, 1988).

MITSCHERLICH-NIELSEN, MARGARETE, 'Gratwanderung zwischen Anspruch und Verstrickung', in *Christa Wolf: Ein Arbeitsbuch. Studien, Dokumente, Bibliographie*, ed. Angela Drescher (Berlin and Weimar: Aufbau, 1989; repr. Frankfurt am Main: Luchterhand, 1990), 114–20.

MITTMAN, ELIZABETH, 'Locating a Public Sphere: Some Reflections on Writers and *Öffentlichkeit* in the GDR', in *WIGY 10*, ed. Jeanette Clausen and Sara Friedrichsmeyer (Lincoln, Neb., and London: University of Nebraska Press, 1995), 19–37.

MÜLLER-RÜCKERT, GABRIELE, *Frauenleben und Geschlechterverhältnis in der ehemaligen DDR: Weibliche Lebenswelten im Spiegel literarischer 'Frauengeschichten' und sozialwissenschaftlicher Auswertung* (Bielefeld: Kleine, 1993).

NAGELSCHMIDT, ILSE, 'Sozialistische Frauenliteratur: Überlegungen zu einem Phänomen der DDR-Literatur in den siebziger und achtziger Jahren', *WB* 35 (1989), 3, 450–71.

NEUHÄUSSER-WESPY, ULRICH, 'Erbe und Tradition in der DDR: Zum gewandelten Geschichtsbild der SED', in *Geschichtswissenschaft in der DDR*, ed. Alexander Fischer and Günther Heydemann (Berlin (FRG): Duncker and Humblot, 1988), i: *Historische Entwicklung, Theoriediskussion und Geschichtsdidaktik*, 129–53.

NORDMANN, INGEBORG, 'Die halbierte Geschichtsfähigkeit der Frau: Zu Irmtraud Morgners Roman *Leben und Abenteuer der Trobadora Beatriz nach Zeugnissen ihrer Spielfrau Laura*', in *DDR-Roman und Literaturgesellschaft*, ed. Jos Hoogeveen and Gerd Labroisse, ABNG 11/12 (Amsterdam: Rodopi, 1981), 419–62.

OEHME, MATTHIAS, 'Ansichten von Caroline', *Temperamente* (1989), 2, 149–52.

OPPEN, KAROLINE VON, *The Role of the Writer and the Press in the Unification of Germany, 1989–1990* (New York: Lang, 2000).

PARRY, CHRISTOPH, 'Zwischen Dekonstruktion, Rekonstruktion und Fiktion', *Ginkgobaum*, 11 (1992), 236–9.

PAUL, GEORGINA, '"Ich meine nichts, was könnte gestrichen werden": Christa Wolf's "Brief über die Bettine"', in *Christa Wolf in Perspective*, ed. Ian Wallace, GM 30 (Amsterdam and Atlanta: Rodopi, 1994), 25–40.

—— 'Schwierigkeiten mit der Dialektik: Zu Christa Wolfs *Medea: Stimmen*', *GLL* 50 (1997), 2, 227–40.

PLAVIUS, HEINZ, 'Gewissensforschung', *NDL* 25 (1977), 1, 139–51.

PLENDERLEITH, H. JANE, '"Der letzte DDR-Roman"? On the Interplay of the Personal and the Political in Sigrid Damm's *Ich bin nicht Ottilie*', in *The New Germany: Literature and Society after Unification*, ed. Osman Durrani, Colin Good, and Kevin Hilliard (Sheffield: Sheffield Academic Press, 1995), 337–48.

PÜSCHEL, URSULA, 'Zutrauen kein Unding, Liebe kein Phantom', *NDL* 27 (1979), 7, 134–9.

REID, J. H., 'Woman, Myth and Magic: On Christa Wolf's *Kassandra* and

Irmtraud Morgner's *Amanda'*, in *Honecker's Germany*, ed. David Childs (London: Allen & Unwin, 1985), 97–117.

—— *Writing Without Taboos: The New East German Literature* (New York: Berg, 1990).

REUFFER, PETRA, *Die unwahrscheinlichen Gewänder der anderen Wahrheit: Zur Wiederentdeckung des Wunderbaren bei Günter Grass und Irmtraud Morgner* (Essen: Verlag Die blaue Eule, 1988).

RICHTER, HANS, 'Moralität als poetische Energie', *SF* 29 (1977), 3, 667–78.

RIEDEL, VOLKER, *Antikerezeption in der Literatur der Deutschen Demokratischen Republik* (Berlin: Akademie der Künste, 1984).

RIETSCH, JÖRN, 'Versuch über einen Versuch: Gedanken über den Blick auf Geschichte in Christa Wolfs Roman *Kindheitsmuster*', *WB* 38 (1992), 1, 68–84.

ROSENBERG, RAINER, 'Was war DDR-Literatur? Die Diskussion um den Gegenstand in der Literaturwissenschaft der Bundesrepublik Deutschland', *ZG* NS 5 (1995), 1, 9–21.

ROSENKRANZ-KAISER, JUTTA, *Feminismus und Mythos: Tendenzen in Literatur und Theorie der achtziger Jahre* (Münster and New York: Waxmann, 1995).

ROTHBAUER, GERHARD, 'Vorgeschichten, Nachgeschichten oder einfach Geschichten?', *NDL* 20 (1972), 1, 163–6.

—— 'Wir könnten so tun, als wäre alles beim alten', *NDL* 23 (1975), 3, 151–4.

RYAN, JUDITH, 'Twilight Zones: Myth, Fairy Tale, and Utopia in *No Place on Earth* and *Cassandra*', in *Responses to Christa Wolf: Critical Essays*, ed. Marilyn Sibley Fries (Detroit: Wayne State University Press, 1989), 312–25.

SAGER, KURT, 'Der Schattenriß einer Frau', *Ginkgobaum*, 10 (1991), 155–62.

SAUER, KLAUS (ed.), *Christa Wolf Materialienbuch* (Darmstadt and Neuwied: Luchterhand, 1979).

SCHACHTSIEK-FREITAG, NORBERT, 'Vom Versagen der Kritik: Die Aufnahme von "Kindheitsmuster" in beiden deutschen Staaten', in *Christa Wolf Materialienbuch*, ed. Klaus Sauer (Darmstadt and Neuwied: Luchterhand, 1979), 117–30.

SCHENKEL, MICHAEL, *Fortschritts- und Modernitätskritik in der DDR-Literatur: Prosatexte der achtziger Jahre* (Tübingen: Stauffenburg, 1995).

SCHEPNITZ, CLAUDIA, 'Sigrid Damm: Cornelia Goethe', *Deutschunterricht*, 42 (1989), 11, 559.

SCHERER, GABRIELA, *Zwischen 'Bitterfeld' und 'Orplid': Zum literarischen Werk Irmtraud Morgners* (Berne: Lang, 1992).

SCHICK, BERND, 'Brief eines Nachgeborenen: Zu Christa Wolf und Annemarie Auer', *SF* 30 (1978), 2, 422–6.

SCHLENKER, WOLFRAM, *Das 'Kulturelle Erbe' in der DDR: Gesellschaftliche Entwicklung und Kulturpolitik 1945–1965* (Stuttgart: Metzler, 1977).

SCHMIDT, RICARDA, 'Im Schatten der Titanin: Minor GDR Women Writers —Justly Neglected, Unrecognised or Repressed?', in *Geist und Macht: Writers and the State in the GDR*, ed. Axel Goodbody and Dennis Tate, GM 29 (Amsterdam and Atlanta: Rodopi, 1992), 151–62.

SCHMITZ-KÖSTER, DOROTHEE, *Trobadora und Kassandra und . . .: Weibliches Schreiben in der DDR* (Cologne: Pahl-Rugenstein, 1989).

SCHUBBE, ELIMAR (ed.), *Dokumente zur Kunst-, Literatur- und Kulturpolitik der SED* (Stuttgart: Seewald, 1972).

SCHUENKE, CHRISTA, 'Viel verlangen: Gespräch mit Brigitte Struzyk', *Temperamente* (1986), 4, 79–82.

SCHULZ, GENIA, 'Kein Chorgesang: Neue Schreibweisen bei Autorinnen (aus) der DDR', in *Bestandsaufnahme Gegenwartsliteratur: Bundesrepublik Deutschland, Deutsche Demokratische Republik, Österreich, Schweiz*, ed. Heinz Ludwig Arnold (Munich: text + kritik, 1988), 212–25.

SCHUSCHENG, DOROTHE, *Arbeit am Mythos Frau: Weiblichkeit und Autonomie in der literarischen Mythenrezeption Ingeborg Bachmanns, Christa Wolfs und Gertrud Leuteneggers* (Frankfurt am Main: Lang, 1987).

SHIRER, ROBERT K., *Difficulties of Saying 'I': The Narrator as Protagonist in Christa Wolf's* Kindheitsmuster *and Uwe Johnson's* Jahrestage (New York: Lang, 1988).

SIBLEY FRIES, MARILYN (ed.), *Responses to Christa Wolf: Critical Essays* (Detroit: Wayne State University Press, 1989).

SILBERMAN, MARC, 'Whose Story is This? Rewriting the Literary History of the GDR', in *Contentious Memories: Looking Back at the GDR*, ed. Jost Hermand and Marc Silberman (New York: Lang, 1998), 25–57.

SMITH, COLIN E., *Tradition, Art and Society: Christa Wolf's Prose* (Essen: Verlag Die blaue Eule, 1987).

STEPHAN, ALEXANDER, 'Von Aufenthalten, Hosenknöpfen und Kindheitsmustern: Das Dritte Reich in der jüngsten Prosa der DDR', in *Studies in GDR Culture and Society 6*, ed. Margy Gerber (Washington: University Press of America, 1981), 127–39.

STRELLER, SIEGFRIED, 'Christa Wolf: Kein Ort. Nirgends', *WB* 29 (1983), 2, 359–62.

TATE, DENNIS, 'Trapped in the Past? The Identity Problems of East German Writers since the *Wende*', in *Germany in the 1990s*, ed. H. J. Hahn, GM 34 (Amsterdam and Atlanta: Rodopi, 1995), 1–16.

——'Writing in the Shadow of Auschwitz: Literary Perspectives on the GDR's Failure to Overcome its Past', in *Reconstructing the Past: Representations of the Fascist Era in Post-War European Culture*, ed. Graham Bartram, Maurice Slawinski, and David Steel (Keele: Keele University Press, 1996), 118–34.

TEUPE, PETER F., *Christa Wolfs* Kein Ort. Nirgends *als Paradigma der DDR-Literatur der siebziger Jahre* (Frankfurt am Main: Lang, 1992).

VERBEECK, GEORGI, 'Confronting the Nazi Experience in the GDR', in *Germany after Unification: Coming to Terms with the Recent Past*, ed. Gert-Joachim Glaeßner, GM 37 (Amsterdam and Atlanta: Rodopi, 1996), 67–85.

VIOLLET, CATHERINE, 'Nachdenken über Pronomina: Zur Entstehung von Christa Wolfs *Kindheitsmuster*', in *Christa Wolf: Ein Arbeitsbuch. Studien, Dokumente, Bibliographie*, ed. Angela Drescher (Berlin and Weimar: Aufbau, 1989; repr. Frankfurt am Main: Luchterhand, 1990), 101–13.

WAGENBACH, KLAUS, 'Wo sind wir zu hause? Gespräch mit Stephan Hermlin', *Freibeuter*, 1 (1979), 1, 47–55.

WALLACE, IAN (ed.), *Christa Wolf in Perspective*, GM 30 (Amsterdam and Atlanta: Rodopi, 1994).

WALTHER, JOACHIM, *Meinetwegen Schmetterlinge: Gespräche mit Schriftstellern* (Berlin: Verlag Der Morgen, 1973).

WASCHESCIO, PETRA, *Vernunftkritik und Patriarchatskritik: Mythische Modelle in der deutschen Gegenwartsliteratur; Heiner Müller, Irmtraud Morgner, Botho Strauß, Gisela von Wysocki* (Bielefeld: Aisthesis, 1994).

WEBER, HERMANN, '"Weiße Flecken" und die DDR-Geschichtswissenschaft', in *Zwischen Parteilichkeit und Professionalität: Bilanz der Geschichtswissenschaft der DDR*, ed. Konrad H. Jarausch (Berlin: Akademie Verlag, 1991), 139–53.

WEEDON, CHRIS, 'Reading Christa Wolf', in *Post-War Women's Writing in German: Feminist Critical Approaches*, ed. Chris Weedon (Providence, RI, and Oxford: Berghahn, 1997), 223–42.

WEHDEKING, VOLKER, *Die deutsche Einheit und die Schriftsteller: Literarische Verarbeitung der Wende seit 1989* (Stuttgart: Kohlhammer, 1995).

WEIGEL, SIGRID, 'Vom Sehen zur Seherin: Christa Wolfs Umdeutung des Mythos und die Spur der Bachmann-Rezeption in ihrer Literatur', in *Christa Wolf: Ein Arbeitsbuch. Studien, Dokumente, Bibliographie*, ed. Angela Drescher (Berlin and Weimar: Aufbau, 1989; repr. Frankfurt am Main: Luchterhand, 1990), 169–203.

WERNER, HANS-GEORG, 'Christa Wolfs Bild der Günderrode: Medium der Selbstbesinnung', in *Christa Wolf in feministischer Sicht*, ed. Michel Vanhelleputte (Frankfurt am Main: Lang, 1992), 43–53.

WEYHMANN, BRIGITTE, 'Helga Schütz: Erziehung zum Chorgesang', *NDH* 28 (1981), 2, 365–8.

WIESEHAN, GRETCHEN, 'Christa Wolf Reconsidered: National Stereotypes in *Kindheitsmuster*', *GR* 68 (1993), 2, 79–87.

WILKE, SABINE, '"Worüber man nicht sprechen kann, darüber muß man allmählich zu schweigen aufhören": Vergangenheitsbeziehungen in Christa Wolfs *Kindheitsmuster*', *GR* 66 (1991), 4, 169–76.

——*Ausgraben und Erinnern: Zur Funktion von Geschichte, Subjekt und geschlechtlicher Identität in den Texten Christa Wolfs* (Würzburg: Königshausen und Neumann, 1993).

WITTSTOCK, UWE, *Über die Fähigkeit zu trauern: Das Bild der Wandlung im Prosawerk von Christa Wolf und Franz Fühmann* (Frankfurt am Main: Athenäum, 1987).

WOODS, ROGER, 'Public Judgement versus Private Reflection: Critical East German Intellectuals as Interpreters of the Past', in *Re-assessing the GDR:*

Papers from a Nottingham Conference, ed. J. H. Reid, GM 33 (Amsterdam and Atlanta: Rodopi, 1994), 101–14.

WURST, KARIN A., 'Sigrid Damm: *Cornelia Goethe*', *GSR* 12 (1989), 1, 167–8.

ZAHLMANN, CHRISTEL, *Christa Wolfs Reise 'ins Tertiär': Eine literaturpsychologische Studie zu* Kindheitsmuster (Würzburg: Königshausen and Neumann, 1986).

ZEHL ROMERO, CHRISTIANE, ' "Remembrance of Things Future": On Establishing a Female Tradition', in *Responses to Christa Wolf: Critical Essays*, ed. Marilyn Sibley Fries (Detroit: Wayne State University Press, 1989), 108–27.

——' "Vertreibung aus dem Paradies?": GDR Women's Writing Reconsidered', in *Retrospect and Review: Aspects of the Literature of the GDR 1976–1990*, ed. Robert Atkins and Martin Kane, GM 40 (Amsterdam and Atlanta: Rodopi, 1997), 108–25.

3. OTHER SOURCES

ABRAMS, LYNN, and HARVEY, ELIZABETH (eds.), *Gender Relations in German History: Power, Agency and Experience from the Sixteenth to the Twentieth Century* (London: University College London Press, 1996).

BARTHES, ROLAND, 'Historical Discourse', trans. Peter Wexler, in *Structuralism: A Reader*, ed. Michael Lane (London: Cape, 1966), 145–55.

——*Mythologies*, trans. Annette Lavers (London: Paladin, 1973).

DE BEAUVOIR, SIMONE, *The Second Sex*, trans. H. M. Parshley (Harmondsworth: Penguin, 1972).

BECKER-CANTARINO, BARBARA, *Der lange Weg zur Mündigkeit: Frauen und Literatur in Deutschland von 1500 bis 1800* (Stuttgart: Metzler, 1987).

BENJAMIN, WALTER, *Gesammelte Schriften*, ed. Rolf Tiedemann and Hermann Schweppenhäuser, 6 vols. (Frankfurt am Main: Suhrkamp, 1972–85).

BENNETT, JUDITH M., 'Feminism and History', *Gender and History*, 1 (1989), 3, 251–72.

BLAU DUPLESSIS, RACHEL, *Writing Beyond the Ending: Narrative Strategies of Twentieth Century Women Writers* (Bloomington, Ind.: Indiana University Press, 1985).

BLUMENBERG, HANS, *Arbeit am Mythos* (Frankfurt am Main: Suhrkamp, 1979; repr. 1986).

BOCK, GISELA, *History, Women's History, Gender History* (San Domenico: European University Institute, 1987).

BOURDIEU, PIERRE, *The Field of Cultural Production: Essays on Art and Literature*, ed. and trans. Randal Johnson (Cambridge and Oxford: Polity, 1993).

BOVENSCHEN, SILVIA, *Die imaginierte Weiblichkeit: Exemplarische Untersuchungen zu kulturgeschichtlichen und literarischen Präsentationsformen des Weiblichen* (Frankfurt am Main: Suhrkamp, 1979).

BRECHT, BERTOLT, *Werke* (Große kommentierte Berliner und Frankfurter Ausgabe), ed. Werner Hecht, Jan Knopf, *et al.*, 30 vols. (Berlin: Aufbau; Frankfurt am Main: Suhrkamp, 1988–2000).

CARROLL, BERENICE A. (ed.), *Liberating Women's History: Theoretical and Critical Essays* (Urbana, Ill.: University of Illinois Press, 1976).

COLLINGWOOD, R. G., *The Idea of History* (Oxford: Clarendon, 1946).

FARGE, ARLETTE, 'Praxis und Wirkung der Frauengeschichtsschreibung', in *Geschlecht und Geschichte: Ist eine weibliche Geschichtsschreibung möglich?*, ed. Michelle Perrot, trans. Wolfgang Kaiser (Frankfurt am Main: Fischer, 1989), 29–45.

FOUQUET, CATHERINE, 'Führt der Weg der Frauengeschichte über die Geschichte des weiblichen Körpers?', in *Geschlecht und Geschichte: Ist eine weibliche Geschichtsschreibung möglich?*, ed. Michelle Perrot, trans. Wolfgang Kaiser (Frankfurt am Main: Fischer, 1989), 47–61.

FREVERT, UTE, *Frauen-Geschichte: Zwischen bürgerlicher Verbesserung und neuer Weiblichkeit* (Frankfurt am Main: Suhrkamp, 1986).

——*'Mann und Weib, und Weib und Mann': Geschlechter-Differenzen in der Moderne* (Munich: Beck, 1995).

GOETHE, CORNELIA, *Briefe und Correspondance secrète, 1767–1769*, ed. and trans. Melanie Baumann *et al.* (Freiburg: Kore, 1990).

GORDON, ANN D., BUHLE, MARI JO, and DYE, NANCY SCHROM, 'The Problem of Women's History', in *Liberating Women's History: Theoretical and Critical Essays*, ed. Berenice A. Carroll (Urbana, Ill.: University of Illinois Press, 1976), 75–92.

GOSSMAN, LIONEL, 'History and Literature: Reproduction or Signification', in *The Writing of History: Literary Form and Historical Understanding*, ed. Robert H. Canary and Henry Kozicki (Madison: University of Wisconsin Press, 1978), 3–39.

GÖTTNER-ABENDROTH, HEIDE, *Die Göttin und ihr Heros* (Munich: Frauen-offensive, 1982).

GREENE, GAYLE, and KAHN, COPPÉLIA, 'Feminist Scholarship and the Social Construction of Woman', in *Making a Difference: Feminist Literary Criticism*, ed. Gayle Greene and Coppélia Kahn (London and New York: Methuen, 1985; repr. Routledge, 1990), 1–36.

HARTMANN, HEIDI, 'The Unhappy Marriage of Marxism and Feminism: Towards a More Progressive Union', in *Women and Revolution: A Discussion of the Unhappy Marriage of Marxism and Feminism*, ed. Lydia Sargent (Montreal: Black Rose Books, 1981), 1–41.

HEILBRUN, CAROLYN G., *Writing a Woman's Life* (New York: Ballantine, 1988; repr. 1989).

HORKHEIMER, MAX, and ADORNO, THEODOR W., *Dialektik der Aufklärung: Philosophische Fragmente* (New York: Social Studies Association, 1944; repr. Frankfurt am Main: Fischer, 1995).

HOSKING, GEOFFREY, and SCHÖPFLIN, GEORGE (eds.), *Myths and Nationhood* (London: Hurst, 1997).

IGGERS, GEORG G., *Historiography in the Twentieth Century: From Scientific Objectivity to the Postmodern Challenge* (Hanover, NH, and London: Wesleyan University Press, 1997).

JACKSON, ROSEMARY, *Fantasy: The Literature of Subversion* (London and New York: Methuen, 1981; repr. Routledge, 1998).

JENKINS, KEITH, *On 'What is History?': From Carr and Elton to Rorty and White* (London and New York: Routledge, 1995).

JÜRß, FRITZ, *Vom Mythos der alten Griechen: Deutungen und Erzählungen* (Leipzig: Reclam, 1988).

KLEMPERER, VICTOR, *LTI: Notizbuch eines Philologen* (Berlin: Aufbau, 1949).

KNOWLES, CAROLINE, 'Caroline Michaelis-Böhmer-Schlegel-Schelling's (1763–1809) Contribution to German Literature', unpublished M.Litt. thesis, University of Oxford, 1992.

KOCH, RAINER, *Geschichtskritik und ästhetische Wahrheit: Zur Produktivität des Mythos in moderner Literatur und Philosophie* (Bielefeld: Aisthesis, 1990).

LACAPRA, DOMINICK, *History and Criticism* (Ithaca, NY, and London: Cornell University Press, 1985; repr. 1996).

LERNER, GERDA, 'New Approaches to the Study of Women in American History', in *Liberating Women's History: Theoretical and Critical Essays*, ed. Berenice A. Carroll (Urbana, Ill.: University of Illinois Press, 1976), 349–56.

——'Placing Women in History: A 1975 Perspective', in *Liberating Women's History: Theoretical and Critical Essays*, ed. Berenice A. Carroll (Urbana, Ill.: University of Illinois Press, 1976), 357–68.

LÜTZELER, PAUL MICHAEL, *Klio oder Kalliope? Literatur und Geschichte: Sondierung, Analyse, Interpretation* (Berlin: Schmidt, 1997).

MACHARDY, KARIN J., 'The Boundaries of History and Literature', in *Fact and Fiction: German History and Literature 1848–1924*, ed. Gisela Brude-Firnau and Karin J. MacHardy (Tübingen: Francke, 1990), 11–25.

MARKS, ELAINE, and COURTIVRON, ISABELLE DE (eds.), *New French Feminisms: An Anthology* (New York: Harvester, 1981).

MARX, KARL, and ENGELS, FRIEDRICH, *Ausgewählte Werke*, 6 vols. (Berlin: Dietz, 1970–2).

PERROT, MICHELLE (ed.), *Geschlecht und Geschichte: Ist eine weibliche Geschichtsschreibung möglich?*, trans. Wolfgang Kaiser (Frankfurt am Main: Fischer, 1989).

PROKOP, ULRIKE, 'Die Melancholie der Cornelia Goethe', in *Schwestern berühmter Männer: Zwölf biographische Portraits*, ed. Luise F. Pusch (Frankfurt am Main: Insel, 1985), 49–122.

RICHEL, VERONICA C., *Louise Gottsched: A Reconsideration* (Berne and Frankfurt am Main: Lang, 1973).

RUNCKEL, DOROTHEE HENRIETTE VON (ed.), *Briefe der Frau Louise Adelgunde Viktorie Gottsched geborene Kulmus*, 3 vols. (Dresden: Harpeter, 1771).

SAMUEL, RAPHAEL, and THOMPSON, PAUL (eds.), *The Myths We Live By* (London and New York: Routledge, 1990; repr. 1993).

SCOTT, JOAN WALLACH, *Gender and the Politics of History* (New York: Columbia University Press, 1988).

——'The Evidence of Experience', *Critical Inquiry*, 17 (1991), 4, 773–97.

SEIDEL, EUGEN, and SEIDEL-SLOTTY, INGEBORG, *Sprachwandel im Dritten Reich* (Halle: Sprache und Literatur, 1961).

SMITH, HILDA, 'Feminism and the Methodology of Women's History', in *Liberating Women's History: Theoretical and Critical Essays*, ed. Berenice A. Carroll (Urbana, Ill.: University of Illinois Press, 1976), 368–84.

STANLEY, LIZ, *The Auto/Biographical I: The Theory and Practice of Feminist Auto/Biography* (Manchester: Manchester University Press, 1992).

STEPHAN, INGE, *Musen und Medusen: Mythos und Geschlecht in der Literatur des 20. Jahrhunderts* (Cologne: Böhlau, 1997).

WAGNER-HASEL, BEATE, '"Das Private wird politisch": Die Perspektive "Geschlecht" in der Altertumswissenschaft', in *Weiblichkeit in geschichtlicher Perspektive: Fallstudien und Reflexionen zu Grundproblemen der historischen Frauenforschung*, ed. Ursula A. J. Becher and Jörn Rüsen (Frankfurt am Main: Suhrkamp, 1988), 11–50.

WAUGH, PATRICIA (ed.), *Postmodernism: A Reader* (London: Arnold, 1992).

WEEDON, CHRIS, *Feminist Practice and Poststructuralist Theory* (Cambridge, Mass. and Oxford: Blackwell, 1987; repr. 1994).

——(ed.), *Post-War Women's Writing in German: Feminist Critical Approaches* (Providence, RI, and Oxford: Berghahn, 1997).

WEIGEL, SIGRID, *Die Stimme der Medusa: Schreibweisen in der Gegenwartsliteratur von Frauen* (Reinbek: Rowohlt, 1989).

WHITE, HAYDEN, *The Content of the Form: Narrative Discourse and Historical Representation* (Baltimore and London: Johns Hopkins University Press, 1987; repr. 1990).

INDEX